ENTERTAINMENT LAW

Adam Epstein

Pearson
Prentice Hall
Legal Series

PEARSON
Prentice
Hall

Upper Saddle River, New Jersey 07458

Library of Congress Cataloging-in-Publication Data

Epstein, Adam.
    Entertainment law / by Adam Epstein.—1st ed.
        p. cm.
    ISBN 0-13-114743-9
    1. Performing arts—Law and legislation—United States. 2. Entertainers—Legal status,
laws, etc.—United States. I. Title.
    KF4290.Z9E67 2006
    344. 73'099—dc22

2004028277

Director of Production and Manufacturing: Bruce Johnson
Senior Acquisitions Editor: Gary Bauer
Editorial Assistant: Jacqueline Knapke
Editorial Assistant: Cyrenne Bolt de Freitas
Senior Marketing Manager: Leigh Ann Sims
Managing Editor—Production: Mary Carnis
Manufacturing Buyer: Ilene Sanford
Production Liaison: Denise Brown
Production Editor: Judy Ludowitz/Carlisle Publishers Services
Composition: Carlisle Communications, Ltd.
Director, Image Resource Center: Melinda Reo
Manager, Rights and Permissions: Zina Arabia
Manager, Visual Research: Beth Brenzel
Manager, Cover Visual Research and Permissions: Karen Sanatar
Image Permission Coordinator: Fran Toepfer
Senior Design Coordinator: Christopher Weigand
Cover Design: Kevin Kall
Cover Photos: Bruce Ayres/Getty Images, Inc.
and Alan Band/Getty Images, Inc.
Cover Printer: Phoenix Color
Printer/Binder: Hamilton Printing

The information provided in this text is not intended as legal advice for specific situations, but is meant solely for educational and informational purposes. Readers should retain and seek the advice of their own legal counsel in handling specific legal matters.

Pearson Education LTD.
Pearson Education Singapore, Pte. Ltd.
Pearson Education, Canada, Ltd.
Pearson Education—Japan

Pearson Education Australia PTY, Limited
Pearson Education North Asia Ltd.
Pearson Educacíon de Mexico, S.A. de C.V.
Pearson Education Malaysia, Pte. Ltd.

10 9 8 7 6 5 4 3 2 1
ISBN 0-13-114743-9

In loving memory of my dear mother
Sharon Schneider

December 6, 2004

Pearson Legal Series

Pearson Legal Series provides paralegal/legal studies students and educators with the publishing industry's finest content and best service. We offer an extensive selection of products for over 70 titles and we continue to grow with more new titles each year. We also provide:

- online resources for instructors and students
- state-specific materials
- custom publishing options from Pearson Custom Publishing group

To locate your local Pearson Prentice Hall representative, visit www.prenhall.com

To view Pearson Legal Series titles and to disocover a wide array of resources for both instructors and students, please visit our website at:

www.prenhall.com/legal_studies

Pearson
Prentice Hall
Legal Series

To Mr. Arthur Stolnitz, an inspiration to me and for many individuals in entertainment circles and beyond.

contents

Chapter 4
CONSTITUTIONAL ISSUES IN ENTERTAINMENT LAW   *72*

Chapter 8
LEGAL ISSUES IN LIVE PERFORMANCES   *182*

This text is designed for undergraduate students. Whether paralegal students or legal studies, broadcast communications, or entertainment industry management majors, the focus of this text is to provide a balanced perspective on fundamental issues related to law and the entertainment industries. Law and graduate students might find this text surprisingly beneficial as well.

The study of law can be an exciting process, but one must have some basic understanding of the U.S. legal system before the advanced study of law. Thus, a brief introduction to U.S. law is offered at the beginning of the text.

Important to the study of entertainment law is the appreciation that the various entertainment industries are often comprised of extremely creative individuals who interact (sometimes unfamiliarly) with for-profit business ventures. This can lead to conflict which has led to litigation, published decisions, change in laws, and so on. The study and appreciation of entertainment law is quite different from merely reading about high-profile individuals and their personal lives at the checkout line of the local grocery store.

The text gives moderate consideration to historical perspectives in the music, radio, television, and motion picture industries. It is important to understand how law changes over time to reflect tremendous technological advances. It is also important to understand that many of the chapters interrelate. The influence that the Internet has had in the entertainment world cannot be underestimated, either, and is addressed where appropriate throughout the text. An appreciation that entertainment continues to move into U.S. households via computer screens, video games, and advanced HDTV broadcasts and plasma television sets is vital.

Understanding that the federal, state, and even city governments regulate the entertainment industries is also crucial to understanding concepts in this text. The role of industry self-regulation cannot be underestimated.

Somewhat erroneously, a few law school traditionalists continue to regard entertainment law as being the same as sports law. This is just not true, though there are inevitable similarities and relationships, particularly in the area of sports television broadcasting and programming. These distinct fields of study also cross paths, especially with the advent of newer and better technologies.

While many law schools and undergraduate programs have adopted courses involving the study of entertainment and sports law, only a small number have experienced faculty or an established curriculum in these areas of the law. This may be mere oversight, but breaking into these fields and obtaining experience can be quite difficult.

Because the study of law is an art rather than a science, and due to the ever-evolving nature of law and technology, it is important for the reader to understand that this text should be used merely as a starting point for further legal research. It is highly advisable that an instructor using this text should have some formal training in the U.S. legal system before presenting the material to students. Cases have been carefully selected, but they have also been edited in order to enhance learning and to avoid becoming bogged down in legalese and less relevant opinions, citations, and other summarizations. The reader should find the original case in order to read the complete and unedited version of the case.

This text is not designed to be a springboard to a musical, television, or motion picture career. It is also not designed for those hoping to enter the entertainment industry as an agent, manager, model, or journalist. The purpose of the text is to expose the reader to various legal issues among the segments of the entertainment industry and, hopefully, to expose readers to entertainment issues that might not have been previously considered in other texts or similar courses in a clear and concise manner. For instructors, this text provides a solid foundation for further assignments, research, forms, and so on, and students and instructors are encouraged to explore further research.

Since laws can change annually, it is highly recommended that this text be used as merely a starting point for further research and exploration, not as a definitive resource on the law. Nothing in this text, therefore, constitutes the giving of legal advice, though real-world documents are provided as concrete starting points for further drafting, review, and consideration.

Of course, I hope you find this text entertaining and informative as well.

— *Adam Epstein*

acknowledgments

I would like to particularly thank Steve Dayton, all the members of the Finance and Law Department at Central Michigan University, and Suzanne Stolnitz, Katherine Baird, Dr. Harry Rutledge, Heather Clapp, and Robert Pimm for their input, support, cooperation, advice, and inspiration regarding the ultimate production of this text after countless revisions. Without their help, this text would just not be the same. I would also like to thank all of the anonymous reviewers and others who provided input and constructive criticism of this work.

Special thanks to the reviewers of this text: Robert Diotalevi, Florida Gulf Coast University; Marissa J. Moran, New York City College of Technology; Taylor L. Morton, Golden West University, CA; Patricia Johnson, Berkeley College, NY; Steven Dayton, Fullerton College, CA; Paul Anderson, Marquette University, WI; and Robert Pimm.

about the author

Adam Epstein earned his B.A., M.B.A., and J.D. from the University of Tennessee. He serves as an Associate Professor in the Department of Finance and Law at Central Michigan University. He has authored a text in the area of sports law and has written numerous other law-related articles. He also worked for the William Morris Agency for a very short period of time. He can be reached at **sportslawprof@aol.com.**

1

INTRODUCTION TO THE AMERICAN LEGAL SYSTEM

AFTER STUDYING THIS CHAPTER YOU SHOULD BE ABLE TO:

1. Describe the phrase entertainment law.
2. Appreciate the differences and similarities between entertainment law and sports law.
3. Identify the major geographic locations in the entertainment industry.
4. Describe the history and role of the American Constitution and common law.
5. Identify the constitutional amendments in the Bill of Rights.
6. Differentiate between criminal law and civil law in the United States.
7. Understand the differences between federal jurisdiction and state jurisdiction.
8. Explain the role of federal administrative agencies.
9. Describe the differences between statutory law and case law.
10. Understand the role of the judiciary in interpreting the Constitution.

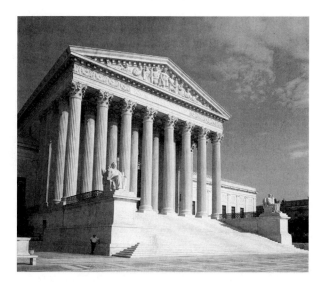

U.S. Supreme Court Building.
eStock Photography LLC.

INTRODUCTION

This chapter is designed to expose readers to the fundamentals of the American legal system. For those who have studied law previously, this chapter might serve as a basic review. For individuals who have not yet studied law, this chapter serves as a springboard for legal basics and the rest of the book.

The initial study of law can be intimidating, as esoteric legal terminology requires students to consult a legal dictionary, such as *Black's Law Dictionary*, quite frequently. Additionally, the failure to understand the basics of the American legal system can potentially send a student into a downward spiral of mass confusion. Therefore, this chapter presumes that little or no formal legal training has been previously attempted by the student.

FOUNDATIONS OF ENTERTAINMENT LAW AND LAWYERS

Entertainment law is simply the general term associated with a variety of business industries and the players within those industries, which include music, radio, television, live performances, movies, videos, publishing, and the like. Entertainment law has its legal and developmental roots in California and New York jurisprudence primarily.

While many people combine **sports law** into another subcategory of entertainment law and the entertainment industry, there is only a partial truth to such categorization. Sport is entertaining and **sports entertainment,** such as the World Wrestling Entertainment's (WWE) scripted athletic performances, provides the best example. Sports law and entertainment law developed much differently and continue to remain relatively distinct fields of law and legal scholarship.[1] Thus, sports law, a similar but distinct field of its own, has its own historical appeal and perspective. However, sports law and industry references will be utilized when necessary throughout the text to enhance chapter insight and further discussion and clarification.

Entertainment lawyers often deal with high-profile legal issues and clientele. Aspects of entertainment law are no different from other areas of legal practice including the more mundane legal concerns involving, for example, criminal law and domestic law issues as opposed to putting together creative entertainment projects and sealing other business deals. Entertainment law is such a broad term that traditional areas of the law such as constitutional law, antitrust, bankruptcy, contracts, wills and estates, general corporate and business issues, federal and state administrative regulatory processes, and intellectual property interests (copyright, trademarks, and patents) are all legitimate concerns in the entertainment industry as a whole. The advent of the boom of technological advances in computers, including the Internet, and current issues such as **piracy** have been the most recent challenges and concerns faced by all involved in the entertainment industry.

Understanding the legal issues in entertainment law requires an appreciation of the traditional areas of law in the context of entertainment. Along the same lines, understanding and appreciating that the artists and performers in the entertainment industry desire to be given credit and control over their work is a vital theme throughout the study of entertainment law. Also, an appreciation of the collective efforts of entertainment **unions** or **guilds** that have negotiated such rights on behalf of artists is equally important. There are also numerous **professional associations** in the entertainment industry that are designed to foster unity and promote issues important to their own cause.

Traditionalists involved in the entertainment industry often prefer to do deals with a handshake. Contemporary players, however, recognize that a handshake is just the first step in putting a deal into a formalized written agreement spelling out the rights and responsibilities of the parties involved. Certainly "who" you know in the entertainment industry is as important as "what" you know, but that could be a true statement in any community or industry around the country. The difference is that the entertainment industry draws so much attention to it, influences so many people, and is viewed as glamorous. Breaking into the industry often requires a lucky break or just hard work.

---

[1] WWE, a publicly traded corporation, produces and promotes wrestling matches for television and live audiences. There are often 12 pay-per-view programs and more than 325 live events each year, including favorites *Raw* and *Smackdown!*

Skyline of New York.
Getty Images Inc.

Los Angeles at night.
Getty Images Inc.-Hulton Archive Photos.

MAJOR ENTERTAINMENT INDUSTRY HUBS

The lifeblood of the entertainment industries focuses in two places: New York and Los Angeles. As such, many of the laws related to entertainment law refer to New York and California statutes. Breaking into the entertainment industry as an attorney often requires becoming admitted to the New York or California bars and relocating to these geographic areas. Still, it is quite possible to be involved in the entertainment industry elsewhere, including Nashville, Atlanta, Washington, D.C., and other North American cities such as Toronto and Vancouver in Canada. Dealing with California and New York attorneys will likely be an eventual prerequisite for developing business, even if the entertainment law practitioner decides not to reside in these communities.

While these other geographic areas have carved out similar, but much smaller, venues for artist representation and management, the heart of the entertainment industries as a whole remains on the east and west coasts regardless of the particular entertainment industry (film, television, publishing, music, theatre, and so on) in which one wishes to participate. With the advent of the reduction of overhead costs associated with technology and technological advances generally, smaller **boutique** firms are able to represent talent around the country in nontraditional cities and settings.

Before exploring the legal issues related to the entertainment industry in this textbook, it is important to have a fundamental understanding of the history of the American legal system and how it works.

HISTORY OF THE AMERICAN LEGAL SYSTEM

American jurisprudence is a direct descendent of **common law** from England. This phrase is used to describe the way in which judges made law throughout

England as a result of the adversarial system of justice. This model is based upon custom and **precedent** (sometimes referred to as **stare decisis**) established by previously decided cases. English law developed by rules and local customs originally established by William the Conqueror in 1066. These rules were significantly modified in 1154 when King Henry II institutionalized common law by creating a unified system of law common to the country. He also is responsible for reinstating a jury system of citizens to investigate criminal accusations and civil claims. The jury reached its verdict through evaluating common local knowledge, and this system remains today in the United States.

Individuals who felt that the early English legal system cheated them could petition the king for damages or an **injunction**—a court order requiring that a party continue or refrain from doing something. This is the basis for modern chancery courts or courts of **equity**—those that render decisions based upon fairness rather than legal redress. While modern statutory law involves written codes and statutes, common law allows judges to interpret law and render decisions on a case-by-case basis.

Common law is still used in the United States, though **codes** and **statutes** continue to grow and expand as ambiguities in the law are filled and trends and technology continue to require changes in the law. Today, only four states—Arkansas, Delaware, Mississippi, and Tennessee—retain separate courts of law and equity. Most states have combined courts of equity today with traditional **circuit** or other trial courts[2] that deal with public disputes involving litigation. In the federal courts, there is no separation between law and equity courts. The trial courts are referred to as the **United States District Courts.**

THE AMERICAN CONSTITUTION

Much of the area of entertainment law involves an understanding of the **Constitution** of the United States (1789), the fundamental and most important of all U.S. legal documents. The Constitution defines the institutions of government and the powers of each institution and establishes the basic rights of U.S. citizens. The purpose of separating powers was to avoid tyranny (as was found in England) and to provide a system of checks and balances in government.

BRANCHES OF GOVERNMENT

The three branches of the American government are the **executive branch,** which includes the president; the **legislative branch,** which includes Congress; and the **judicial branch,** which includes the Supreme Court. **Congress** is the term used to describe the combined efforts of the House of Representatives and

---

[2] Names of trial courts vary around the United States, including circuit courts, courts of common pleas, and so on depending upon the particular state and the jurisdiction of the court.

the Senate. Congress makes the federal laws. The executive branch includes the President of the United States, the Vice President, and the major departments of the government such as the Department of Defense, State Department, Treasury Department, and other **administrative agencies.** The judicial branch is made up of the Supreme Court and other lower courts, and its role is to interpret the laws and apply them to the facts of a given case.

BILL OF RIGHTS

These first ten amendments of the United States Constitution are known as the **Bill of Rights** (1791) and are important in the study and practice of entertainment law today. The study of free speech issues, freedom of the press and of religion, a right to trial by one's peers (jury), protection against cruel and unusual punishment, and protection against unreasonable searches or seizures all emanate directly from these first ten amendments.

INTERPRETATION OF THE CONSTITUTION

The Constitution represents a set of general principles out of which federal and state statutes and codes have emerged. Many believe that the Constitution no longer means what it says—it only means what the Supreme Court of the United States says it means. Such interpretations of the Constitution are the result of changing times, changing ethical views, changing societal values, technological advances, and competing political beliefs. The Supreme Court Justices are supposed to interpret the Constitution apolitically, but one must note that the Justices are appointed by the President of the United States and approved by Congress, both political institutions. In fact, all federal judges are appointed for life terms.

Article I, Section 8, states that Congress shall have the authority "To make all Laws which shall be necessary and proper for carrying into Execution" the various powers allotted to the federal government by the Constitution. This is known as the **Necessary and Proper Clause** and has been a powerful basis for providing Congress with authority to make laws and establish and influence the role of government agencies. Federal administrative agencies such as the Federal Communication Commission (FCC) and the Federal Trade Commission (FTC) play a major role in the regulation of the entertainment industry.

JURISDICTION

In the United States, there are two separate and distinct **jurisdictions** of laws and courts. There are state laws, and there are federal (national) laws. State laws are limited to their own territorial boundaries, and they can regulate, control,

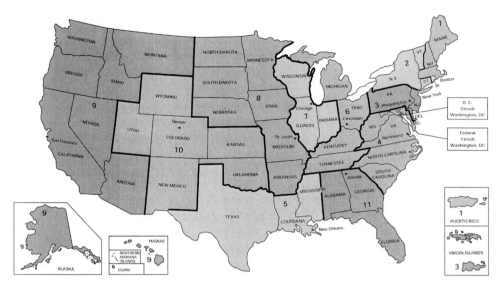

The Federal Circuits.

and govern real and personal property. Federal law encompasses **interstate commerce** concerns and national issues. The fact that there are federal laws and state laws that operate concurrently is often referred to as **federalism**.

FEDERAL COURTS

The Constitution provides that the judicial power of the United States "be vested in one Supreme Court, and in such inferior courts as Congress may from time to time ordain and establish." Over time, Congress established and abolished other federal courts as national needs changed and for judicial efficiency. Supreme Court judges are referred to as **Justices,** while all other federal judges are referred to either as **judges** or **magistrates,** in some instances. The Chief Justice and eight associate Justices of the Supreme Court hear and decide cases involving important questions about the interpretation and fair application of the Constitution and federal laws.

At the top of the federal court system is the Supreme Court of the United States, the highest court. Then, there are 13 United States Courts of Appeals and the U.S. Court of Appeals for the Armed Forces. Below that are 94 U.S. District Courts and specialized courts such as the Tax Court, Court of Federal Claims, Court of Veterans Appeals, and Court of International Trade. There are various routes a case may take to a federal court. Some cases may originate in a U.S. District Court, while others will come from a state court or federal agency as federal law allows.

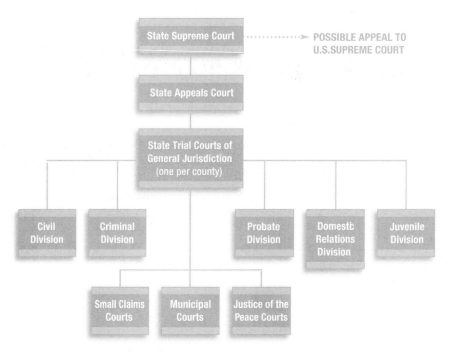

Typical State Court System.

◼ THREE-TIERED SYSTEM

A person, business, or organization involved in a lawsuit in the U.S. court system generally has a three-tiered system at their disposal. State trial courts go by many names, including circuit, chancery, district, and courts of common pleas. State courts have courts of appeal as do the federal District Courts. As a general rule, a plaintiff has one right to appeal as a matter of law and a second right to appeal as a matter of discretion. In other words, if the appellate court is still not favorable to a party, one may petition the Supreme Court for a review of the decision, but only if the Supreme Court chooses to do so under the concept of the **writ of certiorari**—an order by the Supreme Court that it will review the case. That action is entirely discretionary, however, and less than 20 percent of all cases are granted this writ.

This multitiered organization of the courts serves two purposes. First, the courts of appeal can correct errors that have been made in the decisions of trial courts. Second, the Supreme Court can ensure the uniformity of decisions by reviewing cases in which constitutional issues have been decided or in which two or more lower courts or federal circuits have reached different results. Under the Constitution, judges of all federal courts are appointed for life by the President of the United States with the approval of the Senate. Federal judges can be removed from office only through impeachment and conviction by Congress. The federal courts exist to fairly and impartially interpret and apply the law, resolve disputes, and protect the rights and liberties guaranteed by the Constitution. The courts do not make the laws, though judges who forget that principle are referred to as **judicial activists** and are often criticized in public for their decisions.

THE DISTRICT COURTS

Considered the trial courts of the federal judicial system, the 94 U.S. District Courts, located within the 12 regional circuits, hear practically all cases involving federal civil and criminal laws. Decisions of the district courts are typically appealed to the **Courts of Appeal.**

THE U.S. CIRCUITS

1st Circuit—Maine, Massachusetts, New Hampshire, Rhode Island, Puerto Rico

2nd Circuit—Connecticut, New York, Vermont

3rd Circuit—Delaware, New Jersey, Pennsylvania, Virgin Islands

4th Circuit—Maryland, North Carolina, South Carolina, Virginia, West Virginia

5th Circuit—Louisiana, Mississippi, Texas

6th Circuit—Kentucky, Michigan, Ohio, Tennessee

7th Circuit—Illinois, Indiana, Wisconsin

8th Circuit—Arkansas, Iowa, Minnesota, Nebraska, North Dakota, South Dakota

9th Circuit—Alaska, Arizona, California, Guam, Hawaii, Idaho, Montana, Nevada, Northern Mariana Islands, Oregon, Washington

10th Circuit—Colorado, Kansas, New Mexico, Oklahoma, Utah, Wyoming

11th Circuit—Alabama, Florida, Georgia

D.C. Circuit—The administrative agency law capital of the federal circuits

Federal Circuit—Patent, trademark, and international issues

THE CIRCUIT COURTS OF APPEAL

Each of the 12 regional circuits has one U.S. Court of Appeals that hears appeals to decisions of the district courts located within its circuit and appeals to decisions of federal regulatory agencies. The Court of Appeals for the **Federal Circuit** has nationwide jurisdiction and hears specialized cases like patent and international trade cases. (So in essence there are 13 different federal circuits.)

BANKRUPTCY COURTS

The federal courts have jurisdiction over all **bankruptcy** cases. Bankruptcy cannot be filed in state courts. The primary purposes of the law of bankruptcy are: (1) to give an honest **debtor** a fresh start by relieving the debtor of most debts and (2) to repay **creditors** in an orderly manner to the extent that the debtor has property available for payment.

OTHER SPECIAL COURTS

Two courts have nationwide jurisdiction over special types of cases. The U.S. Court of International Trade hears cases involving U.S. trade with foreign countries and customs issues, while the U.S. Court of Federal Claims considers claims for monetary damages made against the U.S. government, federal contract disputes, and disputed taking or claiming of land by the federal government.

CRIMINAL AND CIVIL LAW

In the United States, the goal of **criminal law** is punishment. A crime is committed only if there is a statute that describes the conduct as a criminal act. Often, conduct by individuals may be deemed unethical, but it does not necessarily rise to the level of being criminal unless there is a statute that says it is so. In order to be found guilty of a crime, the **prosecutor** (federal or state) must prove their case to jurors **beyond a reasonable doubt**.[3] Examples of crimes might include tax evasion, money laundering, theft, murder, Internet crimes, and so on.

Contract law, tort law (personal injury involving negligence, product liability, strict liability, and intentional misconduct), constitutional law, tax law, and so on are all considered **civil law.** Private **plaintiffs** and **defendants** are the players in a civil case, whereas prosecutors (district attorneys) and the accused (criminal defendants) are the participants in a criminal case.[4] Similarly,

---

[3] The phrase "beyond a reasonable doubt" is defined as that level of evidence which fully satisfies and entirely convinces to a moral certainty.

[4] The terms plaintiff and defendant are sometimes referred to as petitioner and respondent in some jurisdictions. On appeal, the one appealing the lower court decision is usually referred to as the appellant, and the other party is the appellee.

a plaintiff must prove his or her case by a **preponderance of the evidence** (a much lower standard) in order to recover monetary damages for any wrongdoing by another.

In some instances (as defined by a law or statute), the burden of proof on the plaintiff is by an intermediate standard known as the **clear and convincing evidence** standard. This standard of evidence falls somewhere in between beyond a reasonable doubt and preponderance of the evidence. It is that which will produce in the mind of the adjudicator (a judge or jury) a firm belief or conviction as to the facts alleged. This standard is often used in alleged violations of administrative agency regulations.

FEDERAL ADMINISTRATIVE AGENCIES

Administrative law encompasses laws and legal principles governing the administration and regulation of federal and state agencies. Such agencies are delegated power by Congress (or in the case of a state agency, the state legislature) to act as agents for the executive branch. Federal administrative agencies are given existence and powers by Congress through **enabling legislation.** Their regulations are published in the **Code of Federal Regulations** (C.F.R).

Federal agencies are governed by the federal Administrative Procedures Act (APA), which sets the conditions under which agencies may issue regulations and decisions. The review of agency decisions is heard by the Appeals Board within the agency (if there is one) or the agency itself. Once there is "final agency action" appeals can usually be taken to the appropriate United States Court of Appeals under the concept of **judicial review.** Both the FCC and the FTC play a major role in regulating various aspects of the entertainment industry, especially in radio and television broadcasts. (A discussion of both these agencies is found in Chapter 5.)

STATUTES

Statutes are created by the U.S. Congress and by state legislators in an attempt to lay out the rules of the law. When disputes arise over the meaning of statutes, state and federal courts issue written court **opinions** that interpret the statutes more clearly—this is referred to as **case law.** Some statutory codes are **annotated.** This means that the statutes include more than just the language of the actual statutes—they also provide features such as footnotes, explanatory notes, citations to other cases, summaries of cases, and journal articles that interpret the statutes.

At the federal level, the United States Code (U.S.C.) contains the codification of all general and permanent laws of the United States. The U.S.C. includes federal statutes enacted by the U.S. Congress and signed by the president.[5] A citation to the United States Code (U.S.C.) might look something like this:

15 U.S.C. § 45(a)

(Read: Title 15, United States Code, Section 45, subsection a)

All of the 50 states have their own codified laws as well. These codes also include administrative **regulations** and ordinances at the local level.

CASE LAW

Case law is law made by judges who actually preside over individual cases and then compose opinions of their decisions. Nearly all case law is made by judges on appellate courts, not trial level courts. Case law is published in books called reporters. The **National Reporter System** (published by West) is a set of reporters that divides the 50 states and the District of Columbia into seven regions: Atlantic, North Eastern, North Western, Pacific, South Eastern, South Western, and Southern. The National Reporter System covers the appellate courts of all the states and the District of Columbia. The federal reporters are also part of the National Reporter System.

SECONDARY SOURCES

Secondary sources are books and articles that attempt to explain or comment on the law. They are not the law themselves. There are several different types of secondary sources, including books or **treatises,** articles, encyclopedias, and form books. The **Restatement of Torts, Restatement of Contracts,** and **Corpus Juris Secundum** (C.J.S.) are popular examples of secondary legal sources. Additional resources can be found at the end of this chapter.

CONDUCTING RESEARCH IN ENTERTAINMENT LAW

Exploring and studying law used to require a trip to a law library housing expensive volumes of books and law treatises. With the 1990s technological explosion, researching legal issues or simply exploring the law from home or business has become not only a common practice, but has allowed lawyers and paralegals to gain access to information vital to the practice of entertainment law. The student will find various traditional and computer-based research tools to complement the study of entertainment law as follows.

---

[5] Or laws that are passed over the president's veto.

ENTERTAINMENT PUBLICATIONS

Reading entertainment trade publications is an important practice in entertainment law circles. Whether one subscribes to the print versions or online services, it is expected that one involved in entertainment stay up-to-date on court decisions and current news that could impact their own practice. Two of the largest publications include *The Hollywood Reporter* and *Variety*.

COMPUTER-BASED LEGAL RESEARCH

Legal databases such as www.westlaw.com, www.lexis.com, www.findlaw.com, and many others now provide access to the traditional hard-bound volumes of books. Entertainment lawyers can go online to free (www.findlaw.com) and pay (subscription) sites such as www.lexis.com and www.westlaw.com. Another good source is the www.google.com search engine, though it is not specific to the law. Other efforts to find general research include exploring yahoo.com, netscape.com, askjeeves.com, and so on. Another good source for facts, opinion, and gossip specific to entertainment law is *E! online* found at www.eonline.com. For those involved in the television and radio industries, www.tvweek.com and www.broadcastingcable.com may prove useful. Those interested in entertainment employment opportunities might visit www.ifcome.com, www.showbizjobs.com, and www.entertainmentcareers.com.

CHAPTER SUMMARY

The study of entertainment law requires an appreciation of other areas of law. Understanding the fundamentals of constitutional law and its influence over entertainment issues is vital. Further, an appreciation of the history of the American legal system and the three branches of government puts legal research and writing into its proper focus and perspective. The American three-tiered system of courts at both the federal and state levels is based on the concept of precedent, a direct descendent of the English tradition of common law. The role of the Supreme Court and the various circuits allows for review of judicial decisions as a matter of checks and balances in the American legal system. Becoming familiar with law-related resources, both in print and online, enhances the ability to conduct a successful legal research agenda.

CHAPTER TERMS

Administrative agencies	Bill of Rights	Code of Federal Regulations	Courts of Appeal
Administrative law	Boutique	Codes	Creditor
Annotated	Case law	Common law	Criminal law
Bankruptcy	Circuit	Congress	Debtor
Beyond a reasonable doubt	Civil law	Constitution	Defendant
	Clear and convincing evidence	Corpus Juris Secundum	Enabling legislation
			Entertainment law

Equity | Judicial review | Piracy | Restatement of Torts
Executive branch | Jurisdiction | Plaintiff | Sports entertainment
Federal Circuit | Justices | Precedent | Sports law
Federalism | Legislative branch | Preponderance of the evidence | Stare decisis
Guilds | Magistrates | | Statutes
Injunction | National Reporter System | Professional associations | Treatises
Interstate commerce | | | Unions
Judges | Necessary and Proper Clause | Prosecutor | United States District Courts
Judicial activists | | Regulations |
Judicial branch | Opinions | Restatement of Contracts | Writ of certiorari

REVIEW QUESTIONS

1. What are the various industries involved in the study of entertainment law?
2. Why does the American legal system have its historical roots in the common law of England?
3. What amendments to the Constitution are more formally known as the Bill of Rights?
4. What constitutional amendments are particularly important in the study of entertainment law?
5. Why are there both state and federal court systems?
6. What is the role of federal administrative agencies, particularly the FCC and the FTC, with regard to entertainment?
7. Provide an example of a secondary legal reference or source.
8. What are some examples of print journals to which a lawyer or paralegal may wish to subscribe?
9. What are some law-related Internet Web sites that might be considered by one conducting legal research?
10. Why should nonlawyers have a fundamental understanding of the American legal system?

SELECTED ENTERTAINMENT INDUSTRY AND RELATED WEB SITES

Actors Equity Association (AEA) http://www.actorsequity.org/

American Federation of Musicians (AFM) http://www.afm.org/public/home/index.php

American Federation of Television & Radio Artists (AFTRA) http://www.aftra.org/

American Intellectual Property Law Association http://www.aipla.org/

American Society of Cinematographers http://www.theasc.com/

American Society of Composers, Authors & Publishers (ASCAP) http://www.ascap.com/index.html

Association of Talent Agents (ATA) http://www.agentassociation.com/

Casting Society of America (CSA) http://www.castingsociety.com/

Costume Designers Guild http://www.costumedesignersguild.com/

Directors Guild of America (DGA) http://www.dga.org/index2.php3

International Alliance of Theatrical Stage Employees (IATSE) http://www.iatse-intl.org/splash.html

International Cinematographers Guild http://www.cameraguild.com/

Motion Picture Editors Guild http://www.editorsguild.com/

National Conference of Personal Managers http://www.ncopm.com/

Producers Guild of America http://www.producersguild.org/

Recording Artists Coalition http://www.recordingartistscoalition.com/

Recording Industry Association of America
http://www.riaa.org

Screen Actors Guild (SAG)
http://new.sag.org/sagWebApp/index.jsp

Stuntmen's Association http://www.stuntmen.com

Stuntwomen's Association of Motion Pictures
http://www.stuntwomen.com/

Writers Guild of America (WGA)
http://www.wga.org/

Selected Governmental and Other Web Sites

Copyright Office–Library of Congress
http://www.loc.gov/copyright

Department of Justice (DOJ) http://www.usdoj.gov/

Federal Communications Commission (FCC)
http://www.fcc.gov/

Federal Trade Commission (FTC) http://www.ftc.gov/

International Trademark Association
http://www.inta.org/

United States Patent and Trademark Office
http://www.uspto.gov

World Intellectual Property Organization
http://www.wipo.org

Selected Entertainment and Sports-related Law Journals

Cardozo Arts and Entertainment Law Journal
http://www.cardozo.yu.edu/aelj/index.html

DePaul-LCA Journal of Art & Entertainment Law
http://www.law.depaul.edu/default.asp?Sec=2&Pg=jael/default.htm

Entertainment & Sports Lawyer (ABA Forum on the
Entertainment & Sports Industries)
http://www.abanet.org/forums/entsports/esl.html

Journal of Legal Aspects of Sport
http://law.marquette.edu/cgi-bin/site.pl?2130&pageID=1078

Hastings Communications and Entertainment Law
Journal http://www.uchastings.edu/comment/

Loyola of Los Angeles Entertainment Law Review
http://elr.lls.edu/

Marquette Sports Law Journal
http://law.marquette.edu/cgi-bin/site.pl

Texas Review of Entertainment and Sports Law
http://www.utexas.edu/law/journals/tresl/index.html

UCLA Entertainment Law Review
http://www1.law.ucla.edu/~elr/public_html/

Vanderbilt Journal of Entertainment Law & Practice
http://www.law.vanderbilt.edu/jelp/index.html

Selected Amendments to the Constitution of the United States of America
Amendments I – X are the Bill of Rights

AMENDMENT I

Congress shall make no law respecting an establishment of religion, or prohibiting the free exercise thereof; or abridging the freedom of speech, or of the press; or the right of the people peaceably to assemble, and to petition the Government for a redress of grievances.

AMENDMENT II

A well regulated Militia, being necessary to the security of a free State, the right of the people to keep and bear Arms, shall not be infringed.

AMENDMENT III

No Soldier shall, in time of peace be quartered in any house, without the consent of the Owner, nor in time of war, but in a manner to be prescribed by law.

(continued)

AMENDMENT IV

The right of the people to be secure in their persons, houses, papers, and effects, against unreasonable searches and seizures, shall not be violated, and no Warrants shall issue, but upon probable cause, supported by Oath or affirmation, and particularly describing the place to be searched, and the persons or things to be seized.

AMENDMENT V

No person shall be held to answer for a capital, or otherwise infamous crime, unless on a presentment or indictment of a Grand Jury, except in cases arising in the land or naval forces, or in the Militia, when in actual service in time of War or public danger; nor shall any person be subject for the same offence to be twice put in jeopardy of life or limb; nor shall be compelled in any criminal case to be a witness against himself, nor be deprived of life, liberty, or property, without due process of law; nor shall private property be taken for public use, without just compensation.

AMENDMENT VI

In all criminal prosecutions, the accused shall enjoy the right to a speedy and public trial, by an impartial jury of the State and district wherein the crime shall have been committed, which district shall have been previously ascertained by law, and to be informed of the nature and cause of the accusation; to be confronted with the witnesses against him; to have compulsory process for obtaining witnesses in his favor, and to have the Assistance of Counsel for his defence.

AMENDMENT VII

In Suits at common law, where the value in controversy shall exceed twenty dollars, the right of trial by jury shall be preserved, and no fact tried by a jury, shall be otherwise re-examined in any Court of the United States, than according to the rules of the common law.

AMENDMENT VIII

Excessive bail shall not be required, nor excessive fines imposed, nor cruel and unusual punishments inflicted.

AMENDMENT IX

The enumeration in the Constitution, of certain rights, shall not be construed to deny or disparage others retained by the people.

AMENDMENT X

The powers not delegated to the United States by the Constitution, nor prohibited by it to the States, are reserved to the States respectively, or to the people.

AMENDMENT XI

The Judicial power of the United States shall not be construed to extend to any suit in law or equity, commenced or prosecuted against one of the United States by Citizens of another State, or by Citizens or Subjects of any Foreign State.

AMENDMENT XII

The Electors shall meet in their respective states and vote by ballot for President and Vice-President, one of whom, at least, shall not be an inhabitant of the same state with themselves; they shall name in their ballots the person voted for as President, and in distinct ballots the person voted for as Vice-President, and they shall make distinct lists of all persons voted for as President, and of all persons voted for as Vice-President, and of the number of votes for each, which lists they shall sign and certify, and transmit sealed to the seat of the government of the United States, directed to the President of the Senate;—The President of the Senate shall, in the presence of the Senate and House of Representatives, open all the certificates and the votes shall then be counted;—The person having the greatest Number of votes for President, shall be the President, if such number be a majority of the whole number of Electors appointed; and if no person have such majority, then from the persons having the highest numbers not exceeding three on the list of those voted for as President, the House of Representatives shall choose immediately, by ballot, the President. But in choosing the President, the votes shall be taken by states, the representation from each state having one vote; a quorum for this purpose shall consist of a member or members from two-thirds of the states, and a majority of all the states shall be necessary to a choice. And if the House of Representatives shall not choose a President whenever the right of choice shall devolve upon them, before the fourth day of March next following, then the Vice-President shall act as President, as in the case of the death or other constitutional disability of the President—The person having the greatest number of votes as Vice-President, shall be the Vice-President, if such number be a majority of the whole number of Electors appointed, and if no person have a majority, then from the two highest numbers on the list, the Senate shall choose the Vice-President; a quorum for the purpose shall consist of two-thirds of the whole number of Senators, and a majority of the whole number shall be necessary to a choice. But no person constitutionally ineligible to the office of President shall be eligible to that of Vice-President of the United States.

AMENDMENT XIII

Section 1. Neither slavery nor involuntary servitude, except as a punishment for crime whereof the party shall have been duly convicted, shall exist within the United States, or any place subject to their jurisdiction.

Section 2. Congress shall have power to enforce this article by appropriate legislation.

AMENDMENT XIV

Section 1. All persons born or naturalized in the United States and subject to the jurisdiction thereof, are citizens of the United States and of the State wherein they reside. No State shall make or enforce any law which shall abridge the privileges or immunities of citizens of the United States; nor shall any State deprive any person of life, liberty, or property, without due process of law; nor deny to any person within its jurisdiction the equal protection of the laws.

Section 2. Representatives shall be apportioned among the several States according to their respective numbers, counting the whole number of persons in each State, excluding Indians not taxed. But when the right to vote at any election for the choice of electors for President and Vice-President of the United States, Representatives in Congress, the Executive and Judicial officers of a State, or the members of the Legislature thereof, is denied to any of the male inhabitants of such State, being twenty-one years of age, and citizens of the United States, or in any way abridged, except for participation in rebellion, or other crime, the basis of representation therein shall be reduced in the proportion which the number of such male citizens shall bear to the whole number of male citizens twenty-one years of age in such State.

(continued)

Section 3. No person shall be a Senator or Representative in Congress, or elector of President and Vice President, or hold any office, civil or military, under the United States, or under any State, who, having previously taken an oath, as a member of Congress, or as an officer of the United States, or as a member of any State legislature, or as an executive or judicial officer of any State, to support the Constitution of the United States, shall have engaged in insurrection or rebellion against the same, or given aid or comfort to the enemies thereof. But Congress may by a vote of two-thirds of each House, remove such disability.

Section 4. The validity of the public debt of the United States, authorized by law, including debts incurred for payment of pensions and bounties for services in suppressing insurrection or rebellion, shall not be questioned. But neither the United States nor any State shall assume or pay any debt or obligation incurred in aid of insurrection or rebellion against the United States, or any claim for the loss or emancipation of any slave; but all such debts, obligations and claims shall be held illegal and void.

Section 5. The Congress shall have power to enforce, by appropriate legislation, the provisions of this article.

2

AGENTS AND MANAGERS

AFTER STUDYING THIS CHAPTER YOU SHOULD BE ABLE TO:

1. Define the term agent as applied in the entertainment industry.
2. Describe the roles that talent agents play in entertainment.
3. Distinguish between the various duties one owes as a fiduciary.
4. Describe the various forms of regulation of agents and managers in the entertainment industry.
5. Compare and contrast the differences between California and New York regulation of agents or managers.
6. Identify the types of fees and commission structures associated with representation of talent in the entertainment industry by varying intermediaries.
7. Define the phrase procuring employment.
8. Define and describe the incidental booking exception for talent agents.
9. Differentiate between sports agents and entertainment agents.
10. Discuss various ethical codes and considerations involved in representing talent.

INTRODUCTION

The term **agent** in the entertainment industry is a very general term. Playing the role of an agent can actually mean several different things. For example, there are booking agents, publicists, lawyers, financial advisers, and others who act on behalf of artists. Artists are often described as **talent** in legal circles. If they can afford to, talent often utilize the skills of more than one type of agent (including lawyers) at any given point in their careers. Quality agents of any type have a general understanding of the nature and role of contract law. In some cases, an agent might actually play more than one role on behalf of the talent, especially during the early stages of a career in the entertainment industry. Regardless of the term used to describe these various beneficial intermediaries who play the role of an agent, ultimately the agent's primary goal is the same: to generate as much revenue for the artist as possible by securing as many opportunities for work as possible.

Talent agents and **personal managers** traditionally have performed distinct, albeit similar-sounding, roles in the entertainment industry. Generally speaking, talent agents arrange and negotiate their clients' employment opportunities; personal managers suggest which of those opportunities are worthwhile. Though sometimes talent agents cross over to manage and personal managers cross over to be an agent, there is a distinction between the two, and entertainment unions and state laws actually regulate their differences.

While audiences are able to enjoy the bookings secured by talent agents in thousands of venues in the United States and around the globe, the cities of Los Angeles and New York are the geographic driving forces in the entertainment industry with regard to elite talent representation. Indeed, the entertainment industry is one of California's largest and most well-known industries.

THE ROLE OF TALENT AGENTS

Part of the fun of being a talent agent in entertainment is the uncertainty and taking of risk with an eye toward reaping great financial reward, while maintaining the financial interests of the talented client. Talent agents make money from a **commission** (the most common form of compensation for an agent), **hourly fee,** or **flat fee.** Talent agent fees may be regulated by a state statute or group union, while personal manager fees are often purely a by-product of marketplace negotiations between the client and personal manager.

Once an entertainment career has been solidified by a performer, the focus may be less on number of employment opportunities and more on fewer yet higher paying opportunities to perform. As an artist's career takes off and the term talent often becomes **celebrity,** it is often easier to find avenues for the talent than at the beginning of their often uncertain career, which is generally based upon short-term (though sometimes high profile) projects.

Often, talent and their army of agents part ways during the course of a career, especially in tough times. It is not unheard of, however, for an artist to change agents and later return to the former agent or agency. Due to the dynamic nature of the entertainment industry and the "what have you done for me lately" attitude by both artists and agents, it is very important that the parties negotiate contractual relationships[6] that will allow the termination of agreements with the fewest complications possible.

▋ TRADITIONAL TALENT AGENTS

Talent agents are regulated by states and unions; personal managers are not regulated. Talent agents are marketing intermediaries: their goal is to secure deals on behalf of their clients. Personal managers serve more as advisors. Some of the larger **talent agencies** include The William Morris Agency, ICM (International Creative Management), and CAA (Creative Artists Agency). Though good agents may often create many opportunities for talent to demonstrate their skills, ultimately the talent must decide whether or not to agree to a deal. Usually talent does not object to deals since most deals are of limited duration.

One of the inherent dilemmas of being a talent agent is that more experienced talent agents often avoid unproven talent. This makes sense since there is less of a guarantee on their time and effort as buyers of their talent or buyers of talent at particular **venues** may not know (or wish to know) the ability of a particular unproven entertainer. Since talent agents are usually only paid if they secure a deal which is accepted, there is an incentive to work hard. However, there is little incentive to work for unproven talent other than a potential future payday. That is where personal managers sometimes play the dual role of a talent agent for unknown talent when traditional talent agencies back off until the talent becomes more marketable. Managers who act as talent agents, however, are subject to talent agent laws, though many fail to comply with those regulations, which are discussed later in this chapter.

Talent agents are almost always paid a commission by the artist based upon the **gross earnings,** rather than the net, from a particular deal. Unfortunately, for many artists there are times when it becomes uncertain whose best interest is at heart, creating a potential **conflict of interest.**[7] One might ask whether the

---

[6] Representation contracts go by various names, including representation agreement, general services agreement, and so on.

[7] The Screen Actors Guild and the Association of Talent Agents, for example, have had an agreement to prevent talent agents from also being the producers of films or television shows to avoid potential conflicts of interest.

talent agent is serving the talent's career interest or the talent agent's own financial interest. For example, a talent agent (or talent agency) may have tens or even hundreds (thousands in a few cases) of talent that they represent at any given point in time. If more than one of their clients could be booked for a performance, who does the talent agent push and to whom does the talent agent owe the greatest duty of care? Such questions are not easily answerable and can be troublesome especially in larger talent agencies.

AGENT REGULATION

A few individual states and entertainment unions now set standards for talent agent conduct (as opposed to sports agents, which is discussed later in the chapter). Due to the highly competitive nature of the entertainment industry and due to numerous and egregious cases of **fraud,** talent agents are now specifically regulated in California and New York, the major hubs of the entertainment industries. Talent agencies and their talent agents in essence act like employment agencies.

PRINCIPAL-AGENT

Students of law and business should recognize the importance of the terms **principal** and agent. A principal-agent arrangement exists when a person (the agent) acts on behalf of and in the best interest of another (the principal) and is usually compensated for doing so. The relationship between a principal and agent is special, and this holds true in all industries. For example, lawyers act on behalf of their clients as agents every day. Similarly, shareholders in a corporation elect management to act as agents on behalf of their own financial interests and to maximize shareholder value.

FIDUCIARY DUTIES

Agents owe principals a special legal duty of care as a fiduciary, a hallmark of the principal-agent relationship. A **fiduciary** is someone who owes another a special degree of care and good faith when conducting business transactions. This special relationship forms the trust that binds the relationship that may frequently be tested by changes in attitudes, preferences, or simply market and economic forces. Often, this trust is normally exemplified in a contractual agreement known as an **agreement for representation.** Breach of fiduciary duties often leads to litigation between the parties.

Tom Cruise played a sports agent in *Jerry McGuire*.
Getty Images Inc. –Hulton Archive Photos.

Fiduciary duties that are owed to another are often described in various ways. Some of the descriptions of **duties** in any fiduciary relationship include:

(1) **Duty of Loyalty:** The principle that an employee (agent) may not divert a business opportunity to themselves or to a competitor.
(2) **Duty of Care:** An agent must use reasonable skill and diligence when working for the principal.
(3) **Duty of Accounting:** An agent must keep an account of (and be able to account for) all money and property received and paid out on behalf of a principal.
(4) **Duty of Good Faith:** An agent must be truthful and faithful to promoting the interests of the principal.

One of the reasons that the concept of a fiduciary is so important is that usually one party exercises a more dominant position over another party based upon their knowledge, contacts, and expertise in a particular area or industry. This is very prevalent during the beginning stages of an entertainer's career, but the same concept holds true throughout their career, even when the entertainer becomes more familiar with the industry.

An entertainment agent, manager, or other representative often has considerable control over an artist's affairs at various stages of a career. In fact, talent often selects an agent based upon their contacts within an industry to allow for the utilization of the talent agent's **clout** in order to find employment opportunities and/or negotiation of contracts for the artist. So important is the relationship between talent agents and artists that several states have enacted laws designed to regulate talent agents and, as a result, protect talent from unscrupulous activity, double-dealing, conflicts of interest, and exploitation.

■ SPECIFIC TALENT AGENT DUTIES

In addition to the general fiduciary concepts mentioned previously, a talent agent also owes more specific duties to a principal. A talent agent's duties to his or her clients include:

1. Soliciting public (and possibly private) performances, appearances, and engagements
2. Licensing of rights to creative work and other opportunities that present themselves
3. Pursuing and assisting in the selection of any other opportunities for talent to generate income or revenue

Many consider talent agents to be some of the more powerful people in the entertainment industry. Since so much emphasis is placed on people and personalities in this industry, often a less talented or less marketed artist may get special privileges if they are represented by a talent agent that has considerable contacts and a well-respected reputation within that industry.

■ *MELLENCAMP V. RIVA MUSIC, LTD.*

Sometimes the role of a talent "agent" might not be clearly defined. In such instances, courts might be asked to interpret whether or not a talent agent violated an alleged fiduciary role. In *Mellencamp v. Riva Music, Ltd.*, 698 F. Supp. 1154 (S.D.N.Y. 1988), the federal district court was forced to analyze when a business relationship actually rises to the level of a fiduciary relationship. The court held that obligations assumed by a publisher in an exclusive licensing agreement were <u>not</u> fiduciary duties similar to those of a general talent agent. Popular singer John Mellencamp brought suit against the music publisher that held his composition rights. He alleged that the company automatically became a fiduciary and subsequently failed to promote his songs using their "best efforts." The court disagreed and held that the publishing agreement did not rise to the level of a relationship of "trust and confidence." Thus, the contract created a business (but not) fiduciary relationship and is an often cited case when dealing with the issue of at what point one becomes a fiduciary.

■ UNIONS AND TALENT AGENTS

There are numerous unions in the entertainment industry. Some of the major entertainment related unions include the American Federation of Musicians (AFM), American Federation of Television and Radio Artists (AFTRA), Screen Actors Guild (SAG), National Writer's Union (NWU), and **Author's Guild.** Entertainment unions organized to assert and expand wages and benefits.[8] Their purposes also include protecting artists from unethical or improper activities by their representatives (including limiting the fees that talent agents can charge for their services and utilizing standard contracts) and unethical conduct by employers such as production studios, for example.

■ FEES

Unions often require talent agents to be certified (sometimes called "franchised") in order to represent members of the union such as actors and actresses. Though a talent agent and personal manager do many of the same things, talent agent fees are generally limited to a 10 to 20 percent commission either by state statute, union contract, or simply the competitive marketplace. Personal managers' fees are generally unregulated but tend to hover around 10 to 25 percent. AFTRA and SAG prohibit talent agents from receiving commissions that exceed 10 percent of the artist's gross earnings. AFM allows talent

---

[8] There are many other unions as well, including the American Guild of Musical Artists (AGMA) and the American Guild of Variety Artists (AGVA).

agents to receive commissions of 20 percent for booking one-night engagements and 15 percent for booking longer engagements.

UNIONS AND REPRESENTATION LIMITS

Unions also regulate the duration of the artist-agent relationship. While personal managers prefer longer term relationships in order to maximize the potential return on their input and investment, SAG and AFTRA impose term limits of three years. AFM allows five-year terms in some instances and up to seven-year terms in others. State law, such as California's Labor Code § 2855, limits the term of **personal service** contracts to seven years (discussed further in Chapter 3).

Additionally, various unions do not allow talent agents to **procure employment** for any union member without a certification or **franchise license** agreement from that union. A **license** is the formal granting of permission to do an act (in fact, sometimes it is simply referred to as a permission). These licensing agreements are strict, and any SAG member who engages the services of a talent agent without a franchise license can be subject to disciplinary action. Consequently, the union may seek to impose sanctions on both the artist and the artist's representative for violating union rules.

UNIONS AND MANAGERS

Although these franchise representation agreements regulate talent agents' activities, they do not regulate talent or personal **managers.** Unions and guilds believe that there is less of a need to regulate managers. One reason that managers are not regulated like talent agents is due to the lack of conflict of interest issues that arise between managers and talent, as compared to talent agents. Managers often invest a lot of time and money in assisting talent to reach their goals, and the investment sometimes does not pay for itself. Further, as talent's clout increases, talent might actually "dump" a manager just at the point where they make it big.

CALIFORNIA REGULATIONS

California regulates talent agents and requires licensing in accordance with state law found in its Labor Code. The California **Talent Agencies Act (TAA)** establishes strict licensing requirements for talent agents. The TAA was significantly amended in 1986. The TAA expressly prohibits anyone other than licensed talent agents from procuring (or even merely attempting to procure) employment for talent.

In California, a talent agency is defined to engage in:

> . . . the occupation of procuring, offering, promising or attempting to procure employment or engagements for an artist or artists, except that the activities of

procuring, offering, or promising to procure recording contracts for an artist or artists shall not of itself subject to person or corporation to regulation and licensing under this chapter. California Labor Code § 1700.4(a).

In California, a talent agent must be bonded and obtain a license from the Labor Commissioner. Applicants must be a person of "good moral character" with two years' experience in a business or occupation. Also, applicants must pay a fee of $25, and there is an annual renewal fee of $225. Agent contracts are subject to approval by the Labor Commissioner and may be disregarded if they are deemed "unfair, unjust and oppressive to the artist."

California does not limit talent agent fees **per se** (New York does), but talent agent fees are limited in practice to 10 percent by the various unions. Also, talent agents must maintain separate trust bank accounts for their clients.

EXCEPTIONS TO TAA

The TAA contains two exceptions to the state licensing requirement for talent agents. First, in the music industry, those individuals who procure recording contracts for artists need not obtain a talent agency license. This exception recognizes a difference in the music industry that personal managers often secure and negotiate recording contracts for their clients as well. Second, the TAA provides an exception for negotiating an employment contract when acting in concert with and at the request of a licensed talent agency. Though this may not happen frequently, it still allows personal managers and talent agents to work together if and when necessary by creating a **safe harbor** (an exception) to the rule. A safe harbor affords protection from a penalty for what would otherwise be a violation of the TAA.

PROCURING EMPLOYMENT

Talent agents can procure employment opportunities for talent, while personal managers may not. Still, many believe that such a bright-line distinction is out of touch with reality. In fact, many personal managers will still procure employment for their clients, and talent agents sometimes even ask them to do so. In California, an individual who procures employment for an artist is deemed to be a talent agent. Under the TAA, only talent agents are permitted to procure employment for artists. Consequently, to establish a violation of the TAA, an individual must have engaged in unlicensed procurement activities on behalf of an artist. What "procurement" actually means, however, is often the subject of debate. Many artists could care less about the TAA and just want work, whether it is from talent agents or personal managers.

NEW YORK REGULATIONS

Like California, New York serves a major location and force in the entertainment industry. New York has adopted § 172 of New York's General Business Law

(G.B.L.) which prohibits the operation of an employment agency without a license. Such unlicensed operation is a misdemeanor. New York law regulates **employment agencies,** including theatrical employment agencies.[9] Section 171 defines an employment agency as any individual or company "who, for a fee, procures or attempts to procure employment or engagements for . . . modeling or other entertainments or exhibitions or performances." The same statute excludes from the definition of employment agency "the business of managing . . . where such business only incidentally involves the seeking of employment."

INCIDENTAL BOOKING EXCEPTION

In contrast to California law, New York law has a <u>major</u> exception to licensing known as the **incidental booking exception** for managers. It applies only to representatives who function primarily as personal managers for their clients. This exception to § 171 has been repeatedly held by the courts to mean that the seeking of employment must be incidental to the provision of management services. California talent agents oppose the incidental booking exception in their state, claiming that it would harm their business. Competition for business in California is quite fierce and talent agents understandably do not wish to increase opportunities for personal managers.

Similar to California, New York law requires that all licensed talent agencies must pay a licensing fee to the state or city commissioner. Talent agents must be licensed by the Commissioner of Labor (the Commissioner of Consumer Affairs in New York City). Background and character checks are performed as well. The initial licensing fee is $200 ($400 if the talent agency has more than four employees), and a $5,000 bond is required. A written contract is required, and the maximum fee chargeable for theatrical engagements is 10 percent of the compensation paid to the talent, with an exception allowing a fee of 20 percent for engagements for orchestras and employment or engagements in the opera and concert fields.

The following agreement is an example of a contract between a California talent agency and its client.

TALENT AGENCY GENERAL SERVICES AGREEMENT

AGREED THIS DATE: _____

UNDERSTANDING: *This written agreement confirms our relationship and represents the complete understanding between us. By signing below, you hereby accept the terms of this general services agreement. The pronouns "I" and "me" represents the client and "You" represents the Talent Agency. Wherever the context so requires, the masculine gender shall include and apply to all genders and the singular shall apply to and include, as well, the plural.*

---

[9] The overall New York regulations scheme is found in G.B.L. §§ 170–190.

TERMS:

1. Exclusive Representation. I hereby engage you as my sole and exclusive representative and agent throughout the world for a term of_____ years, commencing with the date written above. This shall be considered the "term" of the agreement. I understand that you may render other or similar services to other persons, firms and corporations. I agree not to engage any other person, firm or corporation to act for me in the capacity in which I have engaged you. Additionally, I hereby represent and warrant that I am free to enter into this Agreement and that I do not have and will not have any contract or obligation that will conflict herewith.

2. Agent's Duties. The agent's duties with regard to this relationship described further hereunder shall be to use all reasonable efforts to procure the engagement of my services, as writer, composer, editor, author, lyricist, musician, artist, performer, designer, consultant, cameraman, technician, director, producer, associate producer, supervisor, or executive, and/or in any other capacity in the entertainment, literary and related fields throughout the world. This includes, but is not limited to, merchandising, testimonials, advertising, infomercials, commercial tie-ups, CD-ROMs, CD-Is, interactive media or any other technology now in existence or hereafter developed or utilized. However, the aforementioned duties outside the United States and its territories may, at your election, be performed by anyone else appointed by you.

3. Fees. I agree to pay you <u>ten percent (10%)</u> of the gross compensation earned or received by me for, or in connection with, (i) any contracts for, or engagements of, my services (collectively and individually hereinafter sometimes referred to as "employment") now in existence, except to such extent that I may be obligated to pay commission on such contracts to another agent, or contracts entered into or negotiated for during the term, including, but not limited to, all gross compensation therefrom, and payments thereon, that are earned or received by me, or become due or payable to me after the expiration of the term, and (ii) for, or in connection with all modifications, renewals, additions, substitutions, supplements, replacements, or extensions of or to such contracts and engagements, whether negotiated during or after the term hereof. You shall continue to perform your obligations hereunder after the term with respect to all employment with respect to which you are entitled to your commission as provided in the immediately preceding sentence.

4. Gross Compensation. "Gross compensation" includes all forms of compensation, money, things of value or other emoluments (including, but not limited to, salaries, earnings, fees, residuals, royalties, bonuses, gifts, monetary and nonmonetary consideration, securities and shares of profits or gross receipts) received by me or any person, firm or corporation, partnership, joint venture or other entity now or hereafter owned or controlled by me (hereafter "my firm") or on which I may have any right, title or interest, on my behalf, from such contracts or engagements and modifications, renewals, additions, substitutions, supplements, replacements, and extensions of or to such contracts or engagements, whether or not procured by you or by anyone else as well as from any form of advertising, commercial tie-ups or infomercials using my name, likeness, or voice.

5. Own Firm. In the event that my firm, if any, has or hereafter during the term acquires, directly or indirectly, any right respecting my services in any of the fields covered by this agreement, then promptly following your request to do so, I shall cause my firm to enter into a written exclusive agency agreement with you with respect to such services upon all of the terms and conditions herein contained, specifically including an agreement by my firm to pay compensation to you as herein provided, based upon the gross compensation paid and/or payable to my firm, directly or indirectly, for furnishing my services. For the purposes of this paragraph, the term "gross compensation" shall be deemed to include gross compensation paid and/or payable to my firm if it would have been gross compensation if paid or payable to me. Notwithstanding the fact that my firm may enter into such agency agreement with you, I shall in all events remain primarily liable, jointly and severally with my firm, to pay compensation to you as provided above, based on the gross compensation paid and/or payable to my firm, directly or indirectly, for furnishing my services; and I shall indemnify you against a failure of my firm to execute said agency agreement, or, if it has executed said agency agreement, any failure of my firm to pay commissions pursuant thereto or otherwise to comply with the provisions thereof, and hold you harmless from any loss, cost, or expense incurred by you as a result of said failure. No waiver, extension, change or amendment with respect to said agency agreement or failure for any reason to execute same, shall be deemed to release me of or from any liability hereunder.

6. Notice of Breach. No breach or failure by you to perform the terms hereof, which breach or failure would otherwise be deemed a material breach of this Agreement, shall be considered as such unless within thirty (30) days after I acquire knowledge of such breach or failure or of facts sufficient to put me upon notice thereof, I serve written notice upon you of such breach or failure and you do not cure said breach or failure within a period of ten (10) days after your receipt of the notice. This paragraph shall not be deemed to extend or limit the applicable provisions of Section 1700.44 of the California Labor Code.

7. Payments Due. Your commissions under this Agreement shall be payable as and when gross compensation is received by you or me, my firm, or any other person or entity on my behalf. From all gross compensation subject to this Agreement which you may receive, you shall have the right to deduct the amount of any and all commissions that are due and payable to you hereunder or under any other representation agreement between us. With respect to gross compensation subject to this Agreement which is paid directly to me, my firm, or any other person or entity on my behalf, an amount equal to said commission shall be deemed to be received and held by me or them in trust for you and your commission thereon shall be paid to you promptly after receipt by me or them of such gross compensation.

8. Subsequent Offers. If within four (4) months after the end of the term hereof, I accept any offer on terms similar or reasonably comparable to any offer made to me during the term hereof, from or through the same offeror or any person, firm or corporation directly or indirectly connected with such offeror, the contract resulting therefrom (oral or written) shall be subject to all of the terms hereof, including the payment provisions as aforementioned. As to the proceeds of any motion picture, film, tape, wire, transcription, recording, or other reproduction of my services covered by this Agreement, your right to payment as aforementioned shall continue so long as any of these are used, sold, leased, or otherwise disposed of, whether during or after the term hereof. If I enter into any agreement which would have been otherwise covered by this General Services Agreement within four (4) months after the termination hereof, with any person or business entity as to whom a submission has been made and/or negotiations commenced on my behalf during the term of this Agreement, then in said event any such employment contract entered into shall be deemed to have been entered into during the term hereof.

9. Jurisdiction. Insofar as this Agreement refers to any employment subject to the jurisdiction of the State of California, controversies arising between us under the Labor Code of the State of California and the rules and regulations for the enforcement thereof shall be referred to the Labor Commissioner of the State of California as provided in Section 1700.44 of said in effect may permit the reference of any such controversy to any other forum, person or group of persons.

10. Entire Agreement. This instrument, together with any forms you and I execute, sets forth the entire contracted arrangement between us with respect to the fields of endeavor recited earlier in this Agreement. This Agreement shall not become effective until accepted and executed by you. I hereby represent and warrant in executing this Agreement that I have not relied on any statement, promises, representations or inducements, except as specifically set forth herein. This Agreement may not be changed, modified, waived or discharged in whole or in part except by an instrument in writing signed by you and me; provided further that any substantial changes in this Agreement must first be approved by the California Labor Commissioner unless said changes operate to my advantage. This Agreement shall inure to the benefit of and be binding upon you and me and your and my respective heirs, distributees, executors and administrators.

11. Additional Considerations. Should any provision of this Agreement be void or unenforceable for any reason, such provision shall be deemed omitted and this Agreement with such provision omitted shall remain in full force and effect. If and when the SAG and the ATA agree to a new franchise agreement, said terms shall be automatically deemed incorporated herein and binding on the parties hereto.

12. Right to Terminate. If I am not offered employment which is subject to this Agreement from a responsible employer with respect to my services covered by this Agreement during any period in excess of four consecutive months during the term, during all of which time I am ready, able and willing to accept employment, either party hereto shall have the right to terminate this Agreement by a notice in writing sent to the last known address of the other party by certified mail; provided, however, that such right shall be deemed waived by me (but not as to future four (4) consecutive months of employment) and any exercise thereof by me shall be ineffective if after the expiration of any such four-month period and prior to the time of mailing of the notice, I have accepted an offer for employment by a responsible employer; and provided further that such termination shall not affect your rights or my obligations under the terms of this Agreement.

_____

Client

_____

Address

AGREED TO AND ACCEPTED:

By: _____

Title: _____

Address: _____

Date: _____

This Talent Agency is licensed by the Labor Commissioner of the State of California. The form of this contract has been approved by the State Labor Commissioner on December 5, 2001. The Labor Commissioner has no jurisdiction over recording contracts and "Materials and Packages" agreements and therefore, neither approves nor disapproves the provisions of this agreement which pertain or apply thereto.

APPROVED AS TO FORM

_____/s/_____

STATE LABOR COMMISSIONER: _____

_____

DATE

WAISBREN V. PEPPERCORN PROD., INC.

In *Waisbren v. Peppercorn Prod., Inc.*, 48 Cal. Rptr. 2d 437 (Cal. Ct. App. 1995), the California Court of Appeals affirmed a lower court ruling that even incidental procurement activities require compliance with the California TAA. This case was important because the court rejected the test that had been adopted in an earlier case, *Wachs v. Curry*, 16 Cal. Rptr. 2d 496 (Ct. App. 1993), to determine whether the degree of representation (i.e., how significant) by an unlicensed talent agent required obtaining a license from the state.

After the termination of the business relationship, plaintiff Brad Waisbren filed suit for commissions owed to him by the company as a result of an alleged oral management contract. The trial court granted **summary judgment** for defendant Peppercorn because the court found that the management contract was void because Waisbren had engaged in talent agency services by procuring employment for Peppercorn without having obtained a talent agency license. Thus, under the *Waisbren* decision, personal managers in California may <u>not</u> engage in even limited efforts to procure employment for a client without fulfilling the regulatory and licensing requirements of the TAA.

ENTERTAINMENT LAWYERS

Though the entertainment industry involves a complex mesh of people from a variety of disciplines, the legal profession is a driving force in entertainment. Many firms in California and New York specialize in entertainment law. These attorneys play a vital role in the entertainment industry. Many of these entertainment lawyers were often artists themselves at one time. They are most important to their clients in the various areas of business law, tax and accounting, labor law, intellectual property, criminal law, family law, immigration law, and litigation. Entertainment lawyers usually charge flat fees or hourly rates for their services.

Many students of the law hope to ultimately practice in the arena of entertainment law. Such practitioners are essentially no different from other attorneys outside the entertainment industry except that they must become familiar with the nuances of the industry itself and the people or players involved in entertainment law. The lure of practicing entertainment law often involves a compelling desire to be involved with high dollar and noteworthy individuals and corporations. Entertainment lawyers play significant roles in all areas of entertainment law, but most entertainment law firms do not welcome novices to the industry with open arms.

Breaking into entertainment law is challenging. Some attorneys stumble into entertainment law accidentally. For others, it is clearly by design. The entertainment industry is so huge that representation is not limited to individual talent. Many lawyers also provide advice and support to motion picture studios, recording companies, and distribution outlets. Such lawyers in the industry have been known to package deals, shop talent and creative material, and advise on financial matters even though they are unlicensed or certified in particular areas.

REGULATION OF LAWYERS

Talent agents, personal managers and lawyers provide valuable services to their clients. Regulation of lawyers, however, presents additional legal and ethical issues that do not apply to either talent agents or personal managers. Practicing lawyers must be licensed by the state in which they practice law. Talent agents and personal managers are not licensed, though they are regulated. Lawyers must obtain a law degree, whereas talent agents and personal managers do not.

Lawyers primarily give advice (just like talent agents and personal managers), and their services often may resemble that of a talent agent or personal manager. Still, lawyers become privy to such a wide range of personal issues as a representative that it is not realistic to say that lawyers only give legal advice. Lawyers who represent groups of individuals, such as a band, can be presented with curious situations or, at the very least, conflicts of interest when, for example, the band dissolves and the lawyer is privy to confidential information. Dealing with potential conflicts of interest is important for lawyers to address at the beginning of the lawyer-client relationship. Such relationships should be in writing and signed by all parties because a lawyer could be disqualified from future representation of the group in order to avoid a conflict of interest in litigation.

It is important to lawyers to avoid a violation of an established state code of professional responsibility such as the 1983 draft of the American Bar Association (ABA) **Model Rules of Professional Conduct** (MRPC) or the 1969 draft of the **Model Code of Professional Responsibility** (MCPR). Almost all states use verbatim or variations of the MRPC as the standard for ethical considerations for lawyers. A violation of the relevant state ethical code might be cause to revoke a lawyer's license and put them out of business. For example, MRPC 7.3 governs **advertising** and **solicitation** by lawyers for which talent agents and personal managers are not regulated. A violation of these regulations could put the lawyer out of business.[10] An ethical violation could also subject the lawyer to a claim of **malpractice**.

Lawyers usually charge an hourly fee for representation and that fee must be reasonable according to MRPC 1.5. However, lawyers can agree to a **contingency fee** arrangement (a percentage of a gross income of the deal). Contingency fee arrangements must be in writing and are often preferred for clients who cannot afford up-front fees.

ABA MODEL RULE 7.3 DIRECT CONTACT WITH PROSPECTIVE CLIENTS[11]

(a) A lawyer shall not by in-person, live telephone or real-time electronic contact solicit professional employment from a prospective client when a significant motive for the lawyer's doing so is the lawyer's pecuniary gain, unless the person contacted:

  (1) is a lawyer; or

  (2) has a family, close personal, or prior professional relationship with the lawyer.

(b) A lawyer shall not solicit professional employment from a prospective client by written, recorded or electronic communication or by in-person, telephone or real-time electronic contact even when not otherwise prohibited by paragraph (a), if:

  (1) the prospective client has made known to the lawyer a desire not to be solicited by the lawyer; or

  (2) the solicitation involves coercion, duress or harassment.

(c) Every written, recorded or electronic communication from a lawyer soliciting professional employment from a prospective client known to be in need of legal services in a particular matter shall include the words "Advertising Material" on the outside envelope, if any, and at the beginning and ending of any recorded or electronic communication, unless the recipient of the communication is a person specified in paragraphs (a)(1) or (a)(2).

(d) Notwithstanding the prohibitions in paragraph (a), a lawyer may participate with a prepaid or group legal service plan operated by an organization not owned or directed by the lawyer that uses in-person or telephone contact to solicit memberships or subscriptions for the plan from persons who are not known to need legal services in a particular matter covered by the plan.

---

[10] There is actually a difference between solicitation (in-person and by mail) as opposed to advertising (on radio, television), and state ethical codes governing lawyers often deal with the subtle differences.

[11] http://www.abanet.org/cpr/mrpc/rule_7_3.html.

■ PERSONAL MANAGERS

While lawyers usually focus on legal issues related to an artist, the term personal manager means something slightly different. Rather than charge an hourly fee, personal managers usually charge a commission (as a percentage of income). Personal managers are often the closest persons to the talent during their career and often give input and advice as to how to best seek and ultimately select business opportunities in order to generate the most revenue for their client. Personal managers play the various roles of coach, counselor, publicist, and adviser, and they do not negotiate deals for their clients (or they are not supposed to).

A personal manager shapes and molds the entertainer's career, especially for unproven talent. The role of the personal manager is to package the persona of the entertainer. Interestingly, it is this same personal manager who, after a deal is made, often serves as the coordinator between the artist and the attorney, movie or record company, talent or booking agent, and other business persons, including sponsors.

The personal manager's role is often inglorious and often receives little thanks. They must keep the talent's career on track and are very much involved in making important decisions based upon input from the other various members of the artist's team. Personal managers' input involving career decisions is so vital that they are involved in some of the make-or-break decisions in the entertainment industry. While there is no pure statutory regulation of personal managers, fiduciary duties still exist. Additionally, in California, a personal manager who procures employment must be listed as a talent agency.[12] In New Jersey, a personal manager who finds work for artists must be licensed as a **booking agency.**[13]

In the end, the personal manager assists the artist in goal setting, goal reaching, and many, many other ways that often go uncompensated in the daily activities of the artist. Some personal managers actually charge a fee based upon an ownership interest in the talent. For example, if an actor is paid through royalties from a profitable television show, the personal manager might take a percentage of that profit. Some question the ethics of that practice as being too self-serving for the personal manager rather than the artist. In the end, personal managers do not seek employment like talent agents do, but they do "promote" the best interests of their clients by providing a third-party perspective on career decisions.

■ BUSINESS MANAGERS

Unlike the personal manager, a **business manager** handles the talent's finances. The business manager must know the nuances of investment issues, tax

---

[12] Cal. Lab. Code § 1700 *et seq.*
[13] N.J. Stat. Ann. § 34: 8–43.

Eddie Murphy makes deal with Paramount Pictures.
AP Wide World Photos.

implications, contract law, and estate planning matters. Many business managers become involved with talent at the point when exposure and revenues increase for the artist. Certainly, understanding the particular industry (e.g., music, television, film) and its own vernacular is very helpful in order to properly converse with talent over financial matters. The giving of financial advice may require state licensure or certification as well.

BOOKING AGENTS

Talent agents are often (and sometimes erroneously) synonymous with **booking agent.** However, most booking agents are those who focus on and arrange for live performances for talent. Thus, the slight difference might be whereas a booking agent contracts for live appearances, talent agents often negotiate more general contracts or [product] endorsements, if they present themselves. Much skill is utilized by booking agents to coordinate a **tour** so that talent may travel in an efficient manner while on the road. For example, it would likely be unwise to schedule a concert date in Los Angeles, then the next stop in New York, and then back to southern California in that order. This is sometimes referred to as **routing.**

SPORTS AGENTS

Sports agents are regulated much differently than talent agents, personal managers, and other intermediaries in entertainment. At one time, sports agents were not regulated at all at the state or federal level.[14] Beginning in the 1980s, states began to regulate sports agent activity specifically with regard to the recruiting of student athletes as clients at colleges and universities around the country, who had remaining eligibility to participate. The purpose was to avoid sanctions from the **National Collegiate Athletic Association** (NCAA). NCAA rules provide for loss of remaining eligibility if a student athlete signs a contract for representation with a sports agent. Unscrupulous agents were also found to have provided **extra benefits** to the student athlete. Unfortunately, some states took this issue more seriously than others and what developed was a myriad of inconsistent and confusing state sports agent laws with which most sports agents still did not comply.

Today, the legal landscape governing sports agents has changed considerably. In order to avoid confusion, the **National Conference of Commissioners on Uniform State Laws** (NCCUSL) drafted a model act (2000) for states to adopt known as the **Uniform Athlete Agents Act** (UAAA). The UAAA focuses on activity by a sports agent who recruits a student athlete with remaining collegiate eligibility in a particular sport.

AS OF FEBRUARY, 2005, THE UAAA HAD BEEN PASSED IN 31 STATES AND TWO TERRITORIES:[15]

Alabama
Arizona
Arkansas
Connecticut
Delaware
District of Columbia
Florida
Georgia
Idaho
Indiana
Kansas
Kentucky
Louisiana
Maryland
Minnesota
Mississippi
Missouri
Montana

---

[14] In October 2004, President George W. Bush signed into law the **Sports Agent Responsibility and Trust Act** (SPARTA), to protect student-athletes from losing NCAA eligibility for unethical behavior by sports agents. The FTC has jurisdiction now through its unfair and deceptive acts rules. See 15 U.S.C. § 7801 *et seq.*

[15] http://www1.ncaa.org/membership/enforcement/agents/uaaa/history.html

Nevada
New York
North Carolina
North Dakota
Oklahoma
Pennsylvania
Rhode Island
South Carolina
Tennessee
Texas
Utah
U.S. Virgin Islands
Washington
West Virginia
Wisconsin

THREE STATES HAD ACTIVE UAAA LEGISLATION IN ITS LEGISLATIVE CHAMBERS:

Hawaii
New Hampshire
South Dakota

SIX STATES HAD EXISTING, NON-UAAA LAWS DESIGNED TO REGULATE ATHLETE AGENTS:

California
Colorado
Iowa
Michigan
Ohio
Oregon

THIRTEEN STATES AND ONE TERRITORY HAD NO EXISTING LAW REGULATING ATHLETE AGENTS:

Alaska
Hawaii
Illinois
Maine
Massachusetts
Nebraska
New Hampshire
New Jersey
New Mexico

Puerto Rico
South Dakota
Vermont
Virginia
Wyoming

Reprinted with permission from the NCAA.

The **big four** professional leagues of the NFL, NBA, MLB, and NHL do have a required **certification** process in the event a sports agent desires to negotiate a salary for a professional athlete in the respective league. Uncertified agents may not negotiate contracts in that sport, but they may pursue other outside endorsement opportunities. Fees for sports agents vary and include a high of 20 percent for **endorsement** income to a low of 1 percent per salary and bonus, the latter being directly regulated by the big four leagues (usually capped at 3 to 4 percent of base salary depending upon the league; check with the leagues and players' associations).

WALTERS AND BLOOM

An egregious example of where sports agents and the entertainment world collided involved Norby Walters and his partner Lloyd Bloom. Walters, also an entertainment booking agent (for singer Dionne Warwick) and a nightclub owner, turned to the world of sports agency to expand business opportunities. They offered money to student athletes (many of whom still had collegiate eligibility remaining). Accepting money was (and still is) a clear violation of NCAA rules. In a three-year period, over 50 former student athletes were signed for representation agreements from numerous schools across the country. In 1990, Walters and Bloom were convicted by jury trial of racketeering, conspiracy, and two counts of mail fraud. An appeals court overruled the conviction, however.[16] The activities by Walters and Bloom (and many, many other sports agents) caused many states to adopt laws related to sports agent misconduct, including the adoption of the UAAA.

CHAPTER SUMMARY

The entertainment industry involves the complex interrelationship between talent, talent agents, lawyers, and personal managers. The industry, which generally includes a broad spectrum—from music to film to television—has had a history of conflicts of interest among its players, necessitating forms of regulation. Any representative of talent owes a special duty of care, known as a fiduciary duty, to their clients.

---

[16] *U.S. v. Walters*, 913 F.2d 388 (7th Cir. 1990).

In the entertainment industry, the roles of talent agents and personal managers are often intertwined. While acts such as the Talent Agencies Act and other union rules require that talent agents be talent agents and personal managers be personal managers, sometimes it is very difficult to remain on only one side of the fence. The roles of talent agent and personal manager can often be confusing and have changed over time. The advent of technology has contributed to the change. Still, a history of unscrupulous conduct by talent agents and personal managers has led to state-specific statutes governing talent agents.

While personal managers may not procure employment for talent in California, the New York rule allows for the "incidental booking exception." While personal managers certainly provide invaluable services to the entertainer, personal manager activities are essentially unregulated. Still, many artists seek invaluable advice from personal managers which could lead to work.

CHAPTER TERMS

Advertising
Agent
Agreement for
    representation
Author's Guild
Big four
Booking agency
Booking agent
Business manager
Celebrity
Certification
Clout
Commission
Conflict of interest
Contingency fee
Duties
Duty of Accounting
Duty of Care
Duty of Good Faith

Duty of Loyalty
Employment agencies
Endorsement
Extra benefits
Fiduciary
Flat fee
Franchise license
Fraud
Gross earnings
Hourly fee
Incidental booking
    exception
License
Malpractice
Managers
Model Code of
    Professional
    Responsibility
    (MCPR)

Model Rules of
    Professional
    Conduct (MRPC)
National Collegiate
    Athletic Association
    (NCAA)
National Conference of
    Commissioners on
    Uniform State Laws
    (NCCUSL)
Per se
Personal manager
Personal service
Principal
Procure employment
Routing
Safe harbor

Solicitation
Sports agent
Sports Agent
    Responsibility
    and Trust Act
Summary judgment
Talent
Talent agencies
Talent Agencies Act
    (TAA)
Talent agent
Tour
Uniform Athlete
    Agents Act (UAAA)
Venues

ADDITIONAL CASES

Anderson v. D'Avola, Cal. Lab. Comm'r Case No. TAC 63–93, Slip Op. at 11–12 (Feb. 24, 1995)

Buchwald v. Superior Court, 62 Cal. Rptr. 364 (Ct. App. 1967)

Chinn v. Tobin, Cal. Labor Comm'r Case No. 17–96 (1997)

Croce v. Kurnit, 565 F. Supp. 884 (S.D.N.Y. 1982)

Davenport v. AFH Talent Agency, Cal. Labor Comm'r Case No. TAC 43–94 (Cal. 2001)

Derek v. Callan, Cal. Lab. Comm'r Case No. TAC 18–80, Slip Op. at 2 (Jan. 14, 1982)

H. A. Artists & Assocs., Inc. v. Actors' Equity Ass'n, 451 U.S. 704 (1981)

Hall v. X Mgmt., Inc., Cal. Lab. Comm'r Case No. TAC 19–90, Slip Op. at 3–5 (Apr. 24, 1992)

Humes v. Margil Venture, Inc., 220 Cal. Rptr. 186 (Ct. App. 1985)

Lee On v. Long, 234 P.2d 9 (Cal. 1951)

Lewis & Queen v. N.M. Ball Sons, 308 P.2d 713 (Cal. 1957)

Mandel v. Liebman, 100 N.E.2d 149 (N.Y. 1951)

Park v. Deftones, 84 Cal. Rptr. 2d 616 (Cal. Ct. App. 1999)

Pine v. Laine, 321 N.Y.S.2d 303 (App. Div. 1971)

Pryor v. Franklin, Cal. Lab. Comm'r Case No. TAC 17 MP114, Slip Op. at 2–3 (Aug. 2, 1982)

Raden v. Laurie, 262 P.2d 61 (Cal. App. 1953)

Strouse v. Corner of the Sky, Inc., Cal. Labor Comm'r Case No. TAC 13–00 (Cal. 2001)

T.C. Theatre Corp. v. Warner Bros. Pictures, 113 F. Supp. 265 (S.D.N.Y. 1953)

Waisbren v. Peppercorn Prod., Inc., 48 Cal. Rptr. 2d 437 (Cal. Ct. App. 1995)

Wong v. Tenneco, Inc., 702 P.2d 570 (Cal. 1985)

REVIEW QUESTIONS

1. What is the role of a talent agent in the entertainment industry?

2. What are the fiduciary duties owed by a talent agent to the client?

3. How does a personal manager differ from a talent agent?

4. What is the role of unions (guilds) in the entertainment industry? Provide examples.

5. What two states regulate talent agents more than any other state in the entertainment industry and why?

6. What is the incidental booking exception in New York? Why do you believe that New York adopted this exception?

7. What are examples of codes of ethics that lawyers must follow to maintain their law license?

8. How do sports agents differ from talent agents or personal managers?

9. What is the Uniform Athlete Agents Act and what was the impetus behind its enactment?

10. Should sports agents be regulated at the federal level or is it best left up to the states?

11. How could the Internet affect the role and effectiveness of a talent agent?

EXHIBIT 2.1

California's Talent Agencies Act*

California Labor Code §1700

(Selected Provisions)

Scope and Definitions

1700. As used in this chapter, "person" means any individual, company, society, firm, partnership, association, corporation, limited liability company, manager, or their agents or employees.

1700.1. As used in this chapter:

(a) "Theatrical engagement" means any engagement or employment of a person as an actor, performer, or entertainer in a circus, vaudeville, theatrical, or other entertainment, exhibition, or performance.

(b) "Motion picture engagement" means any engagement or employment of a person as an actor, actress, director, scenario, or continuity writer, camera man, or in any capacity concerned with the making of motion pictures.

(c) "Emergency engagement" means an engagement which has to be performed within 24 hours from the time when the contract for such engagement is made.

1700.2. (a) As used in this chapter, "fee" means any of the following:

(1) Any money or other valuable consideration paid or promised to be paid for services rendered or to be rendered by any person conducting the business of a talent agency under this chapter.

    (2) Any money received by any person in excess of that which has been paid out by him or her for transportation, transfer of baggage, or board and lodging for any applicant for employment.

    (3) The difference between the amount of money received by any person who furnished employees, performers, or entertainers for circus, vaudeville, theatrical, or other entertainments, exhibitions, or performances, and the amount paid by him or her to the employee, performer, or entertainer.

(b) As used in this chapter, "registration fee" means any charge made, or attempted to be made, to an artist for any of the following purposes:

    (1) Registering or listing an applicant for employment in the entertainment industry.

    (2) Letter writing.

    (3) Photographs, film strips, video tapes, or other reproductions of the applicant.

    (4) Costumes for the applicant.

    (5) Any activity of a like nature.

1700.3. As used in this chapter:

(a) "License" means a license issued by the Labor Commissioner to carry on the business of a talent agency under this chapter.

(b) "Licensee" means a talent agency which holds a valid, unrevoked, and unforfeited license under this chapter.

1700.4. (a) "Talent agency" means a person or corporation who engages in the occupation of procuring, offering, promising, or attempting to procure employment or engagements for an artist or artists, except that the activities of procuring, offering, or promising to procure recording contracts for an artist or artists shall not of itself subject a person or corporation to regulation and licensing under this chapter. Talent agencies may, in addition, counsel or direct artists in the development of their professional careers.

(b) "Artists" means actors and actresses rendering services on the legitimate stage and in the production of motion pictures, radio artists, musical artists, musical organizations, directors of legitimate stage, motion picture and radio productions, musical directors, writers, cinematographers, composers, lyricists, arrangers, models, and other artists and persons rendering professional services in motion picture, theatrical, radio, television and other entertainment enterprises.

Licenses

1700.5. No person shall engage in or carry on the occupation of a talent agency without first procuring a license therefor from the Labor Commissioner. The license shall be posted in a conspicuous place in the office of the licensee. The license number shall be referred to in any advertisement for the purpose of the solicitation of talent for the talent agency. Licenses issued for talent agencies prior to the effective date of this chapter shall not be invalidated thereby, but renewals of those licenses shall be obtained in the manner prescribed by this chapter.

1700.6. A written application for a license shall be made to the Labor Commissioner in the form prescribed by him or her and shall state:

(a) The name and address of the applicant.

(b) The street and number of the building or place where the business of the talent agency is to be conducted.

(continued)

(c) The business or occupation engaged in by the applicant for at least two years immediately preceding the date of application.

(d) If the applicant is other than a corporation, the names and addresses of all persons, except bona fide employees on stated salaries, financially interested, either as partners, associates, or profit sharers, in the operation of the talent agency in question, together with the amount of their respective interests. If the applicant is a corporation, the corporate name, the names, residential addresses, and telephone numbers of all officers of the corporation, the names of all persons exercising managing responsibility in the applicant or licensee's office, and the names and addresses of all persons having a financial interest of 10 percent or more in the business and the percentage of financial interest owned by those persons. The application shall be accompanied by two sets of fingerprints of the applicant and affidavits of at least two reputable residents of the city or county in which the business of the talent agency is to be conducted who have known, or been associated with, the applicant for two years, that the applicant is a person of good moral character or, in the case of a corporation, has a reputation for fair dealing.

1700.7. Upon receipt of an application for a license the Labor Commissioner may cause an investigation to be made as to the character and responsibility of the applicant and of the premises designated in such application as the place in which it is proposed to conduct the business of the talent agency.

1700.8. The commissioner upon proper notice and hearing may refuse to grant a license. The proceedings shall be conducted in accordance with Chapter 5 (commencing at Section 11500) of Part 1 of Division 3 of Title 2 of the Government Code and the commissioner shall have all the power granted therein.

1700.9. No license shall be granted to conduct the business of a talent agency:

(a) In a place that would endanger the health, safety, or welfare of the artist.

(b) To a person whose license has been revoked within three years from the date of application.

1700.10. The license when first issued shall run to the next birthday of the applicant, and each license shall then be renewed within the 30 days preceding the licensee's birthday and shall run from birthday to birthday. In case the applicant is a partnership, such license shall be renewed within the 30 days preceding the birthday of the oldest partner. If the applicant is a corporation, such license shall be renewed within the 30 days preceding the anniversary of the date the corporation was lawfully formed. Renewal shall require the filing of an application for renewal, a renewal bond, and the payment of the annual license fee, but the Labor Commissioner may demand that a new application or new bond be submitted. If the applicant or licensee desires, in addition, a branch office license, he shall file an application in accordance with the provisions of this section as heretofore set forth.

1700.11. All applications for renewal shall state the names and addresses of all persons, except bona fide employees on stated salaries, financially interested either as partners, associates or profit sharers, in the operation of the business of the talent agency.

1700.12. A filing fee of twenty-five dollars ($25) shall be paid to the Labor Commissioner at the time the application for issuance of a talent agency license is filed. In addition to the filing fee required for application for issuance of a talent agency license, every talent agency shall pay to the Labor Commissioner annually at the time a license is issued or renewed:

(a) A license fee of two hundred twenty-five dollars ($225).

(b) Fifty dollars ($50) for each branch office maintained by the talent agency in this state.

1700.13. A filing fee of twenty-five dollars ($25) shall be paid to the Labor Commissioner at the time application for consent to the transfer or assignment of a talent agency license is made but no license fee shall be required upon the assignment or transfer of a license. The location of a talent agency shall not be changed without the written consent of the Labor Commissioner.

1700.14. Whenever an application for a license or renewal is made, and application processing pursuant to this chapter has not been completed, the Labor Commissioner may, at his or her discretion, issue a temporary or provisional license valid for a period not exceeding 90 days, and subject, where appropriate, to the automatic and summary revocation by the Labor Commissioner. Otherwise, the conditions for issuance or renewal shall meet the requirements of Section 1700.6.

1700.15. A talent agency shall also deposit with the Labor Commissioner, prior to the issuance or renewal of a license, a surety bond in the penal sum of ten thousand dollars ($10,000).

1700.16. Such surety bonds shall be payable to the people of the State of California, and shall be conditioned that the person applying for the license will comply with this chapter and will pay all sums due any individual or group of individuals when such person or his representative or agent has received such sums, and will pay all damages occasioned to any person by reason of misstatement, misrepresentation, fraud, deceit, or any unlawful acts or omissions of the licensed talent agency, or its agents or employees, while acting within the scope of their employment.

1700.17. [Section repealed 1982.]

1700.18. All moneys collected for licenses and all fines collected for violations of the provisions of this chapter shall be paid into the State Treasury and credited to the General Fund.

1700.19. Each license shall contain all of the following:

(a) The name of the licensee.

(b) A designation of the city, street, and number of the premises in which the licensee is authorized to carry on the business of a talent agency.

(c) The number and date of issuance of the license.

1700.20. No license shall protect any other than the person to whom it is issued nor any places other than those designated in the license. No license shall be transferred or assigned to any person unless written consent is obtained from the Labor Commissioner.

1700.20a. The Labor Commissioner may issue to a person eligible therefor a certificate of convenience to conduct the business of a talent agency where the person licensed to conduct such talent agency business has died or has had a conservator of the estate appointed by a court of competent jurisdiction. Such a certificate of convenience may be denominated an estate certificate of convenience.

1700.20b. To be eligible for a certificate of convenience, a person shall be either:

(a) The executor or administrator of the estate of a deceased person licensed to conduct the business of a talent agency.

(continued)

(b) If no executor or administrator has been appointed, the surviving spouse or heir otherwise entitled to conduct the business of such deceased licensee.

(c) The conservator of the estate of a person licensed to conduct the business of a talent agency. Such estate certificate of convenience shall continue in force for a period of not to exceed 90 days, and shall be renewable for such period as the Labor Commissioner may deem appropriate, pending the disposal of the talent agency license or the procurement of a new license under the provisions of this chapter.

1700.21. The Labor Commissioner may revoke or suspend any license when it is shown that any of the following occur:

(a) The licensee or his or her agent has violated or failed to comply with any of the provisions of this chapter.

(b) The licensee has ceased to be of good moral character.

(c) The conditions under which the license was issued have changed or no longer exist.

(d) The licensee has made any material misrepresentation or false statement in his or her application for a license.

1700.22. Before revoking or suspending any license, the Labor Commissioner shall afford the holder of such license an opportunity to be heard in person or by counsel. The proceedings shall be conducted in accordance with Chapter 5 (commencing at Section 11500) of Part 1 of Division 3 of Title 2 of the Government Code, and the commissioner shall have all the powers granted therein.

Operation and Management

1700.23. Every talent agency shall submit to the Labor Commissioner a form or forms of contract to be utilized by such talent agency in entering into written contracts with artists for the employment of the services of such talent agency by such artists, and secure the approval of the Labor Commissioner thereof. Such approval shall not be withheld as to any proposed form of contract unless such proposed form of contract is unfair, unjust and oppressive to the artist. Each such form of contract, except under the conditions specified in Section 1700.45, shall contain an agreement by the talent agency to refer any controversy between the artist and the talent agency relating to the terms of the contract to the Labor Commissioner for adjustment. There shall be printed on the face of the contract in prominent type the following: "This talent agency is licensed by the Labor Commissioner of the State of California."

1700.24. Every talent agency shall file with the Labor Commissioner a schedule of fees to be charged and collected in the conduct of that occupation, and shall also keep a copy of the schedule posted in a conspicuous place in the office of the talent agency. Changes in the schedule may be made from time to time, but no fee or change of fee shall become effective until seven days after the date of filing thereof with the Labor Commissioner and until posted for not less than seven days in a conspicuous place in the office of the talent agency.

1700.25. (a) A licensee who receives any payment of funds on behalf of an artist shall immediately deposit that amount in a trust fund account maintained by him or her in a bank or other recognized depository. The funds, less the licensee's commission, shall be disbursed to the artist within

30 days after receipt. However, notwithstanding the preceding sentence, the licensee may retain the funds beyond 30 days of receipt in either of the following circumstances:

    (1) To the extent necessary to offset an obligation of the artist to the talent agency that is then due and owing.

    (2) When the funds are the subject of a controversy pending before the Labor Commissioner under Section 1700.44 concerning a fee alleged to be owed by the artist to the licensee.

(b) A separate record shall be maintained of all funds received on behalf of an artist and the record shall further indicate the disposition of the funds.

(c) If disputed by the artist and the dispute is referred to the Labor Commissioner, the failure of a licensee to disburse funds to an artist within 30 days of receipt shall constitute a "controversy" within the meaning of Section 1700.44.

(d) Any funds specified in subdivision (a) that are the subject of a controversy pending before the Labor Commissioner under Section 1700.44 shall be retained in the trust fund account specified in subdivision (a) and shall not be used by the licensee for any purpose until the controversy is determined by the Labor Commissioner or settled by the parties.

(e) If the Labor Commissioner finds, in proceedings under Section 1700.44, that the licensee's failure to disburse funds to an artist within the time required by subdivision (a) was a willful violation, the Labor Commissioner may, in addition to other relief under Section 1700.44, order the following:

    (1) Award reasonable attorney's fees to the prevailing artist.

    (2) Award interest to the prevailing artist on the funds wrongfully withheld at the rate of 10 percent per annum during the period of the violation.

(f) Nothing in subdivision (c), (d), or (e) shall be deemed to supersede Section 1700.45 or to affect the enforceability of a contractual arbitration provision meeting the criteria of Section 1700.45.

1700.26. Every talent agency shall keep records in a form approved by the Labor Commissioner, in which shall be entered all of the following:

    (1) The name and address of each artist employing the talent agency.

    (2) The amount of fee received from the artist.

    (3) The employments secured by the artist during the term of the contract between the artist and the talent agency, and the amount of compensation received by the artist pursuant thereto.

    (4) Any other information which the Labor Commissioner requires. No talent agency, its agent or employees, shall make any false entry in any records.

1700.27. All books, records, and other papers kept pursuant to this chapter by any talent agency shall be open at all reasonable hours to the inspection of the Labor Commissioner and his agents. Every talent agency shall furnish to the Labor Commissioner upon request a true copy of such books, records, and papers or any portion thereof, and shall make such reports as the Labor Commissioner prescribes.

1700.28. Every talent agency shall post in a conspicuous place in the office of such talent agency a printed copy of this chapter and of such other

(continued)

statutes as may be specified by the Labor Commissioner. Such copies shall also contain the name and address of the officer charged with the enforcement of this chapter. The Labor Commissioner shall furnish to talent agencies printed copies of any statute required to be posted under the provisions of this section.

1700.29. The Labor Commissioner may, in accordance with the provisions of Chapter 4 (commencing at Section 11370), Part 1, Division 3, Title 2 of the Government Code, adopt, amend, and repeal such rules and regulations as are reasonably necessary for the purpose of enforcing and administering this chapter and as are not inconsistent with this chapter.

1700.30. No talent agency shall sell, transfer, or give away to any person other than a director, officer, manager, employee, or shareholder of the talent agency any interest in or the right to participate in the profits of the talent agency without the written consent of the Labor Commissioner.

1700.31. No talent agency shall knowingly issue a contract for employment containing any term or condition which, if complied with, would be in violation of law, or attempt to fill an order for help to be employed in violation of law.

1700.32. No talent agency shall publish or cause to be published any false, fraudulent, or misleading information, representation, notice, or advertisement. All advertisements of a talent agency by means of cards, circulars, or signs, and in newspapers and other publications, and all letterheads, receipts, and blanks shall be printed and contain the licensed name and address of the talent agency and the words "talent agency." No talent agency shall give any false information or make any false promises or representations concerning an engagement or employment to any applicant who applies for an engagement or employment.

1700.33. No talent agency shall send or cause to be sent, any artist to any place where the health, safety, or welfare of the artist could be adversely affected, the character of which place the talent agency could have ascertained upon reasonable inquiry.

1700.34. No talent agency shall send any minor to any saloon or place where intoxicating liquors are sold to be consumed on the premises.

1700.35. No talent agency shall knowingly permit any persons of bad character, prostitutes, gamblers, intoxicated persons, or procurers to frequent, or be employed in, the place of business of the talent agency.

1700.36. No talent agency shall accept any application for employment made by or on behalf of any minor, as defined by subdivision (c) of Section 1286, or shall place or assist in placing any such minor in any employment whatever in violation of Part 4 (commencing with Section 1171).

1700.37. A minor cannot disaffirm a contract, otherwise valid, entered into during minority, either during the actual minority of the minor entering into such contract or at any time thereafter, with a duly licensed talent agency as defined in Section 1700.4 to secure him engagements to render artistic or creative services in motion pictures, television, the production of phonograph records, the legitimate or living stage, or otherwise in the entertainment field including, but without being limited to, services as an actor, actress, dancer, musician, comedian, singer, or other performer or entertainer, or as a writer, director, producer, production executive, choreographer, composer, conductor or designer, the blank form of which has been approved by the Labor Commissioner pursuant to Section 1700.23, where such contract has been approved by the superior court of the county where such minor resides or is employed. Such approval may be given by the superior court on the petition of either party to the contract after such reasonable notice to the other party thereto as may be fixed by said court, with opportunity to such other party to appear and be heard.

1700.38. No talent agency shall knowingly secure employment for an artist in any place where a strike, lockout, or other labor trouble exists, without notifying the artist of such conditions.

1700.39. No talent agency shall divide fees with an employer, an agent or other employee of an employer.

1700.40.   (a) No talent agency shall collect a registration fee. In the event that a talent agency shall collect from an artist a fee or expenses for obtaining employment for the artist, and the artist shall fail to procure the employment, or the artist shall fail to be paid for the employment, the talent agency shall, upon demand therefor, repay to the artist the fee and expenses so collected. Unless repayment thereof is made within 48 hours after demand therefor, the talent agency shall pay to the artist an additional sum equal to the amount of the fee.

(b) No talent agency may refer an artist to any person, firm, or corporation in which the talent agency has a direct or indirect financial interest for other services to be rendered to the artist, including, but not limited to, photography, audition tapes, demonstration reels or similar materials, business management, personal management, coaching, dramatic school, casting or talent brochures, agency-client directories, or other printing.

(c) No talent agency may accept any referral fee or similar compensation from any person, association, or corporation providing services of any type expressly set forth in subdivision (b) to an artist under contract with the talent agency.

1700.41. In cases where an artist is sent by a talent agency beyond the limits of the city in which the office of such talent agency is located upon the representation of such talent agency that employment of a particular type will there be available for the artist and the artist does not find such employment available, such talent agency shall reimburse the artist for any actual expenses incurred in going to and returning from the place where the artist has been so sent unless the artist has been otherwise so reimbursed.

1700.42. [Section repealed 1982.]

1700.43. [Section repealed 1982.]

1700.44.   (a) In cases of controversy arising under this chapter, the parties involved shall refer the matters in dispute to the Labor Commissioner, who shall hear and determine the same, subject to an appeal within 10 days after determination, to the superior court where the same shall be heard de novo. To stay any award for money, the party aggrieved shall execute a bond approved by the superior court in a sum not exceeding twice the amount of the judgment. In all other cases the bond shall be in a sum of not less than one thousand dollars ($1,000) and approved by the superior court. The Labor Commissioner may certify without a hearing that there is no controversy within the meaning of this section if he or she has by investigation established that there is no dispute as to the amount of the fee due. Service of the certification shall be made upon all parties concerned by registered or certified mail with return receipt requested and the

(continued)

certification shall become conclusive 10 days after the date of mailing if no objection has been filed with the Labor Commissioner during that period.

(b) Notwithstanding any other provision of law to the contrary, failure of any person to obtain a license from the Labor Commissioner pursuant to this chapter shall not be considered a criminal act under any law of this state.

(c) No action or proceeding shall be brought pursuant to this chapter with respect to any violation which is alleged to have occurred more than one year prior to commencement of the action or proceeding.

(d) It is not unlawful for a person or corporation which is not licensed pursuant to this chapter to act in conjunction with, and at the request of, a licensed talent agency in the negotiation of an employment contract.

1700.45. Notwithstanding Section 1700.44, a provision in a contract providing for the decision by arbitration of any controversy under the contract or as to its existence, validity, construction, performance, nonperformance, breach, operation, continuance, or termination, shall be valid:

(a) If the provision is contained in a contract between a talent agency and a person for whom the talent agency under the contract undertakes to endeavor to secure employment, or

(b) If the provision is inserted in the contract pursuant to any rule, regulation, or contract of a bona fide labor union regulating the relations of its members to a talent agency, and

(c) If the contract provides for reasonable notice to the Labor Commissioner of the time and place of all arbitration hearings, and

(d) If the contract provides that the Labor Commissioner or his or her authorized representative has the right to attend all arbitration hearings. Except as otherwise provided in this section, any arbitration shall be governed by the provisions of Title 9 (commencing with Section 1280) of Part 3 of the Code of Civil Procedure. If there is an arbitration provision in a contract, the contract need not provide that the talent agency agrees to refer any controversy between the applicant and the talent agency regarding the terms of the contract to the Labor Commissioner for adjustment, and Section 1700.44 shall not apply to controversies pertaining to the contract. A provision in a contract providing for the decision by arbitration of any controversy arising under this chapter which does not meet the requirements of this section is not made valid by Section 1281 of the Code of Civil Procedure.

1700.46 [Section repealed 1982.]

1700.47. It shall be unlawful for any licensee to refuse to represent any artist on account of that artist's race, color, creed, sex, national origin, religion, or handicap.

There are additional laws related to talent agents in California as well, including the California Labor Code and California Code of Regulations, Title 8 California Code of Regulations Chapter 6. Group 3. Employment Agencies.

REFERENCES FOR ADDITIONAL RESEARCH AND DISCUSSION

Biederman, D.E., *Agents v. Managers Revisited*, 1 Vand. J. Ent. L. & Prac. 5 (1999).

Birdthistle, W.A., *A Contested Ascendancy: Problems with Personal Managers Acting as Producers*, 20 Loy. L.A. Ent. L. Rev. 493 (2000).

Cox, L., *Targeting Sports Agents with the Mail Fraud Statute: United States v. Norby Walters & Lloyd Bloom*, 1992 Duke L.J. 1157 (1992).

Devlin, G.E., *The Talent Agencies Act: Reconciling the Controversies Surrounding Lawyers, Managers, and Agents Participating in California's Entertainment Industry*, 28 Pepp. L. Rev. 381 (2001).

Giordano, M.T., *Boxing Basinger: Oral Contracts and the Manager's Privilege on the Ropes in Hollywood*, 9 UCLA Ent. L. Rev. 285 (2002).

O'Brien, J.M., *Regulation of Attorneys under California's Talent Agencies Act: A Tautological Approach to Protecting Artists*, 80 Calif. L. Rev. 471 (1992).

Remis, R., & Sudia, D., *Athlete Agent Legislation in The New Millennium: State Statutes and the Uniform Athlete Agents Act*, 11 Seton Hall J. Sports L. 263 (2001).

Zarin, H.B., *The California Controversy over Procuring Employment: A Case for the Personal Mangers Act*, 7 Fordham Intell. Prop. Media & Ent. L.J. 927 (1997).

Zelenski, D., *Talent Agents, Personal Managers, and Their Conflicts in the New Hollywood*, 76 S. Cal. L. Rev. 979 (2003).

C H A P T E R

ENTERTAINMENT CONTRACTS

AFTER STUDYING THIS CHAPTER YOU SHOULD BE ABLE TO:

1. Define the term boilerplate with regard to contracts.
2. Describe the importance of the phrase freedom of contract and its role in entertainment deals.
3. Describe the various approaches to dealing with minors and entertainment agreements.
4. Discuss the importance and difficulty of utilizing the concept of promissory estoppel in contract law.
5. Apply the principles found in the concept of the statute of frauds to ensure that a written agreement is executed by the parties.
6. Describe California's seven-year statute with regard to entertainment contracts.
7. Define the term contract rider and what role it plays in entertainment contracts.
8. Identify the various remedies associated with a breach of contract.
9. Define the term emancipated minor.
10. Describe why waivers on ticket stubs are not usually enforceable.

INTRODUCTION TO ENTERTAINMENT CONTRACTS

This chapter introduces the student to contract law fundamentals and explores some interesting issues involving contracts and contract disputes in the entertainment industry. Contracts in entertainment law vary greatly. Understanding contract formation, elements, terminology, and the general nature and role of contracts is important in any industry. As in many industries, entertainment industry contracts can be **boilerplate** in nature. This means that they utilize standardized, preprinted forms where usually the only terms to negotiate include dates, dollars, times, and duration of the agreement. Boilerplate contracts are sometimes referred to as "fill-in-the-blank" contracts. The existence of boilerplate contracts is in part a result of successful negotiations evolving from the various unions or guilds involved in the entertainment industry.

Negotiating.
Getty Images Inc. –Stone Allstook.

ORAL CONTRACTS

Numerous contracts in the entertainment industry emanate from **handshake deals.** Historically, the entertainment industry thrived on **oral contracts.** Some members of the Hollywood community take great pride in proclaiming that the rigid rules of written contracts do not apply to them because the industry often regulates itself. One who did not fulfill their obligation was often squeezed out of the industry. Times have changed, however, and formal contracts or agreements (often involving entertainment lawyers) are usually a standard part of most deals.

Oral contracts often prove effective in close-knit industries such as the various segments of entertainment. Still, when things go wrong (for example, one party breaches their promise to another), most wish that the oral contract had been reduced to a written contract from the beginning, so as to establish a better position in litigation or for a settlement to avoid a lawsuit. While oral contracts can be valid under certain conditions, they are still not favored by industry practitioners or courts. Critics of these oral "handshake deals" often note that sometimes oral agreements are made by the party with greater bargaining power in order to find a way out of an agreement, if they decide to no longer pursue the production of the agreement. In other words, the party with the greater bargaining power knows exactly what they are doing by not putting the arrangement in writing. This leaves the artist in limbo with little proof of an agreement if the studio or company backs out or makes a decision to terminate pursuit of that relationship.

Oral agreements are not often found in the music and recording industry. This is due to the higher prevalence of long-term agreements and royalty calculation issues discussed in Chapter 8. Sometimes band members fail to put their group arrangement in writing. This can lead to unfortunate disagreements over who was entitled to what percentage of income in the event of the dissolution of a band and so on.

GENERAL CONTRACT LAW PRINCIPLES

Virtually every business relationship involves a contract. The essence of contract law is to enforce the duties or obligations that were mutually agreed upon by two or more parties. Contract law allows parties to an agreement to agree to almost anything. This principle is often referred to as the **freedom of contract.** Contracts that are fully performed (nothing remains to be done) are often referred to as **executed** contracts, while contracts that are still being performed are often referred to as being **executory.** If parties to a contract cannot reach a definitive (express) agreement, courts do not look favorably on the allegation of the existence of a contract. Therefore, **agreements to agree**—since they lack definiteness—are not valid contracts.

On occasion, a court may imply a contract under the theory of **quantum meruit.** Under this theory, the law imputes the existence of a contract based upon one party having performed services under circumstances in which the parties must have understood and intended compensation to be paid. This prevents one party from unjustly enriching another party for free. Still, proof of the existence of a contract under this theory can be a nightmare.

DEFINITION OF A CONTRACT

A contract is a legally binding agreement. A contract represents the **meeting of the minds** of the parties. A contract must be serious, definite, and legal (as opposed to being for an illegal purpose).

DRAFTING AN ENTERTAINMENT CONTRACT

Good contract drafters are aware of fundamental contract drafting techniques and realize that it is an acceptable art to borrow clauses from one contract that may suit the needs of their own agreement. It is important to remember when drafting a contract that it is often a solid policy to be a pessimist: think of what can go wrong. A rule of thumb for any contract drafter may be to predict what might go wrong, provide for it in the agreement, and protect your client, who may be yourself.

Though most contracts start out as a beneficial relationship between the parties, it is well known that over time attitudes and behaviors can change. Therefore, the contract drafter should use exceptional care to ensure that policies and procedures are provided for in order to address situations and legal issues that might arise when something does go wrong. Good contract drafters protect their client in the event such a situation might occur. Consideration should be given to **alternative** forms of **dispute resolution** (ADR), including **mediation** and **arbitration.**

VALID, VOID, VOIDABLE

All contracts are valid, void, or voidable. A **valid** contract is an agreement that is legally binding and enforceable. A **void** contract is one that is not binding and not enforceable. This may be due to an agreement made for an illegal purpose, for example. A **voidable** contract is binding and enforceable, but one of the parties to the agreement may exercise their **option** to reject the agreement later upon the occurrence of a particular condition. An **option contract,** however, is generally considered to be the right of one of the parties to accept a contract at their option for a limited period of time. Option contracts are very common in entertainment circles (particularly in the television industry) since an artist's market value can go up (or down) during the course of a career, just like the ratings of a particular television show.

MINORS

While minors (those under 18 years of age) may generally void contracts at their option, in the entertainment industry there are certain statutory exemptions and conditions related to minors, as will be discussed later in this chapter. Minors are employed in the entertainment industry quite often, and it is important to appreciate the role that the law plays in legislating and enforcing contract law related to minors in this industry.

OFFER, ACCEPTANCE, CONSIDERATION

All contracts are subject to the principles of **offer, acceptance,** and **consideration.** Additionally, a contract must be for a legal purpose, and the parties to the agreement must have the legal **capacity** or authority to enter into the agreement. If any of these elements is missing in an alleged contractual relationship, no contract exists.

An offer is made by the **offeror** (promisor) to an **offeree** (promisee). The offeror is the "master" of the offer. This means that the offeror can create the parameters of the who, when, where, and how of the proposed contractual situation. Once an offer is made, there are only four things an offeree can do:

(1) Accept (a legally binding contract is created)
(2) Reject (the offer is automatically terminated)
(3) Counteroffer (in which case the original offeror is now the offeree)
(4) Nothing (the law will terminate the contract offer after a "reasonable time")

Any ambiguities that are created when making an offer will be construed against the offeror, if an acceptance is made. With the advent of improved technology such as facsimile and electronic communication (e-mail), contracts can even be made over the Internet.

CONSIDERATION

Consideration is the "price of the promise," and it is a vital element of a contract in the law of contracts. It is the reason a party enters into the agreement. Consideration usually involves the payment of money for a product, service, option, or the forbearance of an act. Consideration involves an exchange of promises. In other words, a party to an agreement "gives" something of value to another when there was no previous obligation to do so.

STATUTE OF FRAUDS

Certain contracts must be in writing to be enforceable. This is the fundamental principle established by what is known as the **statute of frauds.** Historically, the statute of frauds developed from seventeenth century English law (1677) known as the English Statute of Frauds and Perjuries. This principle required that certain kinds of transactions be evidenced by something in writing. The writing also required a signature by the parties or their agent.

Contracts requiring a record to be enforceable include:

(1) Contracts for the sale of real estate
(2) Contracts which <u>cannot</u> be performed within one year

(3) Contracts in which one party acts as **guarantor** or **surety** for another party's debts

(4) Under the **Uniform Commercial Code** (U.C.C.), contracts for the sale of **goods** worth more than $5,000.[17]

(5) Contracts by the executor of a will

(6) Contracts in consideration of marriage

Contracts that are not put in writing might <u>not</u> be valid if the agreement violated the statute of frauds. California's Statute of Frauds, found at Cal. Civ. Code § 1624, provides that certain contracts "are invalid, unless the same, or some note or memorandum thereof, is in writing and subscribed by the party to be charged or by the party's agent."[18] There only need be some written evidence of the contract (even a memorandum) which is signed by the party to be charged. Studios, production companies, designers, and others involved in the sale of goods in the entertainment industry fall under the purview of the U.C.C. Still, since many entertainment contracts involve personal services, the U.C.C. would not apply unless the deal is for longer than one year in duration or if the contract has options which entitle one party to extend the term of an agreement.

PROMISSORY ESTOPPEL

State laws do recognize exceptions to the concept of the statute of frauds. One example of an exception is termed **promissory estoppel.** An oral promise whose enforcement is barred by the statute of frauds might be enforced in a separate cause of action under this doctrine, if a court is agreeable to it. However, many courts use this concept only sparingly and in extreme or extraordinary cases only, to avoid unjust results and where an injustice can be avoided only by enforcing the oral promise.

Under the doctrine of promissory estoppel, a party who has reasonably relied to his or her detriment based upon another's promise may still be able to enforce that promise (or part of the promise) to the extent of the reliance (out-of-pocket costs incurred in order to start a project, for example). The plaintiff must demonstrate that the oral promise was made, however, and this can be extremely difficult. Even if successful, the plaintiff may still not recover the full **benefit of the bargain** of the alleged contract, but it still might be worth pursuing a claim under this doctrine if there are witnesses and other types of proof of the existence of an oral agreement.

STATUTE OF LIMITATIONS

The phrase **statute of limitations** means the time limit set by law during which a person must bring legal action on a case. Under California law, a party

---

[17] U.C.C. § 2–201 (Revised).

[18] New York's version is found at N.Y. Gen. Oblig. Law § 5–701.

has four years in which to file suit for breach of a written contract.[19] In contrast, the statute of limitations is only two years in California, if the contract is an oral agreement. The limitations period for **breach of contract** can vary a lot among the states. For example, it is six years under both Tennessee[20] and New York[21] law, while it is five years in Florida.[22] Oral contracts will require substantially more evidence to overcome the burden of proving that a contract actually existed.

GOOD FAITH

In any contract, there must be an underlying theme of good faith **(bona fide)**, reasonableness, and trust. When a party violates the sanctity of the contractual relationship or breaches the duties required under the contract, such a breakdown of the contract can lead to litigation. Additionally, ambiguities that are created when a contract is formed or issues that were not foreseen by a contract drafter can lead to confusion and discord. The offeror has the duty to avoid creating ambiguities in an offer to an offeree. Otherwise, such ambiguities will likely be construed against the offeror if brought to court.

It is recognized that when dealing with the sales of goods, the U.C.C. requires good faith when it comes to the buying and selling of goods (tangible moveable items at the time of sale). However, the U.C.C. does not apply when it comes to services or personal services contracts. Since the talent in question is unique, such services cannot be **assigned** to another person to complete the same task or obligation.

CALIFORNIA'S SEVEN YEAR STATUTE

California's Labor Code § 2855 (also known as the **Seven Year Statute**) limits the amount of time anyone can be held to a contract for personal services to a maximum of seven years. This seven year limitation law is known as the **De Havilland law.**[23] Recording artists, however, are not covered in the statute and can be sued for breach of contract, if they do not live up to their end of the bargain to deliver a minimum number of productions. In 1987, "Subsection b" was added, which provided a limited exception to the statute for recording contracts. Recording artists are now the only class of personal service workers in California who cannot take advantage of Labor Code § 2855.

---

[19] Cal. Civ. Proc. Code § 312 *et seq.*

[20] Tenn. Code Ann. § 28–3–101 *et seq.*

[21] N.Y. C.P. L.R. § 201 *et seq.*

[22] Fla. Stat. Ann. § 95.011 *et seq.*

[23] As a result of the favorable ruling handed down by California courts in Olivia de Havilland's lawsuit against Warner Bros. Studios in 1945, in which her studio contract could not be extended beyond seven years.

■ PERSONAL SERVICES CONTRACTS

Contracts to secure talent are usually personal service contracts. A personal service contract is one in which the parties (or the party to perform) must possess special knowledge or a unique skill, such that no performance except that of the contracting party could meet the obligations of the contract. A celebrity actor, musician, band, author, and so on are examples of personal service contracts.

■ CONTRACT RIDERS

Sometimes called **technical riders, riders,** or merely **addenda** to a contract, contract riders include the unique and quite particular aspects of a deal. This includes food, beverage, and lodging accommodations; other individual requests by talent; stage specifications, light and sound requirements, and electrical power requirements for set designers; and so on. Some riders can include very thorough (yet extremely ridiculous) requests, though they are usually legal.

The following is an example of a contract rider to a contract for a musical performance.

CONTRACT RIDER FOR MUSICAL ARTIST

This rider, a legal document, is hereby attached to and made part of the original contract dated _____, between _____ ("Artist") and _____ ("Purchaser") for Artist's engagement located at _____ on this date _____.

Purchaser understands that the items required below are reasonable and necessary in order for the Artist to provide the best possible show for the Purchaser and his or her customers. Purchaser also understands that Artist cannot perform without all of the following paragraphs, and that the failure to provide any of the items could result in the Purchaser being held in default of this contract rider. While flexible, any additions or deletions to this agreement must be signed and dated by both parties to be binding.

1. **Production.** Purchaser agrees to furnish, at his or her sole cost, the following: a raised performance area (stage) which is at least four (4') feet above the floor of the arena floor or main seating level. This stage is to be not less than forty (40') feet deep and fifty-six (56') feet wide. It is to be free of all obstructions and of a sound physical construction. Should the facility not be riggable, the following additional stage pieces will be required: Two (2) sound wings, each sixteen (16') feet wide and sixteen (16') feet deep. One is to be placed on each side of the stage, attached to the stage at the front (downstage) most edge. Stair units are required for both sides of the stage. Small light units are requested for these stair units. A Stage Diagram shall be attached to this agreement to visually demonstrate all terms contained within this Rider.

2. **Consoles.** An area not less than twenty-four (24') feet wide by ten (10') feet deep is to be reserved, with tickets pulled before going on sale, for lighting and sound consoles. This area is to be at the house center, not less than thirty (30') feet from the stage. Furthermore, it shall not exceed one-half (1/2) the length of the arena floor, under any circumstances.

3. **Personnel Requirements.** The assistance of not less than 12 stagehands, 3 riggers, 4 truck loaders, 1 qualified licensed electrician, 1 forklift operator, and 2 additional stagehands are required for load-in and load-out. All personnel related to the production shall NOT be drinking alcoholic beverages. Any Runner and others involved in transporting Artist must have a valid driver's license. All machinery should be in the best possible mechanical/working condition. Plenty of fuel should be on hand. All precautions should be taken to insure that the machinery is as safe as possible. Fork is to have minimum lift capacity of 6,000 pounds and a lift range of 14 feet. Electrician is to be qualified and licensed and familiar with the venue. He or she must be on hand at all times, and an emergency number should be available. All of the personnel involved in the production are to be able-bodied, English-speaking adults. No minors are allowed. A runner is required for the first call time until the end of the show. The runner must be able to provide a vehicle that can comfortably fit 6 people. Runner is to report to Artist's stage manager before and after each run is made. Purchaser or his or her representative must be present and available from load-in through load-out and must have copies of this entire contract and rider during this engagement.

4. **Venue.** Purchaser agrees that the venue (auditorium, coliseum, theatre or club) shall be available to Artist's production staff and set-up, at least 12 hours prior to show time. Said venue shall not be open to the public until 1 hour before show time. Loading areas and backstage areas should be cleared of all vehicles and equipment prior to the arrival of Artist's entourage. Two clean separate dressing rooms with mirrors, soap, sinks and 36 towels is a must. A shower with hot water and toilet facilities are also to be provided (portable toilet facilities are unacceptable). These facilities must be located backstage and away from public access and sightlines. A production office must be provided for Artist's staff with a direct phone line, long distance privileges, and cell phones if better served. Parking for 3 buses and two trucks with at least one security guard will be offered during the performance. If parking is available only on the street, spaces must be blocked off by 5:00 AM of the day of the show.

5. **Lights & Sound.** Four spotlights and 8 experienced operators will be available during the performance to assist in Artist's own sound equipment. Additionally, 1 400 amp per leg, 208 volt, three-phase service will be provided within 50 feet of stage left. One 100 amp, 100 volt, single-phase service will be provided within 100 feet of stage right. Artist's own sound engineer shall operate the house mixing console. Additionally, colored fill lighting (red, blue, amber) and dimmer controls must be functional on all stage lighting.

6. **Security.** Purchaser shall provide an adequate security staff of experienced, properly trained, unarmed, easily identifiable and nonuniformed personnel who will work in connection with the Artist's security requests. The security

must be stationed at the backstage and dressing room 3 hours prior to show time. Four security guards must be available to Artist before, during and after each performance. Artist will provide all stage passes, which will be the only passes honored in the backstage area. Purchaser agrees that any passes issued by Artist will be recognized by his or her security personnel. No person without the proper pass is to be admitted to any nonpublic areas. Should the performance span multiple days, security must be provided for the equipment on a 24-hour basis. Artist retains the right to demand substitution of any security guard who, in the Artist's sole judgment, is not physically, mentally or emotionally capable of performing their assigned duties. Purchaser will provide a list of guests to Artist prior to house opening.

7. **Advertising and Promotion.** Artist requires only the trademarked, custom-produced advertising materials be used in their entirety. For radio, Artist will provide at its own cost 1 60-second or 30-second "presale" commercial, 1 60-second or 30-second "week of show" commercial, 1 60-second or 30-second "day of show" commercial, and, if appropriate, 1 60-second or 30-second "welcoming station" commercial. For television, 1 30-second commercial. For newspaper, 1 3" by 6" ad slick. Plus, 100 four-color posters, 21" by 14" in size. Purchaser agrees not to commit Artist to any personal appearances, interviews or photos or any other type of promotional purpose without prior approval. Purchaser shall also not represent that this engagement is copromoted or cosponsored by any third party without written permission of Artist. Artist is to receive 100% Star Billing in all advertisement and publicity.

8. **Other.** Purchaser agrees that there shall be no signs, placards, banners or other advertising materials on or near the stage at any time when the audience is in the building. During the performance, vending is not permitted in the audience. Purchaser agrees to make building and concessions management aware of these requirements. Additionally, the recording, broadcasting or filming of the live performance will not be permitted unless previously authorized in writing, including the working press backstage. This prohibition applies to patrons as well. Artist does not perform in the round. There shall be no intermission and Artist will play between 60 and 90 minutes.

9. **Merchandise.** Artist shall have the right to sell merchandise at the show site on the day of the show. No other sales or distribution of material pertaining to Artist will be allowed without prior written consent. Buyer agrees to provide adequate space for Artist or designee to vend such material.

10. **Master of Ceremonies.** No announcer or Master of Ceremonies (Emcee) shall appear without prior approval by Artist or stage manager.

11. **Tickets.** Purchaser is to use no more than 50 complimentary tickets for advertising or working press. All (any) unused tickets shall be returned for sale to the public no later than 2 hours before the performance.

12. **Force Majeure/Inclement Weather.** Artist's obligation to perform is specifically subject to (i.e., conditional upon) cancellation due to sickness, physical injury (or other inability to perform), accident, and considerable

delay in transportation to venue, fire, riot, strikes, or any other unexpected interference with the performance of the show. Purchaser shall not be responsible for payment to Artist for any other fee other than the relinquishment of the down payment (previously paid) in the event such occurrence characterized by Artist as a force majeure or Act of God are raised. However, in the unfortunate event that the show cannot be presented due to weather, Artist must still be paid in full. Determination of whether any weather conditions shall render the performance(s) unsafe must be made in good faith but is at the sole discretion of the Artist.

13. **Times.** Show times may only be changed with Artist's written approval.

14. **Amendment.** This agreement may be modified up to 30 days prior to the show. Any modifications must be in writing, signed by both parties.

15. **Cancellation.** Artist shall have the right to cancel the performance, without any liability, upon written notice to the Purchaser, not less than 30 days prior to the date of performance.

16. **Payments.** All payments must be made in the form of a cashier's check made payable to:

    _____. Down payments must be received by
    _____ in accordance with the agreement that this contract rider amends.

17. **Gross Receipts.** The term "gross receipts" shall mean box office receipts less federal, state or local admission taxes; commissions and discounts in connection with season ticket sales, credit card charges, remote box offices, parking fees, food, merchandise or other concession income.

18. **Insurance.** Purchaser agrees to provide public liability insurance coverage to protect against injuries to persons or property prior to, during, and subsequent to the performance. This comprehensive policy must cover not less than Two Million Dollars ($2,000,000) per occurrence. Artist shall be individually covered under this policy as well and paid for by Purchaser. Purchaser also agrees to maintain worker's compensation insurance for all of its employees. Insurance for Force Majeure and "Act of God" is highly recommended as Purchaser risks cancellation due to the aforementioned acts but only in good faith.

19. **Hospitality Meals.** Purchaser shall provide the following for the Artist:

Six Hours Prior to Performance
Please place all perishable items on ice or keep refrigerated.

Ten (10) Bottles of room temperature bottled water (noncarbonated only)
Full Roasted Coffee and tea set—to include real ceramic coffee mugs
Honey
Variety of Teas/herbal
Spoons
One (1) 6-pack of Coke or Pepsi (not diet)
One (1) Pint of Whole Milk
One (1) Gallon of Skim Milk
One (1) Box of Honey Smacks cereal

One (1) Package of Mozzarella or Cheddar Cheese

One (1) Bottle of Echinacea Capsules

One (1) Small Fruit Platter of Raspberries, Blueberries, Strawberries, Plums and Whole Bananas

One (1) Small Tray of Fresh Roasted Turkey, Chicken and Roast Beef Deli Only (No pressed or processed meats)

One (1) Small Veggie Tray with Carrots, Cherry Tomatoes, Red Peppers, Cauliflower, Celery, and Blue Cheese Dip

Assorted Raw Almonds, Banana Chips, Dried Cranberries

Assortment of energy bars of various brand names

One (1) Small Bottle of Multivitamins

One (1) Small Bottle of Chewable Flintstones Vitamin "C" Tablets

One (1) Small Cheese Platter with Cheddar, Jack, Gouda and Swiss

Platter Assortment of Gums and Mints

One (1) Roll of Film/200 Speed Exposure

Six (6) Clean Large Bath Towels

Display of Fork, Knives, Spoons, Plates (Not Plastic)

One (1) 1/2 Pint of Fat Free Small Curd Cottage Cheese

One (1) Container of "Coffee Mate" Non-dairy Creamer

Twelve (12) Solo Cups

Four (4) votive candles with matches

Two (2) Chicken or turkey club sandwiches (white bread with bacon, lettuce and tomato)

No less than six (6) bottles of water

Chocolate chip or Oreo cookies

After Performance

Twelve (12) bottles of very cold water

Eight (8) bottles of ice-coffee

Eight (8) cans of diet cola

Two (2) 6-packs of other assorted soda and ice teas

Fresh made deli sandwiches: assorted turkey, roast beef or chicken

Fresh Fruit

Cookies

Signatures:

AGREED (sign and date):

_____

Purchaser

_____

Artist

MINORS AND ENTERTAINMENT CONTRACTS

As in all industries, children employed in the entertainment industry receive special treatment under the law. The entertainment industry deals with contracts to persons under age 18 regularly. Under general contract law principles, minors may void or disaffirm contracts. States such as New York, California, Florida, Tennessee, and others have enacted laws that govern entertainment contracts with minors since minors (or sometimes described as **infants**) may **disaffirm** contracts. Minors often serve as models in commercials and advertising media. Hundreds of famous child actors have benefited from the entertainment industry's reliance on minors for the generation of revenue and profits. Unions such as SAG, AFTRA, and the Actors Equity Association (AEA) have adopted special work rules that may apply to minors in connection with their services in the industry.

Child actors of all ages are thrust into an often harsh world with complex issues. While the first child labor laws in the United States were passed in Massachusetts in 1836, the advent of the industrial revolution and growth of cities and factories forced other states and the federal government to pass laws that focused on employment of children, including wages and working conditions. Both New York and California have specific laws that regulate minors' employment in the entertainment industries. California's regulation is the most comprehensive.

California

In 1927, California became the first state to regulate minors' contracts in entertainment. Similar to the Talent Agencies Act, California has adopted statutes that protect minors' contracts in the entertainment industry.[24] Minors' contracts are regulated in two sections: §§ 6750–53 of the Family Code and § 2855 of the Labor Code. California's law governing minors includes services of an "actor, actress, dancer, musician, comedian, singer, or other performer or entertainer, or as a writer, director, producer, production executive, choreographer, composer, conductor, or designer."[25] The California superior court system must approve or disapprove of minors' contracts. If the Superior Court affirms a minor's contract, the minor cannot disaffirm it.

Under California law, there is no limitation on the length of the term of a minor's contract, and there is no requirement that a limited **guardian** be appointed. Under California law, a maximum of only 50 percent of net earnings will be set aside in a blocked account until the infant becomes 18 years old (New York has no limit on what portion the court sets aside).[26] California courts would have jurisdiction over the action if the minor either resides or is employed in California or if any party to the contract has its principal office in that state. The maximum term of a minor's employment pursuant to an entertainment employment contract is seven years, similar to California's Seven Year

---

[24] California laws related to child actors are often referred to as Coogan's Law, named after Jackie Coogan, a silent-picture child actor in the 1920s whose earnings disappeared.
[25] Cal. Fam. Code § 6750(a)(1).
[26] Cal. Fam. Code § 6752.

Statute. Once the minor turns eighteen years old, he or she may apply for the money in that account. Also, the Family Code entitles the minor's parents to the earnings of their child (the other 50 percent) under § 7500 of the Family Code.

New York

New York law also provides for judicial approval of certain contracts for services of minors.[27] In New York, the **Child Performers Education and Trust Act of 2003** was sponsored to reflect California's laws. The provisions of the statute specifically relate to performing artists and professional athletes. A proceeding for judicial approval of a minor's contract is commenced by the filing of a verified petition by a parent, the guardian, a relative of the infant, or any interested person on the infant's behalf. The petition may be made to the Supreme Court or the Surrogate's Court in the county in which the infant resides. Approval of the contract may be withheld until the parent(s), who may be entitled to the minor's earnings, or the infant, if the infant is entitled to those earnings, consents to set aside a portion of the infant's earnings and place them under the control of a guardian pursuant to court order in a net earnings account. Net earnings are defined as gross earnings less taxes, support, care, education, training, professional management, and reasonable fees and expenses paid in connection with the proceeding, the contract, and its performance.[28]

EMANCIPATION OF MINORS

In California, **emancipated** minors may enter binding contractual agreements, Cal. Fam. Code § 7050(e)(2). Emancipated minors are those who have gone through court proceedings to be legally separated and freed from the control of their parents. In California, minors seeking employment in the entertainment industry must also obtain an **Entertainment Work Permit.** They must obtain written verification from the appropriate school district that the minor has satisfied that district's requirements with respect to age, school record, attendance, and health. The permit is not valid for more than six months, Cal. Admin. Code Title. 8, § 11753(a) and (b). In New York, the termination of parental rights is found in Soc. Serv. Law §§ 384–b 358–a(3)(b).

TERMINATION OF A CONTRACT

A contract may end when each party to the contract simply does what they promised to do. Another way to terminate an agreement is by contract, when each party agrees to end the contract prematurely. In the event one party breaks (breaches) the contract or unilaterally cancels the contract, litigation or other form of dispute resolution may be necessary to enforce the agreement.

---

[27] N.Y. Arts & Cult. Aff. Law § 35.03 *et seq.*
[28] N.Y. Arts & Cult. Aff. Law § 35.03(3)(c).

▉DAMAGES AND REMEDIES FOR A BREACH OF CONTRACT

Generally speaking, when there is a breach of contract, contract law uses a variety of methods to repair the damage. Courts attempt to place the injured party in the position that he would have been in had the contract been performed. Examples of breach of contract are numerous in the entertainment industry. Talent agents not being paid by their artists, allegations of miscalculations of royalty payments by musicians, and studios seeking monetary damages for failure of a designer to prepare a set are all examples of breaches of contract.

Remedies

There are several kinds of contract remedies available when a breach of contract occurs:

(1) Compensatory damages
(2) Specific performance
(3) Consequential damages
(4) Liquidated damages
(5) Punitive damages

Compensatory Damages. Compensatory damages can be defined as the amount of money necessary to make up for the economic loss caused as a result of the breach of contract. Monetary damages are intended to compensate the plaintiff for losses suffered as a result of a breach of contract. **General damages** or noneconomic damages include compensation for pain, suffering, mental anguish, disability, and disfigurement. **Special damages** or economic losses consist of medical expenses, loss of income, and other direct economic losses.

Specific Performance. Specific performance is an order by the court requiring the party that breached the contract to perform its obligation. Similar to an injunction, specific performance orders performance, whereas an injunction orders nonperformance. Assuming a court orders specific performance as a remedy to a breach of contract, the breaching party must do what it agreed to do in the contract. This remedy is <u>not</u> afforded to personal services contracts, since forcing talent to perform would constitute a modern-day form of enslavement or involuntary servitude. However, sales of goods and products could certainly fall within the scope of specific performance as a remedy.

Consequential Damages. Consequential damages are economic losses caused <u>indirectly</u> by a breach of contract. Consequential damages are those which arise from the intervention of "special circumstances" not ordinarily predictable. As a general rule, they are compensable only if it is determined that the circumstances were within the contemplation of both parties at the time the contract was executed and therefore foreseeable by both. When an alleged breach of contract is an unexcused delay in completion of a project or performances, for example, damages as a result of the delay (or breach) could be recoverable.

Liquidated Damages. Liquidated damages are damages specified in the contract itself and are often referred to as "agreed-upon" damages. These damages are a sum of money agreed upon by both buyer and seller prior to contract signing as a substitute for actual damages for breach of contract. This sum is to be paid in lieu of actual damages in the event of a specific contract breach. While not considered a penalty, the parties to the contract do agree prior to the performance of the contract what the damages would be for a breach. Liquidated damages clauses are wise considerations for contract drafters in any contract case since it provides certainty for damages by the parties to a contract.

Punitive Damages. Punitive damages (sometimes called **exemplary damages**) are damages that punish the wrongdoer in a **tort** or personal injury action. Usually punitive damages are <u>not</u> recoverable in a contract action since the goal of contract law is to make "whole" rather than to punish (the goal of the criminal law). Also, unlike compensatory damages, punitive damages are not based on actual economic loss but are designed to make an example out of a party for wrongful (and sometimes intentional) misconduct. Such damages are often used to prevent a future breach by the same parties and/or to send a message to the community (or society) at large that such conduct is unacceptable.

MITIGATION OF DAMAGES

The duty to mitigate damages means that the victim of a breach of contract cannot simply let economic losses pile up and later sue the other party to pay all of those losses as well. The victim of a breach of contract must attempt to reduce the amount of economic loss. Failing to reduce one's damages leads to waste and is not favored by courts.

WAIVERS

A **waiver** is the voluntary relinquishment of a privilege or a right. Good contract drafters often include waivers in any express agreement. Waivers or **release** of liability is a clause in a contract or its own document designed to protect a party from legal liability for injuries that may occur to others. Waivers may be used as protection from liability for accidents, activities carrying certain inherent risks, and even ordinary **negligence** or other unintentional conduct in certain circumstances.

To avoid liability for defamation and invasion of privacy claims (discussed in greater detail in Chapter 4), a common waiver/disclaimer for fictitious works—based more on tort law than contract law—found in motion pictures, television, and publishing industries includes a conspicuous waiver such as the following: "The characters and events depicted in this motion picture are fictional.

Any similarity to any actual person, living or dead, or to any actual events, firms, and institutions or other entities, is coincidental and unintentional."[29]

Tickets and Waivers

In theatres, concert halls, arenas, and elsewhere, ticket holders are entitled to observe an event. However, ticket holders always risk getting injured when so many people gather together. Often printed on tickets are **disclaimers (exculpatory clauses)** of liability in the event of injury during an event. Disclaimers are sometimes short and simple, while other times the waiver might be long and complex.

A ticket might display the following waiver, for example.

Holder voluntarily assumes all risks and danger incidental to the event for which the ticket is issued, whether occurring prior to, during or after the event, including, but not limited to, the danger of being injured by thrown, batted, kicked, shot, struck, by objects such as instruments, equipment, and flying objects, or by other spectators or performers. Holder voluntarily agrees that the management, facility, venue, participants, clubs, and all of their respective agents, officers, directors, owners and employees are expressly released by holder from any claims arising from such activity.

Courts generally do not uphold ticket stub waivers as a matter of public policy. Plaintiffs can challenge the enforceability of express assumption-of-risk language on the back of tickets in several other ways, including that the disclaimer was not clear or **conspicuous**, the spectator was not notified of the language on the ticket and therefore there was no agreement, there was no signature by the ticket holder, and the conduct that caused injury was grossly negligent or **reckless** which cannot be waived. Waivers on the back of ticket stubs might serve as a deterrent to a plaintiff suing but are not usually an effective complete defense to a claim of negligence.

■ COLLECTIVE BARGAINING AGREEMENTS

A **collective bargaining agreement** is a contract that spells out the terms of employment between a labor union and an employer. This negotiated contract between a labor organization and the employer concerns wages, hours of work, and all other terms and conditions of employment. This also includes provisions for grievance and arbitration if there are disputes over the contract. Collective bargaining agreements are often the by-product of serious negotiations

---

[29] *See, e.g., Smith v. Huntington Publ. Co.*, 410 F. Supp. 1270, 1274 (S.D. Ohio 1975), where no reasonable person could have believed an article was about plaintiff when there was even a statement by author in boldface print that names used in article were fictitious), *aff'd mem.*, 535 F.2d 1255 (6th Cir. 1976).

in the entertainment industry and include examples, as discussed further in the text, such as the Screen Actors Guild, Writers Guild, and Directors Guild **Basic Agreement**.

■ BANKRUPTCY AND CONTRACTS

Voluntarily petitioning the bankruptcy court in federal district court for financial relief is usually an option for debtors who cannot live up to their contractual obligations for various reasons. Bankruptcy courts are quite lenient for petitioners, but the *trustee* in bankruptcy has great power. Whether Chapter 7 (liquidation) or Chapters 11 and 13 (reorganization), the trustee has the ultimate say as to whether to discharge contractual obligations owed to creditors. Once a petition for bankruptcy has been made, all creditors must immediately stop pursuing collection of their debts under the concept of the **automatic stay** (11 U.S.C. § 362). The trustee in bankruptcy then is in charge of handling the petition and the bankruptcy estate.

■ *IN RE CARRERE*

The case *In re Carrere*, 64 B.R. 156 (Bankr. C.D. Cal. 1986) represents a failed attempt to use the bankruptcy courts to reject an otherwise legitimate contract.[30] Actress Tia Carrere filed bankruptcy under Chapter 11 of the bankruptcy code in an attempt to reject an executory contract (pursuant to 11 U.S.C. § 365). The purpose of her filing bankruptcy was to avoid a personal services contract and to pursue a more lucrative one with another television show. In August 1985, Carrere entered into a personal services contract with American Broadcasting Company (ABC), agreeing to perform in the television series *General Hospital* from that time until August 1988.

While the contract with ABC was still in effect, Carrere agreed to make an appearance on the television show *A Team*. Under the terms of her agreement with Steven J. Cannell Productions, if she became a regular on *A Team*, she would make more money than on *General Hospital*. In March 1986, Carrere filed her voluntary bankruptcy petition under Chapter 11 and attempted to reject the ABC contract. Carrere made it clear (in the court's eyes) that her primary motivation in seeking the protection of this court was to reject the contract with ABC in order to make more money. ABC felt that the bankruptcy petition was filed in bad faith. Ultimately, the court denied her motion and noted that it would not be fair to allow her to file for bankruptcy for the primary purpose of rejecting this personal services contract.

---

[30] *In re* means "In the matter of" or "Regarding" in Latin.

CHAPTER SUMMARY

Understanding the fundamentals of contract law in any industry is vital. While contracts generally may be oral or written, having a written agreement is important especially if a party to the contract ends up breaching the arrangement. Some members of Hollywood continue to prefer to do business with "handshake deals," but there is a trend away from unwritten contractual agreements these days, even if they are sometimes more efficient than written contracts. Many contracts are boilerplate. One of the unique aspects of entertainment contracts is the appreciation for the role that minors play in this industry. Several states have drafted laws that are specific to minors and entertainment contracts.

CHAPTER TERMS

Acceptance
Addenda
Agreements to agree
Alternative dispute resolution (ADR)
Arbitration
Assigned
Automatic stay
Basic Agreement
Benefit of the bargain
Boilerplate
Bona fide
Breach of contract
Capacity
Child Performers Education and Trust Act of 2003
Collective bargaining agreement

Compensatory damages
Consequential damages
Consideration
Conspicuous
De Havilland law
Disaffirm
Disclaimers
Emancipated
Entertainment Work Permit
Exculpatory clauses
Executed
Executory
Exemplary damages
Freedom of contract
General damages
Goods

Guarantor
Guardian
Handshake deals
Infants
Liquidated damages
Mediation
Meeting of the minds
Negligence
Offer
Offeree
Offeror
Option
Option contract
Oral contracts
Promissory estoppel
Punitive damages
Quantum meruit

Reckless
Release
Riders
Seven Year Statute
Special damages
Specific performance
Statute of frauds
Statute of limitations
Surety
Technical riders
Tort
Uniform Commercial Code (U.C.C.)
Valid
Void
Voidable
Waiver

ADDITIONAL CASES

Columbia Pictures Corp. v. De Toth, 197 P.2d 580 (Cal. Ct. App. 1948)

Coppola v. Warner Bros., No. B154280, 2003 Cal. App. Unpub. LEXIS 1782 (Ct. App. Feb. 25, 2003)

Danforth v. Cohen, 498 U.S. 1103 (1991)

De Havilland v. Warner Brothers Pictures, 153 P.2d 983 (Cal. Ct. App. 1944)

Effects Assoc., Inc. v. Cohen, 908 F.2d 555 (9th Cir. 1990), *cert. denied*, 498 U.S. 1103 (1991)

Johnston v. 20th Century-Fox Film Corp., 187 P.2d 474 (9th Cir. 1947)

Ketcham v. Hall Syndicate, Inc., 236 N.Y.S.2d 206 (Sup. Ct. N.Y. County 1962)

MCA Records, Inc. v. Newton-John, 153 Cal. Rptr. 153 (Ct. App. 1979)

Metro-Goldwyn-Mayer, Inc. v. Scheider, 360 N.E.2d 930 (N.Y. 1976)

People ex rel. Cort Theatre Co. v. Thompson, 119 N.E. 41 (Ill. 1918)

PMC, Inc. v. Saban Entm't, Inc., 45 Cal. App. 4th 579 (1996)

Scott Eden Mgmt. v. Kavovit, 563 N.Y.S.2d 1001 (Sup. Ct. N.Y. County 1990)

Warner Bros. Pictures, Inc. v. Brodel, 192 P.2d 949 (Cal. 1948)

Warner Bros. Pictures, Inc. v. Bumgarner, 17 Cal. Rptr. 171 (Ct. App. 1961)

REVIEW QUESTIONS

1. What are the fundamental elements required to form a contract?
2. What is the importance of having a "meeting of the minds"?
3. Are oral contracts still used in the entertainment industry? What are the pitfalls of agreeing to terms orally rather than in writing?
4. What are the concerns related to minors and contracts in the entertainment industry?
5. Are there any laws related specifically to minors and entertainment?
6. Discuss the various remedies related to a breach of contract. Should punitive damages be allowed for breaches of contract?
7. What are some examples of collective bargaining agreements in entertainment law?
8. Why does the statute of frauds only apply to certain types of agreements?
9. Are tickets and ticket stubs considered contracts? Should they be?
10. Should bankruptcy courts have the power to avoid certain types of contracts?

The following contract represents an example of an agreement between a publishing company and an author.

Sample Publishing Agreement

This Agreement is by and between _____ "Author" and _____ "Publisher" collectively, the parties.

WHEREAS the parties desire to publish a work tentatively entitled "_____" (the "Work");

NOW, THEREFORE, in consideration of the premise and the mutual covenants contained herein, the Publisher and the Author, intending to be legally bound, agree as follows:

1. Author's Duties. The Author, at his/her own expense, shall create, prepare and deliver to the Publisher on or before February 1, 2005, a computer diskette and manuscript of the Work in the English language satisfactory to Publisher, together with any charts, diagrams, review questions and indexes suitable for reproduction and necessary for the completion and publication of the Work. The Work shall be designed as a textbook with accompanying instructor's manual. The manuscript of the Work shall consist in length of at least 200 computer-typed, single-spaced pages in Microsoft Word. If the Author incorporates in the Work any copyrighted material, he shall procure at his/her own expense and deliver to the Publisher written permission from the copyright owner to reprint, reproduce, distribute and display all such copyrighted material incorporated in the Work. If the Author fails or refuses to perform any reasonable correction or revision of the manuscript within a reasonable the time specified by the Publisher, or if any manuscript that is delivered is not approved by the Publisher, the Publisher may terminate this Agreement by giving written notice to the Author. The Publisher shall not unreasonably withhold approval of the manuscript.

2. Assignment. If the manuscript is satisfactory to the Publisher, the Publisher shall notify the Author that the Work has been accepted for publication, and the Author shall execute an assignment to the Publisher of the copyright on the Work. If the manuscript is approved by the Publisher, the Publisher shall publish the Work in any such style and manner, under such imprint, at such price and in such print runs as is reasonable in an effort to market and sell the Work are the property of the Publisher. The Author hereby grants to the Publisher the right to refer to the Author as the author of the Work and to use the Author's name, likeness,

(continued)

and biographical information in the Work and in all publicity and promotion for the Work. The Publisher shall have the right to contract in its own name for all rights pertaining to the Work and to conclude any contracts relating to the Work. The Work shall be created solely for the Publisher. All assignments and licenses that the Author grants to Publisher shall be exclusive to Publisher from the date of this Agreement, and the Author shall not retain or grant to any other person any right or license in or to the Work.

3. Additional Duties. The Author agrees to retain one (1) complete computer file of the manuscript at all times before publication of the Work. In the event of any loss or destruction of the manuscript, the Author shall deliver to the Publisher the duplicate copy of the manuscript and instructor's manual that he retained. If requested by the Publisher, the Author will complete a promotional questionnaire. If requested by the Publisher, the Author agrees to read, revise, correct and return promptly all proofs of the Work while the Work is being prepared for publication. The Author will pay the expense incurred by the Publisher's and printer's errors) requested by the Author and approved by the Publisher that are in excess of ten percent (10%) of the cost of original composition.

4. Representations. The Author represents and warrants to Publisher that the Work is or shall be his/her original creation, that there has been no prior publication of the Work or any part thereof, copyrights of to others and that the Work does not violate any right of privacy and that it is not libelous. The Author further represents and warrants to the Publisher that he is the owner of all the rights granted to Publisher herein and that he has not previously assigned, pledged or otherwise encumbered said rights in conflict with this Agreement.

5. Indemnification. The Author shall indemnify the Publisher against any costs or expenses, including reasonable attorneys' fees, incurred in defending or compromising any action arising by reason of either Author's breach of any warranty or representation contained herein, including, but not limited to, actions for copyright infringement, plagiarism, literary piracy, unfair competition, misappropriation or rights, libel, or any other matter. The Author also shall indemnify the Publisher against any judgment for damages in any action arising by reason of his/her breach of any warranty or representation contained herein. The Author's warranties and indemnities contained herein shall survive the termination of this Agreement.

6. Conflicts. Publisher warrants that it is not contracted with and will not contract with another author for a writing of the same title as the Work or substantially similar to the Work, unless or until this Agreement is terminated in accordance with this agreement or five (5) years from the date of this Agreement, whichever comes first. Without written permission from the Publisher, the Author shall not print, publish, sell or distribute another writing of the same title as the Work, or substantially similar to the Work, or allow another to do so, for five (5) years after the date of this Agreement.

7. Freebies. On publication of the Work, the Publisher shall give ten (10) free copies of the Work to the Author. In addition, the Author may purchase ten (10) copies of the Work at a discount of fifty percent (50%) from the retail price.

8. Royalties. The Publisher agrees to pay to the Author a royalty of thirteen percent (13%) of the actual selling price on all copies sold of the Work. "Actual selling price" for purposes of this Agreement means selling price less trade or other discounts, returns, shipping charges, and sales taxes. If author completes the entire Work ahead of schedule, a bonus of two percent (2%) of the Publisher's net receipts on all copies of the Work sold will be paid less any returns. Royalty percentages for revised editions will be reviewed. No royalty shall be paid on copies of the Work furnished gratis to the Author or to others for review, advertising, or promotional purposes. Royalty reports will be prepared by the Publisher semi-annually beginning with the next period ending on June 30 or December 31 of each year. The Publisher agrees to furnish such accounting and pay any royalties due within sixty (60) days thereafter. Royalty checks will be made payable to _____.

9. Other Concerns. In the absence of written request from the Author prior to publication, the Publisher may, after publication of the Work, dispose of the original manuscript and proofs. The validity, interpretation and performance of this Agreement shall be determined in accordance with the copyright laws of the United

States and the laws of the State of Tennessee, the state in which this Agreement is executed. This Agreement is performable in whole or in part in Knox County, Tennessee. Any disputes arising from this Agreement shall be mediated. If mediation fails, arbitration or court action may be pursued. This Agreement shall be binding upon the heirs, executors, administrators and assigns of the parties.

10. Entire Agreement. This Agreement contains the complete and entire understanding of the parties, and no representations are relied on by any party other than those expressly stated herein. No modification or waiver of any provision shall be valid unless in writing and signed by all parties. Should any provision of this Agreement or the application thereof to any extent be held invalid or unenforceable, the remainder of this Agreement and the application thereof shall not be affected thereby and shall continue in effect.

IN WITNESS WHEREOF, each of the parties hereby executes this Agreement under penalty of perjury to be effective on this _____ day of _____, 2005.

_____ Publishing Company

By: _____
President

_____
Author
_____

Reprinted with permission of Athena Group.

REFERENCES FOR ADDITIONAL RESEARCH AND DISCUSSION

Baumgartner, N., *Record Companies Can Fire Us, But We Can't Fire Them: The Balance Between Recording Artists and Recording Companies: A Tip in Favor of the Artists?* 5 Vand. J. Ent. L. & Prac. 73 (2003).

Carlisle, S.M. & Wolfe, R.C., *Florida's New Child Performer and Athlete Protection Act or What To Do When Your Client Is a Child, Not Just Acting Like One,* 69 Fla. B.J. 93, (1995).

Cook, R., *The Impact of Digital Distribution on the Duration of Recording Contracts,* 6 Vand. J. Ent. L. & Prac. 40 (2003).

Ellis, L., *Talking About My Generation: Assumption of Risk and the Rights of Injured Concert Fans in the Twenty-First Century,* 80 Tex. L. Rev. 607 (2002).

Hardin, T., *The Regulation of Minors' Entertainment Contracts: Effective California Law or Hollywood Grandeur?* 19 J. Juv. L. 376 (1998).

Krieg, J., *There's No Business Like Show Business: Child Entertainers and the Law,* 6 U. Pa. J. Lab. & Emp. L. 429 (2004).

Letowsky, R.C., *Broke or Exploited: The Real Reason Behind Artist Bankruptcies,* 20 Cardozo Arts & Ent. L.J. 625 (2002).

Siegel, E., *When Parental Interference Goes Too Far: The Need for Adequate Protection of Child Entertainers and Athletes,* 18 Cardozo Arts & Ent. L.J. 427 (2000).

CONSTITUTIONAL ISSUES IN ENTERTAINMENT LAW

AFTER STUDYING THIS CHAPTER YOU SHOULD BE ABLE TO:

1. Describe the role of the First Amendment and how it applies to the entertainment industry.
2. Discuss the phrases freedom of speech and freedom of expression.
3. Distinguish between a public figure and a public official.
4. Define the concept of defamation and its various categories, including slander and libel.
5. Identify defenses of a claim to defamation.
6. Define the tort of intentional infliction of emotional distress.
7. Discuss the role of a retraction after a possible defamatory statement has been made.
8. Distinguish between the right of privacy and the term invasion of privacy.
9. Describe the reasons behind the development of stalking laws.
10. Define the term paparazzi.

INTRODUCTION

Freedom of speech and **freedom of the press** are freedoms that cut to the core of constitutional issues involved in the entertainment industry, an industry that thrives on the communication and expression of ideas. Whether entertainers and artists play roles in films or television, play music, or simply serve as spokespersons for products or services, those involved in the entertainment industry ultimately live and die on their performances. Their speech, commentary, and expressions often undergo great public scrutiny and criticism.

In this age of instantaneous and free public debate in electronic chat rooms and Web sites, those involved in the entertainment industry have become even greater targets of public discussion, admiration, hatred, or ridicule. Cable, satellite, and pay-per-view television have given viewers more exposure to entertainers than at any point in the industry's history. The common notion that "it's a free country and I can say whatever I want" has been pushed to the legal limit and beyond in many cases. The Supreme Court of the United States has, however, carved out rules related to the limits of certain speech as it has interpreted the Constitution.

Elizabeth Taylor and Richard Burton hounded by paparazzi.
Getty Images Inc. –Hutton Archive Photos.

Since entertainers voluntarily place themselves in the spotlight, a question arises as to what extent can comments made by the various media (radio, television, newspapers, and Web sites) and others (including private citizens in letters to the editor) be free from a lawsuit in the event that the entertainer believes lies or defamatory statements were made?

(continued)

What if the person being ridiculed in the public eye is not an entertainer at all and is merely a private citizen who was thrust into the public eye involuntarily? Such issues often arise as the subject of a lawsuit and become prime targets for public debate as to what extent commentary can be made, even if untrue, about persons in the spotlight.

This chapter explores the tort of defamation, including libel and slander, and the tort of intentional infliction of emotional distress in the context of the protection afforded by the U.S. Constitution's freedom of the press and freedom of speech. This chapter also addresses the potential liability of the entertainment industry for the promotion of violent music, film, television, and so forth and its effect on society. Recent issues in journalistic fraud are presented as well to demonstrate that false speech is not protected under the Constitution.

▉ FIRST AMENDMENT

The United States Constitution states:

> "Congress shall make no law . . . abridging the freedom of speech, or of the press." U.S. Const. amend. I.

Notice the free speech and free press clauses in the First Amendment. If a newspaper or other media defendant is sued for the publication of alleged defamatory statements, the First Amendment is almost always utilized as the first line of defense. Courts give great deference to the media and what it says, especially when it is a matter of opinion as opposed to fact. The American legal system generally frowns on **censorship**—government regulation of speech.

First Amendment protection for the freedom of speech is strong, but it is not an absolute defense. This chapter will demonstrate that not all speech is protected and that the government may have a legitimate reason to regulate certain types of speech. For example, inciting a riot, using fighting words,[31] and promoting child pornography or things deemed obscene are not forms of protected speech. Inciting a riot is not protected speech.[32] The federal government may regulate broadcast speech as well. For example, the FCC may still curtail speech that constitutes a clear and present danger which would likely incite or produce imminent lawless action.[33]

---

[31] In *Chaplinsky v. New Hampshire*, 315 U.S. 568, 572 (1942), the U.S. Supreme Court held that the First Amendment does not protect fighting words—"those which by their very utterance inflict injury or tend to incite an immediate breach of the peace."

[32] Justice Oliver Wendell Holmes wrote: "The most stringent protection of free speech would not protect a man in falsely shouting fire in a theatre and causing a panic." *Schenck v. United States*, 249 U.S. 47 (1919).

[33] *Brandenburg v. Ohio*, 395 U.S. 444 (1969).

FREEDOM OF EXPRESSION

Though the First Amendment provides for freedom of speech, what constitutes "speech" is not always certain. Speech includes much more than words alone and has been interpreted to mean the use of symbols or expression as well. For example, the wearing of armbands with a peace symbol during the Vietnam War era was protected speech under the First Amendment. *Tinker v. Des Moines School Dist.*, 393 U.S. 503 (1969). On the other hand, the burning of a draft card was <u>not</u> considered protected speech and violated the Selective Service rules. *United States v. O'Brien*, 391 U.S. 367 (1968).

FOURTEENTH AMENDMENT

Equally important to the understanding of the Constitution is the appreciation of the Fourteenth Amendment, which states, in part:

> "No State shall make or enforce any law which shall abridge the privileges or immunities of citizens of the United States; nor shall any State deprive any person of life, liberty, or property, without due process of law; nor deny to any person within its jurisdiction the equal protection of the laws." U.S. Const. amend. XIV.

Notice the **privileges and immunities, due process**, and **equal protection** clauses found in the Fourteenth Amendment. Such protections entitle citizens to the same protections afforded them by the federal government, and states cannot abridge those rights. This is very important in the entertainment industry, especially where the various states might legislate constitutional matters in various ways.

PUBLIC AND PRIVATE PLAINTIFFS

Those individuals who are categorized by courts as **public figure** plaintiffs are required to show **actual malice** on the part of the defendant in order to have any financial recovery for alleged defamatory statements. Actual malice is a standard of proof that means the publication of defamatory material was made "with knowledge that it was false or reckless disregard of whether it was false or not."[34] Courts now require a plaintiff who is a public figure to demonstrate actual malice by the intermediate clear and convincing evidence standard discussed in Chapter 1. Determining who is a public figure, however, is not always an easy task, and courts must decide whether or not an individual may be classified as such in litigation.

---

[34]*New York Times Co. v. Sullivan*, 376 U.S. 254 (1964).

Interestingly, even a private plaintiff seeking recovery for a defamatory publication concerning a public issue may not recover damages without a showing of actual malice. However, the actual malice standard is not required for a private plaintiff suing for "private issue" defamation. Courts sometimes struggle in terms of categorizing who is a public figure and who is a private person in defamation suits.

OFFICIALS AND PUBLIC FIGURES

At one time, courts differentiated between public figures and **public officials** (those who are elected or appointed) for the purposes of potential liability to the media for public discussion over such individuals. However, the distinction between the two has virtually become extinct for purposes of enforcing the actual malice standard, which applies to both public officials and figures now.

Courts consistently require public plaintiffs to prove more harm than their private counterparts. The courts are concerned that if the media is continually in fear that their commentary over public persons might expose them to liability, this would have a "chilling" effect on public debate in the media, including talk shows. A private person has a lower burden of proof when proving defamation which is an issue of state law. Each state has wide latitude in adopting its own standard of proof in defamation actions brought by private persons.

TORT OF DEFAMATION

Defamation has evolved into a civil wrong (tort) as the act of making untrue statements about another which damages his or her reputation and/or deters others from working with or association with the defamed party. Simply put, defamation is an attack on the good reputation of a person or a person's business by slander or libel. Similar to the concept of actual malice, nowhere in the Constitution is the term defamation found. Such concepts are terms developed by the Supreme Court as it has interpreted the Constitution.

If the defamatory statement is written, printed, or otherwise broadcast over the various forms of media it is considered **libel.** Spoken defamation is considered **slander.** One of the difficulties with this tort for plaintiffs is the demonstration that he or she suffered damages for the statement or publication by the defendant. Sometimes damages may not be physical but may involve humiliation, anguish, and suffering, even if no harm was proven to their reputation. Punitive damages may be appropriate for defamation, especially if the plaintiff may show that the statements were meant to be malicious. Of course, truth is always a defense to what would otherwise be a defamatory publication, even if it is harmful to a person's reputation. What is "true," however, is often the subject of debate.

NEW YORK TIMES CO. V. SULLIVAN

In the very important defamation case *New York Times Co. v. Sullivan*, 376 U.S. 254 (1964), the Supreme Court of the United States held that the First Amendment prohibited a public official from recovering any damages for defamation based on criticism of official conduct unless the official proved the statement was made with actual malice. The Supreme Court of the United States overturned an Alabama jury award of $500,000 entered against the *New York Times* for publication of a political advertisement that allegedly defamed Montgomery County (Alabama) Commissioner L. B. Sullivan and criticized the handling of civil rights demonstrators. In order to meet the actual malice standard, the Court held that he was required to establish that the defendant published the defamatory material with knowledge of its falsity or acted with reckless disregard for the truth or falsity of the publication.

OTHER DEFAMATION CASES

In *Curtis Publishing Co. v. Butts*, 388 U.S. 130 (1967), the Supreme Court held that the *New York Times Co. v. Sullivan* standard would apply to public figures as well as public officials. In *Gertz v. Robert Welch, Inc.*, 418 U.S. 323 (1974), the Court held that private citizens may sue for defamation even if they are not a public figure or public official, but punitive damages may only be recovered upon the showing of actual malice. In *Time, Inc. v. Hill*, 385 U.S. 374 (1967), a case which involved private individuals thrust into the public spotlight (not public figures) who were the subject of false media reports in LIFE magazine or otherwise newsworthy events, private individuals had to prove that a story's description of them was false or that it was published with knowledge of the falsity or reckless disregard for the truth (the *New York Times* standard).

FACT AND OPINION

The test for determining which statements are facts and which statements are opinions has not been definitively established. Similar to what is true and what is not "truth," the line between fact and opinion is not always clear. However, once a statement is labeled an opinion either expressly by the speaker or by the court, it is entitled to absolute protection under the First Amendment and cannot be the basis of a defamation claim.

LIBEL

Libel is defamation in writing, print, or pictures. It is written defamation that causes injury to another person. If proved, damages, including injury to reputation and emotional harm, may be awarded, including (possibly) the requiring of a retraction by the publisher. The Internet has created new problems for the law of libel because it is so easy for anyone to publish comment or criticism to a virtually limitless and worldwide audience.

▮ SLANDER

Slander, essentially an oral communication, requires proof of special damages unless the defamatory statement falls within certain common law categories of slander per se. If a plaintiff in a slander action is unable to prove either special damages or slander per se, the plaintiff is barred from recovery.

▮ LIBEL PER SE AND SLANDER PER SE

Some statements, such as an accusation of having committed a crime, having a feared disease, or being unable to perform one's occupation, are referred to as **libel per se** or **slander per se** and can lead to damage awards involving punitive damages. Most states provide for a demand for a printed retraction of defamation and only allow a lawsuit if there is no such admission of error.

▮ RETRACTIONS

One of the greatest measures of protection for media defendants is called the **retraction**. It is a defense to defamation. If a publication is made that is false, states may allow the publisher to retract the statement without imposition of penalty. This is important especially for inadvertent statements due to human error. Retractions occur frequently in the press for a variety of reasons, including the publication of incorrect facts that are not necessarily defamatory.

For example, in 2004, after the Tampa Bay Lightning of the NHL won the Stanley Cup in game 7 against the Calgary Flames, the *Tampa Tribune* actually published the wrong outcome of the event with a lengthy editorial praising the team and fans for a successful season.[35] Though no defamatory statements were made, it did present a huge embarrassment for the newspaper. The press may exercise a retraction in the event an otherwise defamatory statement is made as well. The following represents California's retraction law:

---

[35] http://sports.espn.go.com/nhl/playoffs2004/news/story?id=1817985. Also, http://www.usatoday.com/news/politicselections/nation/president/2004-07-07-post-corrected_x.htm

CALIFORNIA LIBEL RETRACTION STATUTE

Cal. Civ. Code § 48a (2004)

§ 48a. Demand for publication or broadcast of correction

1. In any action for damages for the publication of a libel in a newspaper, or of a slander by radio broadcast, plaintiff shall recover no more than special damages unless a correction be demanded and be not published or broadcast, as hereinafter provided. Plaintiff shall serve upon the publisher, at the place of publication or broadcaster at the place of broadcast, a written notice specifying the statements claimed to be libelous and demanding that the same be corrected. Said notice and demand must be served within 20 days after knowledge of the publication or broadcast of the statements claimed to be libelous.

2. If a correction be demanded within said period and be not published or broadcast in substantially as conspicuous a manner in said newspaper or on said broadcasting station as were the statements claimed to be libelous, in a regular issue thereof published or broadcast within three weeks after such service, plaintiff, if he pleads and proves such notice, demand and failure to correct, and if his cause of action be maintained, may recover general, special and exemplary damages; provided that no exemplary damages may be recovered unless the plaintiff shall prove that defendant made the publication or broadcast with actual malice and then only in the discretion of the court or jury, and actual malice shall not be inferred or presumed from the publication or broadcast.

3. A correction published or broadcast in substantially as conspicuous a manner in said newspaper or on said broadcasting station as the statements claimed in the complaint to be libelous, prior to receipt of a demand therefor, shall be of the same force and effect as though such correction had been published or broadcast within three weeks after a demand therefor.

4. As used herein, the terms "general damages," "special damages," "exemplary damages" and "actual malice," are defined as follows:

(a) "General damages" are damages for loss of reputation, shame, mortification and hurt feelings;

(b) "Special damages" are all damages which plaintiff alleges and proves that he has suffered in respect to his property, business, trade, profession or occupation, including such amounts of money as the plaintiff alleges and proves he has expended as a result of the alleged libel, and no other;

(c) "Exemplary damages" are damages which may in the discretion of the court or jury be recovered in addition to general and special damages for the sake of example and by way of punishing a defendant who has made the publication or broadcast with actual malice;

(d) "Actual malice" is that state of mind arising from hatred or ill will toward the plaintiff; provided, however, that such a state of mind occasioned by a good faith belief on the part of the defendant in the truth of the libelous publication or broadcast at the time it is published or broadcast shall not constitute actual malice.

STATUTES OF LIMITATION

The statute of limitation for slander and libel claims is generally short. Most states provide that a suit must be brought within one year of the publication. Other states extend the time limitation up to two years. For slander, some states place only a six-month time limit to bring a suit. Due to the short duration of these statutes, plaintiffs sometimes attempt to circumvent the defamation claim and sue, instead, under the tort of **intentional infliction of emotional distress,** which usually has a longer time limitation to file a claim.

PARODY AND SATIRE

Satire is a form of literature that uses humor and imitation to ridicule individuals' moral and character traits and flaws. A **parody** is similar, but it can be found in literature, music, art, or film for humorous purposes. These two methods have been used for centuries to criticize public figures and politics generally. Sometimes referred to as "humorous speech," cases involving what would otherwise be considered defamatory statements are given much leeway by courts, as long as a reasonable person would know that the statements are made in jest. Thus, statements that are meant to be funny or encourage laughter are all part of living life and are not actionable in a court of law. This is how tabloid magazines and newspapers and their journalists have been able to defend many (but not all) claims against them for what might otherwise have been defamation.

Jay Leno in monologue.
AP Wide World Photos.

INTENTIONAL INFLICTION OF EMOTIONAL DISTRESS

Though public figures and public officials must meet the actual malice standard as established in *New York Times Co. v. Sullivan* in order to recover for a claim of defamation, one method to avoid having to meet such a high legal standard is by suing under a different tort: the tort of intentional infliction of emotional distress. This unique tort has four elements: (1) the defendant must act intentionally or recklessly; (2) the defendant's conduct must be **extreme and outrageous;** and (3) the conduct must be the cause (4) of severe emotional distress.

At one time, proof of physical illness and injury was required to accompany a claim under this tort, but that standard is no longer required other than in some states for claims of the similar tort of **negligent infliction of emotional distress.** In order for liability to be established, the defendant's conduct must be outrageous in character and extreme in degree as to go beyond all possible bounds of decency and to be regarded as atrocious and utterly intolerable in a civilized society.

HUSTLER MAGAZINE V. FALWELL

This is the case that established that an individual could sue for the tort of intentional infliction of emotional distress against the media.[36] The plaintiff Jerry Falwell, a "televangelist," sued the publisher of *Hustler Magazine* for intentional infliction of emotional distress due to a 1983 advertisement insinuating that his first sexual encounter was with his mother in an outhouse. The advertisement was entitled, "Jerry Falwell talks about his first time" and was meant to look similar to a popular alcohol drink advertisement. This parody contained a disclaimer, "Ad parody—not to be taken seriously."

Still, Falwell contended that the defendant was liable for his emotional distress. He argued that the defendant's intention, namely to harm him, precluded any First Amendment protection and that free expression does not permit one to inflict injury solely for injury's sake. The Supreme Court unanimously disagreed with Falwell. The Court found Falwell to be a public figure and held that sharp criticism—even when false—was protected by the First Amendment. In 1988, the Supreme Court reversed an award of $200,000.

OTHER DEFENSES AND PRIVILEGES

There are several defenses that will defeat a defamation claim. Truth is always a defense. Certain persons and proceedings (such as a judge in his or her courtroom, witnesses testifying about a relevant issue in a case, and certain communications by legislators) are said to be privileged forms of speech, and such communications are protected from defamation claims.

---

[36] *Hustler Magazine v. Falwell*, 485 U.S. 46 (1988).

Also, courts clearly have demonstrated that items deemed **newsworthy** are afforded high First Amendment protection, thus making defenses on grounds of newsworthiness almost impossible to defeat. What is and what is not newsworthy is subject to great debate, but it seems that if statements are made as commentary on both public figures and on items of legitimate public interest, then courts view this in a freedom of speech light. Thus, it seems that as long as an event is newsworthy, media speech related to it is protected.

RIGHT OF PUBLICITY (COMMERCIAL MISAPPROPRIATION)

The **right of publicity,** sometimes referred to as **commercial misappropriation,** is a court-based legal doctrine that prevents the unauthorized commercial use of an individual name, likeness, or other recognizable aspects of one's persona. Obviously, this tort doctrine relates to well-known celebrities in the entertainment industry. It gives an individual the exclusive right to license the use of their identity for commercial and consequently financial promotion. The right of publicity has been identified by courts as the inherent right of every human being to control the commercial use of his or her own identity. Right of publicity statutes typically prohibit an individual from using another's name, voice, signature, photograph, or likeness in products or advertisements without that person's permission.

CALIFORNIA RIGHT OF PUBLICITY STATUTES

California Civil Code § 3344 recognizes a person's identification value and protects a celebrity's right of publicity. This statute makes it illegal to knowingly use "another's name, voice, signature, photograph, or likeness, in any manner, on or in products, merchandise, or goods, or for purposes of advertising or selling, or soliciting purchases of, products, merchandise, goods or services, without such person's prior consent." This statute does not apply to any news, public affairs, or sports broadcast or account or any political campaign.

Interestingly, even after a celebrity dies, the state of California also protects the right of publicity for a time in § 3344.1. This makes it a tort to use a "deceased personality's name, voice, signature, photograph, or likeness, in any manner, on or in products, merchandise, or goods, or for purposes of advertising or selling, or soliciting purchase of products, merchandise, goods, or services, without prior consent" from the person or the estate. This statute is sometimes referred to as the **dead celebrity** statute.

CARSON V. HERE'S JOHNNY PORTABLE TOILETS, INC.

In *Carson v. Here's Johnny Portable Toilets, Inc.,* 698 F.2d 831 (6th Cir. 1983), the defendant marketed portable toilets under the brand name *Here's*

Johnny—popular late night talk show host Johnny Carson's familiar *Tonight Show* introduction—without Carson's permission. The company also used the phrase *The World's Foremost Commodian* in connection with the sale of its product. The district court had dismissed Carson's Michigan common law right of publicity claim because the defendants had not used Carson's "name or likeness." In reversing the district court, the Sixth Circuit Court of Appeals found that the district court's conception of the right of publicity was "too narrow" and held that the defendant had appropriated Carson's identity by using the phrase "Here's Johnny" without permission.

WHITE V. SAMSUNG ELECTRONICS AMERICA, INC.

In *White v. Samsung Electronics America, Inc.*, 971 F.2d 1395 (9th Cir. 1992), Vanna White of the game show *Wheel of Fortune* sued Samsung for creating an advertisement for a videocassette recorder that included a robot in a blond wig and fancy dress standing on a game show set similar to the set used on the television show. The text of the advertisement read, "Longest-running game show. 2012 A.D." This depiction was part of Samsung's advertising campaign which depicted events in the early twenty-first century that involved celebrities in order to show the durability of their products. Vanna White sued Samsung for a violation of the Lanham Act and California's common law right of publicity. The Ninth Circuit Court of Appeals rejected the defense of parody. This decision gave legal force to celebrities such as Vanna White against those who seek to use celebrity identity in a commercial fashion, even if as a parody.

JOURNALISTIC FRAUD

So many court cases have been won by journalists and the media throughout the years that one might believe that journalists have almost free rein on their reporting conduct. This is not true, however. In 2004, false reports by journalists led to harsh criticism of the media. Fictional characters were brought to life in several instances as being true. This led to a continuing discourse on freedom of speech and First Amendment issues with regard to journalism. For example, reporter Jayson Blair "committed frequent acts of journalistic fraud" covering the Washington, D.C., sniper case and the war with Iraq, according to the *New York Times*.[37] This publication found problems in at least 36 of the 73 articles written by Blair from late October to his resignation on May 1, 2003. The 7,500-word story was accompanied by an editor's note apologizing to *New York Times*

---

[37] http://www.foxnews.com/story/0,2933,86551,00.html.

readers.[38] Blair admitted his errors and subsequently published a related book entitled, *Burning Down My Masters' House.*

ANONYMOUS SOURCES

While traditionally journalists have written (or otherwise reported) stories based upon confidential or anonymous sources, courts might be beginning to break down that journalistic protection when an alleged defamatory statement has been made.[39] For example, in 2003, writer Don Yeager was ordered to disclose his sources that he used in a story in *Sports Illustrated* (owned by Time, Inc.) regarding the brief tenure of the University of Alabama head football coach Mike Price. Alabama's press shield law expressly protects reporters from newspapers, radio, and television stations from having to disclose sources during a legal proceeding (Ala. Code § 12–21–142). However, the law does not mention magazine reporters, and the case was appealed to the Alabama Supreme Court to determine whether Time, Inc. had the right to protect its sources. U.S. District Judge Lynwood Smith sought assistance from the Alabama Supreme Court on how to interpret the Alabama statute. However, the Alabama Supreme Court declined to rule on the question.[40]

In *Atlanta Journal-Constitution v. Jewell*, 555 S.E.2d 175 (2001), attorneys argued that reporters must be forced to reveal confidential sources naming Richard Jewell as the suspect in the detonation of a bomb at the 1996 Summer Olympics in Atlanta (later proved to be false). In January 1997, Mr. Jewell sued the newspaper for libel. In 1999, a state court judge declared that two *Atlanta Journal-Constitution* reporters would have to name the confidential law enforcement sources which provided information leading to this story. In the end, though, the Georgia Court of Appeals vacated the requirement that reporters identify their sources.

RIGHT OF PRIVACY

The phrase **right of privacy** is not explicit in the Constitution. However, Justice Brandeis acknowledged this right in the decision of *Olmstead v. United States.*[41] Brandeis argued that despite the lack of specific language in the Constitution, the framers conferred the right to be left alone as the "most comprehensive of rights" and the "right most valued by civilized men." This right of privacy is not to be confused with the Fourth Amendment guard against unreasonable searches and seizures by the government (or police). This is the tort of

---

[38] *USA Today* reporter Jack Kelley and *Chicago Tribune* reporter Uli Schmetzer drew criticism for alleged violations of journalistic ethics in 2004, leading to their leaving their respective positions as well.
[39] Often characterized as an interview "on the condition of anonymity" by journalists.
[40] *Price v. Time, Inc.*, 304 F. Supp. 2d 1294 (N.D. Ala. 2004).
[41] *Olmstead v. United States*, 277 U.S. 438 (1928).

invasion of privacy, and celebrities will sue for the tort of invasion of privacy, which encompasses the right of privacy due to the unyielding nature of some of the members of the media or fans and the like and due to alleged libelous statements that place the plaintiffs in a **false light.**

Since entertainers and artists lead public lives and are continually observed and critiqued by members of the general public, they generally have a lower expectation of privacy than a private citizen. Still, courts have recognized that there are instances when even the most public entertainers might have their privacy rights violated. There are four types of invasions of privacy: (1) intrusion, (2) appropriation of name or likeness, (3) unreasonable publicity, and (4) false light. The tort of false light invasion of privacy is often utilized in litigation by a celebrity in conjunction with a claim of defamation.

CELEBRITY TARGETS

Even though celebrities live life in the limelight, they do not relinquish rights granted to them under the Constitution and other state and federal laws. For example, actor Tom Cruise won a $10 million judgment from his 2001 defamation action against a man who made gay wrestling and sex movies under the pseudonym of Kyle Bradford.[42] Cruise had originally sued for $100 million in Los Angeles Superior Court after a French magazine had been told by the defendant that he had been in a sexual relationship with Cruise. Cruise had previously sued Michael Davis, who had claimed that he had a videotape depicting Cruise engaging in homosexual sex, but the suit was dropped when Davis recanted his story and admitted he did not have such a videotape.[43]

In another case involving celebrities and the tort of invasion of privacy, Pamela Anderson and Bret Michaels, lead singer for the group Poison, reached an out-of-court settlement with Internet Entertainment Group (IEG) over a stolen videotape. Both filed lawsuits against IEG to keep the online site from publishing the videotape. The lawsuits also claimed copyright infringement and misappropriation. The videotape was never widely distributed because a federal judge blocked the release shortly after the suits were filed. Reportedly, the out-of-court settlement required that IEG would pay the pair a seven-figure sum and destroy all copies of the videotape, in addition to an apology. IEG was also sued by Anderson and husband, Tommy Lee, former Mötley Crüe drummer, over a homemade videotape known for its nudity.[44] Though that case had been originally dismissed, a court of appeals overturned the decision, and the plaintiffs were awarded $1,481,786 in addition to attorney fees and court costs.

---

[42] http://www.courttv.com/people/2003/0509/litigious_ctv.html.

[43] http://news.bbc.co.uk/1/hi/entertainment/showbiz/1686039.stm.

[44] http://www.eonline.com/News/Items/0,1,8344,00.html *See also* http://www.starswelove.com/scriptsphp/news.php?newsid=1493.

■ THE DRIVER'S PRIVACY PROTECTION ACT

An unfortunate example of privacy issues and celebrities culminated in the death of an actress in the 1980s. Congress enacted the **Driver's Privacy Protection Act** (DPPA)[45] in 1994, after the murder of actress Rebecca Schaeffer, star of the sitcom *My Sister Sam* in 1989. The assailant obtained her address from the California Department of Motor Vehicles, and he went to her apartment and murdered her in the doorway of her California apartment. The DPPA represents the codification of law as a direct result of privacy issues related to celebrities.

The DPPA prohibits states from disclosing personal information that their drivers submit in order to obtain a driver's license, including an individual's photograph, social security number, driver identification number, name, address (but not 5-digit zip code), telephone number, and medical or disability information. Information on vehicular accidents, driving violations, and driver's status is not "personal information." In 2000, the DPPA was amended to create a new class of "highly restricted personal information." This includes an individual's photograph or image, social security number, and medical or disability information.

■ STALKING LAWS

The crime of **stalking** is no laughing matter. Stalking is a crime, and it affects both males and females in all walks of life, including celebrities. All states have now enacted antistalking laws. Many states have both criminal and civil antistalking laws, including some having telephone and online stalking statutes referred to as electronic or **cyberstalking.**[46] The appropriate remedy for stalking is a **restraining order** (sometimes referred to as an **order of protection**), but such remedies make situations public, cost money, and are ultimately served at the discretion of a judge.

Stalking involves repetitive misconduct involving harassing, annoying, threatening, and sometimes potentially deadly behavior. It can create immense mental and emotional distress upon its victims. For an antistalking statute to pass constitutional requirements of interpretation, the statute must clearly define what behavior is disallowed. Critics of stalking laws claimed that these statutes were overly vague and should be unconstitutional in that they violated the First, Fifth, and Fourteenth Amendments of the Constitution. However, well-drafted statutes have avoided this problem.

California enacted the first antistalking statute in 1990, primarily in response to the public outcry over the stalking and murder of Rebecca Schaeffer. Numerous other celebrities, including, but not limited to, Halle Berry, Britney Spears, Madonna, and David Letterman, have had highly publicized instances of resorting to the help of the police and courts in order to prevent continued stalking misconduct.[47]

---

[45] 18 U.S.C. §§ 2721–2725. Effective September 13, 1997.
[46] Alaska, California, Indiana, and West Virginia, just to name a few.
[47] *See, e.g.*, http://www.kron4.com/Global/story.asp?S=1824610&nav=5D7zMgl0.

EXHIBIT 4.1

California Stalking Laws

Cal. Civil Code § 1708.7

(a) A person is liable for the tort of stalking when the plaintiff proves all of the following elements of the tort:

    (1) The defendant engaged in a pattern of conduct the intent of which was to follow, alarm, or harass the plaintiff. In order to establish this element, the plaintiff shall be required to support his or her allegations with independent corroborating evidence.

    (2) As a result of that pattern of conduct, the plaintiff reasonably feared for his or her safety, or the safety of an immediate family member. For purposes of this paragraph, "immediate family" means a spouse, parent, child, any person related by consanguinity or affinity within the second degree, or any person who regularly resides, or, within the six months preceding any portion of the pattern of conduct, regularly resided, in the plaintiff's household.

    (3) One of the following:

        (A) The defendant, as a part of the pattern of conduct specified in paragraph (1), made a credible threat with the intent to place the plaintiff in reasonable fear for his or her safety, or the safety of an immediate family member and, on at least one occasion, the plaintiff clearly and definitively demanded that the defendant cease and abate his or her pattern of conduct and the defendant persisted in his or her pattern of conduct.

        (B) The defendant violated a restraining order, including, but not limited to, any order issued pursuant to Section 527.6 of the Code of Civil Procedure, prohibiting any act described in subdivision (a).

(b) For the purposes of this section:

    (1) "Pattern of conduct" means conduct composed of a series of acts over a period of time, however short, evidencing a continuity of purpose. Constitutionally protected activity is not included within the meaning of "pattern of conduct."

    (2) "Credible threat" means a verbal or written threat, including that communicated by means of an electronic communication device, or a threat implied by a pattern of conduct or a combination of verbal, written, or electronically communicated statements and conduct, made with the intent and apparent ability to carry out the threat so as to cause the person who is the target of the threat to reasonably fear for his or her safety or the safety of his or her immediate family.

    (3) "Electronic communication device" includes, but is not limited to, telephones, cellular telephones, computers, video recorders, fax machines, or pagers. "Electronic communication" has the same meaning as the term defined in Subsection 12 of Section 2510 of Title 18 of the United States Code.

    (4) "Harass" means a knowing and willful course of conduct directed at a specific person which seriously alarms, annoys, torments, or terrorizes the person, and which serves no legitimate purpose. The course of conduct must be such as would cause a reasonable person to suffer substantial

(continued)

emotional distress, and must actually cause substantial emotional distress to the person.

(c) A person who commits the tort of stalking upon another is liable to that person for damages, including, but not limited to, general damages, special damages, and punitive damages pursuant to Section 3294.

(d) In an action pursuant to this section, the court may grant equitable relief, including, but not limited to, an injunction.

(e) The rights and remedies provided in this section are cumulative and in addition to any other rights and remedies provided by law.

(f) This section shall not be construed to impair any constitutionally protected activity, including, but not limited to, speech, protest, and assembly.

Cal. Penal Code § 422

422. Any person who willfully threatens to commit a crime which will result in death or great bodily injury to another person, with the specific intent that the statement, made verbally, in writing, or by means of an electronic communication device, is to be taken as a threat, even if there is no intent of actually carrying it out, which, on its face and under the circumstances in which it is made, is so unequivocal, unconditional, immediate, and specific as to convey to the person threatened, a gravity of purpose and an immediate prospect of execution of the threat, and thereby causes that person reasonably to be in sustained fear for his or her own safety or for his or her immediate family's safety, shall be punished by imprisonment in the county jail not to exceed one year, or by imprisonment in the state prison. For the purposes of this section, "immediate family" means any spouse, whether by marriage or not, parent, child, any person related by consanguinity or affinity within the second degree, or any other person who regularly resides in the household, or who, within the prior six months, regularly resided in the household. "Electronic communication device" includes, but is not limited to, telephones, cellular telephones, computers, video recorders, fax machines, or pagers. "Electronic communication" has the same meaning as the term defined in Subsection 12 of Section 2510 of Title 18 of the United States Code.

Cal. Penal Code § 646.9

646.9. (a) Any person who willfully, maliciously, and repeatedly follows or harasses another person and who makes a credible threat with the intent to place that person in reasonable fear for his or her safety, or the safety of his or her immediate family, is guilty of the crime of stalking, punishable by imprisonment in a county jail for not more than one year or by a fine of not more than one thousand dollars ($1,000), or by both that fine and imprisonment, or by imprisonment in the state prison.

(b) Any person who violates subdivision (a) when there is a temporary restraining order, injunction, or any other court order in effect prohibiting the behavior described in subdivision (a) against the same party, shall be punished by imprisonment in the state prison for two, three, or four years.

(c) Every person who, having been convicted of a felony under this section, commits a second or subsequent violation of this section shall be punished by imprisonment in the state prison for two, three, or four years.

(d) In addition to the penalties provided in this section, the sentencing court may order a person convicted of a felony under this section to register as a sex offender pursuant to subparagraph (E) of paragraph (2) of subdivision (a) of Section 290.

(e) For the purposes of this section, "harasses" means a knowing and willful course of conduct directed at a specific person that seriously alarms, annoys, torments, or terrorizes the person, and that serves no legitimate purpose. This course of conduct must be such as would cause a reasonable person to suffer substantial emotional distress, and must actually cause substantial emotional distress to the person.

(f) For purposes of this section, "course of conduct" means a pattern of conduct composed of a series of acts over a period of time, however short, evidencing a continuity of purpose. Constitutionally protected activity is not included within the meaning of "course of conduct."

(g) For the purposes of this section, "credible threat" means a verbal or written threat, including that performed through the use of an electronic communication device, or a threat implied by a pattern of conduct or a combination of verbal, written, or electronically communicated statements and conduct made with the intent to place the person that is the target of the threat in reasonable fear for his or her safety or the safety of his or her family and made with the apparent ability to carry out the threat so as to cause the person who is the target of the threat to reasonably fear for his or her safety or the safety of his or her family. It is not necessary to prove that the defendant had the intent to actually carry out the threat. The present incarceration of a person making the threat shall not be a bar to prosecution under this section.

(h) For purposes of this section, the term "electronic communication device" includes, but is not limited to, telephones, cellular phones, computers, video recorders, fax machines, or pagers. "Electronic communication" has the same meaning as the term defined in Subsection 12 of Section 2510 of Title 18 of the United States Code.

(i) This section shall not apply to conduct that occurs during labor picketing.

(j) If probation is granted, or the execution or imposition of a sentence is suspended, for any person convicted under this section, it shall be a condition of probation that the person participate in counseling, as designated by the court. However, the court, upon a showing of good cause, may find that the counseling requirement shall not be imposed.

(k) The sentencing court also shall consider issuing an order restraining the defendant from any contact with the victim, that may be valid for up to 10 years, as determined by the court. It is the intent of the Legislature that the length of any restraining order be based upon the seriousness of the facts before the court, the probability of future violations, and the safety of the victim and his or her immediate family.

(l) For purposes of this section, "immediate family" means any spouse, parent, child, any person related by consanguinity or affinity within the second degree, or any other person who regularly resides in the household, or who, within the prior six months, regularly resided in the household.

(m) The court shall consider whether the defendant would benefit from treatment pursuant to Section 2684. If it is determined to be appropriate, the court shall recommend that the Department of Corrections make a certification as provided in Section 2684. Upon the certification, the defendant shall be evaluated and transferred to the appropriate hospital for treatment pursuant to Section 2684.

(continued)

646.91. (a) Notwithstanding any other law, a judicial officer may issue an ex parte emergency protective order where a peace officer, as defined in Section 830.1 or 830.2, asserts reasonable ground to believe that a person is in immediate and present danger of stalking based upon the person's allegation that he or she has been willfully, maliciously, and repeatedly followed or harassed by another person who has made a credible threat with the intent of placing the person who is the target of the threat in reasonable fear for his or her safety, or the safety of his or her immediate family, within the meaning of Section 646.9.

(b) A peace officer who requests an emergency protective order shall reduce the order to writing and sign it.

(c) An emergency protective order shall include all of the following:

(1) A statement of the grounds asserted for the order.

(2) The date and time the order expires.

(3) The address of the superior court for the district or county in which the protected party resides.

(4) The following statements, which shall be printed in English and Spanish:

(A) "To the protected person: This order will last until the date and time noted above. If you wish to seek continuing protection, you will have to apply for an order from the court at the address noted above. You may seek the advice of an attorney as to any matter connected with your application for any future court orders. The attorney should be consulted promptly so that the attorney may assist you in making your application."

(B) "To the restrained person: This order will last until the date and time noted above. The protected party may, however, obtain a more permanent restraining order from the court. You may seek the advice of an attorney as to any matter connected with the application. The attorney should be consulted promptly so that the attorney may assist you in responding to the application."

(d) An emergency protective order may be issued under this section only if the judicial officer finds both of the following:

(1) That reasonable grounds have been asserted to believe that an immediate and present danger of stalking, as defined in Section 646.9, exists.

(2) That an emergency protective order is necessary to prevent the occurrence or reoccurrence of the stalking activity.

(e) An emergency protective order may include either of the following specific orders as appropriate:

(1) A harassment protective order as described in Section 527.6 of the Code of Civil Procedure.

(2) A workplace violence protective order as described in Section 527.8 of the Code of Civil Procedure.

(f) An emergency protective order shall be issued without prejudice to any person.

(g) An emergency protective order expires at the earlier of the following times:

(1) The close of judicial business on the fifth court day following the day of its issuance.

(2) The seventh calendar day following the day of its issuance.

(h) A peace officer who requests an emergency protective order shall do all of the following:

(1) Serve the order on the restrained person, if the restrained person can reasonably be located.

(2) Give a copy of the order to the protected person, or, if the protected person is a minor child, to a parent or guardian of the protected child if the parent or guardian can reasonably be located, or to a person having temporary custody of the child.

(3) File a copy of the order with the court as soon as practicable after issuance.

(i) A peace officer shall use every reasonable means to enforce an emergency protective order.

(j) A peace officer who acts in good faith to enforce an emergency protective order is not civilly or criminally liable.

(k) A peace officer who requests an emergency protective order under this section shall carry copies of the order while on duty.

(l) "Judicial officer" as used in this section, means a judge, commissioner, or referee.

(m) Nothing in this section shall be construed to permit a court to issue an emergency protective order prohibiting speech or other activities that are constitutionally protected or protected by the laws of this state or by the United States or activities occurring during a labor dispute, as defined by Section 527.3 of the Code of Civil Procedure, including but not limited to, picketing and hand billing.

(n) The Judicial Council shall develop forms, instructions, and rules for the scheduling of hearings and other procedures established pursuant to this section.

(o) Any intentional disobedience of any emergency protective order granted under this section is punishable pursuant to Section 166. Nothing in this subdivision shall be construed to prevent punishment under Section 646.9, in lieu of punishment under this section, if a violation of Section 646.9 is also pled and proven.

Cal. Penal Code § 653m

653m. (a) Every person who, with intent to annoy, telephones or makes contact by means of an electronic communication device with another and addresses to or about the other person any obscene language or addresses to the other person any threat to inflict injury to the person or property of the person addressed or any member of his or her family, is guilty of a misdemeanor. Nothing in this subdivision shall apply to telephone calls or electronic contacts made in good faith.

(b) Every person who makes repeated telephone calls or makes repeated contact by means of an electronic communication device with intent to annoy another person at his or her residence, is, whether or not conversation ensues from making the telephone call or electronic contact, guilty of a misdemeanor. Nothing in this subdivision shall apply to telephone calls or electronic contacts made in good faith.

(c) Every person who makes repeated telephone calls or makes repeated contact by means of an electronic communication device with the intent to annoy another person at his or her place of work is guilty of a misdemeanor punishable by a fine of not more than one thousand dollars ($1,000), or by imprisonment in

(continued)

a county jail for not more than one year, or by both the fine and imprisonment. Nothing in this subdivision shall apply to telephone calls or electronic contacts made in good faith. This subdivision applies only if one or both of the following circumstances exist:

(1) There is a temporary restraining order, an injunction, or any other court order, or any combination of these court orders, in effect prohibiting the behavior described in this section.

(2) The person makes repeated telephone calls or makes repeated contact by means of an electronic communication device with the intent to annoy another person at his or her place of work, totaling more than 10 times in a 24-hour period, whether or not conversation ensues from making the telephone call or electronic contact, and the repeated telephone calls or electronic contacts are made to the workplace of an adult or fully emancipated minor who is a spouse, former spouse, cohabitant, former cohabitant, or person with whom the person has a child or has had a dating or engagement relationship or is having a dating or engagement relationship.

(d) Any offense committed by use of a telephone may be deemed to have been committed where the telephone call or calls were made or received. Any offense committed by use of an electronic communication device or medium, including the Internet, may be deemed to have been committed where the electronic communication or communications were originally sent or first viewed by the recipient.

(e) Subdivision (a), (b), or (c) is violated when the person acting with intent to annoy makes a telephone call requesting a return call and performs the acts prohibited under subdivision (a), (b), or (c) upon receiving the return call.

(f) If probation is granted, or the execution or imposition of sentence is suspended, for any person convicted under this section, the court may order as a condition of probation that the person participate in counseling.

(g) For purposes of this section the term "electronic communication device" includes, but is not limited to, telephones, cellular phones, computers, video recorders, fax machines, or pagers. "Electronic communication" has the same meaning as the term defined in Subsection 12 of Section 2510 of Title 18 of the United States Code.

Reprinted with permission of LexisNexis.

VIOLENT SPEECH IN ENTERTAINMENT

One of the most interesting yet controversial areas of the entertainment law is the clash between the First Amendment protections of freedom of speech and expression against the alleged negative effect and influence of the glamorization of violence in society in various forms of the media. Movies, television shows, videos, and other forms of media often contain violent content that seems to encourage fighting, sex, and other forms of speech, expression, or even gestures that might influence the behaviors of members of society, particularly young people. At issue is whether freedom of speech outweighs any governmental interest in regulating "hate speech," for example.

◼ SUBLIMINAL SPEECH

In summer 1990, the rock band Judas Priest was involved in a trial for allegedly being responsible for suicide attempts five years earlier by two Nevada teenage residents.[48] The plaintiffs claimed that the song, *Better by You Better Than Me* contained a **subliminal** (subconscious) message which said, "Do it," and it was the proximate cause of their suicide attempts.[49] The trial judge ruled that **subliminal speech** or music on record albums did <u>not</u> deserve First Amendment protection and that people have the right to be free from this type of speech. Therefore, the plaintiffs could sue under a form of the tort of invasion of privacy. The plaintiffs lost, however, because they could not prove intent.

◼ *WALLER V. OSBOURNE*

In another subliminal message case, *Waller v. Osbourne*, 763 F. Supp. 1144 (M.D. Ga. 1991), the plaintiffs brought a wrongful death action asserting that their son had been incited to commit suicide through the music, lyrics, and subliminal messages contained in the song "Suicide Solution" on the album *Blizzard of Ozz.* by John "Ozzy" Osbourne. The court noted that the presence of a subliminal message (similar to false and misleading commercial speech) has little social value. If the song had subliminal messages, the music would then have no First Amendment protection.

The Court concluded that the most important characteristic of a subliminal message is that it enters into the brain while the listener is unaware that he or she has heard anything at all. If the message is heard to <u>any</u> extent, then the listener is not dealing with a subliminal message. Ultimately, the Court held the plaintiff had failed to produce evidence from which one could even infer that there was a subliminal message in the song.

The *Waller v. Osbourne* case follows:

Waller v. Osbourne

763 F. Supp. 1144 (M.D. Ga. 1991)

DUROSS FITZPATRICK, UNITED STATES DISTRICT JUDGE:

Plaintiffs Thomas and Myra Waller in the above captioned action allege that the defendants proximately caused the wrongful death of their son Michael Jeffery Waller by inciting him to commit suicide through the music, lyrics, and subliminal messages contained in the song

---

[48] *See Vance v. Judas Priest*, No. 86-5844/86-3939, 1990 WL 130920 (D.C. Nev. August 24, 1990). The suit was brought by the parents.
[49] Album *Stained Class* (1978).

"Suicide Solution" on the album "Blizzard of Ozz." Defendants deny all allegations of wrongdoing on their part and now have pending before the court a joint motion for summary judgment.

I. BACKGROUND FACTS

Plaintiffs filed their original complaint in this case on April 28, 1988, following the death of their son Michael Jeffery Waller on May 3, 1986, as the result of a self-inflicted pistol wound to his head. In that original complaint, plaintiffs alleged that their son's suicide occurred after he had repeatedly listened to an Ozzy Osbourne cassette tape which contained audible and perceptible lyrics that directed Michael Waller to take his own life.

Defendants Ozzy Osbourne, CBS Inc., and CBS RECORDS Inc., responded to the plaintiffs' complaint by moving the court to dismiss the complaint because it failed to state a claim upon which relief could be granted. Before the court acted on the motion to dismiss, however, plaintiffs filed a motion to amend their complaint which the court authorized.

The modified complaint, (Plaintiffs' Amended Complaint), discarded the claim that the lyrics which allegedly incited their son to commit suicide were audible and perceptible and instead charged that those same lyrics represent a subliminal message that is consciously intelligible only when the music is electronically adjusted. The amended complaint further alleges that as a result of the dissemination of the music, lyrics, and subliminal message in the song "Suicide Solution" on the album "Blizzard of Ozz," defendants are liable to the plaintiffs for causing the pain and suffering of their deceased son; inciting his wrongful death; encouraging persons to physically harm themselves or commit suicide; and engaging in fraud, invasion of privacy, and nuisance.

Defendants responded to plaintiffs' amended complaint by filing a joint motion to dismiss plaintiffs' complaint as amended. In addressing defendants' motion to dismiss in an order dated

July 20, 1989, the court distilled plaintiffs' complaint down to the dispositive issue of whether or not the alleged subliminal message actually existed and, if so, were the defendants nevertheless protected from liability by the first amendment to the United States Constitution. The court granted plaintiffs the opportunity to pursue that issue through discovery and therefore denied defendants' motion to dismiss with the proviso that upon the completion of discovery the motion could be renewed in the form of a summary judgment motion.

As the discovery phase of the case began, plaintiffs were confident that a subliminal message existed within a twenty-eight second interlude on the song "Suicide Solution." Plaintiffs asserted, however, that the existence of the subliminal message could "only be confirmed by having an opportunity to test the multi-track masters and stereo masters of the entire tape of the album "Blizzard of Ozz." Plaintiffs therefore requested that they be given the opportunity to have their expert examine the master tapes of the "Blizzard of Ozz" album. Defendants consented to plaintiffs' request and on August 27, 1990, delivered the twenty-four track and stereo master tapes of the "Blizzard of Ozz" album to the studio of the expert plaintiffs had hired to analyze the tapes.

The expert plaintiffs employed to examine the master tapes, Martin Hall, is a Santa Barbara High School graduate who has completed upper level history courses at the University of California at Santa Barbara. Mr. Hall is not an expert in mastering and mixing rock music, however, he had previously tested the commercial release of "Suicide Solution" for the plaintiffs in the case of *McCollum v. CBS, Inc.*, 202 Cal. App. 3d 989, 249 Cal. Rptr. 187 (1988). That examination of "Suicide Solution" by Mr. Hall led him to conclude that the song did not contain subliminal messages but rather something he identified as "preconscious suggestions." This is a term he uses to describe something which is not the same as a subliminal message since, according to Hall, a subliminal message is not audible while a preconscious suggestion can be heard though not necessarily understood.

The preconscious suggestions Mr. Hall found were a series of lyrics which are "clearly audible but mostly unintelligible." Mr. Hall noted at that time, however, that his version of the alleged preconscious lyrics did involve "guess work" which could only be confirmed by examining the master tape of "Suicide Solution." After conducting tests on the master tapes, Mr. Hall did not find any subliminal messages in the song "Suicide Solution." In his report prepared for plaintiffs' attorney, Mr. Hall stated that the alleged subliminal lyrics are actually lyrics that are "preconscious, in that the vocal performance [of the lyrics in question] is audible (and is, therefore, not subliminal per se) but not immediately intelligible." The method of testing that plaintiffs in this case had assured the court on numerous occasions was the only means of confirming the existence of a subliminal message in the song "Suicide Solution" determined with certainty that no subliminal messages existed anywhere on the entire tape.

Plaintiffs' other expert, Victoria Evans, a computer science lecturer who has no experience in music recording or sound engineering, attempted to identify subliminal messages in the song "Suicide Solution" through the use of a MacIntosh computer and a software package called DigiDesign AudioMedia. While Ms. Evans credits the computer system with enabling her to discover what she has labelled a subliminal message in the song "Suicide Solution," the MacIntosh computer and the AudioMedia program did not, and could not, identify any of the words in the song; nor could it indicate any distinction between the lyrics and music contained on the record album. The computer system assisted Ms. Evans by allowing her to copy the music onto a "sound file" and then slow it down so she could carefully listen to the lyrics. The only manner, however, in which Ms. Evans actually identified what she has labeled a subliminal message in the song "Suicide Solution" was by literally hearing the words with her own ears.

Those words Ms. Evans heard on "Suicide Solution," which she labelled as a subliminal message, are an almost identical listing of the words that plaintiffs initially identified as, and Mr. Hall currently claims are, audible lyrics.

Ms. Evans' findings indicate that she also has determined that the lyrics, which plaintiffs assert represent a subliminal message that incited their son to commit suicide, are words that are audible though not immediately intelligible. However, unlike plaintiffs' other expert, Mr. Hall, who failed to find a subliminal message because he realized that if the words are audible they cannot be subliminal, Ms. Evans found what she had labelled a subliminal message for the plaintiffs by failing to recognize the true meaning of subliminal and instead defining it for her purposes as any words contained in music that are barely heard but not decipherable.

Other than the expert witnesses Hall and Evans, plaintiffs produced two other affidavits in support of their case. The affidavits, however, fail to add any additional information not already provided by plaintiffs' other experts and merely indicate that they found lyrics in the song "Suicide Solution" unintelligible. Soon after those affidavits were taken, discovery in the case was closed and defendants filed the instant joint motion for summary judgment now before the court.

II. DISCUSSION

In determining whether or not the court should grant the joint summary judgment motion of the defendants in this case, the court must initially resolve the issue of whether, as a matter of law, the song "Suicide Solution" on the album "Blizzard of Ozz" contains subliminal messages as alleged by plaintiffs. The court finds this step necessary because it is convinced that the presence of a subliminal message, whose surreptitious nature makes it more akin to false and misleading commercial speech and other forms of speech extremely limited in their social value, would relegate the music containing such to a class worthy of little, if any, first amendment constitutional protection.

Plaintiffs attempt to establish the presence of subliminal messages in the song "Suicide Solution" contained on the "Blizzard of Ozz" album primarily through the deposition testimony of two expert witnesses. Plaintiffs' expert, Mr. Hall, however, fails to create an issue of fact concerning the existence of a subliminal message when his specific finding is that since the lyrics in question in this case are audible, they cannot be a subliminal message as plaintiffs allege.

Plaintiffs' other expert, Ms. Evans, is equally unsuccessful in creating a genuine issue of fact since she contends that the lyrics in question are a subliminal message precisely because they are barely heard but not decipherable. While the court was unable to find a precise legal definition of a subliminal message, it is clear from the definition of subliminal that lyrics which are audible enough to make one consciously aware of their presence, though they may not necessarily be intelligible, do not qualify as a subliminal message.

According to *Webster's Ninth New Collegiate Dictionary*, (1985 Edition), subliminal is actually defined as "inadequate to produce a sensation or perception" and "existing or functioning below the threshold of conscious awareness." *Random House Dictionary* (1987 Edition) defines subliminal as "existing or operating below the threshold of consciousness; being or employing stimuli insufficiently intense to produce a discrete sensation but often being or designed to be intense enough to influence the mental processes or the behavior of the individual." If, as defined, a subliminal message must exist below the threshold of conscious awareness then it must follow that lyrics distinct enough to be heard and reacted to—even though garbled or unclear, are not a subliminal message. The most important character of a subliminal message is that it sneaks into the brain while the listener is completely unaware that he has heard anything at all. If the message is heard to any extent, even if garbled and unintelligible, the listener consciously attempts to discern a meaning from that which he hears. One is then dealing, not with a subliminal message, but

rather the interpretation of an abstract medium which is akin to spotting objects in cloud formations.

Possibly a visual subliminal message such as the words "eat popcorn" on a reel of movie film can be proved more easily than an audio one such as the one alleged here. If the film is stopped and one holds each frame up to the light somewhere there must be at least one frame that says "eat popcorn." Here, there is nothing that says what the plaintiffs contend unless one uses his imagination. Therefore, despite her desire to label the lyrics contained in the twenty-eight second interlude on the song "Suicide Solution" a subliminal message, the fact that Ms. Evans found that those lyrics are audible means that she has proved just the opposite—that the lyrics are not a subliminal message.

Furthermore, honoring Ms. Evans definition of subliminal message would mean that all rock music, or any music for that matter, which contains unintelligible lyrics could be found to contain a subliminal message, thereby, subjecting an endless number of performers and producers to possible law suits. It would be an understatement to say such a ruling would open the flood gates of litigation.

Ms. Evans' expert opinion that the song "Suicide Solution" contains a subliminal message directly contradicts the opinion rendered by plaintiffs' other expert, Mr. Hall. Moreover, in light of the definition of subliminal and the manner in which she defines subliminal message, it is clear that her opinion lacks any credible support and as such fails to create a genuine issue of fact concerning whether the song "Suicide Solution" on the album "Blizzard of Ozz" contains subliminal messages.

Plaintiffs have steadfastly predicted that given the opportunity to thoroughly examine the song "Suicide Solution" they would be able to prove the existence of a subliminal message in the song. After their experts were given an unrestricted opportunity to find a subliminal message in the music in question, however, plaintiffs have been unable to produce any evidence which creates a genuine issue of fact concerning whether the song "Suicide Solution" on the album "Blizzard of Ozz" contains a subliminal message. Plaintiffs have simply failed to produce any evidence from which one could even infer that there is a subliminal message in the song "Suicide Solution" on the album "Blizzard of Ozz."

The court noted in its order denying defendants' motion to dismiss that the plaintiffs would be hard-pressed to avoid summary judgment in this action absent the presence of a subliminal message in the music of the defendants. Such is the case because music in the form of entertainment represents a type of speech that is generally afforded first amendment constitutional protection.

The first amendment protection that shields those who produce, perform, and distribute music is not, however, absolute. Music legally classified as obscene or defamatory, or that which represents fighting words or incites imminent lawless activity is either entitled to diminished first amendment constitutional protection or none at all. Therefore, even though the court has found that defendants' music does not contain subliminal messages, plaintiffs can strip away the first amendment protection defendants now stand behind if they can demonstrate that defendants' music fits into one of the above categories.

Plaintiffs contend that the song "Suicide Solution" on the album "Blizzard of Ozz" is properly categorized as speech which incites imminent lawless activity, thereby depriving defendants of any legitimate claim to first amendment protection. The removal of first amendment protection from defendants' music on such a basis is contingent on a finding that it was "directed to inciting or producing imminent lawless action and is likely to incite or produce such action." *Brandenburg*, 395 U.S. at 447, 89 S.Ct. at 1829. Subsequent Supreme Court decisions have further indicated that in making such a finding the primary focus of the court should be on the imminence of the threat. *Hess v. Indiana*, 414 U.S. 105, 94 S.Ct. 326, 38 L.Ed. 2d 303 (1973).

In *Hess*, the Court was forced to decide whether an antiwar demonstrator's first amendment rights were violated when the state of Indiana arrested him for shouting, "We'll take the fucking street later [or again]," to a crowd the police were attempting to disperse. In upholding the demonstrator's first amendment right to make that statement the court concluded that since the uncontroverted evidence showed that Hess' statement was not directed to any person or group of persons, it cannot be said that he was advocating, in the normal sense, any action. And since there was no evidence or rational inference from the import of the language, that his words were intended to produce, and likely to produce, *imminent* disorder, those words could not be punished by the state on the ground that they had 'a tendency to lead to violence.'

A careful examination of the defendants' music in accordance with the test developed in *Brandenburg* and refined in *Hess* leads this court to conclude that the defendants did not engage in culpable incitement. There is no indication whatsoever that defendants' music was directed toward any particular person or group of persons. Moreover, there is no evidence that defendants' music was intended to produce acts of suicide, and likely to cause *imminent* acts of suicide (noting that there, in fact, is no evidence nor even any allegations in this case that Michael Jeffery Waller committed suicide immediately after listening to defendants' music), nor could one rationally infer such a meaning from the lyrics.

Viewing the facts in a light most favorable to the plaintiffs, the song "Suicide Solution" can be perceived as asserting in a philosophical sense that suicide may be a viable option one should consider in certain circumstances. And a strong argument can certainly be made that in light of the almost epidemic proportion of teenage suicides now occurring in this country it is irresponsible and callous for a musician with a large teenage following such as Ozzy Osbourne to portray suicide in any manner other than a tragic occurrence. Nevertheless, an abstract discussion of the moral propriety or even moral necessity for a resort to suicide, is not the same as indicating to someone that he should commit suicide and encouraging him to take such action. That, however, is what the law requires the plaintiffs to demonstrate in order to hold the defendants liable for inciting their son to commit suicide through the dissemination of their music. Plaintiffs have made no such showing and have failed to demonstrate any manner in which defendants' music can be categorized as speech which incites imminent lawless activity. Accordingly, the court finds as a matter of law that defendants are protected by the first amendment from liability for culpable incitement.

Absent the allegation that defendants' music represents speech that incites imminent lawless activities, plaintiffs have no other plausible basis in this case upon which they can overcome the broad first amendment protection generally afforded speech in the form of music. Plaintiffs put forth other theories of liability such as negligence, nuisance, fraud, and invasion of privacy. However, all of those tort based theories, as asserted by plaintiffs, fail to overcome the defendants' imposition of a valid first amendment defense.

Numerous courts have pointed out that any attempt to impose tort liability on persons engaged in the dissemination of protected speech involves too great a risk of seriously chilling all free speech. In *Walt Disney Productions, Inc., v. Shannon*, 247 Ga. 402, 276 S.E.2d 580 (1981), the court found that the imposition of tort liability on defendants who were charged with broadcasting statements which invited children to engage in conduct that posed a foreseeable risk of injury would open a Pandora's box and chill the flow of protected speech. The Fifth Circuit Court of Appeals indicated in *Herceg v. Hustler Magazine, Inc.*, 814 F.2d 1017, 1024 (5th Cir. 1987), *cert. denied* 485 U.S. 959, 99 L.Ed. 2d 420, 108 S.Ct. 1219 (1988) that placing tort liability on some forms of protected speech would require the hopelessly complicated endeavor of differentiating between different categories of protected speech raising the possibility that "the worthiness of speech might be judged by majoritarian notions of political and social propriety and morality."

In the case of *Zamora v. Columbia Broadcasting System*, 480 F. Supp. 199 (S.D. Fla. 1979), plaintiffs urged the court to impose tort liability on the defendants for their negligent broadcast of violent shows which allegedly caused a susceptible minor to engage in unlawful conduct. In noting that the broadcasts represented speech which did not incite nor in any other way qualify for less than full constitutional protection, the court determined that plaintiffs were in essence asking the court to fashion a new cause of action for the dissemination of protected speech which caused "an untoward reaction on the part of any 'susceptible' person." *Id.* at 206. The court in *Zamora* declined to take such a step asserting that it would be an unconstitutional imposition of a generally undefined and undefinable duty. *Id.*

Plaintiffs do cite the case of *Weirum v. RKO General, Inc.*, 15 Cal. 3d 40, 123 Cal. Rptr. 468, 539 P.2d 36 (1975), in which a wrongful death action was brought against a radio station for broadcasting promotional announcements encouraging listeners to race to a certain site, as supporting its argument that tort liability can and should be imposed in this action. The *Weirum* decision is distinguishable from the instant case, however, because the California Supreme Court never made a finding in the case that it was dealing with protected speech entitled to full first amendment protection.

In the final analysis, the court simply has no basis upon which to impose tort liability on the defendants when, as in this case, the alleged wrongful acts are based on the defendants' dissemination of protected speech. The court, therefore, finds as a matter of law that the defendants' first amendment rights protect them from being held liable under plaintiffs' claims of negligence, nuisance, fraud, and invasion of privacy.

III. CONCLUSION

In all candor the court must also observe that the lyrics of a great many songs that come under the heading of rock music seem to foster an outlook on life that emphasizes alienation, cynicism, rebellion, and futility. Many young people find just as much relaxation and pleasure from rock music without the dreary lyrics of "Suicide Solution" as the rest of us get from the music of Beethoven, Gamble Rogers, Whitney Houston, or Hank Williams—as the case may be. In a world full of traps for the unwary teenager such as rampant drug and alcohol abuse and a "new morality" that stresses the importance of doing anything that feels good, an addiction to music of this sort could be another step in a path to self destruction. Nevertheless, whether the defendants' album "Blizzard of Ozz" could fit this description, or whether the court approves of rock music in general or of this particular brand of it, is irrelevant. The sole duty of this court in this lawsuit is to determine whether subliminal messages appear in the song and whether the music in question is afforded first amendment protection.

Plaintiffs' case is predicated almost entirely upon the allegation that defendants incited their son to commit suicide by the use of a subliminal message in the song "Suicide Solution" on the album "Blizzard of Ozz." They asserted with confidence that a subliminal message did exist and if given the opportunity to test the master tapes of the song they could identify it. However, after being given every opportunity to find the subliminal message, using tests they stated were the only ways to confirm its existence, plaintiffs failed to present any evidence from which a reasonable fact finder could even infer that a subliminal message existed within the song "Suicide Solution" on the album "Blizzard of Ozz."

Plaintiffs failed to demonstrate the existence of a subliminal message or that defendants' music incites imminent lawless activity, and were thereby left with the difficult task of attempting to impose liability on the defendants based on their dissemination of speech fully protected by the first amendment. It was a task plaintiffs were unable to accomplish.

Having ruled on the matter before the court, this order cannot be signed without an expression of sympathy for the parents of Michael Jeffery Waller who have shown their devotion to his memory by the filing and prosecution of this lawsuit. The court has no doubt as to the sincerity of their motives in following through with what must be an extremely painful course of action. The death of anyone before he has had a full measure of life is tragic and especially so if the person is a much loved teenaged son. If the death is by suicide the pain and grief to those left behind is almost unbearable. Although the court must render all its decisions without regard to sympathy, that does not mean it loses its capacity to experience that emotion.

Accordingly, for the foregoing reasons, defendants' Joint Motion for Summary Judgment is GRANTED as the court finds that there are no genuine issues of material fact concerning the claims put forth by plaintiffs in this action and defendants are entitled to judgment as a matter of law.

SO ORDERED, this day of May, 1991.

COLUMBINE TRAGEDY

Did the violent video game *Doom* serve as the impetus behind students at Columbine High School in Colorado killing other members of that school on April 20, 1999? In 2000, a federal judge dismissed a lawsuit against several video game distributors for the event at the high school. The lawsuit had been filed by the family of one of the teachers at the school and other victims. Twelve students

Princess Diana pursued by photographers.
Getty Images, Inc –Liason.

were killed, and many others were wounded. The dismissal stated that there was no way that the makers of video games were to blame for the deaths or the shootings.[50]

PAPARAZZI

Public tragedies such the shootings at Columbine High School and the death of Princess Diana on August 31, 1997, demonstrate that the media can be its own worst enemy when it comes to the rush to capture and ultimately publish news-worthy events. The term **paparazzi** is used to describe overzealous photogra-phers who allegedly invade the privacy of their subjects (whether celebrities, victims, or those involved in scandals) in hope of capturing a photograph to sell for a profit. They are often involved in physical confrontations, and many mem-bers of the media blamed the paparazzi photographers for the death of Princess Diana. However, in 1999 a French judge ruled that the paparazzi were not the cause of Princess Diana's death, but rather the driver of the automobile in-volved in the accident was under the influence of alcohol.[51] Paparazzi are often the recipients of physical confrontations and other displays of violent behavior by persons whose pictures they are trying to take. Some now refer to the pa-parazzi as the stalkerazzi.

[50] http://www.gamespot.com/features/6090892/p-7.html
[51] http://www.cnn.com/WORLD/europe/9909/03/france.diana/

CHAPTER SUMMARY

As an industry that thrives on freedom of speech and freedom of expression of ideas, the entertainment industry and the Constitution often clash when it comes to how far the various media may go when entertaining and reporting events. While courts give great deference to the media when reporting newsworthy events, there are times when journalists cross the line. Though parody and satire are forms of protected speech, courts have carved out torts such as defamation (libel and slander) for plaintiffs who allege falsities generated in the media. The Supreme Court has also interpreted the Constitution to allow for the right of privacy and the right of publicity when it comes to those persons in the public spotlight. Those same individuals, whether public officials or figures, often will have to demonstrate actual malice on the part of a media defendant when it comes to publication of an allegedly false statement. The Internet has created new problems for the law of libel because it is so easy for anyone to publish comments to a worldwide audience.

Though states provide protection for erroneous reporting in the form of retraction statutes, the media has much leeway in terms of reporting. Unfortunately, tabloid journalists, the paparazzi, and reporters that simply go too far have given the media a bad name. Additionally, the entertainment industry has brought more scrutiny upon itself with the promotion of violent movies, games, and music, and the court of public opinion has essentially coerced the various players in the entertainment industry into police themselves with rating systems.

CHAPTER TERMS

Actual malice
Censorship
Commercial
　misappropriation
Cyberstalking
Dead celebrity
Defamation
Driver's Privacy
　Protection Act
Due process

Equal protection
Extreme and outrageous
False light
Freedom of speech
Freedom of the press
Intentional infliction of
　emotional distress
Invasion of privacy
Libel
Libel per se

Negligent infliction of
　emotional distress
Newsworthy
Order of protection
Paparazzi
Parody
Privileges and
　immunities
Public figure
Public official

Restraining order
Retraction
Right of privacy
Right of publicity
Satire
Slander
Slander per se
Stalking
Subliminal
Subliminal speech

ADDITIONAL CASES

Bosley v. WildWetT.com, 310 F. Supp. 2d 914 (N.D. Ohio 2004)

Brett Michaels v. Internet Entertainment Group, Inc., 5 F. Supp. 2d 823 (1998)

Chaplinsky v. New Hampshire, 315 U.S. 568 (1942)

Eimann v. Soldier of Fortune Magazine, 880 F.2d 830 (5th Cir. 1989)

Elvis Presley Enterprises Inc. v. Capece, 141 F.3d 188 (5th Cir. 1998)

FCC v. Pacifica Found., 438 U.S. 726 (1978)

Herceg v. Hustler Magazine Inc., 814 F.2d 1017 (5th Cir. 1987)

Interstate Circuit, Inc. v. City of Dallas, 390 U.S. 676 (1968)

Jacobellis v. Ohio, 378 U.S. 184 (1964)

Joseph Burstyn, Inc. v. Wilson, 343 U.S. 495 (1952)

Lane v. M.R.A. Holdings, L.L.C., 242 F. Supp. 2d 1205 (M.D. Fla. 2002)

Miller v. California, 413 U.S. 15 (1973)

New York v. Ferber, 458 U.S. 747 (1982)

New York Times Co. v. Sullivan, 376 U.S. 254 (1964)

Roth v. United States, 354 U.S. 476 (1957)

Sable Communications of California, Inc. v. FCC, 492 U.S. 115 (1989)

Skywalker Records, Inc. v. Navarro, 739 F. Supp. 578 (S.D. Fla. 1990)

Spahn v. Julian Messner, Inc. 221 N.E.2d 543 (N.Y. 1966)

Tucker v. Fischbein, 237 F.3d 275 (3d Cir. 2001)

United States v. Paramount Pictures, Inc., 334 U.S. 131 (1948)

United States v. Playboy Entertainment Group, Inc., 529 U.S. 803 (2000)

Weyrich v. New Republic, Inc., 235 F.3d 617 (D.C. Cir. 2001)

Zacchini v. Scripps-Howard Broadcasting Co., 433 U.S. 562, 205 U.S.P.Q. 741 (1977)

REVIEW QUESTIONS

1. Why are constitutional issues relevant to the entertainment industry?

2. Why are parody and satire important in entertainment from a constitutional point of view?

3. Discuss various torts related to constitutional issues in entertainment, including defamation, slander, libel, and the intentional infliction of emotional distress.

4. What is the right of privacy? What is the right of publicity?

5. Do you believe that consideration of using retractions (in advance) are used by the media as a defense knowing that damage has already been done to someone's reputation?

6. How effective do you feel court orders are to end stalking behavior and misconduct?

7. How is broadcast speech regulated by the federal government?

8. What are the concerns related to subliminal speech in entertainment? Should subliminal messages be afforded First Amendment protection?

9. Should the paparazzi be regulated?

REFERENCES FOR ADDITIONAL RESEARCH AND DISCUSSION

Dragas, M.L., *Curing a Bad Reputation: Reforming Defamation Law*, 17 Hawaii L. Rev. 113 (1995).

Duhart, O.R., *When Time Stands Still: An Argument for Restoring Public Figures to Private Status*, 27 Nova L. Rev. 365 (2002).

Firester, R. & Jones, K.T., *Catchin' the Heat of the Beat: First Amendment Analysis of Music Claimed to Incite Violent Behavior*, 20 Loy. L.A. Ent. L. Rev. 1 (2000).

Giftos, A.C., *The Common Law Right of Publicity and Commercial Appropriation of Celebrity Identity: "A Whole New Wardrobe for Vanna,"* 38 St. Louis U. L.J. 983 (1994).

Halcomb Lewis, D.M., *Defamation of Sports Officials*, 38 Washburn L.J. 781 (1999).

Halperin, A.E., *Newsgathering After the Death of a Princess: Do American Laws Adequately Punish and Deter Newsgathering Conduct That Places Individuals in Fear or at Risk of Bodily Harm?*, 6 Vill. Sports & Ent. L.J. 171 (1999).

Jackson, D.M., *The Corporate Defamation Plaintiff in the Era of Slapps: Revisiting New York Times v. Sullivan*, 9 Wm. & Mary Bill Rts. J. 491 (2001).

Lampulgh, D. & Infield, P., *Harmonising Anti-Stalking Laws*, 34 Geo. Wash. Int'l. L. Rev. 853 (2003).

Quinlan, M. & Persels, J., *It's Not My Fault, the Devil Made Me Do It: Attempting to Impose Tort Liability on Publishers, Producers, and Artists for Injuries Allegedly "Inspired" by Media Speech*, 18 S. Ill. U. L.J. 417 (1994).

Radosevich, A.C., *Thwarting the Stalker: Are Anti-Stalking Measures Keeping Pace with Today's Stalker?*, 2000 U. Ill. L. Rev. 1371 (2000).

Rahimi, T.J., *The Power to Control Identity: Limiting a Celebrity's Right to Publicity*, 35 Santa Clara L. Rev. 725 (1995).

Walton, M.D., *The Public Figure Doctrine: A Reexamination of Gertz v. Robert Welch, Inc. in Light of Lower Federal Court Public Figure Formulations*, 16 N. Ill. U. L. Rev. 141 (1995).

CHAPTER 5

ADMINISTRATIVE REGULATION IN BROADCAST ENTERTAINMENT

AFTER STUDYING THIS CHAPTER YOU SHOULD BE ABLE TO:

1. Describe the role of the FCC and FTC in regulating speech.
2. Define the term license and its application in a regulatory context.
3. Differentiate and discuss the terms obscene speech and indecent speech.
4. Define the Miller test.
5. Describe some of the historical and recent enforcement actions taken by the FCC.
6. Explain the purpose of the Fairness Doctrine.
7. Distinguish between regulation and deregulation trends by the federal government.
8. Define the term infomercial.
9. Discuss the FTC's role in false and misleading advertising.
10. Describe the impact of the advent of new broadcasting methods and technologies.

INTRODUCTION

Whether meant to protect children or to influence societal values, the Supreme Court of the United States has interpreted the terms **obscene speech** and **indecent speech** differently. Federal agencies such as the Federal Communications Commission (FCC) and the Federal Trade Commission (FTC) play an integral role in the regulation of radio and television broadcast speech at the federal level.

Obscene language is not a form of protected speech under the Constitution. In fact, it is a violation of federal law to broadcast obscene material in any medium. Programming that is considered indecent, however, is something different and is acceptable under certain conditions. Regulations governing speech broadcast over the airwaves, thus, are legal forms of censorship. Changes in radio and television broadcast technology coupled with the advent of the Internet have given federal courts and agencies even more issues related to broadcast communications regulation, freedom of speech, and so forth. This chapter examines the roles of the FCC and FTC in regulating speech. The end of the chapter also provides a historical context to the development of radio.

President Reagan signing a bill.
The White House Photo Office.

THE FEDERAL COMMUNICATIONS COMMISSION

The **Federal Communications Commission** (FCC) is the federal agency that reports to Congress and regulates interstate and international radio, television, wire, cable, and satellite **broadcasts.** Part of its role is to ensure that obscene language is not broadcast. Congress has given the FCC the responsibility for administratively enforcing 18 U.S.C. § 1464 which legislatively prohibits indecent forms of speech. The FCC is authorized under the Communications Act of 1934 to fine a broadcast licensee or even revoke the license of a station that aired obscene or indecent language. The prohibition against indecent speech does not apply to programming aired on cable-only television channels or the Internet.

LICENSING

One of the most important matters that the FCC governs is the licensing of radio and television stations. In addition to allocating broadcast channels and frequencies, the FCC considers applications to build or sell stations and license renewals. The FCC licenses both for-profit (commercial) stations and not-for-profit (noncommercial) stations as long as the stations serve the public interest, convenience, and necessity (47 U.S.C. § 310(d)). Broadcasters are ultimately held responsible for the material aired by their stations.

The FCC is a **licensor** of the airwaves, and as a result, it may revoke the license of a **licensee** radio or television station, if necessary, as a remedy for a violation. Still, before revoking a license, the FCC must issue an order directing the party to "show cause" why its license should not be revoked. The FCC does not regulate closed-circuit radio or television (such as what is found in retail stores or public sporting arenas). The FCC has no authority over professional sports teams and leagues, and arrangements for broadcasting these types of events are based upon private contract law agreements.

HISTORY OF THE FCC

The FCC was created as part of President Franklin D. Roosevelt's "New Deal" agenda in order to create a rapid, efficient, nationwide, and worldwide wire and radio communication service. Though it receives congressional financial support and appropriations, the FCC can (and does) raise revenue as part of an auctioning process for parts of the invisible broadcast frequency spectrum. The FCC has a chairman and is authorized to have up to five commissioners who are appointed by the president. The FCC's **Media Bureau** administers the rules governing radio and television stations. Other FCC bureaus include the Cable Service Bureau, Common Carrier Bureau, and Private Radio Bureau.

The FCC is responsible for enforcement of the provisions of the **Communications Act of 1934** (Act). This independent federal agency has the broadest authority to regulate and investigate possible broadcast rule violations and to take enforcement action, including issuing fines, if warranted. For antitrust and criminal actions, the FCC refers cases to the U.S. Department of Justice.

The FCC may make such rules it believes necessary to implement the provisions of the Communications Act of 1934 and has a great deal of discretion to adopt whatever procedures it deems most efficient. The Act provides for appeals to the District of Columbia Circuit Court of Appeals from adverse FCC decisions.[52] The applicable standard of judicial review is found in the Administrative Procedure Act (APA) and prohibits agency decisions that are **arbitrary, capricious, unreasonable,** and an **abuse of discretion.**[53]

INTERPRETATIONS

Subsequent to the enactment of the Act, the FCC was involved in numerous cases involving interpretations of the Act and the policies of the FCC. Licenses for rights to the broadcast radio spectrum were limited and subject to an intense renewal process by the FCC in a highly regulated governmental policy, as long as the **public interest** was being served.

OBSCENE BROADCASTING

Obscene broadcasting is not protected by the First Amendment nor under FCC regulations. Media broadcasts using the public airwaves cannot broadcast obscene material at any time whatsoever. Complaints against broadcasters may be filed with the FCC.

In *Miller v. California*, 413 U.S. 14 (1973), the U.S. Supreme Court established a three-pronged test (known as the **Miller test**) for obscenity prohibitions which would violate the First Amendment:

   (a) whether the average person, applying contemporary community standards, would find that the work, taken as a whole, appeals to the prurient interest (arousing lustful feelings);
   (b) whether the work depicts or describes, in a patently offensive way, sexual conduct specifically defined by the applicable state law; and
   (c) whether the work, taken as a whole, lacks serious literary, artistic, political or scientific value.

Of course, this involves a lot of interpreting of the meaning of "average person" and "community standards" which can change from neighborhood

---

[52] 47 U.S.C. § 402(b).
[53] 5 U.S.C. § 706(2)(A).

community to state to region and so on, leaving much interpretation to the courts on a case-by-case basis.

INDECENT BROADCASTING

While the First Amendment protects indecent published material and speech, a broadcast deemed indecent is not without governmental regulation. The FCC restricts the television and radio broadcast times of potentially indecent broadcasts to after 10:00 P.M. and before 6:00 A.M.[54] The FCC has defined indecent broadcasting as language or material that, in context, depicts or describes, in terms patently offensive as measured by the contemporary community standards for the broadcast medium, sexual or excretory organs or activities.[55] Broadcasts violating this rule are subject to indecency enforcement action.

One of the greatest issues facing the FCC and broadcasters is the ambiguity related to what is and what is not indecent speech. For many years, the **National Association of Broadcasters** has desired more clear-cut guidelines for dealing with potentially indecent material. In 2004, the FCC finally cited a four-letter word beginning with the letter "F" as being indecent and profane, even though the FCC previously noted that an occasional use of the F-word was acceptable.[56] The U.S. Senate passed legislation in 2004 to prohibit broadcasters from airing certain indecent words or phrases and to increase the maximum fine for radio and television broadcasters and personalities from a mere $27,500 per incident to $275,000 per incident for FCC license holders and $11,000 for personalities for a maximum fine of $3 million per day.[57]

ENFORCEMENT ACTIONS

The **Enforcement Bureau** of the FCC pursues written complaints of indecent or obscene broadcasting received from the public at large. The Enforcement Bureau was established in late 1999. Under the Act, the FCC may assess a monetary forfeiture against a broadcast station for violation of an FCC regulation. Recall, however, that a broadcaster's right to air indecent (but not obscene) speech is protected between the hours of 10 P.M. and 6 A.M.

---

[54] 47 C.F.R. § 73.3999.

[55] See Action For Children's Television v. FCC, 11 F.3d 170, 172 (D.C. Cir. 1993) and Action For Children's Television v. FCC, 58 F.3d 654 (D.C. Cir. 1995), cert. denied, 116 S. Ct. 701 (1996). See also Industry Guidance on the Commission's Case Law Interpreting 18 U.S.C. § 1464 and Enforcement Policies Regarding Broadcast Indecency, 16 F.C.C.R. 7999 (2001).

[56] http://www.cnn.com/2003/LAW/12/23/findlaw.analysis.hilden.indecency/

[57] Passed by a 99–1 vote in the Senate, but not signed into law by President Bush by the end of 2004. http://www.foxnews.com/story/0,2933,123398,00.html

Complaints to the FCC require the date and time of the alleged broadcast, the call sign of the station involved, and information regarding the details of what was actually said (or depicted) during the alleged indecent or obscene broadcast. If it appears that a violation may have occurred, the Enforcement Bureau staff commences an investigation by sending a **letter of inquiry** to the broadcast station.

FCC V. PACIFICA FOUND

In a pivotal case involving the struggle between freedom of speech and indecent broadcast material, the Supreme Court held in *FCC v. Pacifica Found.*, 438 U.S. 726 (1978), that the FCC can restrict indecent speech on the airwaves even though such speech is otherwise protected under the First Amendment. This case involved an afternoon radio broadcast of George Carlin's 12-minute monologue entitled *Filthy Words*, which listed and repeated a variety of uses of "words you couldn't say on the public airwaves."[58] The Court found the Carlin monologue to be indecent and upheld the FCC ruling that the language was indecent and prohibited by 18 U.S.C. §1464. Still, what is characterized as indecent according to community standards can change over time.

FAIRNESS DOCTRINE

The **fairness doctrine** was an FCC policy from 1949 until 1987. This doctrine required broadcasters, as a condition of getting their licenses from the FCC, to report controversial issues in their community by offering balancing viewpoints. The fairness doctrine's constitutionality was upheld by the U.S. Supreme Court in *Red Lion Broadcasting v. FCC*, 395 U.S. 367 (1969). In *Miami Herald Publishing Co. v. Tornillo*, 418 U.S. 241 (1974), without ruling the doctrine unconstitutional, the Court concluded that the doctrine inescapably dampened the vigor and limits the variety of public debate. In 1984, the Supreme Court finally concluded that the rationale underlying the doctrine was flawed and that the doctrine was limiting the breadth of public debate, in *FCC v. League of Women Voters*, 468 U.S. 364 (1984).

POLITICAL SPEECH

While the FCC supports free speech and commentary in the arena of broadcast journalism, sometimes material broadcast over the airwaves can be extremely

---

[58] Also known as the "Seven Dirty Words."

controversial, especially when it comes to politics. Such speech falls under the FCC's category of **political programming.** In 1967, the FCC promulgated regulations that required stations airing personal attacks[59] and political editorials[60] to give the opposing side an opportunity to respond. In *Radio-Television News Directors Ass'n v. FCC*, 229 F.3d 269 (D.C. Cir. 2000), the District Court for the District of Columbia directed the FCC to repeal the personal attack and political editorial rules, however.

TELECOMMUNICATIONS ACT OF 1996

President Bill Clinton signed the **Telecommunications Act of 1996** into law in February 1996, representing the first major reform since the Communications Act of 1934 (47 U.S.C. § 101 *et seq.*). This 1996 Act affected broadcast radio and television regulation and other forms of communication, including telephone services. As a result of this Act, ownership of broadcast radio and television began to consolidate as national ownership limits for radio were eliminated and local ownership restrictions were based on market size. This Act also reflected the FCC's general policy move away from regulation and toward **deregulation**. With very few exceptions, such as university radio stations, broadcasters still need a federal license from the FCC. Licenses are temporary and do not constitute ownership rights (although stations themselves can be owned).

MEDIA OWNERSHIP

The FCC recently relaxed the government's guidelines for media ownership. Regulation of radio and television broadcasts had been tight, similar to federal policies related to telephone service providers and the airlines. **Cross-ownership** regulations had prevented owners of daily newspapers or multiple broadcast facilities within a single local market from acquiring a license to operate a television station in the same market. Cross-ownership concerns also prevented mergers that might undermine antitrust laws (discussed later in the text). In 2003, media ownership policies changed, and media conglomerates such as Tribune Corp., Time Warner, Clear Channel, and Fox could now own television stations reaching 45 percent of the national audience, rather than the previous 35 percent.[61] Additionally, the same company may be able to own two (and in larger cities three) television stations in the same market.

---

[59] The personal attack rule stated that "if an attack is made on someone's integrity during a presentation of views on a controversial issue of public importance, the licensee must inform that person . . . and provide a reasonable opportunity to respond" (47 C.F.R § 73.1920).

[60] The political editorial rule stated that the broadcaster must provide a "reasonable opportunity" for opposing candidates to respond (47 C.F.R. § 73.1930).

[61] *See* http://www.wired.com/news/business/0,1367,59068,00.html?tw=wn_story_related

RECENT ENFORCEMENT ACTIONS

The FCC has fined a number of radio stations for airing talk radio broadcast discussions and music with indecent lyrics. When the FCC levies a fine, the broadcaster has 30 days to pay the fine or appeal it. In 2004, the FCC proposed a $755,000 fine against Clear Channel Communications for a sexually explicit radio show called *Bubba the Love Sponge*, which aired on four Florida radio stations.[62] It was the second highest fine ever proposed by the FCC. Later the same year, the FCC reached a $1.75 million settlement with Clear Channel over indecency complaints related to radio personality Howard Stern. This was on top of the *Bubba the Love Sponge* fine. Clear Channel adopted a zero tolerance indecency policy which included companywide training and automatic suspensions, including modification of on-air talent to share financial responsibility in the event of a fine by the FCC due to an indecent broadcast.[63]

The following tables list a sample of broadcast indecency-related Notices of Apparent Liability (NALs) and Forfeiture Orders (FOs) issued by the FCC and/or the Enforcement Bureau since November 8, 1999. Some of the NALs and FOs involve indecency complaints that were received by the FCC prior to the creation of the Enforcement Bureau and are indicated with an asterisk (*).[64]

FCC Notices of Apparent Liability

04-08-2004	Clear Channel Broadcasting Licenses, Inc., Citicasters Licenses, L.P., Capstar TX Limited Partnership	$495,000
03-18-2004	Capstar TX Limited Partnership, WAVW(FM), Stuart, Florida	$55,000
03-18-2004	Infinity Broadcasting Operations, Inc., WKRK-FM, Detroit, Michigan	$27,500
03-12-2004	AMFM Radio Licenses, L.L.C., WWDC(FM), Washington, DC; Clear Channel Broadcasting Licenses, Inc., WRXL(FM), Richmond, Virginia; Capstar TX Limited Partnership, WOSC(FM), Bethany Beach, Delaware	$247,500
01-27-2004	Clear Channel Broadcasting Licenses, Inc., Citicasters Licenses, L.P., Capstar TX Limited Partnership	$755,000
01-27-2004	Young Broadcasting of San Francisco, Inc., KRON-TV, San Francisco, California	$27,500
10-02-2003	Infinity Broadcasting Operations, Inc., Infinity Radio Operations, Inc., Infinity Radio Subsidiary Operations, Inc., Infinity Broadcasting Corporation of Dallas, Infinity Broadcasting Corporation of Washington, DC, Infinity Holdings Corporation of Orlando, Hemisphere Broadcasting Corporation	$357,500
10-02-2003	AMFM RADIO LICENSES, LLC	$55,000
04-03-2003	Infinity Broadcasting Operations, Inc., WKRK-FM, Detroit, Michigan	$27,500
12-13-2002	Edmund Dinis, WJFD(FM), New Bedford, MA	$22,400

---

[62] $715,000 for airing indecent programming and $40,000 for recordkeeping violations.

[63] *See* http://www.usatoday.com/money/media/2004-02-25-clearchannel-decency_x.htm

[64] http://www.fcc.gov/eb/broadcast/NAL.html

08-02-2002	Rubber City Radio Group, WONE-FM, Akron, OH	$7,000
06-28-2002	Emmis Radio License Corporation, WKQX(FM), Chicago, IL	$7,000
06-07-2002	Infinity Broadcasting Operations, Inc., WNEW(FM), New York, NY	$21,000
05-01-2002	GA-MEX Broadcasting, Inc., WAZX(AM) Smyrna, GA; WAZX-FM, Inc., WAZX(FM), Cleveland, GA	$7,000
03-21-2002	Emmis Radio License Corporation, WKQX(FM), Chicago, IL	$21,000
01-28-2002	Entercom Seattle License, LLC, KNDD(FM), Seattle, WA	$14,000
06-01-2001	Citadel Broadcasting Company, KKMG(FM), Pueblo, CO	$7,000
05-17-2001	The KBOO Foundation, KBOO-FM, Portland, OR	$7,000
04-06-2001	Emmis FM License Corp. of Chicago, WKQX(FM), Chicago, IL	$14,000
04-03-2001	Citicasters Co., KEGL(FM), Fort Worth, TX	$14,000
03-30-2001	Telemundo of Puerto Rico License Corp.	$21,000
02-08-2001	WLDI, Inc., WCOM(FM), Bayamon, PR	$21,000
01-18-2001	Capstar TX Limited Partnership, WZEE(FM), Madison, WI	$7,000
* 12-05-2000	CBS Radio License, Inc., WLLD(FM), Holmes Beach, FL	$7,000
* 10-06-2000	Capstar TX Limited Partnership, KTXQ(FM), Fort Worth, Texas	$7,000
09-26-2000	Citicasters Co., KSJO(FM), San Jose, CA	$7,000
* 09-26-2000	Citicasters Co., KSJO(FM), San Jose, CA	$7,000
* 09-07-2000	Regent Licensee of Flagstaff, Inc., KZGL(FM), Cottonwood, AZ	$6,000
* 07-14-2000	Communicast Consultants, Inc., KRXK(AM), Rexburg, Idaho	$7,000
* 04-28-2000	Three Eagles of Columbus, Inc., KROR(FM), Hastings, Nebraska	$7,000

FCC Forfeiture Orders[65]

02-18-2004	Emmis Radio License Corporation, WKQX(FM), Chicago, Illinois	$7,000
12-08-2003	Infinity Broadcasting Operations, Inc., WKRK-FM, Detroit, Michigan	$27,500
11-01-2002	Emmis Radio License Corporation, WKQX(FM), Chicago, IL	$21,000
09-27-2002	Entercom Seattle License, LLC, KNDD(FM), Seattle, WA	$12,000
01-08-2002	Emmis FM License Corp. of Chicago, WKQX(FM), Chicago, IL	$14,000
05-11-2001	WLDI, Inc., WCOM(FM), Bayamon, PR	$16,800
* 03-02-2001	Infinity Radio License, Inc., WLLD(FM), Holmes Beach, FL	$7,000
* 10-12-2000	Communicast Consultants, Inc., KRXK(AM), Rexburg, Idaho	$7,000
* 08-24-2000	Three Eagles of Columbus, Inc., KROR(FM), Hastings, Nebraska	$6,000
* 06-28-2000	Citicasters Co., WXTB(FM), Clearwater, FL	$7,000
* 06-27-2000	Citicasters Co., WXTB(FM), Clearwater, FL	$23,000
* 06-13-2000	Infinity Broadcasting Corporation of Los Angeles, KROQ-FM, Pasadena, CA	$2,000
* 01-28-2000	WQAM LLP, WQAM(AM), Miami, Florida	$35,000

---

[65] http://www.fcc.gov/eb/broadcast/FO.html

Janet Jackson and Justin Timberlake at Super Bowl 2004.
AP Wide World Photos.

SUPER BOWL 2004

Ethical standards related to broadcast television were brought to the forefront in 2004 when singer Janet Jackson's breast was revealed on CBS national network television, with the help of performer Justin Timberlake, during the Super Bowl half-time show on February 1, 2004.[66] This event thrust the FCC into the national spotlight with regard to broadcast regulations. One individual from Knoxville, Tennessee filed a lawsuit (though later withdrawn) against Viacom International, Inc., CBS Broadcasting, Inc., MTV Networks Enterprises, Inc., Janet Jackson, and Justin Timberlake, alleging violations of FCC regulations and demanding punitive damages for suffering outrage, anger, and embarrassment for the deed.[67] A Utah lawyer later sued Viacom for $5,000 in small claims court for the same event, claiming false advertising, but a judge dismissed his claim.[68]

OTHER FCC REGULATIONS

The FCC does not regulate licensee advertising rates or rates charged for broadcast time. Still, if a licensee broadcasts information about a contest, the broadcast must not be false or misleading and must fully and accurately disclose the

[66] FCC Chairman Michael Powell called the event "a classless, crass and deplorable stunt." *See* http://www.cbs.sportsline.com/nfl/story/7055467. Jackson later issued an apology for the stunt, while Timberlake declared the incident was due to a "wardrobe malfunction." http://www.cnn.com/2004/US/02/02/superbowl.jackson/

[67] http://www.rollingstone.com/news/newsarticle.asp?nid=19299

[68] http://www.msnbc.msn.com/id/5077854/

material terms of the contest. Broadcasting hoaxes (false information concerning a crime or catastrophe) violate FCC rules if (1) the licensee knew this information was false, (2) it was foreseeable that the broadcast would cause substantial public harm, and (3) broadcast of the information did in fact directly cause substantial public harm. The FCC also regulates lottery information broadcasts (with a few exceptions).[69] Finally, the FCC has held that the use of subliminal broadcasting techniques (see Chapter 4) is contrary to the public interest and ultimately a deceptive form of programming.

RELIGIOUS BROADCASTS

As of this writing, there is no federal law that gives the FCC the authority to prohibit radio and television stations from broadcasting religious programs.

WEBCASTING

Broadcasting radio and television over the Internet has become known as **webcasting.** Webcasting involves the traditional over-the-air radio broadcasters who transmit their actual broadcast signals on the Internet in "real time" from the station's Web site. Webcasting is also made up of purely Internet-based broadcasters sometimes referred to as **cybercasters.** Congress enacted the Communications Decency Act (CDA) to ban indecency on the Internet, just as the FCC and the *Pacifica* case dealt with regulating indecent speech over the traditional airwaves. However, the Supreme Court struck down the CDA entirely in 1997, thereby granting the highest level of First Amendment protection to the Internet.[70]

THE FEDERAL TRADE COMMISSION

The **Federal Trade Commission (FTC)** is a consumer protection agency with mandates under the Federal Trade Commission Act (15 U.S.C. §§ 41–51) to guard the marketplace from unfair methods of competition and to prevent unfair or deceptive acts or unfair business practices that harm consumers. The FTC protects the American consumer. When food and drugs are part of an advertising campaign, the Food and Drug Administration (FDA) will likely be involved. Federal law prohibits advertising for cigarettes, little cigars (15 U.S.C. §§ 1331–1340), and smokeless or chewing tobacco (15 U.S.C. §§ 4401–4408)

---

[69] 47 C.F.R. § 73.1217.
[70] *Reno v. ACLU*, 521 U.S. 844 (1997).

on any medium of communication that is regulated by the FCC.[71] There are no federal laws that prohibit broadcasting advertising for alcoholic beverages.

FTC AND INFOMERCIALS

The Bureau of Competition of the Federal Trade Commission and the Antitrust Division of the U.S. Department of Justice share responsibility for enforcing laws that promote competition in the marketplace. The FTC has the authority to prohibit **deceptive acts and practices** and unfair methods of competition. Many media outlets, especially magazines and television, run advertisements or **infomercials** to induce the sales of products. Infomercials include weight-loss products, exercise equipment, hair-loss products, financial and other self-improvement programs, and numerous other potentially untested and/or misleading products or services. While some products clearly are misleading, others are not as well-defined. The FTC has handled numerous cases involving these infomercials, their producers, and in some instances the media that broadcast the claims.

ADDITIONAL CONSIDERATIONS IN BROADCAST ENTERTAINMENT

Voice of America

From using radio signals in search and rescue missions at sea to the utilization of radio-based walkie-talkies, the American military has utilized radio technology heartily, including the promotion of the **Voice of America (VOA)** broadcasts, a government radio network that broadcasts in over 40 languages around the world. The VOA, in addition to the Armed Forces Radio Network, began during World War II to keep soldiers and citizens informed of the status of battles, the war generally, and conditions back home in the United States. Today, the VOA sponsors television broadcasts as well and falls under the jurisdiction of the International Broadcasting Board, part of the U.S. State Department. Under U.S. law, the Voice of America is forbidden to broadcast directly to American citizens (22 U.S.C. § 1461).

Wireless Communications

Though not considered "radio" by most consumers, other forms of transmitting and receiving information, such as mobile telephones (cell phones), use radio or satellite communication services within their assigned **spectrum** block, including a designated geographic area. (The FCC delineated 128 markets into

---

[71] Federal Cigarette Labeling and Advertising Act and the Comprehensive Smokeless Tobacco Health Education Act of 1986.

which the blocks of the spectrum are divided into four groups labeled A through D, with subdivisions for Major Economic Areas and Regional Economic Area Groupings.) 47 C.F.R. 2. 106. Sending and receiving e-mails, pictures, and other data without the use of a telephone line (such as with a personal digital assistant) is referred to as wireless communication and operates between 2305–2320 MHz (Megahertz) and 2345–2360 MHz of the spectrum.

Satellite Digital Audio Radio Service

Today, **Satellite Digital Audio Radio Service (SDARS)** is an effective means of transmitting information via radio waves. This satellite-based system utilizes digitally encoded technology to broadcast to Earth-based receivers. In 1997, the FCC adopted service rules for only two SDARS authorizations. This includes CD Radio, Inc. (now known as Sirius Satellite Radio) and American Mobile Radio Corporation (XM Satellite Radio). It is important to note that the FCC decided in late 2004 that subscription satellite radio services such as XM and Sirius do not have to abide by the same on-air FCC indecency standards as traditional broadcast stations. Interestingly, Howard Stern has plans to move his broadcasts to Sirius beginning January, 2006. See (http://money.cnn.com/2004/12/15/news/newsmakers/stern_fcc/).

SDARS is similar to FM radio in that it requires a line of sight for effective broadcasting. A studio on Earth creates the program and transmits the audio to the space station or satellite, which relays the program to a station or receiver such as a car radio. Even though a broadcast is sent from above via satellite, cities with tall buildings can interfere with satellite signals. As a consequence, SDARS utilizes terrestrial repeaters to relay the signal around tall buildings. In late 2003, the National Football League (NFL) and Sirius

The new Sirius Satellite Radio, pictured here inside a BMW SUV, can pick up satellite signals from anywhere in the country plus provide television reception.
© Brant Ward/The San Francisco Chronicle/Corbis Saba.

Satellite Radio announced a seven-year agreement for Sirius to broadcast all NFL games live nationwide and for Sirius to become the official satellite radio partner of the NFL. As part of the agreement, Sirius created the NFL Radio Network.

High Definition Digital Radio

In early 2004, radio transmissions joined other broadcast industries and began offering high definition (HD) digital radio. Special models of radios can receive CD-quality sound on FM stations and FM-quality sound on AM stations.[72]

K and W Call Letters

After the federal government began the licensing of radio broadcast stations in 1912, stations were given identification letters referred to as **call letters** or call signs. These four-letter codes identified the geographic origin of broadcast of the radio station. Since 1927, the alphabet has been divided among countries for basic call sign use. The United States, for example, is assigned the three letters N, K, and W to serve as initial call letters for the exclusive use of its radio stations. It also shares the initial letter A with some other countries. The letter A is assigned to the Army and Air Force; N is assigned to the Navy and Coast Guard, and K and W are assigned to domestic stations, both government and nongovernment.

Generally speaking, stations west of the Mississippi River were classified with the first letter "K," while stations east of the Mississippi River began with the letter "W." Alaska and Hawaii were treated as western states receiving K call signs. In addition, Puerto Rico, currently a U.S. commonwealth, and the Virgin Islands have been treated as eastern states receiving W call signs. Numerous exceptions exist for these call letters including for historical reasons and due to radio stations moving their base operations from one side of the Mississippi River to the other. Station KDKA, Pittsburgh, Pennsylvania, is one example.

Corporation for Public Broadcasting

To provide an alternative to private commercial broadcasting, Congress passed the Public Broadcasting Act of 1967,[73] which established the **Corporation for Public Broadcasting (CPB),** a private government corporation. It is a nonprofit organization that funds over 1,000 public television and radio stations nationwide using an annual appropriation from Congress. Ninety-five percent of this money goes to support local television and radio stations, programming, and improvements to the public broadcasting system as a whole. The CPB provides the largest source of funds for radio programming and television programming for broadcast on National Public Radio (NPR) and the Public Broadcasting Service (PBS), a private, nonprofit enterprise owned and operated by member stations. CPB invests in quality programming, particularly for

---

[72] The company iBiquity Digital developed and licenses HD digital radio.
[73] 47 U.S.C. § 396.

children. There are nearly 700 public radio stations and more than 350 public television stations.

National Association of Broadcasters

Founded in 1923, the National Association of Broadcasters (NAB) serves as the broadcast lobbying representative organization for radio and television stations. Based in Washington, D.C., this trade organization remains instrumental in influencing governmental policy regulating the airwaves. It represents approximately 900 television stations and 5,000 radio stations.

CHAPTER SUMMARY

The study of radio and its importance in the entertainment industry cannot be underestimated. The FCC, from its beginnings to an era of high regulation to an era of deregulation, represents a change in attitude by the federal government over the control of the airwaves. As the sole licensor for the broadcast spectrum, the FCC has considerable power, though it maintains a policy of deregulation. The FTC also plays a role in regulating speech and advertising via the various broadcast media. Understanding the differences between obscene and indecent forms of speech are vital if one is to appreciate legalized regulation of speech known as censorship. From the original fundamental radio transmissions to the current use of the Internet and satellites to transmit radio waves, the broadcast industry, including radio and television, continues to present a variety of legal challenges for all involved in the industry.

CHAPTER TERMS

Abuse of discretion
Arbitrary
Broadcasts
Call letters
Capricious
Communications Act of 1934
Corporation for Public Broadcasting (CPB)
Cross-ownership
Cybercasters

Deceptive acts and practices
Deregulation
Enforcement Bureau
Fairness doctrine
Federal Communications Commission (FCC)
Federal Trade Commission (FTC)
Indecent speech

Infomercials
Letter of inquiry
Licensee
Licensor
Media Bureau
Miller test
National Association of Broadcasters (NAB)
Obscene speech
Political programming
Public interest

Satellite Digital Audio Radio Service (SDARS)
Spectrum
Telecommunications Act of 1996
Unreasonable
Voice of America (VOA)
Webcasting

ADDITIONAL CASES

Anti-Defamation League of B'nai B'rith v. FCC, 4 F.C.C.2d 190 (1966)

Ashbacker Radio Corp. v. FCC, 326 U.S. 327 (1945)

Bosley v. WildWetT.com, 2004 U.S. Dist. LEXIS 5124

Citizens Comm. Center v. FCC, 447 F.2d 1201 (D.C. Cir. 1971)

Citizens Comm. to Save WEFM v. FCC, 506 F.2d 246 (D.C. Cir. 1974)

FCC v. League of Women Voters of Cal., 468 U.S. 364 (1984)

FCC v. National Citizens Comm. for Broadcasting, 436 U.S. 775 (1978)

FCC v. Pottsville Broadcasting Co., 309 U.S. 134 (1940)

FCC v. RCA Communications, 346 U.S. 86 (1953)

FCC v. Sanders Bros. Radio Station, 309 U.S. 470 (1940)

FCC v. WNCN Listener's Guild, 450 U.S. 582 (1981)

Federal Radio Comm'n v. Nelson Bros. Bond & Mortgage Co., 289 U.S. 266 (1933)

Fox TV Stations, Inc. v. FCC, 280 F.3d 1027 (D.C. Cir 2002)

Gross v. FCC, 480 F.2d 1288 (2d Cir. 1973)

Hawaiian Tel. Co. v. FCC, 498 F.2d 771 (D.C. Cir. 1974)

In re Use of the AM Carrier Signals, 100 F.C.C.2d 5 (1984)

National Ass'n of Broadcasters v. FCC, 740 F.2d 1190 (D.C. Cir. 1984)

National Broadcasting Co. v. United States, 319 U.S. 190 (1943)

Office of Communication of the United Church of Christ v. FCC, 707 F.2d 1413 (D.C. Cir. 1983)

Red Lion Broad. Co. v. FCC, 395 U.S. 367 (1969)

Syracuse Peace Council v. FCC, 867 F.2d 654 (D.C. Cir. 1989).

Time Warner Entm't Co. v. FCC, 240 F.3d 1126 (D.C. Cir. 2001)

Turner Broadcasting System, Inc. v. FCC, 520 U.S. 180 (1997)

REVIEW QUESTIONS

1. What are the specific roles of the FCC and the FTC?
2. What is the difference between obscene speech and indecent speech in broadcasting?
3. Do you believe that the time limitation for broadcasting indecent speech is effective? Why or why not?
4. What is the Miller test? Is it clear-cut?
5. What was the importance of the decision in the *Pacifica* case?
6. Why was the fairness doctrine instituted and later repealed?
7. What does the term webcasting mean?
8. May the FCC refuse to allow the broadcasting of religious programs?
9. How did the Telecommunications Act of 1996 amend the Communication Act of 1934?
10. What is the role of the FTC and infomercials?
11. How is SDARS different from traditional radio broadcasting?

REFERENCES FOR ADDITIONAL RESEARCH AND DISCUSSION

Barron, J.A., *The Open Society and Violence in the Media,* 33 McGeorge L. Rev. 617 (2002).

Price, M.E., *Public Broadcasting and the Crisis of Corporate Governance,* 17 Cardozo Arts & Ent. L.J. 417 (1999).

Rigney, J.T., *Avoiding Slim Reasoning and Shady Results: A Proposal for Indecency and Obscenity Regulation in Radio and Broadcast Television,* 55 Fed. Comm. L.J. 297 (2003).

Tramont, B.N., *Too Much Power, Too Little Restraint: How the FCC Expands Its Reach Through Unenforceable and Unwieldy "Voluntary" Agreements,* 53 Fed. Comm. L.J. 49 (2000).

Vander Wilt, E., *Considering COPA: A Look at Congress's Second Attempt to Regulate Indecency on the Internet,* 11 Va. J. Soc. Pol'y & L. 373 (2004).

ANTITRUST REGULATION IN ENTERTAINMENT LAW

AFTER STUDYING THIS CHAPTER YOU SHOULD BE ABLE TO:

1. Define the terms antitrust and monopoly and the relationship to anticompetitive conduct.
2. Explain the joint role of the U.S. Department of Justice, FTC, and FCC in enforcing antitrust laws.
3. Describe the role of the Sherman and Clayton antitrust acts.
4. Differentiate between the per se rule and rule of reason antitrust analyses.
5. Discuss the role of the U.S. Department of Justice in regulating mergers.
6. Describe the terms horizontal and vertical mergers and how they apply in entertainment.
7. Define the phrase block booking and apply the concept and its historical role in movies.
8. Discuss the term siphoning in the context of television and sports broadcasting.
9. Explain the NFL's blackout rule as an exemption to antitrust laws.
10. Discuss other issues related to antitrust in broadcasting and music.

INTRODUCTION

This chapter introduces the student to the antitrust laws and discusses federal laws related to the regulation of monopolistic behavior and how these issues have affected the entertainment industry. **Antitrust** regulation also has had a history of involvement in the sports industry from both an organizational and broadcasting perspective. The United States is the land of capitalism and free markets. The American dream fosters the spirit of individuals to pursue the best life and occupation possible. Fundamental to the American economy are the laws of supply and demand and the theory of freedom of competition. As the industrial revolution and big business created monopolies in industries such as sugar and cotton (among others), a concerned U.S. Congress enacted **antitrust laws:** laws designed to prevent anticompetitive behavior in business in order to promote competition and ultimately drive down prices for consumers and to offer better quality and greater choices at the same time.

Generally speaking, defendants in antitrust cases are usually large companies, while plaintiffs will be consumers, smaller businesses, or the government pursuing a claim on behalf of the public at large. Antitrust principles and concerns apply in the various entertainment industries, and government agencies have worked together to ensure that no one organization controls a product, price, or output.

DEPARTMENT OF JUSTICE

The mission of the Antitrust Division of the U.S. Department of Justice has been to promote and protect competition through the enforcement of the antitrust laws. The antitrust laws apply to virtually all industries and to every level of business. Antitrust laws prohibit a variety of practices that **restrain trade,** such as **price-fixing** conspiracies, corporate mergers likely to reduce competition in particular markets, and **predatory** acts designed to achieve or maintain **monopoly** power. The antitrust laws describe unlawful practices in general terms, leaving it to the courts to decide what specific practices are illegal based on the facts and circumstances of each case. Serious and/or willful violations of the antitrust laws are pursued by filing criminal suits that can lead to large fines and jail sentences. Where criminal prosecution is not appropriate, the U.S. Department of Justice institutes a civil action seeking a court order forbidding future violations of the law and requiring steps to remedy the anticompetitive effects of past violations. The FTC and the Antitrust Division of the U.S. Department of Justice share responsibility for enforcing laws that promote competition in the marketplace.

Bill Gates. Chairman and Chief Software Architect.
Corbis/Bettman.

■ MONOPOLIES

While it is not illegal to have a monopoly in a given market, the antitrust laws make it unlawful to maintain or attempt to create a monopoly through tactics that either unreasonably exclude firms from the market or significantly impair their ability to compete. A single firm may commit a violation through its own actions, or a violation may result if a group of firms work together to monopolize a market. A common complaint is that some companies try to monopolize a market through predatory or **below-cost** pricing. This can drive out smaller firms that cannot compete at those prices. The government and courts tend to get involved only when predatory activities lead to higher prices for consumers.

■ SHERMAN ANTITRUST ACT OF 1890

The **Sherman Antitrust Act of 1890** (Sherman Act) is the most fundamental federal law that governs anticompetitive business behavior. Congress enacted the Sherman Act to regulate business practices among competitors affecting interstate commerce. In other words, whenever commerce or trade crosses states lines, antitrust laws apply. The primary purpose of the Sherman Act is to promote competition and to deter monopolistic practices that ultimately hurt consumers.

Section 1 of the Sherman Act forbids contracts, combinations, or conspiracies that may unreasonably restrain trade. Section 2 of the Sherman Act prohibits monopolization of trade and commerce. The Supreme Court has implemented two separate and primary standards in deciding whether a particular restraint on trade is unreasonable: the **per se rule** and the **rule of reason.** Violations of the Sherman Act may subject the wrongdoer to criminal penalties. Individuals may be fined by the government up to $350,000 per violation, while corporations may be fined up to $10,000,000 per violation. The government may also pursue civil damages for violations of the Sherman Act, and such damages are automatically tripled. Additionally, reasonable costs and attorneys' fees may be awarded.

CLAYTON ACT

Congress passed the **Clayton Act** in 1914. This additional antitrust act provides that labor unions and labor activities are exempt from the Sherman Act. Section 6 of the Clayton Act states that labor is not to be considered commerce. Still, § 16 of the Clayton Act allows the government or a private plaintiff to obtain an injunction against anticompetitive behavior if necessary.

PER SE RULE

When a court utilizes the per se rule analysis to determine whether there has been a violation of antitrust law, any labor practices that are inherently unreasonable restraints of trade will be invalidated. In *Northern Pacific Railway Co. v. United States*, 356 U.S. 1 (1958), the Supreme Court stated that there are certain agreements or practices which, because of their pernicious effect on competition, are conclusively presumed to be unreasonable and therefore illegal. For example, price-fixing is a per se violation of antitrust laws. Price-fixing is anticompetitive and hurts consumers.

RULE OF REASON

Under the rule of reason analysis, a court must examine the alleged anticompetitive practice at issue and determine whether it is reasonable or unreasonable. Some restraints may be necessary as a legitimate business practice in order to simply stay in business, for example. Still, if a restraint of trade fails the per se test, further examination of the labor practice is <u>not</u> then necessary under an independent rule of reason analysis. When a court utilizes a rule of reason analysis, the defendant has the advantage because proving a violation requires large governmental expense, massive discovery, a lengthy trial, and expert testimony as to whether or not what the defendant did had or did not have legitimate business purposes that do (or do not) outweigh the anticompetitive effects.

QUICK LOOK ANALYSIS

The Supreme Court in *California Dental Association v. F.T.C.*, 526 U.S. 756 (1999), upheld the FTC's use of another form of antitrust analysis known as the **quick look** or structured rule of reason approach. In recent years, courts have fashioned an abbreviated or quick look rule of reason analysis designed for restraints that do not fall within the narrow categories of restraints deemed per se unlawful, but that are sufficiently anticompetitive that they do not require a full-blown rule of reason inquiry either. The Court ruled that the California Dental Association's rules restricting members' price and quality advertising should not have been invalidated on the basis of an abbreviated, quick look antitrust analysis. However, this decision lacks clarity as to when a quick look would be allowed and what it entails.

MERGERS AND ANTITRUST

In the various entertainment industries such as television, radio, music, and film production, there are often mergers and acquisitions which consolidate formerly separate businesses under a single umbrella. Some of the largest entertainment-related mergers include Time, Inc. with Warner, Turner Broadcasting System (TBS) with America Online (AOL), Paramount with Viacom and CBS television, and ABC-Capital Cities with Walt Disney Company.[74] Such multimedia mergers are so large that they could, theoretically, violate antitrust laws by creating a by-product that is anticompetitive. The government's role in identifying and challenging anticompetitive mergers is a difficult task that can take thousands of hours of investigative work and often litigation. Most mergers actually benefit competition and consumers by allowing firms to operate more efficiently. Still, mergers likely lessen competition. That, in turn, can lead to higher prices, reduced availability of goods or services, lower quality of products, and less innovation. Indeed, some mergers create a concentrated market in which the few members may be tempted to **collude,** while others enable a single firm to raise prices.

Premerger Notification

To combat anticompetitive big-time mergers after the fact, the **Hart-Scott-Rodino Antitrust Improvements Act of 1976** (15 U.S.C. § 18(a)) was passed by Congress. This Act is a set of amendments to the antitrust laws and was signed into law by President Gerald R. Ford. It provides that certain larger

---

[74] In 2000, AOL merged with Time Warner.

companies seeking to acquire or merge with another company must file advance notice of their intentions with the FTC and the Assistant Attorney General in charge of the Antitrust Division of the U.S. Department of Justice at least 30 days prior to consummation of such a transaction. Title III of this Act allows states to sue companies in federal court for monetary damages under antitrust laws on behalf of their citizens. Companies must now file premerger notification forms if the transaction value threshold of the merger is over $50 million. Fees must be paid to the government for the application based upon the increased size of the merger. The government may then use this information to determine if the proposed transaction may be anticompetitive and to take enforcement action, if appropriate, to prevent the consummation of the transaction.

Horizontal Mergers

In a **horizontal merger,** the acquisition of a competitor could increase market concentration and increase the likelihood of collusion. The elimination of head-to-head competition between two leading firms may result in unilateral anticompetitive effects. A recent example of this involved Staples, Inc., a superstore retailer of office supplies. Staples attempted to acquire Office Depot, another giant retailer in the same industry and clearly a competitor. In many areas of the country, the merger would have reduced the number of superstore competitors, often leaving Staples as the only superstore in the area. The FTC subsequently blocked the merger and avoided potentially harmful effects such as increased costs to profits, though Staples would have benefited highly from the merger.

Vertical Mergers

Vertical mergers involve firms in a buyer-seller relationship. Put another way, a **vertical merger** is a merger between two firms, one of which is a supplier or distributor for the other. This can harm competition by making it difficult for competitors to gain access to an important component product or to an important channel of distribution. This is sometimes referred to as a **bottleneck.**

For example, when Time Warner, Inc. (HBO and others) and Turner Corp. (CNN, TBS, etc.) attempted to merge in 1996, the FTC was concerned that Time Warner could refuse to sell (or sell at outrageous rates) video programming to competitors of cable TV companies owned or affiliated with Time Warner or Turner. That would allow the merging companies to maintain monopolies against their competitors such as satellite broadcasters and newer wireless cable technologies. The FTC approved the merger but required a restructuring of the acquisition by Time Warner Inc. of Turner Broadcasting System, Inc. (TBS), originally valued at $7.5 billion. Time Warner agreed to the restructuring to settle FTC charges that the merger would restrict competition in cable television programming and distribution.

BLOCK BOOKING

The term **block booking** is an example of illegal anticompetitive conduct.[75] Prior to the Supreme Court declaring the practice illegal, motion picture studios forced rental agencies (theatre owners) to pay for a group of films (a block), thus giving the studio a guarantee of a financial return on any film. The theatre owner was required to rent a block of films in order for the studio to agree to distribute the one "A" film that audiences wanted to see. Studios sold their films in packages on an all-or-nothing basis. This made it extremely difficult for independent producers of films to get their movies into theatres. Block booking is, of course, no longer legal.

In 1938, the Roosevelt administration ordered the U.S. Department of Justice to file suit against Hollywood's Big Eight studios to make such a practice illegal. The Supreme Court decision in *U.S. v. Paramount Pictures*, 334 U.S. 131 (1948), dealt the final blow to the Hollywood studios and their practice of block booking. It ended years of a profitable practice by the Hollywood studio system elite. The influence of independent film producers and the rise of the Society of Independent Motion Picture Producers (SIMPP) played a major role in the abolishment of the block booking practice.

H. A. ARTISTS & ASSOCS. V. ACTORS' EQUITY ASS'N

As mentioned in Chapter 2, unions often require talent agents to be certified (i.e., franchised) in order to represent members of the union such as actors and actresses. The actor's union, **Actors' Equity Association (AEA)**, represented most of the stage actors and actresses in the United States and entered into collective bargaining agreements with major theatrical producers throughout the country. The AEA had established minimum (scale) wages and other conditions of employment for those represented by the union. In 1928, the AEA unilaterally established a licensing system for the regulation of theatrical agents due to abuses in excessive fees and commissions charged for representation. It also prohibited union members from using a theatrical agent who had not obtained a license from the union.

In *H. A. Artists & Assocs. v. Actors' Equity Ass'n*, 451 U.S. 704 (1981), plaintiff-theatrical agents refused to obtain union licenses, and a lawsuit was brought that alleged violations of §§ 1 and 2 of the Sherman Act. The Court of Appeals affirmed a district court decision which determined that the union's franchising system was immune from antitrust challenge. The Supreme Court agreed. This represented a legitimate form of private regulation, rather than state or federal regulation of theatrical agents.

The *H. A. Artists & Assocs. v. Actors' Equity Ass'n* case follows.

---

[75] Sometimes referred to as a tying arrangement.

H. A. Artists & Assocs. v. Actors' Equity Ass'n

451 U.S. 704 (1981)

Supreme Court of the United States

Certiorari to the United States Court of Appeals for the Second Circuit.

JUSTICE STEWART delivered the opinion of the Court:

The respondent Actors' Equity Association (Equity) is a union representing the vast majority of stage actors and actresses in the United States. It enters into collective-bargaining agreements with theatrical producers that specify minimum wages and other terms and conditions of employment for those whom it represents. The petitioners are independent theatrical agents who place actors and actresses in jobs with producers. The Court of Appeals for the Second Circuit held that the respondents' system of regulation of theatrical agents is immune from antitrust liability by reason of the statutory labor exemption from the antitrust laws. We granted certiorari to consider the availability of that exemption in the circumstances presented by this case.

I

A

Equity is a national union that has represented stage actors and actresses since early in this century. Currently representing approximately 23,000 actors and actresses, it has collective-bargaining agreements with virtually all major theatrical producers in New York City, on and off Broadway, and with most other theatrical producers throughout the United States. The terms negotiated with producers are the minimum conditions of employment (called "scale"); an actor or actress is free to negotiate wages or terms more favorable than the collectively bargained minima.

Theatrical agents are independent contractors who negotiate contracts and solicit employment for their clients. The agents do not participate in the negotiation of collective-bargaining agreements between Equity and the theatrical producers. If an agent succeeds in obtaining employment for a client, he receives a commission based on a percentage of the client's earnings. Agents who operate in New York City must be licensed as employment agencies and are regulated by the New York City Department of Consumer Affairs pursuant to New York law, which provides that the maximum commission a theatrical agent may charge his client is 10% of the client's compensation.

In 1928, concerned with the high unemployment rates in the legitimate theater and the vulnerability of actors and actresses to abuses by theatrical agents, including the extraction of high commissions that tended to undermine collectively bargained rates of compensation, Equity unilaterally established a licensing system for the regulation of agents. The regulations permitted Equity members to deal only with those agents who obtained Equity licenses and thereby agreed to meet the conditions of representation prescribed by Equity. Those members who dealt with nonlicensed agents were subject to union discipline.

The system established by the Equity regulations was immediately challenged. In *Edelstein v. Gillmore,* 35 F.2d 723, the Court of Appeals for the Second Circuit concluded that the regulations were a lawful effort to improve the employment conditions of Equity members. In an opinion written by Judge Swan and joined by Judge Augustus N. Hand, the court said:

"The evils of unregulated employment agencies (using this term broadly to include also the personal representative) are set forth in the defendants' affidavits and are corroborated by common knowledge. . . . Hence the requirement that, as a condition to writing new business with Equity's members, old contracts with its members must be made to conform to the new standards, does not seem to us to justify an inference that the primary purpose of the requirement is infliction of injury upon plaintiff, and other personal representatives in a similar situation, rather than the protection of the supposed interests of Equity's members. *The terms they insist upon are calculated to secure from personal representatives better and more impartial service, at uniform and cheaper rates, and to improve conditions of employment of actors by theater managers.* Undoubtedly the defendants intend to compel the plaintiff to give up rights under existing contracts which do not conform to the new standards set up by Equity, but, as already indicated, *their motive in so doing is to benefit themselves and their fellow actors in the economic struggle.* The financial loss to plaintiff is incidental to this purpose." *Id., at* 726 (emphasis added).

The essential elements of Equity's regulation of theatrical agents have remained unchanged since 1928. A member of Equity is prohibited, on pain of union discipline, from using an agent who has not, through the mechanism of obtaining an Equity license (called a "franchise"), agreed to comply with the regulations. The most important of the regulations requires that a licensed agent must renounce any right to take a commission on an employment contract under which an actor or actress receives scale wages. To the extent a contract includes provisions under which an actor or actress will sometimes receive scale pay—for rehearsals or "chorus" employment, for example—and sometimes more, the regulations deny the agent any commission on the scale portions of the contract. Licensed agents are also precluded from taking commissions on out-of-town expense money paid to their clients. Moreover, commissions are limited on wages within 10% of scale pay, and an agent must allow his client to terminate a representation contract if the agent is not successful in procuring employment within a specified period. Finally, agents are required to

pay franchise fees to Equity. The fee is $200 for the initial franchise, $60 a year thereafter for each agent, and $40 for any subagent working in the office of another. These fees are deposited by Equity in its general treasury and are not segregated from other union funds.

In 1977, after a dispute between Equity and Theatrical Artists Representatives Associates (TARA)—a trade association representing theatrical agents—a group of agents, including the petitioners, resigned from TARA because of TARA's decision to abide by Equity's regulations. These agents also informed Equity that they would not accept Equity's regulations, or apply for franchises. The petitioners instituted this lawsuit in May 1978, contending that Equity's regulations of theatrical agents violated §§ 1 and 2 of the Sherman Act, 26 Stat. 209, as amended, 15 U.S.C. §§ 1 and 2.

B

The District Court found, after a bench trial, that Equity's creation and maintenance of the agency franchise system were fully protected by the statutory labor exemptions from the antitrust laws, and accordingly dismissed the petitioners' complaint. Among its factual conclusions, the trial court found that in the theatrical industry, agents play a critical role in securing employment for actors and actresses:

"As a matter of general industry practice, producers seek actors and actresses for their productions through agents. Testimony in this case convincingly established that an actor without an agent does not have the same access to producers or the same opportunity to be seriously considered for a part as does an actor who has an agent. Even principal interviews, in which producers are required to interview all actors who want to be considered for principal roles, do not eliminate the need for an agent, who may have a greater chance of gaining an audition for his client.

. . . .

"Testimony confirmed that agents play an integral role in the industry; without an agent, an actor would have significantly lesser chances of gaining employment." *Id.,* at 497, 502.

The court also found "no evidence to suggest the existence of any conspiracy or illegal combination between Actors' Equity and TARA or between Actors' Equity and producers," and concluded that "[the] Actors Equity franchising system was employed by Actors' Equity for the purpose of protecting the wages and working conditions of its members." *Id.* at 499.

The Court of Appeals unanimously affirmed the judgment of the District Court. It determined that the threshold issue was, under *United States v. Hutcheson,* 312 U.S. 219, 232, whether Equity's franchising system involved any combination between Equity and any "non-labor groups" or persons who are not "parties to a labor dispute." If it did, the court reasoned, the protection of the statutory labor exemption would not apply.

First, the Court of Appeals held that the District Court had not been clearly erroneous in finding no agreement, explicit or tacit, between Equity and the producers to establish or police the franchising system. *Ibid.* Next, the court turned to the relationship between the union and those agents who had agreed to become franchised, in order to determine whether those agreements would divest Equity's system of agency regulation of the statutory exemption. Relying on *Musicians v. Carroll,* 391 U.S. 99, the court concluded that the agents were themselves a "labor group," because of their substantial "economic inter-relationship" with Equity, under which "the union [could] not eliminate wage competition among its members without regulation of the fees of the agents." Accordingly, since the elimination of wage competition is plainly within the area of a union's legitimate self-interest, the court concluded that the exemption was applicable.

After deciding that the central feature of Equity's franchising system—the union's exaction of an agreement by agents not to charge commissions on certain types of work— was immune from antitrust challenge, the Court of Appeals turned to the petitioners' challenge

of the franchise fees exacted from agents. Equity had argued that the fees were necessary to meet its expenses in administering the franchise system, but no evidence was presented at trial to show that the costs justified the fees actually levied. The Court of Appeals suggested that if the exactions exceeded the true costs, they could not legally be collected, as such exactions would be unconnected with any of the goals of national labor policy that justify the labor antitrust exemption. Despite the lack of any cost evidence at trial, however, the appellate court reasoned that the fees were sufficiently low that a remand to the District Court on this point "would not serve any useful purpose." *Id.* at 651.

II

A

Labor unions are lawful combinations that serve the collective interests of workers, but they also possess the power to control the character of competition in an industry. Accordingly, there is an inherent tension between national antitrust policy, which seeks to maximize competition, and national labor policy, which encourages cooperation among workers to improve the conditions of employment. In the years immediately following passage of the Sherman Act, courts enjoined strikes as unlawful restraints of trade when a union's conduct or objectives were deemed "socially or economically harmful." *Duplex Printing Press Co. v. Deering,* 254 U.S. 443, 485 (Brandeis, J., dissenting). In response to these practices, Congress acted, first in the Clayton Act, 38 Stat. 731, and later in the Norris-LaGuardia Act, 47 Stat. 70, to immunize labor unions and labor disputes from challenge under the Sherman Act.

Section 6 of the Clayton Act, 15 U.S.C. § 17, declares that human labor "is not a commodity or article of commerce," and immunizes from antitrust liability labor organizations and their members "lawfully carrying out" their "legitimate [objectives]." Section 20 of the Act prohibits injunctions against specified employee activities, such as strikes and boycotts, that are undertaken in the employees' self-interest and that occur in the course of disputes "concerning terms or conditions of employment," and states that none of the specified acts can be "held to be [a] [violation] of any law of the United States." 29 U.S.C. § 52. This protection is re-emphasized and expanded in the Norris-LaGuardia Act, which prohibits federal-court injunctions against single or organized employees engaged in enumerated activities, and specifically forbids such injunctions notwithstanding the claim of an unlawful combination or conspiracy. While the Norris-LaGuardia Act's bar of federal-court labor injunctions is not explicitly phrased as an exemption from the antitrust laws, it has been interpreted broadly as a statement of congressional policy that the courts must not use the antitrust laws as a vehicle to interfere in labor disputes.

[In] *United States v. Hutcheson,* 312 U.S. 219, the Court held that labor unions acting in their self-interest and not in combination with nonlabor groups enjoy a statutory exemption from Sherman Act liability. After describing the congressional responses to judicial interference in union activity, the Court declared that "[so] long as a union acts in its self-interest and does not combine with non-labor groups, the licit and the illicit under § 20 [of the Clayton Act] are not to be distinguished by any judgment regarding the wisdom or unwisdom, the rightness or wrongness, the selfishness or unselfishness of the end of which the particular union activities are the means." *Id.* at 232 (footnote omitted).

The Court explained that this exemption derives not only from the Clayton Act, but also from the Norris-LaGuardia Act, particularly its definition of a "labor dispute," see n. 14, *supra,* in which Congress "reasserted the original purpose of the Clayton Act by infusing into it the immunized trade union activities as redefined by the later Act." Thus under *Hutcheson,* no federal injunction may issue over a "labor dispute," and "§ 20 [of the Clayton Act] removes all such allowable conduct from the taint of being a 'violation of any law of the United States,' including the Sherman [Act]." *Ibid.*

The statutory exemption does not apply when a union combines with a "non-labor group." *Hutcheson, supra,* at 232. Accordingly, antitrust immunity is forfeited when a union combines with one or more employers in an effort to restrain trade. In *Allen Bradley Co. v. Electrical Workers,* 325 U.S. 797, for example, the Court held that a union had violated the Sherman Act when it combined with manufacturers and contractors to erect a sheltered local business market in order "to bar all other business men from [the market], and to charge the public prices above a competitive level." The Court indicated that the union efforts would, standing alone, be exempt from antitrust liability, *ibid.,* but because the union had not acted unilaterally, the exemption was denied. Congress "intended to outlaw business monopolies. A business monopoly is no less such because a union participates, and such participation is a violation of the Act."

B

The Court of Appeals properly recognized that the threshold issue was to determine whether or not Equity's franchising of agents involved any combination between Equity and any "non-labor groups," or persons who are not "parties to a labor dispute" (quoting *Hutcheson,* 312 U.S., at 232). And the court's conclusion that the trial court had not been clearly erroneous in its finding that there was no combination between Equity and the theatrical producers to create or maintain the franchise system is amply supported by the record.

The more difficult problem is whether the combination between Equity and the agents who agreed to become franchised was a combination with a "nonlabor group." The answer to this question is best understood in light of *Musicians v. Carroll,* 391 U.S. 99. There, four orchestra leaders, members of the American Federation of Musicians, brought an action based on the Sherman Act challenging the union's unilateral system of regulating "club dates," or one-time musical engagements. These regulations, *inter alia,* enforced a closed shop; required orchestra leaders to engage a minimum number of "sidemen," or instrumentalists; prescribed minimum prices for local engagements; prescribed higher minimum prices for traveling orchestras; and permitted leaders to deal only with booking agents licensed by the union.

Without disturbing the finding of the Court of Appeals that the orchestra leaders were employers and independent contractors, the Court concluded that they were nonetheless a "labor group" and parties to a "labor dispute" within the meaning of the Norris-LaGuardia Act, and thus that their involvement in the union regulatory scheme was not an unlawful combination between "labor" and "nonlabor" groups. The Court agreed with the trial court that the applicable test was whether there was "job or wage competition or some other economic interrelationship affecting legitimate union interests between the union members and the independent contractors."

The Court also upheld the restrictions on booking agents, who were *not* involved in job or wage competition with union members. Accordingly, these restrictions had to meet the "other economic interrelationship" branch of the disjunctive test quoted above. And the test was met because those restrictions were "'at least as intimately bound up with the subject of wages' . . . as the price floors." *Id.* at 113 (quoting *Teamsters v. Oliver,* 362 U.S. 605, 606). The Court noted that the booking agent restrictions had been adopted, in part, because agents had "charged exorbitant fees, and booked engagements for musicians at wages . . . below union scale."

C

The restrictions challenged by the petitioners in this case are very similar to the agent restrictions upheld in the *Carroll* case. The essential features of the regulatory scheme are identical: members are permitted to deal only with agents who have agreed (1) to honor their fiduciary obligations by avoiding conflicts of interest, (2) not to charge excessive commissions, and (3) not to book members for jobs paying less than the union minimum. And as in *Carroll,* Equity's regulation of agents

developed in response to abuses by employment agents who occupy a critical role in the relevant labor market. The agent stands directly between union members and jobs, and is in a powerful position to evade the union's negotiated wage structure.

The peculiar structure of the legitimate theater industry, where work is intermittent, where it is customary if not essential for union members to secure employment through agents, and where agents' fees are calculated as a percentage of a member's wage, makes it impossible for the union to defend even the integrity of the minimum wages it has negotiated without regulation of agency fees. The regulations are "brought within the labor exemption [because they are] necessary to assure that scale wages will be paid. . . ." *Carroll,* 391 U.S. at 112. They "embody . . . a direct frontal attack upon a problem thought to threaten the maintenance of the basic wage structure." *Teamsters v. Oliver,* 358 U.S. 283, 294. Agents must, therefore, be considered a "labor group," and their controversy with Equity is plainly a "labor dispute" as defined in the Norris-LaGuardia Act: "representation of persons in negotiating, fixing, maintaining, changing, or seeking to arrange terms or conditions of employment, regardless of whether or not the disputants stand in the proximate relation of employer and employee." 29 U.S.C. § 113c.

Agents perform a function—the representation of union members in the sale of their labor—that in most nonentertainment industries is performed exclusively by unions. In effect, Equity's franchise system operates as a substitute for maintaining a hiring hall as the representative of its members seeking employment.

Finally, Equity's regulations are clearly designed to promote the union's legitimate self-interest. In a case such as this, where there is no direct wage or job competition between the union and the group it regulates, the *Carroll* formulation to determine the presence of a nonlabor group— whether there is "'some . . . economic interrelationship affecting legitimate union interests . . . ,"' 391 U.S. at 106 (quoting District Court opinion)—necessarily resolves this issue.

D

The question remains whether the fees that Equity levies upon the agents who apply for franchises are a permissible component of the exempt regulatory system. We have concluded that Equity's justification for these fees is inadequate. Conceding that *Carroll* did not sanction union extraction of franchise fees from agents, Equity suggests, only in the most general terms, that the fees are somehow related to the basic purposes of its regulations: elimination of wage competition, upholding of the union wage scale, and promotion of fair access to jobs. But even assuming that the fees no more than cover the costs of administering the regulatory system, this is simply another way of saying that without the fees, the union's regulatory efforts would not be subsidized—and that the dues of Equity's members would perhaps have to be increased to offset the loss of a general revenue source. If Equity did not impose these franchise fees upon the agents, there is no reason to believe that any of its legitimate interests would be affected.

III

For the reasons stated, the judgment of the Court of Appeals is affirmed in part and reversed in part, and the case is remanded for proceedings consistent with this opinion. *It is so ordered.*

Material has been adapted for this text. Used with the permission of LexisNexis.

FEDERAL BASEBALL

The sport of professional baseball has held a unique exemption from antitrust laws in accordance with the controversial interpretation of the Supreme Court in *Federal Baseball Club of Baltimore, Inc. v. National League of Professional Baseball Clubs*, 259 U.S. 200 (1922). The Court held that antitrust laws do not apply to professional baseball as baseball did not involve interstate commerce. Even though players traveled across state lines, Justice Oliver Wendell Holmes held that it was only incidental to the game and that baseball was "purely a state affair" and held to remain exempt from antitrust laws. Baseball utilized the reserve clause which precluded players from jumping to another baseball league, the Federal Baseball League. Therefore, since the court held that antitrust laws did not apply to baseball, baseball's reserve clause was acceptable and did not constitute an antitrust violation.

THE CURT FLOOD ACT OF 1998

The **Curt Flood Act of 1998** (15 U.S.C. § 27(a)) was an attempt by Congress to legislatively override the antitrust ruling in the *Federal Baseball* case. However, the Curt Flood Act is limited only to certain activities of baseball and has very little effect on prior court decisions or other practical applications. For example, section (a) of the Act states,

A major league baseball stadium.
Getty Images/Time Life Pictures.

"the conduct, acts, practices, or agreements of persons in the business of organized professional baseball directly relating to or affecting employment of major league baseball players to play baseball at the major league level are subject to the antitrust laws to the same extent such conduct, acts, practices, or agreements would be subject to the antitrust laws if engaged in by persons in any other professional sports business affecting interstate commerce." 15 U.S.C. § 27a(a).

Thus, the antitrust exemption is only repealed as to employment-related activities. In addition, section (b)(2) of the Curt Flood Act specifically excludes the Major League Baseball Constitution from antitrust coverage, including its dealings with minor league baseball. 15 U.S.C. § 27a(b)(2).

ANTITRUST AND TELEVISION

The FCC, as part of its agenda to serve the public interest, adopted regulations coined **antisiphoning** to protect programming found on free (i.e., noncable or satellite) broadcast television. Antisiphoning rules prevented cable television systems (a.k.a. subscription television) from **siphoning off** (drawing an audience away) programming for pay cable channels that otherwise would be seen on **conventional broadcast** television. These antisiphoning rules stated that only movies no older than three years and sports events not ordinarily seen on television could be cablecast. Siphoning rules have been an issue particularly with regard to the broadcasting of sports—namely, whether sports should be free for the public at large or whether cable organizations such as ESPN and others should be able to charge a fee for major sporting events. Many critics of antisiphoning legislation raise concerns regarding the First Amendment implications of such rules.

HOME BOX OFFICE, Inc v. FCC

In *Home Box Office, Inc. v. FCC*, 567 F.2d 9 (D.C. Cir. 1977), the FCC attempted to justify rules that would prevent the siphoning of programming material from free (conventional) broadcast television to pay cable television broadcasts. The FCC wanted to ensure that the general public receives free access to certain programming on broadcast television. The FCC maintained that it was obligated to impose its antisiphoning rules because the overall level of public enjoyment of television entertainment would be reduced if sports events were shown only on pay cable or shown on conventional television only after some time delay. The United States Court of Appeals for the District of Columbia Circuit disagreed and found no reasonable public interest justification for imposing siphoning restrictions on cable with regard to sports programming.

The Court identified three separate grounds for vacating the FCC's antisiphoning rules. First, although the Supreme Court allowed the FCC to regulate cable television through the Communications Act of 1934, only those objectives which had been long established in broadcast television or had been congressionally approved justified any regulation. Although the government could adopt reasonable regulations separating broadcasters and cable providers who compete and interfere with each other for the same audience, those regulations must pass scrutiny under the four-part test set out by the Supreme Court in *United States v. O'Brien.*[76] Under the **O'Brien test,** the FCC regulations:

1. must fall within the constitutional power of the government,
2. must further an "important or substantial governmental interest,"
3. must be "unrelated to the suppression of free expression," and
4. must impose no greater restriction on First Amendment freedoms "than is essential to the furtherance" of the governmental interest.

THE SPORTS BROADCASTING ACT OF 1961

The **Sports Broadcasting Act of 1961**[77] generally exempts television agreements entered into by professional football, baseball, basketball, and hockey leagues from the federal antitrust laws. In 1968, FCC established strict limitations on the sale of sports programming to pay television operators in order to protect the television structure at that time. These limits prohibited "specific events" (such as the NCAA men's March Madness basketball tournament and the Super Bowl) from being sold to anyone other than broadcast television. Additionally, the *O'Brien* decision held that the antisiphoning agenda with regard to sports programming did not further an important or substantial governmental interest because the record indicated no conflict or controversy between the

---

[76] 391 U.S. 367 (1968).
[77] 15 U.S.C. § 1291.

two groups. Had the FCC adequately demonstrated the siphoning to be harmful, the Court might have come to a different conclusion.

Although Congress granted sports leagues the privilege of operating beyond the scope of antitrust scrutiny, Congress has maintained a keen eye toward the policies of the leagues and their potential to bypass the over-the-air broadcast networks in search of pay television revenues. Numerous bills have been introduced which have attempted to restrain the move of sports programming away from mass-market conventional broadcast television. In fact, in § 26 of the **Cable Act of 1992,**[78] Congress directed the FCC to conduct an ongoing study on the carriage of local, regional, and national sports programming by broadcast stations, cable programming networks, and pay-per-view services.

N.C.A.A. V. BOARD OF REGENTS OF UNIV. OF OKLA.

In *N.C.A.A. v. Board of Regents of Univ. of Okla.*, 468 U.S. 85 (1984), the Supreme Court of the United States held that the NCAA's conduct of awarding television rights of college football games to only two networks (ABC and CBS) violated antitrust laws. These networks could not televise a particular college or university football team more than four times nationally and six times overall during any two-year period of the plan, limiting the number of times a team could be featured on television. The Universities of Oklahoma and Georgia brought an action alleging that the NCAA's television control violated § 1 of the Sherman Act. The Court concluded that the NCAA's television plan did, in fact, unreasonably restrain competition.

NFL BLACKOUT RULE

The National Football League (NFL) does have a very limited antitrust exemption of its own which can be found at 15 U.S.C. § 1291 and § 1292. The NFL is allowed to pool and sell a unitary video package to television networks (§ 1291). The NFL is also allowed to issue blackouts of nonlocal games when local teams are being telecast and when there has not been a sellout (§ 1292). More specifically, the **NFL blackout rule** stipulates that games will not be broadcast in home markets (i.e., within a 75-mile radius) unless they are sold out 72 hours in advance of the opening kickoff. The NFL and the commissioner have complete control to extend or suspend the deadline. The NFL has always maintained that the television blackout rule is necessary to sell tickets because home fans would not watch the games in person if they knew they could watch them on television for free.

The *Stoutenborough v. National Football League* case follows.

---

[78] Formally known as the Cable Television Consumer Protection and Competition Act of 1992, 47 U.S.C. § 521, it amended the Communications Act of 1934.

Stoutenborough v. National Football League

59 F.3d 580 (6th Cir. 1995)

United States Court of Appeals for the Sixth Circuit

OPINION: BOYCE F. MARTIN, JR., Circuit Judge.

Thomas Stoutenborough and Self-Help for Hearing Impaired Persons, an unincorporated association of individuals with hearing impairments, appeal the district court order granting the defendants' motion to dismiss for failure to state a claim upon which relief can be granted. They argue that the Americans With Disabilities Act, 42 U.S.C. § 12101, *et seq.,* and other federal statutes apply to the National Football League's "blackout rule" and require the defendants to provide some "auxiliary aid or service" to assure that hearing impaired persons have equal access to some form of telecommunication of the affected football games in areas of public accommodation. For the following reasons, we affirm the judgment of the district court.

Stoutenborough is a hearing-impaired resident of Cleveland, Ohio and the managing director of Self-Help for Hearing Impaired Persons. On September 15, 1993, Stoutenborough and Self-Help for Hearing Impaired Persons filed a class-action complaint in federal district court against the National Football League, Inc., the Cleveland Browns Football Club, Inc., National Broadcasting Company, Inc., American Broadcasting Company, Inc., Columbia Broadcasting Systems, Inc., W.K.Y.C. - T.V. 3, W.J.W. - T.V. 8, and W.E.W.S. - T.V. 5. The complaint, as subsequently amended, alleged that the National Football League's "blackout rule," which prohibits the live local broadcast of home football games that are not sold out seventy-two hours before game-time, violates the Americans With Disabilities Act of 1990, the Television Decoder Circuitry Act of 1990, the Communications Act of 1934, and the Rehabilitation Act of 1973. This timely appeal followed.

On appeal, Stoutenborough and Self-Help for Hearing Impaired Persons claim that their action is based "primarily and fundamentally" upon Title III of the Americans With Disabilities Act. In essence, they argue that the "blackout rule" unlawfully discriminates against them in a disproportionate way because they have no other means of accessing the football game "via telecommunication technology." Thus, they are denied the "substantially equal" access that they claim the Americans With Disabilities Act requires. Stoutenborough and Self-Help for Hearing Impaired Persons also argue that the "service" at issue is the live television transmission of football games that are offered as services, benefits, or privileges in places of public accommodation.

At the outset, the defendants contend that the National Football League's "blackout rule" is not discriminatory: it applies equally to both the hearing and the hearing-impaired populations. We agree. The "blackout rule" prohibits both the hearing and the hearing-impaired from viewing "blacked out" home football games. As the defendants also point out, the fact that hearing individuals may be able to listen to a "blacked out" game, if it is broadcast by radio, is irrelevant, because the "blackout rule" neither reaches nor impacts radio broadcasting. Thus, the radio broadcast of "blacked-out" games does not render the "blackout rule" discriminatory, because the rule itself impacts only the televised broadcast of home football games. Moreover, with the advent of devices that make radio transmissions accessible to persons with hearing impairments, the hearing and the hearing-impaired populations attain equal footing as radio broadcasts become available to both.

The defendants also maintain that none of the statutes upon which Stoutenborough and Self-Help for Hearing Impaired Persons rely provides them a cause of action, in light of the plain language of those statutes. *E.g., United States v.*

Ron Pair Enters., Inc., 489 U.S. 235, 241, 103 L. Ed. 2d 290, 109 S. Ct. 1026 (1989). Again, we agree. Title III of the Americans With Disabilities Act provides, in relevant part:

No individual shall be discriminated against on the basis of disability in the full and equal enjoyment of the goods, services, facilities, privileges, advantages, or accommodations of any place of public accommodation by any person who owns, leases (or leases to), or operates a place of public accommodation. 42 U.S.C. § 12182(a).

The district court correctly observed:

The discrimination against which the statute is directed is based on the practices or procedures of the public accommodation itself which may deny the handicapped equal access to a service which that accommodation offers. The televised broadcast of football games is certainly offered through defendants, but not as a service of public accommodation. It is all of the services which the public accommodation offers, not all services which the lessor of the public accommodation offers, which fall within the scope of Title III.

First, none of the defendants falls within any of the twelve "public accommodation" categories identified in the statute. 42 U.S.C. § 12181(7). Also, the prohibitions of Title III are restricted to "places" of public accommodation, disqualifying the National Football League, its member clubs, and the media defendants. As the applicable regulations clarify, a "place" is "a facility, operated by a private entity, whose operations affect commerce and fall within at least one of the" twelve "public accommodation" categories. 28 C.F.R. § 36.104. "Facility," in turn, is defined as "all or any portion of buildings, structures, sites, complexes, equipment, rolling stock or other conveyances, roads, walks, passageways, parking lots, or other real or personal property, including the site where the building, property, structure, or equipment is located." *Id.*

In addition, the "service" that Stoutenborough and Self-Help for Hearing Impaired Persons seek to obtain—the televised broadcast of "blacked-out" home football games—does not involve a "place of public accommodation." Although a game is played in a "place of public accommodation" and may be viewed on television in another "place of public accommodation," that does not suffice. Moreover, the plaintiffs' argument that the prohibitions of Title III are not solely limited to "places" of public accommodation contravenes the plain language of the statute.

Titles I and II of the Americans With Disabilities Act are also inapplicable. Title I prohibits employment discrimination by a "covered entity," which is defined as "an employer, employment agency, labor organization, or joint labor-management committee." 42 U.S.C. § 12111(2). Title II prohibits discrimination by a "public entity," which is defined as any state and local government and its agencies and instrumentalities, as well as the National Railroad Passenger Corporation and any commuter authority. 42 U.S.C. §§ 12131(1) and 12132. By their terms, then, these statutes are inapplicable to the factual situation before us.

Plaintiffs' argument that Title IV of the Americans With Disabilities Act, when read in conjunction with the Television Decoder Circuitry Act, is broad enough to protect hearing-impaired individuals in the context of television broadcast services, is similarly unavailing. The provisions of Title IV amend the Communications Act of 1934, to accommodate the hearing impaired in the provision of telephone services and to require closed captioning in certain types of television announcements. Section 401 of the Americans With Disabilities Act requires certain "common carriers" to provide telecommunications relay services. However, because the Title IV definition of "common carriers" is premised upon the Communications Act of 1934 definition at 47 U.S.C. § 153(h), it is clear that the "common carriers" referred to in Title IV do not include television broadcasters. *See* 47 U.S.C. § 225(a)(1). Section 402 requires television public service announcements that are produced or funded by a federal agency to include closed captioning. 47 U.S.C. § 611.

Therefore, these provisions are irrelevant to the broadcast of National Football League games and the "blackout rule."

Moreover, the Communications Act of 1934, 47 U.S.C. § 151 *et seq.,* which established the regulatory scheme governing the Federal Communications Commission, does not indicate congressional intent to apply the Americans With Disabilities Act to the "blackout rule." The "public interest" standard articulated in Section 309(a) of the Communications Act does not create a private cause of action. *E.g., Schnapper v. Foley,* 215 U.S. App. D.C. 59, 667 F.2d 102, 116–17 (D.C. Cir. 1981), *cert. denied,* 455 U.S. 948 (1982). This standard does not incorporate the Americans With Disabilities Act's anti-discrimination requirement so as to prohibit the "blackout rule."

Finally, the Television Decoder Circuitry Act of 1990, which simply requires that all television sets manufactured in or used in the United States having thirteen-inch screens and above,

must "be equipped with built-in decoder circuitry designed to display closed captioned television transmission," 47 U.S.C. § 303(u), is inapplicable. None of the defendants meet the "manufacturer" criterion set forth in this statute.

We have accepted the facts alleged in the complaint as true, as we must under a 12(b)(6) motion to dismiss for failure to state a claim. *Nishiyama v. Dickson County,* 814 F.2d 277, 283 (6th Cir. 1987). The law as we have reviewed it is clear. These facts simply do not establish the violation of a protected right. Therefore, we believe that the district court was correct in finding that Stoutenborough and Self-Help for Hearing Impaired Persons failed to state a cognizable claim.

Accordingly, the judgment of the district court is AFFIRMED.

Material has been adapted for this text. Used with the permission of LexisNexis.

ANTITRUST ISSUES IN THE MUSIC INDUSTRY

Since 1934, the U.S. Department of Justice has concerned itself with competitive issues particularly in the licensing of music performance rights by the nation's two largest performing rights organizations, the American Society of Composers, Authors, and Publishers (ASCAP) and Broadcast Music Inc. (BMI).

In *Broadcast Music, Inc. v. Columbia Broadcasting System, Inc.*, 441 U.S. 1 (1979), Columbia Broadcasting System, Inc. (CBS) brought an action against ASCAP and BMI and their members and affiliates, alleging that the issuance by ASCAP and BMI to CBS of **blanket licenses** to copyrighted musical compositions at fees negotiated by them violated antitrust laws as a form of illegal price-fixing. Blanket licenses give the licensees the right to perform any and all of the compositions owned by the members or affiliates as often as the licensees desire for a stated term and price.

The District Court in the case had dismissed the complaint, holding that the blanket license was not price-fixing and not a per se violation of the Sherman Act. The Court of Appeals reversed and remanded the case for consideration of the appropriate remedy, holding that the blanket license issued to television networks was a form of price-fixing illegal per se under the Sherman Act and established copyright misuse. The Supreme Court of the United States reversed again and held that the issuance by ASCAP and BMI of blanket licenses does not constitute price-fixing and is not per se unlawful under the antitrust laws.

RECENT SETTLEMENT IN THE MUSIC INDUSTRY

In another example of antitrust issues and the music industry, in late 2003, U.S. District Court Judge D. Brock Hornby (Maine) approved a $143 million settlement of a lawsuit that accused major record companies and large music retailers of conspiring to set minimum music prices in violation of federal antitrust laws.[79] The lawsuit, which was signed by the **attorneys general** of 43 states and territories, accused major record labels and large music retailers facing competition from superstore discount retailers like Target and Wal-Mart of conspiring to set minimum music prices. Under the settlement, the defendants agreed to make sales practice changes to ensure strong market competition, provide consumer compensation, and make available approximately 7 million CDs of various musical genres for distribution by the state attorneys general to public libraries, schools, and charitable groups for the benefit of all consumers.[80]

ANTITRUST AND RADIO

The growth and development of radio and the wireless industry were not without their own antitrust issues. The federal government watched with concern as to what was happening with the Radio Corporation of America (RCA), as it gained a considerable stronghold over the radio industry. RCA became so powerful that it licensed other companies to make receivers. This list included companies such as Philco, Zenith, Emerson, and Sylvania, all of which are popular industry names today. The federal government's primary concern involved monopolistic behavior and unfair competitive dealings by RCA and David Sarnoff. In the early 1930s, the U.S. Department of Justice filed an antitrust suit against the company. In a 1932 **consent decree**,[81] the organization's operations were separated, and GE, AT&T, and Westinghouse were forced to sell their interests in the company. Sarnoff then helped form the National Broadcasting Company (NBC) which, like all other networks at the time, broadcast in AM radio.

CLEAR CHANNEL AND AMFM

In 2000, the U.S. Department of Justice announced that Clear Channel Communications Inc. and AMFM Inc. agreed to sell 99 radio stations in 27 markets

---

[79] See http://www.musiccdsettlement.com/english/default.htm

[80] http://www.musiccdsettlement.com/english/default.htm. Class action claims for consumers in other states also were settled by private counsel. Defendants included Sony Music Entertainment, EMI Music Distribution, Warner-Elektra-Atlantic Corp., Universal Music Group, and Bertelsmann Music Group, as well as retailers Tower Records, Musicland Stores, and Transworld Entertainment.

[81] An out-of-court legal settlement whereby the accused party agrees to modify or change their behavior rather than plead guilty or go through an administrative hearing on charges brought before a court.

nationwide after the Department of Justice expressed antitrust concerns about Clear Channel's $23.5 billion merger with AMFM, the largest radio transaction ever reviewed. The Department of Justice said that the transaction would have led to a loss of head-to-head competition between the two companies, resulting in increased prices for radio advertising.[82] The action exemplifies the role that the government plays in the enforcement of antitrust laws in order to promote competition in the consumer marketplace.

CHAPTER SUMMARY

Though the American dream fosters freedom of competition, Congress has granted the federal government the authority to regulate anticompetitive business practices. The U.S. Department of Justice and the Federal Trade Commission are the primary watchdogs for large-scale business mergers, acquisitions and practices that could harm consumers in the form of higher prices. Since the enactment of the Sherman and Clayton Acts, the Supreme Court has utilized its discretion to interpret the laws by applying the per se, rule of reason, and quick look analyses to determine if there has been a violation of antitrust laws. Whether a merger is a horizontal merger or vertical merger, governmental administrative agencies keep a keen eye for potentially harmful conduct to consumers, as a matter of public interest.

Film, radio, television, and music have had their share of antitrust issues with the federal government, as have professional sports, particularly professional baseball and football. Baseball has maintained a long-time exemption from antitrust laws, and even the National Football League has been granted limited exception to antitrust activity in the form of its blackout rule.

CHAPTER TERMS

Actors' Equity
    Association (AEA)
Antisiphoning
Antitrust
Antitrust laws
Attorney general
Below-cost
Blanket license
Block booking
Bottleneck

Cable Act of 1992
Clayton Act
Collude
Consent decree
Conventional broadcast
Curt Flood Act of 1998
Hart-Scott-Rodino
    Antitrust
    Improvements Act
    of 1976

Horizontal merger
Monopoly
NFL blackout rule
O'Brien test
Per se rule
Predatory
Price-fixing
Quick look
Restraint of trade

Rule of reason
Sherman Antitrust Act
    of 1890
Siphoning off
Sports Broadcasting Act
    of 1961
Vertical merger

ADDITIONAL CASES

American Football League v. National Football League, 323 F.2d 124 (4th Cir. 1963)

ASCAP v. Showtime/The Movie Channel, Inc., 912 F.2d 563 (2d Cir. 1990)

Berger v. Heckler, 771 F.2d 1556 (2d Cir. 1985)

BMI v. Columbia Broadcasting System, Inc., 441 U.S. 1 (1979)

Buffalo Broadcasting Co. v. ASCAP, 744 F.2d 917 (2d Cir. 1985), *cert. denied*, 469 U.S. 1211 (1985)

Century Communications v. FCC, 835 F.2d 292, 302 (D.C. Cir. 1987)

Columbia Broadcasting System, Inc. v. ASCAP, 400 F. Supp. 737 (S.D.N.Y. 1977)

---

[82] http://www.usdoj.gov/atr/public/press_releases/2000/5183.htm

Columbia Broadcasting System, Inc. v. ASCAP, 620 F.2d 930 (2d Cir. 1980), *cert. denied*, 450 U.S. 970 (1981)

United States v. ASCAP, 157 F.R.D. 173 (S.D.N.Y. 1994)

United States v. ASCAP, 331 F.2d 117 (2d Cir. 1964), *cert. denied*, 377 U.S. 997 (1964)

United States v. Midwest Video Corp., 406 U.S. 649 (1972)

United States v. O'Brien, 391 U.S. 367 (1968)

United States Football League v. National Football League, 842 F.2d 1335 (2d Cir. 1988)

REVIEW QUESTIONS

1. What are some of the specific practices that antitrust laws are designed to prevent?
2. Are all monopolies illegal?
3. What are the major federal laws related to antitrust?
4. What tests do courts use to determine whether or not an antitrust violation has occurred?
5. Why are mergers special concerns for the government's role in protecting the public interest?
6. What is the difference between a horizontal merger and a vertical merger?
7. How does the sport of professional baseball have an antitrust exemption?
8. What is block booking and is it legal today?
9. Why did the FCC establish antisiphoning regulations?
10. What is the NFL blackout rule?

REFERENCES FOR ADDITIONAL RESEARCH AND DISCUSSION

Baker, S., *The Casey Martin Case: Its Possible Effects on Professional Sports*, 34 Tulsa L.J. 745 (1999).

Bautista, P.R., *Congress Says, "Yooou're Out!!!" to the Antitrust Exemption of Professional Baseball: A Discussion of the Current State of Player-Owner Collective Bargaining and the Impact of the Curt Flood Act of 1998*, 15 Ohio St. J. on Disp. Resol. 445 (2000).

Borteck, A.E., *The Faux Fix: Why a Repeal of Major League Baseball's Antitrust Exemption Would Not Solve Its Severe Competitive Balance Problems*, 25 Cardozo L. Rev. 1069 (2004).

Chi, E.C., *Star Quality and Job Security: The Role of the Performers' Unions in Controlling Access to the Acting Profession*, 18 Cardozo Arts & Ent. L.J. 1 (2000).

Greene, S.M., *Regulating the NCAA: Making the Calls under the Sherman Antitrust Act and Title IX*, 52 Me. L. Rev. 81 (2000).

Mitten, M.J., *Applying Antitrust Law to NCAA Regulation of "Big Time" College Athletics: The Need to Shift from Nostalgic 19th and 20th Century Ideals of Amateurism to the Economic Realities of the 21st Century*, 11 Marq. Sports L. Rev. 1 (2000).

Rosenthal L.J., *From Regulating Organization to Multi-Billion Dollar Business: The NCAA Is Commercializing the Amateur Competition It Has Taken Almost a Century to Create*, 13 Seton Hall J. Sport L. 321 (2003).

Siok, K., & Wilson, T., *Talent Agents as Producers: A Historical Perspective of Screen Actors Guild Regulation and the Rising Conflict with Managers*, 21 Loy. L.A. Ent. L.J. 401 (2001).

INTELLECTUAL PROPERTY ISSUES IN ENTERTAINMENT LAW

AFTER STUDYING THIS CHAPTER YOU SHOULD BE ABLE TO:

1. Define the distinct intellectual property terms copyright, trademark, and patent.
2. Discuss the impact and effect of the Sonny Bono Copyright Term Extension Act of 1998.
3. Distinguish between the legal effects of works copyrighted before and after 1998.
4. Define the term infringement in the context of intellectual property.
5. Discuss the fair use doctrine and defenses, including the de minimis defense.
6. Discuss the role of licensing in intellectual property.
7. Explain the different types of categories of trademarks.
8. Define the Madrid Protocol and its role in international registration.
9. Discuss the role of the World Intellectual Property Organization (WIPO) in resolving disputes.
10. Discuss the concerns over piracy of intellectual property, including cybersquatting and other Internet-related concerns.

INTRODUCTION

Protecting the creative rights of **intangible property** of authors, computer programmers, designers, artists, and entertainers is vital in the entertainment industry. Consumers who purchase video games, CDs, and DVDs, or those who attend public performances where a fee is charged, are paying for the right to hear or see something created, manufactured, or distributed by the artist, writer, musician, movie studio, recording studio, and so on. Paying for the right to view or listen to various forms of entertainment is what drives the entertainment industry, and ensuring that others do not copy original works without permission invites numerous legal issues and concerns.

Traditional **intellectual property** courses focus on the fundamental aspects of securing copyrights, patents, and trademarks and protecting against their infringement. With the advent of the Internet, however, a whole new world has been created in which the entertainment industry is threatened as never before by a world in which computers and their users are sharing (i.e., infringing), in a "virtual reality," copyrighted, trademarked, and patented visual and audio information and products for free and without the consent of the original authors.

As a result of unauthorized piracy via computers and other advanced technology, lawsuits were brought by the Recording Industry Association of America (RIAA) in 2003 against **file-sharers** of downloaded music in a highly publicized campaign against "pirates" of original material. Piracy over the Internet is almost effortless and is only a few keystrokes away for infringers. Most consumers realize that downloading such material is not legal, while others risk getting caught for an infringement.

This chapter introduces the student to the traditional cornerstones of intellectual property: copyright, trademark, and patent law. The chapter also discusses contemporary infringement issues and offers the latest legal attempts to protect against piracy, including modification and amendments to the major intellectual property laws. Though the various forms of digital technologies (CDs, DVDs, MP3s, etc.) and the Internet will continue to wreak havoc for the entertainment industry in the short run, attempts have been made to minimize the effects of piracy on lost revenues for the studios, labels, and artists themselves.

COPYRIGHT

The Constitution gives Congress the authority to regulate **copyrights** (U.S. Const. art. I, § 8, cl. 8). Important to writers, publishers, videographers,[83] and other creative individuals who are authors of "original works of authorship," a copyright gives the copyright owner the exclusive right to reproduce the copyrighted work, to prepare **derivative works,** to distribute copies of the copyrighted work, and to perform or display the copyrighted work publicly under § 106 of the Copyright Act of 1976.

Understanding copyright is obviously important for those individuals who reduce their ideas to a written form. This could be the author of a novel seeking to break into the publishing world, the author of a screenplay hoping to get adopted by a studio, and composers of lyrics, just to name a few. Those who seek to publish textbooks, those who participate in self-publishing efforts by creating course packets for colleges or schools, and even those involved in electronic publishing, including **blogging**[84] on the Internet, should consider potential copyright issues.

Copyright includes literary, artistic, dramatic, musical, graphic arts, and other creations, including computer software. Movie producers and musicians must concern themselves with copyright issues, especially if someone else's

The Copyright Symbol.
Brand X Pictures

---

[83] Documentary and wedding videographers, for example.
[84] A blog is a journal that is available on the Internet and is short for web + log. The activity of updating a blog is "blogging," and someone who keeps or maintains a blog is a "blogger."

work is intentionally (or in some cases unintentionally) used in the production of a motion picture, on television, or even in videos.

THE COPYRIGHT ACT

The current U.S. Copyright Act of 1976 (Act) is codified at 17 U.S.C. §§ 101–810. It is the federal law enacted by Congress to protect the original writings of authors. A work is covered under the Act whether or not a copyright notice © is attached and whether or not the work is registered with the federal Copyright Office of the Library of Congress (37 C.F.R. §§ 201–204).[85]

Although it is no longer necessary today, the placing of a notice on copyrighted material avoids questions as to whether or not it is copyrighted. It is also not necessary to register the work. The essential elements of copyright notice include the term Copyright (or "Copr."), copyright symbol, year of copyright, name of the copyright holder, and the phrase "All Rights Reserved." For example:

Copyright © 2004 Adam Epstein. All Rights Reserved.

Nearly every original, **tangible** (written or recorded) expression is copyrighted immediately once it is created, though a more formal process is required for a patent, discussed later in this chapter.

WORKS NOT PROTECTED

Several categories of material are generally not eligible for federal copyright protection. These include:

1. Works that have not been fixed in a tangible form of expression (for example, choreographic works that have not been notated or recorded or improvisational acceptance speeches or performances);
2. Titles, names, short phrases, and slogans; familiar symbols or designs; mere variations of typographic ornamentation, lettering, or coloring; mere listings of ingredients or contents;
3. Ideas, procedures, methods, systems, processes, concepts, principles, discoveries, or devices, as distinguished from a description, explanation, or illustration;

[85] For sound recordings, the copyright symbol is represented by the letter P enclosed in a circle Ⓟ, which stands for phonorecords or phonogram in the U.K.

4. Works consisting entirely of information that is common property and containing no original authorship (for example, standard calendars, height and weight charts, tape measures and rulers, and lists or tables taken from public documents or other common sources).[86]

SONNY BONO COPYRIGHT TERM EXTENSION ACT OF 1998

The Sonny Bono Copyright Term Extension Act of 1998 amended the copyright laws by extending the duration of copyright protection an additional twenty years.[87] A summary of the effects of this Act is as follows:[88]

For works created after January 1, 1978, copyright protection will endure for the life of the author plus an additional 70 years after the author's death. In the case of a joint work, the term lasts for 70 years after the last surviving author's death. For *anonymous* and *pseudonymous* works and *works made for hire,* the term will be 95 years from the year of first publication or 120 years from the year of creation, whichever expires first.

For works created but not published or registered before January 1, 1978, the term endures for life of the author plus 70 years after the author's death, but in no case will expire earlier than December 31, 2002. If the work is published before December 31, 2002, the term will not expire before December 31, 2047.

For pre-1978 works still in their original or renewal term of copyright, the total term is extended to 95 years from the date that copyright was originally secured.

COPYRIGHT INFRINGEMENT

The term **infringement** is used when there is an unauthorized use of another's work. Copyright infringement is the tort in which a plaintiff attempts to demonstrate that the protected work has been copied without permission. Those individuals who violate copyright laws <u>and</u> do not have a defense under the fair use doctrine (discussed following) are subject to a court-ordered injunction, the collection and destruction of the infringing articles, payment to the true owner of monetary damages realized by the infringer, attorney's fees, and possible penalties for criminal infringement.

The following case exemplifies a battle involving copyright infringement.

---

[86] http://www.copyright.gov/circs/circ1.html#wnp.

[87] 17 U.S.C. § 302.

[88] http://web.missouri.edu/~ascwww/copyterm.html.

Mattel, Inc. v. Goldberger Doll Mfg. Co.

365 F.3d 133 (2d Cir. 2004)

OPINION: LEVAL, Circuit Judge:

Plaintiff Mattel, Inc., appeals from a grant of summary judgment by the United States District Court for the Southern District of New York (Rakoff, J.) in favor of the defendant Radio City Entertainment ("Radio City"). Mattel is the creator of, and owns copyrights in, the world famous "Barbie doll," whose current sales exceed $1 billion per year worldwide. Defendant Radio City operates the Radio City Music Hall theater in New York City, which features the widely renowned Rockettes chorus line. To celebrate the millennium, Radio City (together with its co-defendants) created a doll, which it named the "Rockettes 2000" doll. Mattel brought this suit alleging that in designing the Rockette doll, Radio City infringed its copyrights by copying facial features from two different Barbie dolls-"Neptune's Daughter Barbie," registered in 1992, and "CEO Barbie," registered in 1999. It is not reasonably subject to dispute that the Rockette doll is, in several respects including central features of the face, quite similar to the Barbie dolls.

The district court granted the defendant's motion for summary judgment. The court assumed for the purposes of the summary judgment motion that the defendant had copied the Rockette doll's eyes, nose, and mouth from Barbie. It concluded, however, "When it comes to something as common as a youthful, female doll, the unprotectible elements are legion, including, e.g., full faces; pert, upturned noses; bow lips; large, widely spaced eyes; and slim figures" (internal quotation marks omitted). Believing that copyright protection did not extend to Barbie's eyes, nose, and mouth, the court excluded similarity as to those features from the determination whether there was substantial similarity between plaintiff's and defendant's dolls. It concluded in comparing the other parts of the respective heads that there was no substantial similarity and therefore

entered summary judgment for the defendant. Mattel brought this appeal.

Discussion

The court's conclusion that the eyes, nose, and mouth of the registered Barbie faces were not protected by copyright was erroneous.

In explanation of this conclusion, the court relied on our 1966 opinion in *Ideal Toy Corp. v. Fab-Lu Ltd.*, 360 F.2d 1021 (1966). In that case, the district court had denied a preliminary injunction to one doll manufacturer who accused another of copying. On appeal, we found that the district court had not abused its discretion in finding that the plaintiff had failed to show a likelihood of success on the merits, and therefore affirmed. Comparing the dolls at issue, we observed that "similarities exist as to standard doll features such as the full faces; pert, upturned noses; bow lips; large, widely spaced eyes; and slim figures." *Id.* at 1023. On the other hand we noted that there were "distinct differences" as to the neck, hair style, chin structure, overall craftsmanship, and head design, the last of which was "the gravamen of [the] infringement claim." *Id.* We thus concluded that the district court had not abused its discretion in its assessment that the plaintiff had not shown a likelihood of success on the "substantial similarity" prong of its claim.

Although in *Ideal Toy* we described the facial features of the dolls then before us as "standard," we did not say that those facial features were not protected by copyright. To the contrary, we included those features in our comparison of the dolls, noting both the similarity in those features and the differences in others. When the case returned to the district court for trial, following our affirmance of the denial of the preliminary injunction, the defendant, which had previously denied copying, now admitted it. Judge Weinfeld then found infringement and imposed liability. In describing the respects in which the defendant's dolls were substantially similar to those of the plaintiff, i.e. the similarities that sustained the judgment of liability, Judge Weinfeld specifically noted the similarity in the "large widely spaced eyes, . . . pert upturned noses, [and] bow lips." *Id.* Judge Weinfeld clearly did not understand our prior ruling as suggesting that the features we described as standard were unprotected.

The proposition that standard or common features are not protected is inconsistent with copyright law. To merit protection from copying, a work need not be particularly novel or unusual. It need only have been "independently created" by the author and possess "some minimal degree of creativity." *Feist Publ'ns, Inc. v. Rural Tel. Serv. Co.,* 499 U.S. 340, 345, 113 L. Ed. 2d 358, 111 S. Ct. 1282 (1991). As the Supreme Court has explained, "requisite level of creativity is extremely low; even a slight amount will suffice. The vast majority of works make the grade quite easily, as they possess some creative spark, no matter how crude, humble or obvious it might be." *Id.* (internal quotation marks omitted). There are innumerable ways of making upturned noses, bow lips, and widely spaced eyes. Even if the record had shown that many dolls possess upturned noses, bow lips, and wide-spread eyes, it would not follow that each such doll-assuming it was independently created and not copied from others-would not enjoy protection from copying. We have often affirmed entitlement to copyright protection so long as the work was in fact created by its author, notwithstanding "lack of creativity," *Thomas Wilson & Co. v. Irving J. Dorfman Co.,* 433 F.2d 409, 411 (2d Cir. 1970) (lace design, although not a "work of art," possessed "more than the faint trace of originality required"), "lack of artistic merit," *Rushton v. Vitale,* 218 F.2d 434, 435–36 (2d Cir. 1955) (chimpanzee doll showed more than "merely trivial" originality), and absence of anything "strikingly unique or novel," *Alfred Bell & Co. v. Catalda Fine Arts, Inc.,* 191 F.2d 99, 102–03 (2d Cir. 1951) ("All that is needed . . . is that the author contributed something more than a merely trivial variation,

something recognizably his own. Originality in this context means little more than a prohibition of actual copying. No matter how poor artistically the author's addition, it is enough if it be his own.") (internal quotation marks omitted).

On Radio City's motion for summary judgment, we must view the evidence in the light most favorable to Mattel. Uncontradicted evidence shows the Barbie visage was independently created by Mattel. Nothing in the record gives reason to doubt that its creation involved whatever minimal creativity or originality is needed to satisfy the requirement of authorship. The evidence Mattel submitted is sufficient to justify copyright protection for the central expressive features of Barbie's face.

The protection that flows from such a copyright is, of course, quite limited. The copyright does not protect ideas; it protects only the author's particularized expression of the idea. *See Attia v. Soc'y of the N.Y. Hosp.,* 201 F.3d 50, 55 (2d Cir. 1999) (architect's copyright was not infringed by copying of his "concepts and ideas"); *Peter Pan Fabrics, Inc. v. Martin Weiner Corp.,* 274 F.2d 487, 489 (2d Cir. 1960) (L. Hand, J.) ("There can be no copyright in the 'ideas' disclosed but only in their 'expression.'"); *Nichols v. Universal Pictures Corp.,* 45 F.2d 119, 121 (2d Cir. 1930) (L. Hand, J.) (a playwright's copyright was not violated by a movie script on similar themes). Thus, Mattel's copyright in a doll visage with an upturned nose, bow lips, and widely spaced eyes will not prevent a competitor from making dolls with upturned noses, bow lips, and widely spaced eyes, even if the competitor has taken the idea from Mattel's example, so long as the competitor has not copied Mattel's particularized expression. An upturned nose, bow lips, and wide eyes are the "idea" of a certain type of doll face. That idea belongs not to Mattel but to the public domain. *See Mattel, Inc. v. Azrak-Hamway Int'l, Inc.,* 724 F.2d 357, 360 (2d Cir. 1983) (creator of a muscle-bound action doll has copyright in "particularized expression [such as] the decision to accentuate certain muscle groups relative to others" even though imitator is free to make dolls expressing same general idea). But

Mattel's copyright will protect its own particularized expression of that idea and bar a competitor from copying Mattel's realization of the Barbie features.

The distinction between the idea and the expression, although famously difficult to apply, is of great importance. One artist's version of a doll face with upturned nose, bow lips, and widely spaced eyes will be irresistible to an eight-year-old collector. Another artist's version, which to a grownup may look very like the first, will be a dud to the eight-year-old. The law of copyright guarantees to the designer of the successful version that, although its *idea* for a certain type of work is freely available to others who would imitate it, the designer cannot be deprived of the benefit of its successful design by others' copying it.

We can surmise that in the highly competitive, billion-dollar doll industry, getting the doll's face and expression exactly right is crucial to success. Mattel's evidence showed that it frequently produces revisions and adjustments to the particular realization of the Barbie face in an effort to continue to appeal to its young customers, as their tastes change with time. It is entitled by its copyright not to have its design copied by competitors.

We express no view as to whether the Rockette doll was copied from Barbie. However, because the district court erred in concluding that the defendant could freely copy the central facial features of the Barbie dolls without infringing Mattel's copyright, we vacate the grant of summary judgment and remand for trial.

Conclusion

The judgment is vacated and the case remanded for further proceedings.

Material has been adapted for this text. Used with the permission of LexisNexis.

FIRST SALE DOCTRINE

The Copyright Act of 1976 (§ 106) grants the owner of a copyright six exclusive rights: reproduction, preparation of derivative works, distribution, public performance, public display, and digital transmission performance. However, a copyright owner's right of distribution is limited by the **first sale doctrine** found in § 109(a). Copyright owners used to have the exclusive right to sell or distribute (vend) copies of their works. But copyright laws changed, and today the copyright owner's right to control the sale of a particular copy of a work ends after the owner's first transfer of that copy.

Thus, under the first sale doctrine, ownership after a legal purchase (i.e., a "first sale") of a physical copy of any copyrighted work, such as a book, compact disc, and so on, permits lending, reselling, disposing, or doing whatever the owner wishes to do with it, but it does not allow a complete copying of it. The growth of digital technology and the advent of the Internet and online communications, however, has caused considerable discord among courts as to whether this doctrine should apply to newer technologies such as CDs, DVDs, MP3s, and so on. In 2001, the U.S. Copyright Office reported to Congress on the impact of electronic commerce and technological protection measures on the first sale doctrine. The report concluded that it was too soon to say what the effects of e-commerce would be on this doctrine and recommended a "wait and see" approach. There is still uncertainty as to the first sale doctrine with respect to the Digital Millennium Copyright Act (DMCA), discussed later in this chapter.[89]

FAIR USE DOCTRINE

The **fair use doctrine**[90] allows someone to use a copyrighted work without fear of being sued. It is a defense to a claim of copyright infringement (17 U.S.C. § 107). As mentioned previously, one of the exclusive rights of a copyright holder is the right to authorize the preparation of these derivative works based upon the original copyrighted work. A derivative work is defined as one "based upon one or more preexisting works, such as translation, musical arrangement . . . or any other form in which a work may be recast, transformed, or adapted."

Section 107 provides four factors to be considered in determining whether the use of another work is, in fact, a fair use:

1. the purpose and character of the use, including whether such use is of commercial nature or is for nonprofit educational purposes;
2. the nature of the copyrighted work;
3. the amount and substantiality of the portion used in relation to the copyrighted work as a whole; and
4. the effect of the use upon the potential market for or value of the copyrighted work.

While the preceding may seem simple, litigation over the phrase "fair use" abounds because of the extremely large gray area in the law as to whether or not fair use may apply. There is no **bright-line test** in fair use cases. This has caused much debate as to what is (and is not) fair use in professional, academic, and other educational circles who use photocopies of articles and studies to enhance the learning environment at a seminar, conference, or in the classroom.[91] However, if a subsequent work causes the original owner to lose money or if the original owner is offended by the use, there is a greater likelihood of a lawsuit. When in doubt (or if possible), one may wish to contact the copyright holder for a permission to use the work.

FAIR USE CASES

As previously mentioned, one of the biggest concerns among students of copyright law is the lack of consistency in the application of the fair use doctrine.

---

[89] http://www.copyright.gov/reports/studies/dmca/dmca_study.html.
[90] Not to be confused with the fairness doctrine discussed in Chapter 5.
[91] *See American Geophysical Union v. Texaco Inc.*, 802 F. Supp. 1 (S.D.N.Y. 1992), for example.

Courts have created a system that allows for extreme unpredictability and opinion as to whether or not using another's work is a fair use. There is no bright-line test as to what is and what is not fair use, and each instance of potential fair use must be judged on its own merits. Numerous cases have attempted to better define what fair use is, and courts have differed upon its interpretation. (Notice the number of cases found at the end of this chapter).

Hustler Magazine, Inc. v. Moral Majority, Inc.

It was held to be a fair use when publisher Larry Flynt made disparaging statements in the form of a parodied advertisement about the Reverend Jerry Falwell in an edition of *Hustler* magazine (discussed in Chapter 4). Ironically, Falwell thereafter made several hundred thousand photocopies of the page with the advertisement and distributed them as part of a fund-raising effort for his organization's cause. Flynt was later sued by *Hustler* magazine for making the copies of the advertisement and distributing them. *Hustler* magazine alleged that the copies were not a fair use. The court sided with Falwell in *Hustler Magazine, Inc. v. Moral Majority, Inc.*, 606 F. Supp. 1526 (C.D. Cal. 1985).

Video Pipeline, Inc. v. Buena Vista Home Entertainment, Inc.

In *Video Pipeline, Inc. v. Buena Vista Home Entertainment, Inc.*, 192 F. Supp. 2d 321 (D.N.J. 2002), the District Court of New Jersey granted a preliminary injunction against Video Pipeline and prevented them from distributing promotional previews over the Internet made from copyrighted motion pictures. Buena Vista Entertainment originally granted a license to Video Pipeline for its use of some trailers in video stores, but Video Pipeline then broadcasted the trailers (i.e., short previews to draw a viewer's interest) over the Internet without permission. This allowed consumers to view them from home or work, rather than having to come into the store. The court determined that Video Pipeline's clip previews were derivative works under § 106(2) and found that Internet display was a public (as opposed to private) performance. Therefore, the court held that Video Pipeline had infringed the copyright and that it was not a fair use. An injunction was granted because the court felt that there would be irreparable harm if it did not and that the public interest would not be harmed by granting a preliminary injunction.

WORK FOR HIRE

Although the general rule is that the person who creates a work is its author, there is an exception to that principle called the **work for hire.** Sometimes abbreviated WMFH (work made for hire), this is a work prepared by an employee within the scope of his or her employment or a work specially ordered or **commissioned** in certain specified circumstances. When a work qualifies as a work made for hire, the employer or contractor is considered to be the author, rather than the person who came up with the idea or concept (the employee or subcontractor). Persons (writers, composers) who come up with ideas, lyrics, or scripts are often well paid by fixed or contingent fees in WMFH situations. The concept of work for hire is certainly vital to authors and writers in the publishing industry and to those who write lyrics and movie and television scripts. Even though they are compensated for their creative work, the work becomes the property of the employer.

FAIR USE AND HOME RECORDING

In *Sony Corp. of Am. v. Universal City Studios, Inc.*, 464 U.S. 417 (1984), also known as the Betamax case, the plaintiffs Universal Studios and Walt Disney Productions alleged that the ability of a home videotape recorder (VTR) to record programming from home violated federal copyright laws and constituted an infringement. Sony defended its product by asserting that a consumer had the absolute right to record programs at home for private use. In 1984, the Supreme Court held that the videotaping of programs from home was legal, in a 5–4 decision. Thus, consumers do not violate federal copyright law when they use videocassette recorders to tape television programs for their own use. Additionally, companies that manufacture or sell the VTRs (i.e., VCRs) do not violate the copyright law by making them available to the public.

FAIR USE AND MUSIC

It was held to be a fair use when the rap group 2 Live Crew borrowed the opening musical tag and the words (but not the melody) from the first line of the song "Pretty Woman" ("Oh, pretty woman, walking down the street"). The rest of the lyrics and the music were different. *See Campbell v. Acuff-Rose Music*, 510 U.S. 569 (1994). As a general rule, parodying more than a few lines of a song lyric is unlikely to be excused as a fair use. Comedian performers such as Weird Al Yankovic, who earn a living by humorously modifying hit songs, seek permission of the songwriters before recording their parodies.

COPYRIGHT LICENSE

One way to generate money from a copyrighted work is to license the material to someone else so that they can use it for their own purposes, such as on Internet sites, in catalogs and books, and so forth. A license is the formal grant of the right to use copyrighted material by the author (licensor) and usually is conditioned upon payment of a fee or a royalty by the licensee. Use of computer software and interactive computer games usually requires a license. In 1998, Congress passed the Fairness In Music Licensing Act.[92] The Act was opposed vehemently by ASCAP, BMI, and all other composer and performing rights organizations. The result of the Act is easier access to music by smaller businesses and their patrons, while at the same time reducing potential profits for songwriters, performers, and these licensing agents.

This Act exempts smaller businesses that perform background music only from radio, television, cable, and satellite sources and that do not transmit beyond their establishments (and do not charge admission) from licensing fees. Thus, all restaurants, bars, and so forth containing less than 3,750 square feet and all nonfood service and beverage establishments containing less than 2,000 square feet are exempt from paying for a license under this Act. Those businesses where square footage exceeds these limits are still exempt, if they use six or fewer speakers with no more than four speakers in any one room or, where they use audio/visual equipment, if they use no more than four televisions with no more than one television in each room, with no television having a diagonal screen size greater than 55 inches, while meeting the preceding speaker restrictions.

DE MINIMIS DEFENSE

In some cases, the amount of material copied is so small (**de minimis**) that a court may permit it without even conducting a fair use analysis. For example, in the motion picture *Seven*, several copyrighted photographs appeared in the film, prompting the copyright owner of the photographs to sue the producer of the movie. The court held that the photographs "appear fleetingly and are obscured, severely out of focus, and virtually unidentifiable" and permitted the use of the photographs as de minimis, and a fair use analysis was not required.[93]

EDUCATIONAL COURSE PACKS

Educational course packs consist of selected readings from books, magazines, or journals. They are prepared for specific college courses by an instructor who takes the material to a copy shop that copies and then sells the educational course packs to the students. They are not illegal per se, but there have been numerous lawsuits or settlements involving the use of course packets in the educational setting to determine whether there is a fair use or not.

---

[92] 17 U.S.C. § 110(5)(B).
[93] *Sandoval v. New Line Cinema Corp.*, 973 F. Supp. 409 (S.D.N.Y. 1997), 147 F.3d 215 (2d Cir. 1998).

Student reviewing books.
Photoedit

In *Basic Books, Inc. v. Kinko's Graphics Corp.*, 758 F. Supp. 1522 (S.D.N.Y. 1991), a Kinko's copy center was held to be infringing copyrights when it photocopied book chapters for sale to students as educational course packs for their university classes. Since the copying was done by Kinko's, the copying was for commercial purposes as opposed to educational purposes. Additionally, 5 to 25 percent of original books were being copied, and the court found that to be excessive and that the educational course packs competed directly with the potential sales of the original books.

Netpaks

One recent instance involved **Netpaks,** a term used to describe educational course packs that utilize Adobe pdf files rather than paper. In 2004, a settlement was reached with copy shops Abel's Copies and Speedway Copying with the Copyright Clearance Center, which was used as a licensing agent for publishing giants Elsevier, John Wiley & Sons, Pearson Education, Princeton University Press, Sage Publications, and the University of Chicago Press. The copy shops had been sued for false advertising as well by using "academic-use waivers," leading the public to believe that copyright fees do not have to be paid.[94]

PUBLIC DOMAIN

One may use works deemed to be in the **public domain** without permission and without infringement concerns. Public domain contains all works that for

---

[94] *See* http://www.copyright.com/News/PressRelease2004February10.asp and http://www.copyright.com/News/PressRelease2004March30.asp.

whatever reason are not protected by copyright. As such, they are free for all to use without permission. Works in the public domain include characteristics such as: a lost copyright, an expired copyright, owned or authored by the federal government, specifically granted to public domain, or just noncopyrightable. Some of the frequently cited examples of public domain works include classics such as *Hamlet* and other plays by William Shakespeare, and Beethoven's *Fifth Symphony.*

In the United States, for example, the public domain now includes works published before January 1, 1923, and also works published between 1923 and 1978 that did not contain a valid copyright notice or works published between 1923 and 1978 for which the copyright was not renewed. Public domain also includes works authored by employees of the federal government or works that the copyright owner has freely granted to the public domain. Because of the duration of copyright protection established in the 1976 revision of the U.S. Copyright Act, no works published after January 1, 1978, will pass into the public domain until at least the year 2048.

TRADEMARK

A trademark is a word (or **brand name**[95]), logo or package design, or a combination of the two. A trademark is used by a **merchant** or a manufacturer to identify and distinguish their goods from others. The word **trademark** is commonly used broadly to describe all types of marks that are protected under the law: trademarks, service marks, certification marks, and collective marks. A trademark serves to identify the source of goods and services. Words, names, sounds, colors, scents, symbols, and shapes (including combinations) have been held to be legitimate trademarks.[96]

Whereas the Constitution contemplates copyrights and patents by giving Congress the power to enact laws to "promote the Progress of Science and useful Arts" by granting exclusive rights in "Writings and Discoveries" to "Authors and Inventors," (U.S. Const. art. 1, § 8, cl. 8), there is no mention of trademarks in the Constitution. A trademark registered under the federal **Lanham Act** (the Trademark Act) has nationwide protection.[97] There are only two sources of trademark protection under the Lanham Act: the U.S. Patent and Trademark Office (USPTO) opinions and decisions of judges overseeing litigation over allegations of trademark violations.

---

[95] A brand name identifies goods.
[96] For color, *see Qualitex Co. v. Jacobson Prods. Co.*, 514 U.S. 159 (1995). As long as the public associates the color of the product with the source of goods in question, it could be protected by trademark. For sounds, certificates of registration have been issued for the MGM lion's roar and the distinctive NBC chimes.
[97] 15 U.S.C. § 1051 *et seq.*

THE LANHAM ACT

Similar to copyright infringement issues, trademarks are governed by the Lanham Act, sometimes just referred to as the Trademark Act. Section 43(a) of the Lanham Act (15 U.S.C. § 1125(a)) creates a federal cause of action for a false designation of origin or other misleading information used in connection with the sale of a good or service, including misleading advertising. The Lanham Act was designed to prevent trademark infringement and prohibits uses of trademarks, trade names, and trade dress that are likely to cause confusion about the source of a product or service. Infringement law protects consumers from being misled by the use of infringing marks and also protects producers from unfair practices by an imitating competitor. Under the Lanham Act, an owner of a trademark applies to the Patent and Trademark Office (PTO) to register the trademark. Under state law, trademarks are protected as part of the common law of unfair competition. Generally speaking, registration is not required at the state level.

FUNCTIONS

Trademarks perform four functions that are protected by courts:

1. To identify one seller's goods and distinguish them from goods sold by others;
2. To signify that all goods bearing the trademark come from or are controlled by a single, albeit anonymous, source;
3. To signify that all goods bearing the trademark are of an equal level of quality; and
4. To serve as a prime instrument in advertising and selling the goods.

Trademark rights stem from use of the trademark, not from the registration process. In fact, rights in a trademark may exist in common law without a registration. Similarly, the ownership of a registration does not guarantee that there does not exist a prior, unregistered user whose rights may be superior to those of the registrant.

LIKELIHOOD OF CONFUSION

The key issue in determining infringement is whether there is a likelihood of confusion caused by the alleged infringer's use of the owner's trademark (or something similar). Courts look to factors such as (1) strength of the trademark;

(2) degree of similarity between the two trademarks; (3) proximity of the products being sold; (4) likelihood the plaintiff will bridge the gap between the products being sold; (5) evidence of actual confusion; (6) good faith of the defendant in using the trademark; (7) quality of the defendant's trademark; and (8) sophistication of the relevant consumer market.[98]

CATEGORIES OF TRADEMARKS

There are several categories of trademarks in the law (all found at 15 U.S.C. § 1127) including **fanciful trademarks** or **arbitrary trademarks** (no meaning before becoming a trademark), **suggestive trademarks** (allude to product quality), **descriptive trademarks** (describe the goods or services), and **generic trademarks** (describe a whole class of products). If a trademark is too descriptive, the U.S. PTO may refuse to register it. Frequent examples of the different types of trademarks include:

Fanciful trademarks: Fanciful trademarks are easy to register and have no obvious association with a good or service. They are essentially "made up."

Yahoo, Ketchup, Xerox, Kodak, Starbucks, Verizon, Reebok

Arbitrary trademarks: Similar to fanciful marks and also easy to register, they do not suggest the goods or services being provided or offered, but the word used actually has a common meaning.

Scrabble, Hard Rock (café), Apple (computers), Blackberry (handheld device)

Suggestive trademarks: Suggestive trademarks are also relatively easy to register, but they suggest (i.e., create in the consumer's mind and/or imagination) an association between their name and that of the good or service.

WordPerfect, 7-Eleven, Caterpillar, Coppertone, Greyhound

Descriptive trademarks: These trademarks actually describe the goods or services they represent.

University of Kentucky, Frosted Mini Wheats, Vision Center

Generic trademarks: These are the weakest of the trademarks and most difficult (most likely because it will be rejected by the U.S. PTO) to register. In essence, generic trademarks do not exist per se, and a company cannot control the name.

Car Wash, Super Glue, Personal Computer, Milk

---

[98]*Polaroid Corp. v. Polarad Elecs. Corp.*, 287 F.2d 492 (2d Cir. 1961).

The McDonalds' Service mark.
© James Leynse/CORBIS SABA.

SERVICE MARKS

A **service mark** is any word, name, symbol, device, or any combination used, or intended to be used, in commerce, to identify and distinguish the services of one provider from services provided by others, and to indicate the source of the services. Service marks are similar to trademarks except that they apply to services rather than goods. The same word or symbol can be both a trademark and a service mark. Examples of service marks include McDonald's (for food service), Federal Express, Amtrak, American Airlines, H. & R. Block, and Marriott. Titles, character names, and other distinctive features of radio or television programs may also be registered as service marks, such as the television show *Survivor.*

CERTIFICATION MARK

A **certification mark** is any word, name, symbol, device, or any combination used, or intended to be used, in commerce with the owner's permission by someone other than its owner, to certify regional or other geographic origin, material, mode of manufacture, quality, accuracy, or other characteristics of someone's goods or services, or that the work or labor on the goods or services was performed by members of a union or other organization. A certification mark certifies that goods and/or services of another meet certain very specific standards of quality. In order to obtain and maintain a certification mark, the certifier must set forth very specific standards that the products it certifies must meet, and the certifier must provide that anyone who makes that category of product may apply for certification. The certifier never uses the mark on any products of its own, it merely licenses others to do so. An example of a certification mark includes the Good Housekeeping Seal of Approval, which is placed on kitchen products.

Collective Mark

A **collective mark** is a trademark or service mark used, or intended to be used, in commerce, by the members of a cooperative, an association, or other collective group or organization, including a mark which indicates membership in a union, an association, or other organization. Collective marks are different from ordinary trademarks because they are used by all of the members of a group, rather than one specific company or individual. Examples of collective marks include the ABA (American Bar Association), AARP, and UAW.

NAMES AS TRADEMARKS

Things can become protectable trademarks in two ways: by being inherently distinctive or by becoming distinctive. **Surnames** (last names) and first names can be protected as trademarks only upon proof that they have acquired **distinctiveness** and **secondary meaning** through use. For instance, if the public has come to associate the name with goods or services that come from a particular source, then the name functions as a trademark and is entitled to protection (such as Ford Motor Company). However, there is generally considered to be a qualified right of an individual to use his or her own name, even if that name has been trademarked by someone else. Courts may require disclaimers or other measures to prevent confusion on the part of the public in such situations.

ACQUIRING A TRADEMARK

In the United States, trademark rights are acquired through use of the trademark on or in connection with the goods or services. Trademark rights are not created by the act of registration alone. A registration will not be issued until the trademark has been used in commerce. There are two types of federal registrations: Principal Register[99] registrations and registrations on the Supplemental Register.[100] Both principal and supplemental registrations confer upon the registrant valuable benefits, including establishing the basis of a lawsuit.

---

[99] The Principal Register is the primary register in the United States. Only trademarks that are distinctive or have acquired distinctiveness may be registered on the Principal Register.
[100] The Supplemental Register is reserved for designations which are deemed to be capable of serving a trademark function, but which do not yet do so, such as descriptive marks and marks that are primarily merely surnames.

The owner may use the ® registration notice, and the mark will be located by trademark examiners who conduct trademark searches.

Prior to obtaining a trademark, one might want to conduct a trademark availability search. A **trademark availability search** is a reasonable and prudent step prior to the adoption of a trademark because it may reveal that use of the trademark would infringe upon a third party's rights. Similarly, performing a trademark availability search may reveal existing trademark registrations that might bar a registration of the proposed trademark. Once a trademark has been acquired, a plaintiff may recover triple damages for an infringement.

TRADEMARK PROHIBITIONS

Section 2 of the Lanham Act (15 U.S.C. § 1052) prohibits registration of a trademark in numerous ways including that which: Consists of or comprises immoral, deceptive or scandalous matter; Consists of matter which may disparage or falsely suggest a connection with persons, living or dead, institutions, beliefs or national symbols or bring them into contempt or disrepute; Consists of or comprises the flag or coat of arms or other insignia of the United States, or any State or municipality, or any foreign nation; Consists of or comprises a name, portrait, or signature of a living individual without his or her consent; Consists of or comprises the name, portrait or signature of a deceased President of the United States during the life of his widow without the consent of the widow; Is confusingly similar to a prior existing mark; Is primarily descriptive or deceptively **misdescriptive** of the goods or services; Is primarily geographically descriptive or deceptively misdescriptive of the origin of the goods or services; Is primarily merely a surname; Comprises matter that, as a whole, is functional.

TRADEMARK RENEWAL

Trademark registrations that were issued or were renewed on or after November 16, 1989 must be renewed every ten years. The renewal application is due on the tenth anniversary of registration. The initial renewal period for registrations that were issued before November 16, 1989 is twenty years, with subsequent renewals due every ten years. Pursuant to § 8 of the Lanham Act, 15 U.S.C. § 1058, the owner of a trademark registration is required to periodically submit a declaration attesting to and demonstrating that the trademark is still in use in commerce. The **declaration of use** must initially be submitted between the fifth and sixth anniversaries of registration and subsequently with or during the same registration year as each renewal.

TRADEMARK NOTICE SYMBOL: ®

The ® symbol may only be used in connection with trademarks that are federally registered with the U.S. PTO and only when used in connection with the goods or services covered by the registration. The symbol should be displayed next to the word, logo, or drawing which is registered at least once in all advertising and promotional materials. In addition or as an alternative, the notation **Marca Registrada** or Registered in the U.S. Patent Office (abbreviated "Reg. U.S. Pat. & Tm. Off.") may also be used. Similarly, a legend may be used stating that the words or logo are "a registered trademark of . . . " or simply using a ® followed by the name of the corporate owner. Failure to include some indication that the trademark is registered may result in a denial of certain damage awards in an infringement action.

TRADEMARK NOTICE SYMBOL: ™ AND ^SM

The ™ and ^SM symbols are symbols that a trademark owner may use to indicate that a term is considered a trademark ™ or service mark ^(SM) when the term has not been registered. Use of these symbols puts third parties on notice that trademark rights are being claimed. The symbols should be used in the same manner that an ® is used for registered trademarks. The ® symbol can be used only in connection with registered trademarks. There are no legal requirements governing the use of the ™ or ^SM symbols. Anyone claiming common law trademark rights may use these symbols.

LOSING TRADEMARK RIGHTS

Unlike copyrights or patents, which have a limited life, trademarks can exist indefinitely (in theory). However, under certain circumstances, trademarks can be lost. A trademark is lost when it ceases to identify the origin or quality of the goods or services on which it is used. The most common ways to lose a trademark are through (1) abandonment; (2) using the trademark in a generic manner; (3) licensing the trademark indiscriminately; and (4) failing to prosecute infringers. In general, nonuse for three consecutive years creates a presumption of abandonment.

Generic Names

A trademark can be lost if it becomes a **generic name.** That is, the trademark is used to describe a product or service, rather than to identify its source and quality. A trademark owner may avoid widespread generic use by:

1. Using it as an adjective as opposed to a noun (i.e., "Kleenex tissue" not "a kleenex");
2. Capitalizing the trademark or otherwise setting it apart from surrounding text; or
3. Using it in conjunction with the term "brand" (i.e., "Scotch brand tape").

When a trademark owner itself uses the trademark as a generic term or allows others to do so, rights are lost, and it becomes available for use by all. Common examples of trademarks that have become generic through descriptive or generic use include trampoline, escalator, thermos, and aspirin.

TRADE SECRETS

A **trade secret** consists of any formula, pattern, device, or compilation of information which is used in one's business and which gives an opportunity to obtain an advantage over competitors who do not know or use it. All rights in a trade secret cease to exist once the trade secret is released to the public.

Trade secret law is primarily state law and provides protection for valuable commercial information that is maintained in secrecy. Theft or publication of an otherwise trade secret allows a cause of action against anyone who reveals such otherwise secret information in breach of a contractual agreement with the trade secret owner. An action for the tort of **misappropriation of a trade secret** is the usual claim.

Trade secrets are different from patents, copyrights, and trademarks. While patents and copyrights require you to disclose your information in the application process, trade secrets require one to keep the information secret. Trade secrets remain valid only as long as no one else has discovered the information independently, the information has not been made public (by employees, for example), and the secret is not discovered by working backward from the original product or process. If the trade secret is revealed in violation of a *nondisclosure agreement,* one can obtain an injunction and sue for damages in a breach of contract action. Nondisclosure agreements are often referred to as **confidentiality agreements** and/or **covenants not to compete.**[101]

Coca-Cola

Pearson Education/PH College

One of the most cited examples of a trade secret is the formula for the soft-drink Coca-Cola. The formula, also referred to as "Merchandise 7X," is known to only a few people involved with that company. These individuals have signed nondisclosure agreements. Interestingly, one could not buy a Coke in India because Indian law required that trade secret information be disclosed, but that law changed in the early 1990s and the product is sold there today.

---

[101] Also sometimes referred to as no compete clauses or noncompete agreements.

UNIFORM TRADE SECRETS ACT

The Uniform Trade Secrets Act (UTSA) was promulgated by the National Conference of Commissioners on Uniform State Laws, similar to other acts such as the Uniform Athlete Agents Act (discussed in Chapter 2). The UTSA has been adopted totally or in part by forty-four state jurisdictions. Also, the Economic Espionage Act (EEA) of 1996 creates a federal crime for theft of a trade secret and encompasses foreign actions as well.[102]

POLICING MARKS

While a trademark can be licensed to another by the owner, the owner must exercise control over the quality of the licensee's goods. Therefore, in order for the owner to license its trademark and keep ownership of it at the same time, the arrangement calls for certain responsibilities. Merely licensing the trademark to another without controlling the quality of the licensee's goods will result in the loss of ownership over the trademark. Such a license is a license in gross or a naked license. Quality control by the licensor can take various forms.

The following are standard provisions that impose some responsibility on the owner of the trademark to maintain control: (1) the owner shall have the right to control the quality of the licensee's products; (2) written specific guidelines or standards must be followed by the licensee; (3) the owner shall have the right to inspect the licensee's premises and production processes; (4) the licensee shall provide product samples to the licensor according to a specific schedule; and (5) the owner shall have the right to disapprove packaging and advertising by the licensee.

UNFAIR COMPETITION

Unfair competition is the creation of a false impression as to the source, origin, sponsorship, or endorsement of products or services without the use of a trademark. There is a federal version of unfair competition embodied in § 43(a) of the Lanham Act, 15 U.S.C. § 1125(a), which prohibits the use, with goods or services, of a false designation of origin or a false or misleading description or representation of fact. A claim of unfair competition may arise from the same facts as a claim for trademark infringement, if a trademark is used in a way that creates a false designation of origin or a false or misleading description or representation of fact.

The following was a real-world complaint involving copyright and trademark issues. The case settled in 2004.

---

[102] 18 U.S.C. §§ 1831–1839.

John B. Koegel (JK-4762)
The Koegel Group LLP
161 Avenue of the Americas
New York, New York 10013
(212) 255-7744

Attorneys for Plaintiff
Samuel Bourdin

UNITED STATES DISTRICT COURT
SOUTHERN DISTRICT OF NEW YORK

SAMUEL BOURDIN,
Plaintiff,

- against -

MADONNA CICCONE p/k/a MADONNA, WARNER BROS. RECORDS INC., WB MUSIC CORP., WEBO GIRL PUBLISHING INC., WARNER CHAPPELL MUSIC INC., MTV NETWORKS, JEAN-BAPTISTE MONDINO and BANDITS PRODUCTIONS,
Defendants.

03 Civ._____ (_)
COMPLAINT
JURY TRIAL DEMANDED

Plaintiff, SAMUEL BOURDIN, by his attorneys, The Koegel Group LLP, as and for his complaint states as follows:

NATURE OF THE ACTION

1.   Guy Bourdin (1928–1991) was a groundbreaking image-maker who had a profoundly influential impact on fashion photography. Most familiar are the works published in French Vogue from the mid-1950s through to the late 1980s which had the greatest impact in the decade of the 1970s. His photographic works are widely recognized and most recently a major exhibition of his work was presented by the Victoria and Albert Museum in London, England. A number of the works relevant to this action were on display in that exhibition. Defendants have produced, displayed, distributed, exploited and in various other ways utilized certain "music videos" and possibly other products which are unlawfully derived from copyright protected works created by Guy Bourdin. This action seeks a permanent injunction, an accounting, and an award of damages and attorneys fees under the Copyright Act of 1976, 17 U.S.C. § 101 *et seq.* and the Lanham Act, 15 U.S.C. § 1051 *et seq.* arising from the Defendants' unlawful commercial piracy.

JURISDICTION AND VENUE

2.   This is an action for copyright infringement arising under the Copyright Act of 1976, 17 U.S.C. § 101 *et seq.* and for violation of the Lanham Act, 15 U.S.C. § 1051 *et seq.* This Court has jurisdiction of the subject matter of this action under 28 U.S.C. § 1338.

3.   Venue is proper in this district under 28 U.S.C. §§ 1391(b), 1391(c) and 1400 in that a substantial part of the events giving rise to the claims occurred in this judicial district, Defendants or their agents may be found in this district and each of the Defendants is subject to personal jurisdiction in this district.

PARTIES

4.   Plaintiff, Samuel Bourdin, is the son of Guy Bourdin. Upon his death, Guy Bourdin's copyright rights to his artistic works passed to the Plaintiff and therefore, since 1991 the Plaintiff has been and still is the sole proprietor of all right, title and interest in and to the copyright rights for the photographic and videographic works of Guy Bourdin.

5.   Upon information and belief, Defendant, Madonna Ciccone, professionally known and hereinafter referred to as "Madonna," wrote and performed a song entitled "Hollywood" (hereinafter the "Song"), and in connection with the Song participated in the production of videos for the Song which infringe Plaintiff's copyright rights and which violate the Lanham Act. Hereinafter all of the infringing videos will be collectively referred to as the "Hollywood Videos."

6.   Upon information and belief, Defendant Jean-Baptiste Mondino conceived of and directed the Hollywood Videos. Defendant Jean-Baptiste Mondino is located *inter alia* at 45 Rue Lévis, 75017 Paris, France.

7.   Upon information and belief, Defendant Bandits Productions produced the infringing Hollywood Videos. Defendant Bandits Productions is located *inter alia* at 34 bis, avenue Bernard Palissy, 92210 Saint Cloud, France.

8.   Upon information and belief, Defendant Warner Bros. Records Inc. is a Delaware corporation and is engaged in promoting the career of Madonna, including but not limited to financing the production of the infringing Hollywood Videos. Defendant Warner Bros. Records Inc. is located *inter alia* at 3300 Warner Boulevard, Burbank, California.

9.   Upon information and belief, Defendants Webo Girl Publishing Inc., WB Music Corp., and Warner Chappell Music Inc. are the publishers/administrators of the Song and authorized the use of the Song in the infringing Hollywood Videos. As the publishers/administrators, these defendants directly benefit from any increased interest in the Song which the Hollywood Videos engender. Defendants Webo Girl Publishing Inc. and WB Music Corp. are located *inter alia* at 15800 N.W. 48th Avenue, Miami, Florida. Warner Chappell Music Inc. is located *inter alia* at 10585 Santa Monica Boulevard, Los Angeles, California.

10.   Upon information and belief, Defendant MTV Networks has exhibited the Hollywood Videos on its television station numerous times and has benefited directly from this widespread exhibition of the infringing Hollywood Videos. MTV Networks, a division of Viacom International Inc., is a Delaware corporation and is located *inter alia* at 1515 Broadway, New York, New York.

11.   Upon information and belief, all Defendants transact or have transacted business within this judicial district, derive substantial revenues from goods and services sold or rendered in this judicial district, and are subject to the jurisdiction of this Court.

THE BOURDIN WORKS

12.   Guy Bourdin is recognized as one of the most influential fashion photographers in history. He is said to be the first fashion photographer to reject the "product shot" in favor of a complex narrative through highly constructed compositions in strange and unusual settings.

13.   This action involves a number of highly expressionistic works created by Guy Bourdin in both photographic and videographic form and as of the date of this complaint Plaintiff is able to identify at least eleven works which have been infringed. Those eleven works are set forth in Exhibit A hereto and will be hereinafter referred to collectively as the "Bourdin Works."

14.   With regard to all of the photographic and videographic works which are relevant to this action, Guy Bourdin and the Plaintiff have complied in all respects with the laws governing copyright, and have secured the exclusive right and privilege in and to the copyright rights in the Bourdin Works.

15.   Since Guy Bourdin's death in 1991, the Bourdin Works have been published under authority or license granted by Samuel Bourdin and have been printed, published, and/or displayed in conformity with the provisions of the Copyright Act of the United States and all other laws governing copyrights.

16.   Pursuant to 17 U.S.C. § 411(a) and 17 U.S.C. § 101, the Bourdin Works are not "United States works" and registration is not a prerequisite to the commencement of this action. Nonetheless, seven of the eleven works set forth in Exhibit A were registered with the United States Copyright Office by the Plaintiff as of March 19, 2002 (Registration # TX5–511–596).

17.   Each of the Bourdin Works is an original work of art and each is subject to protection under the Copyright Laws of the United States pursuant to 17 U.S.C § 104.

18.   Plaintiff is currently and at relevant times has been the sole proprietor of all relevant rights in and to the Bourdin Works.

COUNT I

COPYRIGHT INFRINGEMENT

19.   Upon information and belief, the photographic and videographic works of Guy Bourdin are well known to Defendant Madonna, Defendant Jean-Baptiste Mondino, and Defendant Bandits Productions. Guy Bourdin works generally and all of the photographic Bourdin Works were prominently published well in advance of the production of the Hollywood Videos including, *inter alia,* in two books solely on Guy Bourdin: i) *Exhibit A - Guy Bourdin,* by Fernando Delgado and Samuel Bourdin, © 2001, published by Bullfinch Press and ii) *Guy Bourdin,* edited by Charlotte Cotton and Shelly Verthime, © 2003, published by the Victoria and Albert Museum, London. Given the prominence of Guy Bourdin and his works, it is likely that the other Defendants were aware of Bourdin's photography and of the interest that the Defendants Madonna, Mondino, and Bandits Productions would be likely to have in his work.

20.   The Hollywood Videos are structured as a montage of various scenes. An overwhelming number of all of the scenes in the Hollywood Videos are overtly and substantially derived from the Bourdin Works. In each instance the innovative artistic expression created by Guy Bourdin in each Bourdin Work has been substantially plagiarized. Factors such as composition, background, wardrobe, lighting, narrative, camera angle, décor, and objects depicted are strikingly similar. The aesthetic appeal of the infringing Hollywood Videos is identical to the Bourdin Works and none of the variations between the Bourdin Works and the Hollywood Videos distract from the duplicate overall expression conveyed to the viewer. Both qualitatively and quantitatively the Hollywood Videos are strikingly and substantially similar to the Bourdin Works.

21.   Exhibit A, which sets forth eleven copyright protected works by Guy Bourdin, also sets forth eleven frames or stills from the Hollywood Videos which demonstrate the extensive

appropriation of the Bourdin Works. There are very few scenes or sequences in the Hollywood Videos that are not distinctly derived from the Bourdin Works.

22.   Accordingly, it would appear that the unlawful appropriation of the Bourdin Works and other infringing acts of the Defendants were willful, wanton, deliberate, and/or intentional.

23.   The ongoing piracy of the Bourdin Works and the exploitation of this piracy committed jointly and/or vicariously by the Defendants was without the consent or the permission of the Plaintiff and constitutes a continuing infringement of Plaintiff's copyright rights.

24.   Upon information and belief, Defendants are now engaged in publishing, displaying, distributing, exploiting and in various other ways utilizing the Hollywood Videos in commerce throughout the world including within this judicial district.

25.   Plaintiff has no adequate remedy at law and is suffering irreparable harm and damage as a result of the acts of the Defendants in an amount thus far not determined.

26.   Plaintiff is entitled to recover from Defendants the damages sustained by the Plaintiff as a result of Defendant's wrongful acts in an amount which Plaintiff is presently unable to ascertain.

27.   Plaintiff is further entitled to recover from Defendants the gains, profits or advantages Defendants have obtained as result of the wrongful acts in an amount which Plaintiff is also presently unable to ascertain.

COUNT II

LANHAM ACT INFRINGEMENT

28.   With knowledge of the strong reputation of Guy Bourdin and his work among the public and especially for the unique and distinctive style and content of his works, Defendants have produced, displayed, distributed and otherwise exploited the Hollywood Videos which are confusingly similar to the works of Guy Bourdin.

29.   The Defendants' copying of significant, recognizable features and trade dress from the oeuvre of groundbreaking artistic works created by Guy Bourdin is causing and is likely to continue to cause confusion as to the source of the Hollywood Videos and, therefore, constitutes a false designation of origin of the Hollywood Videos.

30.   Defendants' piracy constitutes a false designation of origin and a false description or representation in violation of Section 43(a) of the Lanham Act, 15 U.S.C. § 1125(a). The unique and innovative perspective consistently and boldly conveyed by Guy Bourdin in his photographic and videographic works constitutes a distinct and recognizable signature of Bourdin authorship. Hence, the use by the Defendants' of Bourdin's characteristic expressions creates a likelihood of confusion as to the source of authorship of the Hollywood Videos.

31.   By reason of the foregoing, Plaintiff is being damaged by the Defendants' use of the Hollywood Videos and Plaintiff will continue to be so damaged unless and until the Defendants are enjoined from any further use of the Hollywood Videos in any direct or derivative manner whatsoever.

32.   Plaintiff is being and will continue to be irreparably injured by and has suffered and will continue to suffer irreparable damage from the acts of the Defendant and Plaintiff has no adequate remedy at law for the continuing harm.

33. In connection with the widespread display of the Hollywood Videos in interstate and foreign commerce, Defendants have in effect represented the Hollywood Videos to have been authorized by the Plaintiff. In fact, the use of Bourdin Works in the Hollywood Videos was not authorized by the Plaintiff.

34. Defendant has used a false description or representation in connection with the Hollywood Videos in violation of 15 U.S.C. § 1125(a), by reason of which Plaintiff has been damaged in an amount to be proved at trial and is entitled to injunctive relief.

WHEREFORE, Plaintiff prays that judgment be entered against the Defendants, jointly and severally, as follows:

A. That Defendants have infringed Plaintiff's copyright rights in violation of 17 U.S.C. § 501.

B. That Defendants have infringed Plaintiff's rights under the Lanham Act.

C. That Defendants be required to account for and relinquish to Plaintiff any and all gains, profits, and advantages derived by Defendants through their infringement of the Bourdin Works, which presently cannot be ascertained.

D. That Defendants be ordered to pay Plaintiff such damages as Plaintiff has sustained or incurred as a consequence of Defendants' copyright infringement and Lanham Act violation.

E. That upon Plaintiff's election, Defendants be ordered to pay such statutory damages as shall be just pursuant to 17 U.S.C. § 504.

F. That Defendants pay to Plaintiff the costs and reasonable expenses incurred in this action, including reasonable attorneys' fees, as provided by law, 17 U.S.C. § 505 and 15 U.S.C. § 1117.

G. That Defendants pay treble damages pursuant to 15 U.S.C. § 1117(b).

H. That, because of the willful, wanton, deliberate and intentional nature of the infringement of Plaintiff's proprietary rights and the passing off of the Hollywood Videos as obviously derived from the work of Guy Bourdin, Plaintiff receive an award of punitive or exemplary damages.

I. That Defendants, along with any agents and servants, and all those persons in active concert or participation with each or any of them, be permanently restrained and enjoined from directly or indirectly infringing Plaintiff's copyright rights in any manner, and from exhibiting, causing, contributing to, or participating in, the unauthorized exhibition or distribution in any manner of the Hollywood Videos or any component part thereof.

J. That Defendants, along with any agents and servants, and all those persons in active concert or participation with each or any of them, be permanently restrained and enjoined from engaging in any conduct that tends falsely to represent that, or is likely to confuse, mislead, or deceive the public that the Hollywood Videos originated from Guy Bourdin, or that the Hollywood Videos have been sponsored, approved or licensed by Plaintiff or are in some way connected or affiliated with Plaintiff and/or his father.

K. That Defendants, their officers, directors, principals, agents, servants, employees, successors and assigns and all those in active concert or participation with them be permanently enjoined and restrained from manufacturing, producing, distributing, circulating, selling, advertising, promoting or displaying anything bearing any simulation, reproduction, derivative adaptation, counterfeit, copy or colorable imitation of any artistic works created by Guy Bourdin including the Hollywood Videos.

   L. That Defendants be required to deliver up for destruction all forms and copies of the Hollywood Videos and all promotional and advertising material and other unauthorized matter which picture, reproduce or utilize any infringing part of the Hollywood Videos.

   M. That Plaintiff be granted such other and further relief as is warranted and justified by the pleadings and the evidence.

JURY TRIAL DEMANDED

   35. Plaintiff hereby demands a trial by jury.

Dated: New York, New York
    September 25, 2003

                By: _____
                John B. Koegel (JK-4762)

                THE KOEGEL GROUP LLP
                Attorneys for Plaintiff
                161 Avenue of the Americas
                New York, New York 10013
                Tel: (212) 255-7744
                Fax: (212) 337-1103

Reprinted with permission from John B. Koegel, Esq.

■ THE FEDERAL TRADEMARK DILUTION ACT OF 1995

The Federal Trademark Dilution Act of 1995, effective January 1996, protects famous trademarks from uses that dilute their distinctiveness.[103] A **dilution** is the lessening of the capacity of a famous trademark to identify and distinguish goods or services. Unlike an action for infringement, a dilution does not focus on whether or not consumers would be confused. Dilution focuses on conduct that weakens the distinctiveness associated with the trademark. This new definition replaced older court interpretations which held that dilution can occur by **blurring** or **tarnishment.**

  Blurring is the unauthorized use of a trademark on dissimilar products or services that causes the trademark to no longer be a unique identifier of the trademark owner's goods. Tarnishment is when the trademark becomes linked with poor quality, unsavory, or unwholesome goods or services. At least twenty-five states also have laws that prohibit trademark dilution. Also, both registered

---

[103] 15 U.S.C. § 1125.

and unregistered trademarks may be protected under this act. Examples of violations of the Act, for example, would include Dupont shoes, Buick aspirin, and Kodak pianos.[104]

TRADE DRESS

The term **trade dress,** similar to trademark, represents the total image of a product as opposed to a product's individual parts or aspects. Trade dress protection may deal with the totality of features such as size, shape, color, color combinations, texture, or graphics. This could involve the design, shape, and appearance of a product, including its packaging as long as it is distinctive.

PATENTS

A **patent** for an invention is the formal grant of a property right to the **inventor,** issued only by the federal government's Patent and Trademark Office. The term of a new patent is generally twenty years from the date on which the application for the patent was filed in the United States. The right conferred by the patent grant is the right to exclude others from making, using, offering for sale, or selling the invention in the United States or "importing" the invention into the United States. When one applies for a patent, the phrase "patent applied for" or "patent pending" may be used on articles or processes and in advertisements.

In order to be patentable, the invention must be novel, not obvious, and it must serve a useful purpose. Patent laws focus on excluding others from using the invention without permission. This is often found in special photographic and musical equipment, electronics, and computer-based software and technology (such as streaming video). Patents go by various names, including utility patents, design patents, and plant patents. A **mask work** is in effect the blueprint of a semiconductor chip, and the holder of the rights to a mask work has the exclusive right to reproduce the mask work and import and distribute semiconductors embodying the mask work.

MADRID PROTOCOL

The 1996 Madrid Agreement **(Madrid Protocol)** is a treaty that facilitates the international registration and maintenance (extensions) of trademarks. The

---

[104] *See* H.R. 1295, July 19, 1995.

United States is now a member. This system gives a trademark owner the possibility to have his trademark protected in several countries by simply filing one application with a single office, in one language, and with one set of fees in one currency. An international registration produces the same effect as an application for registration of the trademark made in each of the countries designated by the applicant. The international registration lasts ten years from the date of the international registration and is renewable for subsequent periods of twenty years.

COUNTERFEITING

A particularly egregious form of trademark infringement is called **counterfeiting.**[105] Counterfeiting consists of the use of a substantially identical copy of a registered trademark on the same goods or services for which the original trademark is registered. There are special remedies for counterfeiting including **ex parte** seizure orders, triple damages, and statutory damages.

PIRACY AND INTELLECTUAL PROPERTY

Piracy is the unauthorized copying of copyrighted, trademarked, or patented materials for personal use or for resale. Piracy and **pirates** have been the bane of the entertainment industry for many years, but advances in computer technology have made it easier than ever to copy original material. As a result, there has been a considerable amount of lost revenue and profit in the entertainment industry. This has become particularly true with regard to CDs, DVDs, MP3s, photographs, computer games and software, and even full-length movies. Internet shareware dot-com Web sites such as KaZaA, Grokster, Morpheus, iMesh, and eDonkey create a virtual world of music file-sharing and sharing of movies from DVD burners. In 2003, Napster began a pay-for-play service to allow users to pick and choose what songs they want to download for a small fee as a deterrent to piracy.

Attempts to Control Piracy

The Recording Industry Association of America (RIAA) developed copyright technology that enables copyright holders and the RIAA to track unauthorized digital copies over the Internet. These systems use embedded signaling, also referred to as watermarking, technology with codes containing unique identification numbers for tracking purposes (by companies such as BigChampagne which tracks Internet file-sharing). Also, "spoofs" which make a high-pitched screeching sound have been added to hinder the P2P (peer-to-peer) downloading process.

---

[105] Lanham Act, § 32(d), 15 U.S.C. § 1116(d).

DIGITAL MILLENNIUM COPYRIGHT ACT

On October 12, 1998 (17 U.S.C. § 512) the U.S. Congress passed the **Digital Millennium Copyright Act (DMCA).**[106] The Act is designed to implement the treaties signed in 1996 at the World Intellectual Property Organization (WIPO) Geneva conference. The DMCA was supported by the software and entertainment industries. The DMCA had as its primary purpose the goal of updating U.S. copyright laws to deal with the digital information age. Major points of the DMCA include, but are not limited to:

1. Makes it a crime to circumvent antipiracy measures found in commercial software and to manufacture, sell, or distribute code-cracking devices used to copy software.
2. Limits Internet service providers (ISPs) from copyright infringement liability for simply transmitting information over the Internet. However, the same ISPs must remove material from users' Web sites that appear to constitute copyright infringement.
3. Provides exemptions from anticircumvention provisions for nonprofit libraries, archives, and educational institutions with some exceptions. It also limits the liability of colleges and universities for copyright infringement by faculty members or graduate students when the schools act as an ISP.
4. Requires that webcasters pay licensing fees to record companies.

ANTI-CYBERSQUATTING REGULATION

In 1999, Congress enacted the **Anti-Cybersquatting Consumer Protection Act (ACPA)** which prohibits certain types of cybersquatting. The statute amended the Lanham Act to make it a type of trademark infringement if a domain name containing a distinctive or famous trademark is registered in bad faith. **Cybersquatting** is the act of registering an Internet address, such as a company name or the name of a famous individual, with the intent of selling it (i.e., extortion) to who the real world would perceive to be the "rightful owner of that address." Cybersquatting began in the mid-1990s. Individuals are referred to as **cybersquatters.**

Typosquatting

Typosquatting is a form of cybersquatting. An owner speculates that someone will misspell an otherwise legitimate domain name and purchases that variation on the name in order to make a profit. For example, registering the domain name yahooo.com (yahoo.com—notice the extra "o") with the hope that someone making a typo will get to that Web site unexpectedly based on the probability

---

[106] Pub. L. No. 105-305, 112 Stat. 2860 (1998).

that a certain number of Internet users will mistype the name of a Web site's URL (Uniform Resource Locator such as http:) when surfing the Internet.

■ WIPO

The World Intellectual Property Organization (WIPO) is an intergovernmental organization based in Geneva, Switzerland, responsible for the promotion of the protection of intellectual rights throughout the world. It is one of the sixteen specialized agencies of the United Nations system of organizations. According to its own Web site, WIPO seeks to harmonize national intellectual property legislation and procedures, provide services for international applications for industrial property rights, exchange intellectual property information, provide legal and technical assistance to developing and other countries, facilitate the resolution of private intellectual property disputes, and marshal information technology as a tool for storing, accessing, and using valuable intellectual property information.[107] Examples of major treaties with which WIPO has been involved include the WIPO Copyright Treaty and the WIPO Performance and Phonograms Treaty, both adopted in late 1996. WIPO is often called upon to settle disputes involving registered Internet domain names.

■ ICANN

The Internet Corporation for Assigned Names and Numbers (ICANN) has established a uniform domain name dispute resolution policy that is applicable to all registrars of .com, .net, and .org domain names. Binding arbitration is the method for dispute resolution in the event a settlement cannot be reached involving the Domain Name System (DNS) such as .com, .org, .biz, and so on. The Uniform Domain Name Dispute Resolution Policy (UDNDRP) lists the rules governing domain name disputes.

Panavision.com

In *Panavision Int'l, L.P. v. Toeppen*, 141 F.3d 1316 (9th Cir. 1998), Panavision sued Toeppen for trademark dilution for registering the domain name Panavision.com. Toeppen had also registered Internet domain names for Delta Airlines, Neiman Marcus, Eddie Bauer, Lufthansa, and more than 100 other popular celebrity and business names. The Ninth Circuit Court of Appeals found that Toeppen had devised this scheme in order to extort money from Panavision—in this instance, $13,000. The court ruled in favor of Panavision. Still, the court of appeals stated that a commercial activity was required to obtain jurisdiction over a cybersquatter, and theoretically, a cybersquatter could

---

[107] http://www.wipo.int/about-wipo/en/gib.htm#P52_8261.

simply register a domain name and wait for an offer for the name, rather than commercially market it as Dennis Toeppen did.[108] This decision created some confusion for the legal community because had Toeppen actually had a commercial activity, the decision might have been different. However, times changed, and the law has changed as well (such as the enactment of the DMCA).

Peterframpton.com

Musician Peter Frampton challenged the registration by a legitimate company named Frampton Enterprises, Inc. over the use of the registered Internet domain name peterframpton.com. Peter Frampton owned a federal registration for the trademark Peter Frampton[109] to use in connection with live musical performances, audio recordings, and audio production and recording studio services. He claimed to have used the trademark in connection with musical equipment, videos, clothing, and numerous forms of commercial merchandise.

Still, the president of Frampton Enterprises, Lyle Peter Frampton, asserted that he also was commonly known as "Peter Frampton" and that his business, a sales and marketing development company, used the domain name peterframpton.com solely to identify him as the company president and not to sell merchandise related to the challenger Peter Frampton. However, the peterframpton.com Web site also offered "Entertainment!" and contained two logos that read "Peter Frampton," copied from Peter Frampton's own Frampton.com Web site, among other similar Web site content.

An arbitrator ordered transfer of the challenged domain name based on his review of the facts alleged by both parties and his conclusion that Lyle Peter Frampton had no rights in or legitimate interest to the domain name and had registered and used the domain name in bad faith.[110] The arbitrator noted that the name Peter Frampton was one of the most internationally famous and acclaimed names in pop music for the past thirty years and was likely to be recognized by a "significant proportion of the world's population" as a source for music and other entertainment services. Thus, it is now established that individuals do not have exclusive rights to use their surnames (i.e., last names) as Internet domain names when such use is likely to confuse or mislead consumers as to the source or sponsor of the Web sites associated with those domain names.

Millertime.com

In *Miller Brewing Co. v. Miller Family*, NAF (National Arbitration Forum) Case FA 104177 (Apr. 15, 2002), an arbitrator found that individuals who had registered and used their surnames as all or part of a domain name with knowledge that the domain name was the well-known trademark of a third party were <u>not</u> entitled to keep the domain names. The arbitrator ordered the domain names

---

[108] There are numerous other examples of cybersquatting involving celebrities including Michael Crichton, Madonna, Julia Roberts, Celine Dion, and countless others. *See* J. Anschell & J. Lucas, *What's in a Name: Dealing with Cybersquatting*, 21 Ent. & Sports L. 3 (2003).

[109] He also owned frampton.com but not peterframpton.com at the time.

[110] Case No. D2002–0141 found at http://arbiter.wipo.int/domains/decisions/html/2002/d2002-0141.html.

transferred by their registrants to the trademark owners (Miller Brewing Company) who had brought the domain name claim.

The Miller Brewing Company, owner of a federal registration and several pending applications for the trademark Miller Time, challenged the registration by a family with the surname "Miller" of the domain name Millertime.com. The Miller family registered the domain name Millertime.com in 1995. The arbitrator found that the Miller family's use of the Millertime.com domain name was not in good faith because at that time the Millers implicitly knew of Miller Brewing's popular Miller Time trademark and intentionally used the fame of the trademark to attract consumers to the goods and services offered on the Web site.[111]

The case *Time Warner Entertainment Company, L.P., and Hanna-Barbera Productions, Inc. v. John Zuccarini, Cupcake Patrol, and The Cupcake Patrol*, WIPO Case No. D2001–0184 follows:

WIPO Arbitration and Mediation Center

ADMINISTRATIVE PANEL DECISION

Time Warner Entertainment Company, L.P., and Hanna-Barbera Productions, Inc. v.
John Zuccarini, Cupcake Patrol, and The Cupcake Patrol

Case No. D2001-0184

1.   The Parties

The Complainants are: Time Warner Entertainment Company, L.P., a limited partnership organized under the laws of the state of Delaware, with its principal place of business in New York, New York, USA., and Hanna-Barbera Productions, Inc., a division of Time Warner Entertainment Company, L.P., incorporated in Delaware with its principal place of business at 15303 Ventura Boulevard, Suite 1400, Sherman Oaks, California 91403, USA. The Complainants are represented in this proceeding by Dennis L. Wilson, Esq., of Keats McFarland & Wilson LLP, 9720 Wilshire Boulevard, Penthouse Suite, Beverly Hills, California 90212, USA.

The Respondents are John Zuccarini, Cupcake Patrol and The Cupcake Patrol, whose address is 957 Bristol Pike, Suite D-6, Analusia, PA 19020, USA. The Respondents are represented by Christopher A. Grillo,

Esq., Law Office of Christopher A. Grillo, 1 East Broward Blvd, 7th Floor, Fort Lauderdale, Florida 33304, USA.

2.   The Domain Names and Registrar

The domain names in dispute are: "harypotter.com", "looneytoones.com", and "scobydoo.com".

The registrar for the disputed domain names is: Core Internet Council of Registrars (CORE), WTC II, 29 route de Pre-Bois, CH-1215, Geneva, Switzerland 1215 CH.

3.   Procedural History

This dispute is to be resolved in accordance with the Uniform Policy for Domain Name Dispute Resolution (the Policy) and Rules (the Rules) approved by the Internet Corporation for Assigned Names and

---

[111] *See* http://www.arbforum.com/domains/decisions/104177.htm.

Numbers (ICANN) on October 24, 1999, and the World Intellectual Property Organization Arbitration and Mediation Center's Supplemental Rules for Uniform Domain Name Dispute Resolution (the Center, the Supplemental Rules).

The Complaint was filed on February 2, 2001. On February 5, 2001, the Center requested that the registrar CORE check and report back on the registrant for the domain names "harypotter.com", "looneytoones.com" and "scobydoo.com". On February 9, 2001, CORE reported to the Center that the registrants were the Respondents, i.e., John Zuccarini, Cupcake Patrol and The Cupcake Patrol.

On February 15, 2001, the Center pointed out to the Complainants that they had specified a three person panel while paying the fee for a single member panel and asked that the Complainants clarify their preference. On the same day the Complainants stated their preference for a single member panel.

On February 20, 2001, the Center forwarded a copy of the Complaint to the Respondents by registered mail and by e-mail and this proceeding officially began. Respondents' Response was filed with the Center on March 10, 2001.

The Administrative Panel submitted a Declaration of Impartiality and Independence on March 29, 2001, and the Center appointed the Panel on March 29, 2001. The Panel finds the Center has adhered to the Policy and the Rules in administering this Case.

This Decision is due by April 11, 2001.

4.   Factual Background

The Complainants own the Looney Tunes family of cartoon characters that include Bugs Bunny, Wile E. Coyote and Daffy Duck. The Complainants have licensed the use of their Looney Tunes characters for the manufacture and sale of a variety of goods such as clothing and toys. The Respondents registered the disputed domain name "looneytoones.com" on February 18, 2000.

Scooby-Doo is the name of a cartoon great dane dog created by the Complainants' Hanna-Barbera division in 1969. Complainants state that as a TV show Scooby-Doo ran some eighteen years, and that it continues to be broadcast in syndication. The name has been licensed by the Complainants for a variety of merchandising. The Respondents registered the disputed domain name "scobydoo.com" on November 10, 1999.

Harry Potter is a central character in a series of books written by the Scottish writer J. K. Rowling. Ms. Rowling has licensed, *inter alia,* movie and merchandising rights to the Complainants, which is the Complainants' basis for contesting the "harypotter.com" (registered on April 13, 2000) domain name in this proceeding.

It does not appear from the record that the Complainants ever tried to convince the Respondents to turn the disputed domain names over to the Complainants. Instead, the Complainants have had recourse directly to this proceeding.

5.   The Parties' Contentions

Complainants' Contentions

— The Looney Tunes characters are famous because they have appeared in over one hundred copyrighted cartoons, television specials, and animated motion pictures produced and distributed by the Complainants.

— The Complainants own many trademarks and other intellectual property based on the Looney Tunes characters.

— All legal rights in the Scooby-Doo character are owned by the Complainant Hanna-Barbera, which is in turn a division of the Complainant Time Warner Entertainment Company, L.P.

— The Complainants have registered trademarks for a number of articles based on the character Scooby-Doo. As a result of the commercial exploitation of the Scooby-Doo trademark, the Complainants have developed tremendous good will in the Scooby-Doo trademark, which has become famous among children and adults in the United States and internationally.

— Pursuant to the exercise of an option in an agreement dated June 1, 1998, the Complainants obtained all rights in all books of the Harry Potter series, including audio visual, copyright, trademark and related good will.

— The Harry Potter character and books are world famous.

— The Complainants have registered a number of trademarks based on the Harry Potter books and characters.

— The Respondents have never been licensed by Complainants to use the Complainants' trademarks, and the Respondents have no legitimate rights to Complainants' trademarks.

— The disputed domain names are identical to Complainants' trademarks Harry Potter, Looney Tunes and Scooby-Doo.

— The Respondents have engaged in a practice of registering misspellings of trademarks and famous domain names which has been labeled "typosquatting."

— All of Respondents' infringing domain names show the viewer additional pop-up windows containing websites and advertising for third parties selling various goods and services, including online games, credit card services, auction services and much more besides. The Respondents are trying to derive benefit from the public's being misled to believe the Complainants are connected with or are endorsing the Respondents' products.

Respondents' Contentions

— This proceeding violates the United States Constitution since it involves a taking of property without due process. Therefore, WIPO lacks the authority to hear or issue a ruling in this proceeding.

— What the Respondents did or did not do with respect to other cases is completely irrelevant.

— The Respondents use typosquatting as a form of free enterprise. Typosquatting is not cybersquatting and, in relation to the Internet, is not trademark infringement.

— The Complainants claim that a misspelling of a name is ipso facto confusingly similar to the correctly spelled name. Who is to say that was not the word the Respondents were trying to spell? The Panel should eschew the imbecility of outlawing sites that are spelled similarly to each other.

— U.S. trademark violations can only be brought for names that are identical to each other, not merely similar to each other.

— The Respondents do not compete with the Complainants' line of products and services, and therefore there is no possibility of confusion.

6. Discussion and Findings

In order for a Complainant to prevail and have a disputed domain name transferred to it, the Complainant must prove the following (the Policy, paragraph 4(a)(i-iii):

— the domain name is identical or confusingly similar to a trademark or service mark in which the Complainant has rights; and

— the Respondent has no rights or legitimate interests in respect of the domain name; and

— the domain name was registered and is being used in bad faith.

Identical or Confusingly Similar

Regarding the Looney Tunes mark, the Complainants have produced copies of United States federal principal register mark registrations that include no. 2419405 for "Looney Tunes WB" registered on January 9, 2001, for use in selling toys and sporting goods; also registration no. 2257588 for "Looney Tunes WB" dated June 29, 1999, for men's, women's and children's clothing (Complaint Exhibit C). The Respondents do not contest that the Looney Tunes cartoon characters were created some seventy years ago.

As to Complainants' trademark rights in the Scooby-Doo cartoon character, the Respondents do not contest that the cartoon character has been appearing on television since 1969. In addition, the Complainants offer other products using this mark and have a number of U.S. federal principal mark register registrations including: service mark registration no. 1579527 dated January 23, 1990 for offering entertainment services (Complaint Exhibit E).

As for the Harry Potter books, with which the Panel is quite familiar, the Complainants have shown at Exhibits H and I that the titles and characters of the Harry Potter books are being used to market a variety of merchandise.

Complaint Exhibits F and G show the record-setting sales of the Harry Potter book series.

The Panel is quite convinced that the Complainants have rights in the marks Harry Potter, Looney Tunes and Scooby-Doo. In registering the disputed domain names "harypotter.com", "looneytoones.com", and "scobydoo.com", the Respondents have deliberately misspelled the marks, but only slightly: the original mark remains almost intact, both visually, phonetically and orthographically. Thus the disputed domain names are confusingly similar to the Complainants' marks in violation of the Policy at 4a(i). The Respondents urge the Panel to consider only identical registrations as being proscribed by the Policy (the Response p. 6), but the Panel rejects this because it is incompatible with the plain language of the Policy at 4a(i): "your domain name is identical *or confusingly similar* (our emphasis) to a trademark or service mark in which the complainant has rights; . . . ."

Legitimate Rights or Interests

The Complainants assert (Complaint p. 11) that the Respondents "have never been licensed by Complainants . . . to use the Complainants' trademarks, and Respondents have no legitimate rights to Complainants' trademarks."

The Respondents, Response p. 7, state: "Respondent does not compete with Complainant. It does not offer similar services or products." However, the Respondents never get around to telling the Panel just what their line of business or use of the disputed domain names is. And the Panel itself is able to see no legitimate right or interest on Respondent's behalf as called for under the Policy at 4a(ii). At one point the Respondents say they use "typosquatting as a form of free enterprise," but the Panel does not find this is a legitimate right or interest under the Policy.

Registered and Used in Bad Faith

Although the Panel finds the Complainants have proved beyond doubt that the Respondents make it a practice to register domain names that infringe famous trademarks, the Panel agrees with the Respondents this is not really pertinent here since it does not appear to the Panel the Respondents were attempting to register the disputed domain names to keep the Complainants from registering them (the Policy at 4b(ii).

However, as the Complaint shows (pp. 13-14), the Respondents are using the disputed domain names to show large volumes of advertising to the web traffic the disputed domain names attract. In the Panel's view, the disputed domain names attract traffic because they contain the good will of the Complainants' famous marks; as the Respondents intend, humans and search engines confuse the Respondents for the Complainants. This violates the Policy at 4b(iv) and leads the Panel to find the Respondents registered and were using the disputed domain names in bad faith (See *Encyclopaedia Britannica, Inc. v. Zuccarini,* ICANN/WIPO Case No. D2000-0330, June 7, 2000; and *Yahoo!Inc. v. Cupcakes,* ICANN/WIPO Case No. D2000-0777, October 2, 2000).

7.   Decision

The Panel finds the disputed domain names are confusingly similar to the Complainants' marks and that the Respondents have no legitimate rights or interests in the disputed names. In addition, the Panel finds the Respondents registered and were using the disputed domain names in bad faith.

Therefore, per the Policy 4(i) and Rule (15), the Panel orders that the disputed domain names, "harypotter.com", "looneytoones.com" and "scobydoo.com" be transferred from the Respondents, John Zuccarini, Cupcake Patrol and The Cupcake Patrol to the Complainants, Time Warner Entertainment Company, L.P., and Hanna-Barbera Productions, Inc.

Dennis A. Foster
Presiding Panelist

Date: April 11, 2001

Decision was rendered in a case administered by the World Intellectual Property Organization (WIPO) Arbitration and Mediation Center. Administrative Panel Decision provided by the World Intellectual Property Organization (WIPO). The Secretariat of WIPO assumes no liability or responsibility with regard to the transformation of this data.

CHAPTER SUMMARY

Protecting the rights of creative individuals is paramount in the entertainment industry, whether in publishing, television, developing computer software, writing lyrics, and so forth. The study of intellectual property therefore requires a basic understanding of copyrights, patents, and trademarks and their relationship to entertainment law. Ultimately, securing rights of intellectual property is financially related, and property holders can generate significant revenues by licensing their ideas to prevent an infringement.

Since the advent of the Internet and advances in technology have occurred so quickly, the entertainment industry has faced a dilemma: while exposure to artists, musicians, authors, and others is easier than before, stealing songs, videos, and games by "pirates" has occurred almost simultaneously. Technology such as CD and DVD burners and freeware and shareware Web sites on the Internet has created a virtual world that threatens the traditional models of revenue generation by the entertainment industry. This has been costly to the industry as a whole.

Modifications to the Lanham Act, including the Digital Millennium Copyright Act and the Anti-cybersquatting Consumer Protection Act, have proved to be legitimate legislative attempts to counterattack a world filled with cybersquatters and typosquatters. Only time will tell if these laws can be effectively enforced.

CHAPTER TERMS

Anti-Cybersquatting
    Consumer
    Protection Act
    (ACPA)
Arbitrary trademark
Blogging
Blurring
Brand name
Bright-line test
Certification mark
Collective Mark
Commissioned
Confidentiality
    agreement
Copyright
Counterfeiting
Covenant not to
    compete

Cybersquatters
Cybersquatting
Declaration of use
De minimus defense
Derivative work
Descriptive trademark
Digit Millennium
    Copyright Act
    (DMCA)
Dilution
Distinctiveness
Ex parte
Fair use doctrine
Fanciful trademark
File-sharers
First sale doctrine
Generic name

Generic trademark
Infringement
Intangible property
Intellectual property
Inventor
Lanham Act
Madrid Protocol
Marca Registrada
Mask work
Merchant
Misappropriation of a
    trade secret
Misdescriptive
Netpaks
Nondisclosure
    agreement
Patent

Pirates
Public domain
Secondary meaning
Service mark
Suggestive trademark
Surname
Tangible
Tarnishment
Trade dress
Trade secret
Trademark
Trademark availability
    search
Typosquatting
Unfair competition
Work for hire

ADDITIONAL CASES

ABKCO Music, Inc. v. Harrisongs Music, 722 F.2d 988 (2d Cir. 1983)

Aimster Copyright Litigation, In re, 334 F.3d 643 (7th Cir. 2003)

American Geophysical Union v. Texaco, Inc., 37 F.3d 881 (2d Cir. 1994)

Apple Computer, Inc. v. Microsoft Corp., 35 F.3d 1435 (9th Cir. 1994), *cert. denied*, 513 U.S. 1184 (1995).

Billy-Bob Teeth, Inc. v. Novelty, Inc., 329 F.3d 586 (7th Cir. 2003)

Bleistein v. Donaldson Lithographing Co., 188 U.S. 239 (1903)

Bright Tunes Music Corp. v. Harrisongs Music, 420 F. Supp. 177 (S.D.N.Y. 1976)

Caesars World, Inc. v. Milanian, 247 F. Supp. 2d 1171 (D. Nev. 2003)

Campbell v. Acuff-Rose Music, Inc., 510 U.S. 569 (1994)

Castle Rock Entertainment, Inc. v. Carol Publ. Group, 150 F.3d 132 (2d Cir. 1998)

Ciccone, p/k/a Madonna v. Parist, WIPO Case No. D2000–0847

Crichton v. Alberta Hot Rods, WIPO Case No. D2002–0872

Cybersell Inc. v. Cybersell Inc., 130 F.3d 414 (9th Cir. 1998)

Dastar Corp. v. Twentieth Century Fox Film Corp., 123 S. Ct. 2041 (2003)

Denker v. Uhry, 820 F. Supp. 722 (S.D.N.Y. 1992)

DirecTV, Inc. v. Karpinsky, 274 F. Supp. 2d 918 (E.D. Mich. 2003)

Dr. Seuss Enterprises, L.P. v. Penguin Books USA, Inc., 109 F.3d 1394 (9th Cir. 1997)

DVD Copy Control Ass'n, Inc. v. Bunner, 4 Cal. Rptr. 3d 69 (2003)

Eldred v. Ashcroft, 537 U.S. 186 (2003)

Elsmere Music, Inc. v. National Broadcasting Co., 482 F. Supp. 741 (S.D.N.Y.), *aff'd*, 632 F.2d 252 (2d Cir. 1980)

ETW Corp. v. Jireh Publishing, Inc., 332 F.3d 915 (6th Cir. 2003)

Fantasy, Inc. v. Fogerty, 664 F. Supp. 1345 (N.D. Cal. 1987)

Federation Internationale de Football Association v. Nike, Inc., 2003 U.S. Dist. LEXIS 17536 (D.D.C. 2003)

Feist Publications v. Rural Telephone Service, 499 U.S. 340 (1991)

Fisher v. Dees, 794 F.2d 432 (9th Cir. 1986)

Fisher-Price, Inc. v. Safety 1st, Inc., 279 F. Supp. 2d 530 (D. Del. 2003)

Frasier v. Adams-Sandler, Inc., 94 F.3d 129 (4th Cir. 1996)

Harper & Row v. Nation Enters., 471 U.S. 539 (1985)

Keep Thomson Governor Comm. v. Citizens for Gallen Comm., 457 F. Supp. 957 (D.N.H. 1978)

Kellogg Co. v. Toucan Golf, Inc., 337 F.3d 616 (6th Cir. 2003)

Kelly v. Arriba Soft Corp., 280 F.3d 934 (9th Cir. 2002)

Lamothe v. Atlantic Recording Corp., 847 F.2d 1403 (9th Cir. 1988)

Leibovitz v. Paramount Pictures Corp., 137 F.3d 109 (2d Cir. 1998)

Litchfield v. Spielberg, 736 F.2d 1352 (9th Cir. 1984)

Los Angeles News Service v. KCAL-TV Channel 9, 108 F.3d 1119 (9th Cir. 1997)

Lotus Dev. Corp. v. Borland International, Inc., 49 F.3d 807 (1st Cir. 1995)

Mattel, Inc. v. Walking Mountain Prods., 353 F.3d 792 (9th Cir. 2003)

Metro-Goldwyn-Mayer Studios, Inc. v. Grokster, Ltd., 259 F. Supp. 2d 1029 (C.D. Cal. 2003)

Michaels v. Internet Entertainment Group, 5 F. Supp. 2d 823 (C.D. Cal. 1998)

Miller v. Universal City Studios, Inc., 650 F.2d 1365 (5th Cir. 1981)

MiTek Holdings, Inc. v. Arce Engineering Co., 89 F.3d 1548 (11th Cir. 1996)

Monster Communications, Inc. v. Turner Broadcasting Sys. Inc., 935 F. Supp. 490 (S.D.N.Y. 1996)

Moseley v. Secret Catalogue, Inc. 537 U.S. 418 (2003)

National Basketball Assn v. Motorola, Inc., 105 F.3d 841 (2d Cir. 1997)

Playboy Enters. Inc. v. Frena, 839 F. Supp. 1552 (M.D. Fla. 1993)

Pro-Football, Inc. v. Harjo, 2003 U.S. Dist. LEXIS 17180, 2003 WL 22246923 (D.C. Cir. Sept. 30, 2003)

Recording Industry Association of America, Inc. v. Verizon Internet Services, Inc., 351 F.3d 1229 (D.D.C. 2003)

Religious Technology Center v. Lerma, 40 U.S.P.Q. 2d 1569 (E.D. Va. 1996)

Religious Technology Center v. Pagliarina, 908 F. Supp. 1353 (E.D. Va. 1995)

Ringgold v. Black Entertainment Television, Inc., 126 F.3d 70 (2d Cir. 1997)

Rosemont Enterprises, Inc. v. Random House, Inc., 366 F.2d 303 (2d Cir. 1966)

Roy Export Co. Estab. of Vaduz v. Columbia Broadcasting Sys., Inc., 672 F.2d 1095 (2d Cir. 1982)

Salinger v. Random House, 811 F.2d 90 (2d Cir. 1987)

Sargent Fletcher, Inc. v. Able Corp., 3 Cal. Rptr. 3d 279 (2003)

Sega Enterprises Ltd. v. Accolade, Inc., 977 F.2d 1510 (9th Cir. 1992)

Selle v. Gibb, 741 F.2d 896 (7th 1984)

Sheldon v. Metro-Goldwyn Pictures Corp., 81 F.2d 49 (2d Cir. 1936)

Shields v. Zuccarini, 254 F.3d 476 (3d Cir. 2001)

Springsteen v. Burgar, WIPO Case No. D2000–1532

Steinberg v. Columbia Pictures Industries, Inc., 663 F. Supp. 706 (S.D.N.Y. 1987)

Three Boys Music v. Bolton, 212 F.3d 477 (9th Cir. 2000)

Ticketmaster Corp. v. Tickets.Com, Inc., 2003 U.S. Dist. LEXIS 6483 2003 WL 21406289 (C.D. Cal. Mar. 7, 2003)

Toys R Us, Inc. v. Step Two, S.A., 318 F.3d 446 (3d Cir. 2003)

Twentieth Century Music Corp. v. Aiken, 442 U.S. 151 (1975)

Twin Peaks v. Publications Int'l, Ltd., 996 F.2d 1366 (2d Cir. 1993)

Universal City Studios v. Sony Corp. of America, 464 U.S. 417 (1984)

Virtual Works Inc. v. Volkswagen of Am. Inc., 238 F.3d 264 (4th Cir. 2001)

Walker v. DC Comics, 67 Fed. Appx. 736 (3d Cir. 2003)

Walt Disney Productions v. Air Pirates, 581 F.2d 751 (9th Cir. 1978)

Wham-O, Inc. v. Paramount Pictures Corp., 286 F. Supp. 2d 1841 (N.D. Cal. 2003)

Wright v. Warner Books, Inc., 953 F.2d 731 (2d Cir. 1991)

REVIEW QUESTIONS

1. What is intellectual property? What are the various categories of intellectual property?
2. What is the fair use doctrine?
3. What is a license and why is this important in entertainment?
4. What are the differences between copyrights, patents, and trademarks?
5. What is a collective mark?
6. What does trade dress mean?
7. Why and how is piracy a concern in the entertainment industry?
8. What is the Digital Millennium Copyright Act of 1998?
9. What are cybersquatting and typosquatting?
10. What is the role of WIPO?

REFERENCES FOR ADDITIONAL RESEARCH AND DISCUSSION

Adeyanju, Y., *The Sonny Bono Copyright Term Extension Act: A Violation of Progress and Promotion of the Arts*, 2003 Syracuse L. & Tech. J. 6 (2003).

Badgley, R.A., *Improving ICANN in Ten Easy Steps: Ten Suggestions for ICANN to Improve Its Anti-cybersquatting Arbitration System*, 2001 U. Ill. J.L. Tech. & Pol'y 109 (2001).

Dolmayan, R., *The Fair Use Doctrine: How Does It Apply to New Technology That May Impinge on Financial Interests of the Copyright Owners?*, 4 J. Legal Advoc. & Prac. 186 (2002).

Farid, N., *Not in My Library: Eldred v. Ashcroft and the Demise of the Public Domain*, 5 Tul. J. Tech. & Intell. Prop. 1 (2003).

Gifford, C.N., *The Sonny Bono Copyright Term Extension Act*, 30 U. Mem. L. Rev. 363 (2000).

Mousley, M.C., *Peer-to-Peer Combat: The Entertainment Industry's Arsenal in Its War on Digital Piracy*, 48 Vill. L. Rev. 667 (2003).

Schulz, M., *Part Two: Marks, Their Protectability and Registrability: Why Different "Marks" in the Lanham Act?*, 12 J. Contemp. Legal Issues 39 (2001).

LEGAL ISSUES IN LIVE PERFORMANCES

AFTER STUDYING THIS CHAPTER YOU SHOULD BE ABLE TO:

1. Discuss the purpose and role of the Actors' Equity Association (AEA).
2. Define the term Equity Waiver Agreement.
3. Discuss the various live awards productions in the entertainment industry.
4. Identify legal issues or concerns related to art displays.
5. Explain why some beauty pageants are regulated by consumer protection laws.
6. Define the term ticket scalping.
7. Discuss live exotic dancing and its relationship to zoning laws.
8. Explain the phrase secondary effects/impacts with regard to regulating adult business establishments.
9. Discuss issues related to seating and live performances.
10. Discuss bona fide occupational qualification (BFOQ) and its relation to live entertainment and entertainment generally.

INTRODUCTION

The goal of this chapter is to introduce the student to various legal and business terms and issues in the "live" entertainment industry, including adult entertainment concerns. Whether one attends the local comedy club, waits outside in a long line for open seating at a favorite concert, or simply watches a live performance from one's own living room broadcast on television (and now via the Internet), performances by artists, musicians, actors, and others give fans a chance to see their favorite performances in an unedited setting. Live performances, however, in addition to being the oldest form of the performing arts, are usually creatures of a contractual relationship between buyers and sellers of services. Ticket sales and regulation of scalping and counterfeit tickets are considered as well.

LIVE THEATRE

Whether one is a **for-profit** enterprise or a **not-for-profit** venture, understanding live theatre issues requires an appreciation for the difference in the various settings.[112] The term **theatre** or **live theatre** has varied meanings and certainly has its own language.[113] Most people think of a Broadway play or musical, the name given to the thirty-something professional theatres near Times Square in New York City. If a live performance appears **on-Broadway,** it usually means that it has the highest production costs but also has the most significant and the broadest public appeal. An off-Broadway production refers to performances away from the Times Square area, but it does not mean that it is not a high-quality production.[114]

Regional (or resident theatre) is the term attributed to professional theatres throughout the United States found primarily in larger cities. Sometimes successful productions appear regionally before moving on to Broadway. Numerous other ways to describe live theatre include roadhouses, **civic light operas,** and **dinner theatres,** where a play or musical is performed while dinner is being served.

---

[112] *See* I.R.C. 501(c)(3).

[113] Theatre and theater are interchangeable spellings.

[114] An example of an off-Broadway production would be COLT: The Chicago Off-Loop Theatre.

Jose Carreras (R) & Teresa Stratas on stage at the Metropolitan Opera.
Getty Images/Time Life Pictures

■EQUITY THEATRE

The Actors' Equity Association (AEA) is the actors' union for stage actors and stage managers. There are a variety of special union contracts (also known simply as Equity) including an Equity contract for children known as the **Theatre for Young Audiences** (TYA). Equity contracts provide the greatest opportunity for live actors to earn the highest wage scale, as opposed to lesser (but still Equity) productions known as **CORST** (Council of Resident/Stock Theatres) or **LORT** (League of Regional Theatres) contracts. Thus, a binding, written contract (often boilerplate in nature) is a driving legal force in live theatre today, as it is in other avenues of entertainment.[115]

For many years Equity actors in Hollywood could not work in smaller nonunion productions. These productions had allowed not only an opportunity to work for less wages, but also allowed actors to practice their skills. In 1972, however, the stage actors' union established a special union contract called the **Equity Waiver Agreement** (sometimes called just Equity Waiver or now the **99-seat plan**). This plan evolved into the City of Los Angeles's small theatre plans of 1988 and 2000, in which actors receive minimal compensation, rehearsal times are limited, and production runs are restricted.

The City of Los Angeles code sets the standard for professional actors' rights by allowing them to work without a salary and in limited numbers of performances in smaller and often much more personable settings.[116] It also affords the public the opportunity to watch celebrity performers hone their skills in a much smaller setting (and at a greatly reduced price) in Equity waiver theatre.

---

[115] For further discussion on contracts see Chapter 3.

[116] New York's version of Equity waiver theatre is called an off-off-Broadway production.

Not all theatre productions are supported by the AEA and these productions are known as **non-Equity** productions. Equity actors may not work in such productions, however, unless they are granted a waiver.

LIVE AWARDS PRODUCTIONS

Awards shows today are big business. Whether the Emmy (television), Oscars (film), Tonys (Broadway theatre only),[117] or Grammys (music), live awards presentations are a combination of scripted and, of course, nonscripted live performances by celebrities and other icons within the specific industry. With the advent of television and now the Internet, selling advertising airtime during such ceremonies can be a highly profitable venture.

Akin to reality television, live awards presentations allow audiences around the world to experience vicarious participation and interaction with some of their favorite performers. These awards also serve as marketing tools for the respective industries themselves, individual or group performers, and writers and directors. Of course, broadcasts of award ceremonies such as the Academy Awards[118] promotes the particular medium of entertainment, not to mention potential sales of related merchandise including videos, DVDs, and other items related to a production. Other profitable live awards productions include the Golden Globe Awards (independent films), the Screen Actors' Guild (SAG) Awards, various Music Television (MTV) Awards, and so on.

BEAUTY PAGEANTS

As a form of live entertainment, beauty pageants are not highly regulated. However, recent concerns over fraudulent conduct related to the results or scoring of beauty pageants have led a few states to consider regulation and licensing of such contests. In Tennessee, for example, The Tennessee Consumer Protection Act § 47–18–201 requires all beauty pageant operators to register with the Tennessee Division of Consumer Affairs each year. Additionally, the beauty pageant operator must be registered and bonded to conduct beauty pageants.

TICKET SCALPING

Viewing live performances usually requires the purchase of a ticket for the right to enter the premises. However, many cities and states have decided to regulate the resale of legitimately purchased tickets. This is known as **ticket scalping. Antiscalping laws** are designed to keep resellers of otherwise legitimate tickets away from venues as matters of the tort of **nuisance,** to avoid the selling of

---

[117] The Pulitzer Prize for drama is often given to non-Broadway productions.

[118] Academy of Motion Picture Arts and Sciences.

Close-up of money changing
hands between ticket scalper
and buyer at 1996 Olympics,
Atlanta, GA.
Photoedit

fraudulent (counterfeit) tickets and to ensure that ticket prices remain afford-able to the typical customer or average fan. Courts have found that antiscalping laws do not violate due process provisions of the Constitution and do not in-terfere with other property rights.

In many states, the laws regarding ticket scalping are in a state of flux. At one time, reselling a ticket for more than a certain percent above its box office price was considered scalping and was prohibited, whether it was done via the Internet online **(cyberscalping)**, from an office, or on the street.

A summary of antiscalping laws follows and is subject to change at any time.

STATE TICKET RESALE (ANTISCALPING) LAWS[119]

Arkansas, Kentucky, Louisiana, Michigan, Minnesota
No more than face value

Connecticut, North Carolina
No more than face value plus $3

Florida
No more than face value plus $1
No sale of multi-day or multi-event tickets that have been used at least once for admission

Georgia
Only the original purchaser, a charity, or a licensed broker may sell for more than face value

Illinois
No more than face value (except that a ticket broker licensed by the state may accept any price, provided that the broker includes in the listing the broker's Illinois registration number)

Massachusetts
No more than face value plus $2 (except that a ticket broker licensed by the state may charge for certain additional expenses related to acquiring and selling the ticket)

Mississippi
No more than face value for events held on state-owned property and athletic contests at Mississippi colleges and universities; no limits on other events

Missouri
No more than face value for sporting events; no limits on other events

New Jersey
No more than face value plus the greater of 20% of the ticket price or $3 (except that a registered ticket broker or a season ticket holder may accept a premium of up to 50% of the price paid to acquire the ticket)

---

[119] http://pages.ebay.com/help/policies/event-tickets.html.

New Mexico

No more than face value for college athletic events; no limits on other events

New York

No more than face value plus the greater of 10% of the ticket price or $5

Pennsylvania

No more than face value plus the greater of 25% of the ticket price or $5

Rhode Island

No more than face value plus the greater of 10% of the ticket price or $3

South Carolina

No more than face value plus $1

Geographic Limitations

Many states, counties, and cities also hold it illegal to resell tickets at any price within 1,000 feet from where the show is taking place. Large venues such as Madison Square Garden and others which can seat over 5,000 people, for example, are rightfully concerned about rampant street scalping and the nuisances it can create to customers, traffic, and others, and such venues have pushed for increasing the **no scalp zone** from 1,000 to 1,500 feet, for example, from the entrance of the arena.[120] The following statute represents California's criminalization of ticket scalping on the event grounds itself.

PENAL CODE

PART 1. Crimes and Punishments

TITLE 9. Of Crimes Against the Person Involving Sexual Assault, and Crimes Against Public Decency and Good Morals

Chapter 12. Other Injuries to Persons

Cal. Pen. Code § 346 (2004)

§ 346. Unauthorized sale ("scalping") of tickets to entertainment event

Any person who, without the written permission of the owner or operator of the property on which an entertainment event is to be held or is being held, sells a ticket of admission to the entertainment event, which was obtained for the purpose of resale, at any price which is in excess of the price that is printed or endorsed upon the ticket, while on the grounds of or in the stadium, arena, theater, or other place where an event for which admission tickets are sold is to be held or is being held, is guilty of a misdemeanor.

Reprinted with permission of Lexis/Nexis.

---

[120] *See* NY CLS Art & Cult. Affr. § 25.11.

COUNTERFEIT TICKETS

Elaborate ticket seals, serial numbers, and watermarks have been instituted to protect against ticket counterfeiting. Unfortunately, fraudulent sales of **counterfeit tickets** are big (and illegal) business. In 2004, a man was arrested for allegedly selling $55,000 worth of Los Angeles Lakers season tickets, with the promise of playoff seats, to buyers who never received them, and was charged with grand theft. The man offered Lakers playoff tickets on eBay if the buyer would purchase season tickets estimated between $15,000 and $25,000. No tickets were ever received by the victims, according to prosecutors.[121]

LAND USE REGULATION

The use of land for entertainment is subject to state laws and county ordinances. Obtaining local permits prior to utilizing land and buildings for entertainment is a prerequisite to doing business. The concept of **municipal police power** is the power of a city or county to enact regulations in order to protect the public health, safety, and welfare. **Zoning** is the way that state and local governments control the physical development of land and the kinds of uses to which each individual property may be put. Zoning laws typically specify the areas in which residential, industrial, recreational, or commercial activities may take place. Thus, zoning laws regulate the geographic location of a business and are part of the normal land use regulatory powers by the government.

If one's desired use of a parcel of land is inconsistent with local zoning laws, a **variance** may be requested. If granted, it permits the owner to use the land in a way that is ordinarily not permitted by the zoning ordinance. A variance is not a change in the zoning law but a waiver of certain requirements found within the zoning ordinance. Zoning and other land use regulations are exercises of municipal police power, the power to regulate historic properties, natural areas, and others, as long as the land use is regulated for a legitimate public purpose.

For example, in New York State the Alcoholic Beverage Control (ABC) laws and regulations of the State Liquor Authority have partial clothing requirements in establishments holding liquor licenses. These ABC laws also require that these establishments maintain their premises certain distances from schools and churches. The same holds true for adult entertainment establishments, but some have avoided this by not serving alcohol.

EXOTIC DANCING

While the phrase **adult entertainment** can refer to bookstores, video stores, and the like, when it comes to live performances, most people refer to **strip clubs** or **exotic dancing** (i.e., nude dancing). Land use regulations are often

[121] http://crossword.uniontrib.com/news/state/20040608-1417-ca-lakers-theft.html

Stripper dancing.
Getty Images Inc. –Stone Allstock

publicly criticized, debated, and sometimes litigated when adult entertainment businesses are involved. Community perceptions on live exotic dancing vary throughout the United States, and states and communities regulate this form of entertainment quite differently.

FIRST AMENDMENT AND POLICE POWER

Many forms of adult entertainment, including printed materials, films, and live entertainment, are protected by the First Amendment of the Constitution, as discussed in greater detail earlier in the text. Municipalities are not permitted to enact local regulations that completely suppress the freedom of expression associated with these activities. Although the constitutional protection of the freedom of expression means municipalities must allow for such uses within their boundaries, this does not mean that municipalities cannot regulate adult uses.

SECONDARY EFFECTS/IMPACTS

Municipalities may use their police power to regulate the potentially negative aspects of the **secondary effects/impacts** of certain live performances. Municipalities can regulate adult uses in a manner that seeks to mitigate these potential secondary effects/impacts (for example, an increase in crime, drug use, lowering of property values, etc.) often associated with adult entertainment.

City of Renton v. Playtime Theatres

In *City of Renton v. Playtime Theatres*, 475 U.S. 41 (1986), the United States Supreme Court utilized a four-part test established previously in *United States v. O'Brien*, 391 U.S. 367 (1968), to determine when zoning regulations for adult businesses do <u>not</u> violate the First Amendment freedom of speech and expression. The case involved a constitutional challenge to a city zoning ordinance enacted by appellant city of Renton, Washington, that prohibited adult motion picture theatres from locating within 1,000 feet of any residential zone, single- or multiple-family dwelling, church, park, or school.

In determining the constitutional validity of an ordinance or zoning restrictions, courts must consider whether:

1. The predominant purpose of the zoning is to suppress the sexually explicit speech itself, or rather, to eliminate the secondary effects of adult uses;
2. The zoning regulation furthers a substantial governmental interest;
3. The zoning regulation is narrowly tailored to affect only those uses that produced the unwanted secondary effects; and
4. The zoning regulations leave open reasonable alternative locations for adult uses.

The city of Renton's zoning ordinance was designed to prevent the occurrence of harmful secondary effects, including the alleged crime associated with adult entertainment by protecting approximately 95% of the city's area from the placement of motion picture theatres emphasizing matter depicting, describing, or relating to "specified sexual activities" or "specified anatomical areas" for observation by patrons.[122] The city of Renton felt it was entitled to rely on the experiences of Seattle and other cities, rather than have to justify it by conducting its own study. The Supreme Court determined that the city of Renton regulations met the *O'Brien* test, and the regulations were upheld.

Some state and city laws require "buffer zones" that restrict how close (measured in feet) an exotic dancer may display their act, "heightened stage requirements," to protect dancers, and a restriction against selling alcoholic beverages at adult establishments. All have been deemed valid forms of regulation by the government.[123]

Hang On, Inc. v. City of Arlington

In another live adult entertainment case, an ordinance of the city of Arlington, Texas, forbade any touching between exotic performers and adult customers. This rule was challenged by the owner of a topless bar on various constitutional grounds. The court in *Hang On, Inc. v. City of Arlington*, 63 F.3d 1248 (5th Cir. 1995), noted that the city of Arlington had amassed studies describing the noxious effects of adult entertainment establishments, and it held that intentional touching is conduct beyond the expressive scope of the dance.

Applying the *O'Brien* test, the court ruled that the city was in compliance. The court, while noting that the Arlington City Council did not make specific

---

[122] 475 U.S. at 44.
[123] *See Colacurcio v. City of Kent*, 163 F.3d 545 (9th Cir. 1998).

findings regarding the no-touch provisions of its ordinance, permitted the city to offer a rationale to justify the no-touch rule in order to prevent prostitution, drug dealing, and assault.

City of Erie v. Pap's A. M.

A more recent United States Supreme Court decision on adult entertainment uses was rendered in *City of Erie v. Pap's A.M.*, 527 U.S. 277 (2000). The Supreme Court has recognized that the First Amendment protects nude erotic dancing as a form of artistic expression. The case was brought by Pap's (doing business as Kandyland), an establishment featuring all nude dancing, against the City of Erie, Pennsylvania, which had enacted an ordinance making it an offense to knowingly or intentionally appear in public in a "state of nudity." The Court of Common Pleas (the trial court) struck down the ordinance as unconstitutional, but the case was reversed by the appellate court. The Pennsylvania Supreme Court reversed again, finding that the ordinance's public nudity sections violated Pap's right to freedom of expression as protected by the First and Fourteenth Amendments.

To comply with the ordinance, dancers at Kandyland had to wear "pasties" and "G-strings" in order to comply with the law. Pap's filed a lawsuit contending that the ordinance violated its right to freedom of expression as protected by the First Amendment. The Court evaluated the city ordinance under the framework set forth in *United States v. O'Brien* for content-neutral restrictions on symbolic speech.

In its decision, the Supreme Court stated that, although being in a "state of nudity" is not an inherently expressive condition, nude dancing is expressive conduct that falls within the outer ambit of the First Amendment's protection. The Supreme Court of the United States subsequently reversed the Pennsylvania Supreme Court. It upheld the city of Erie's ordinance and stated that it met all four factors set forth in the *O'Brien test*.

The 1998 *Buzzetti* case represents how New York City regulated live adult entertainment in the context of constitutional issues.

Buzzetti v. City of New York

140 F.3d 134 (2d Cir. 1998)

United States Court of Appeals for the Second Circuit

Opinion: Leval, Circuit Judge:

Plaintiffs Adele Buzzetti, doing business under the name of her cabaret, Cozy Cabin, which features topless female dancers, and Vanessa Doe, a topless dancer (using a fictitious name for the purposes of this suit), appeal from the dismissal of their complaint in the United States District Court for the Southern District of New York (John S. Martin, J.) seeking declaratory and injunctive relief against the enforcement of a New York City zoning ordinance. The ordinance regulates the permissible locations of commercial establishments featuring various forms of adult entertainment. The plaintiffs argue that because the ordinance applies to female topless entertainment, but not to male topless entertainment, it violates both the First Amendment's Free Speech Clause and the Fourteenth Amendment's Equal Protection Clause. We affirm.

Background

Prior to November 1994, New York City's zoning law did not distinguish between adult entertainment and other commercial establishments. In late 1993, the Department of City Planning (the "DCP") undertook an "Adult Entertainment Study" (the "DCP study") to help the City Planning Commission (the "CPC" or the "Planning Commission") determine whether, like many other municipalities, New York City should adopt zoning regulations directed at adult entertainment establishments. This study was completed in September 1994. The DCP study included both a survey of numerous studies undertaken elsewhere—including Islip, New York; Los Angeles, California; Indianapolis, Indiana; Whittier, California; Austin, Texas; Phoenix, Arizona; Manatee County, Florida; New Hanover County, North Carolina; and the State of Minnesota—and an examination of the nature and effects of adult entertainment establishments in New York City. With respect to New York City, the DCP study referred to previous studies of adult entertainment establishments conducted by other organizations, including an August 1993 Chelsea Action Coalition and Community Board 4 study and an April 1994 study by the Times Square Business Improvement District, as well as to testimony taken at an October 1993 public hearing held by the Borough of Manhattan's Task Force on the Regulation of Sex-Related Businesses. In addition, the DCP conducted its own survey of adult entertainment establishments in New York City, focusing principally on three types of establishments: adult video and book stores, adult theaters, and topless or nude bars.

Based on these sources, the DCP study concluded that adult entertainment constituted a serious and growing problem in New York City. It noted that studies from other cities had documented numerous "negative secondary impacts" of such establishments, including "increased crime rates, depreciation of property values, deterioration of community character and the quality of urban life." DCP Study at 67. These effects were consistent with the experience of those areas of New York City marked by high concentrations of adult entertainment establishments, the study concluded. Even in areas where adult establishments were not heavily concentrated, residents, businesses, and community leaders feared the consequences of possible future proliferation. The DCP study found that there had been a sharp increase in the overall number of adult entertainment establishments in New York City in the previous 10 years, including a 26 percent increase in topless/nude bars. The DCP therefore recommended special zoning restrictions on adult entertainment.

In November 1994, the New York City Council approved a one-year interim zoning moratorium on the opening or enlargement of adult establishments. In March 1995, the DCP and the New York City Council Land Use Committee filed a joint land use review application to amend the city's zoning law to establish permanent zoning regulations applicable to adult establishments. After receiving comments from the city's five borough boards and 39 community boards, and after holding its own public hearings, the CPC approved the proposed permanent regulations on September 18, 1995. Based on the DCP study, other reports, and public testimony, the Planning Commission concluded that there were "substantial adverse secondary effects stemming from the location and concentration of adult uses" in New York, including "the negative impact adult establishments have on economic development and revitalization; their tendency to decrease property value, thereby limiting tax revenue; [the] impediment [created] to economic activity; their tendency to encourage criminal activity, particularly when the establishments are located in concentration; the proliferation of illegal sex-related businesses; their damaging impact on neighborhood character and residents including children; and the costs associated with maintaining and patrolling areas." Following additional public hearings, on October 25, 1995, the City Council approved the permanent restrictions, effective immediately. It is this set of permanent zoning restrictions ("the Zoning Amendment" or "the Amendment") that are at issue in this case.

The Zoning Amendment does not forbid the operation of any category of business. Instead, it restricts the areas in which certain sexually-oriented businesses may operate. The Zoning Amendment's regulatory scheme applies to all "adult establishments," which is defined to mean a commercial establishment, a "substantial portion" of which is used as: an "adult book store," an "adult theater," an "adult eating or drinking establishment," or some "other adult commercial establishment" (or some combination of these). Zoning Amendment, § 12–10. Businesses fall into one of these categories of "adult establishments" if they "regularly feature" or devote a "substantial portion" of their business to entertainment or material emphasizing "specified anatomical areas" or "specified sexual activities." *Id.* For example,

An adult eating or drinking establishment is an eating or drinking establishment which regularly features any one or more of the following:

(1) live performances which are characterized by an emphasis on "specified anatomical areas" or "specified sexual activities"; or

...

(3) employees who, as part of their employment, regularly expose to patrons "specified anatomical areas."

and which is not customarily open to the general public during such features because it excludes minors by reason of age. *Id.*

And:

An adult theater is a theater which regularly features one or more of the following:

...

(2) live performances characterized by an emphasis on "specified anatomical areas" or "specified sexual activities", and

which is not customarily open to the general public during such features because it excludes minors by reason of age. *Id.*

For purposes of this appeal, the following two definitions are pivotal:

"specified sexual activities" are: (i) human genitals in a state of sexual stimulation or arousal; (ii) actual or simulated acts of human masturbation, sexual intercourse or sodomy; or (iii) fondling or other erotic touching of human genitals, pubic region, buttock, anus or female breast.

"Specified anatomical areas" are: (i) less than completely and opaquely concealed: (a) human genitals, pubic region, (b) human buttock, anus, or (c) female breast below a point immediately above the top of the areola; or (ii) human male genitals in a discernibly turgid state, even if completely and opaquely concealed. *Id.* (emphasis added).

Based upon these definitions, the Zoning Amendment regulates the locations at which adult establishments may operate. In addition to the general ban on commercial establishments in residentially-zoned areas of New York City, the Amendment completely forbids adult establishments from operating in certain other specified areas of the city. See Zoning Amendment, §§ 32–01, 42–01. Moreover, in those areas where adult establishments are permitted to locate, the establishments, subject to certain exceptions, may not be located within 500 feet of any school, day care center, or house of worship, nor within 500 feet of the edge of most residential areas. *See id.* In addition, to prevent concentration of adult establishments, the Zoning Amendment generally provides that no adult establishments may be located within 500 feet of any other adult establishment. *See id.* A one-year transition period (with the possibility of additional extensions of time) is provided for non-conforming adult establishments existing at the time of enactment of the Zoning Amendment.

On October 10, 1996, the plaintiffs-appellants filed a complaint alleging that the Zoning Amendment violated the Equal Protection Clause and the First Amendment, and sought injunctive and declaratory relief on that basis. The complaint alleged that Buzzetti's cabaret, Cozy Cabin, which regularly features barechested female dancers, would be economically unable to relocate as required by the Zoning Amendment and therefore would be forced to close. In addition, the complaint alleged that plaintiff Doe is a topless dancer, and that the Zoning Amendment will restrict her ability to earn a livelihood, as well as her ability to express herself through her dancing.

The district court denied plaintiffs' motion for a preliminary injunction, finding that they had not demonstrated a likelihood of success on the merits of their constitutional claims. The district court determined that the New York ordinance was not viewpoint-discriminatory, but rather constituted "a content-neutral time, place, and manner regulation" and, as such, passed constitutional muster if it "'is designed to serve a substantial governmental interest and allows for reasonable alternative avenues of communication.'" This test was met because, the court found, New York's "interest in preventing crime, maintaining property values, and preserving the quality of the city's neighborhoods is both important and substantial" and "the Zoning Amendment also provides for reasonable alternative avenues of communication in numerous zoning districts throughout the city." *Id.* The district court also concluded that the Zoning Amendment did not run afoul of the Equal Protection Clause as "gender-biased." The court noted that the ordinance was aimed at the secondary effects produced by adult entertainment, and "in our culture the public display of female breasts will have far different secondary effects than the public display of male breasts. Rightly or wrongly, our society continues to recognize a fundamental difference between the male and female breast." Finally, the court noted the broad discretion afforded legislative bodies in determining which aspects of general social problems should be targeted for regulation.

Having denied the plaintiffs a preliminary injunction, the district court, pursuant to the parties' joint stipulation, entered final judgment denying plaintiffs' claims for declaratory and injunctive relief and dismissing plaintiffs' complaint. Plaintiffs brought this appeal contending that the Zoning Amendment violates the First Amendment because its regulation of

female topless dancing, but not male topless dancing, constitutes a viewpoint-based restriction on expression suppressing the viewpoint of "female eroticism." In addition, they argue, the Zoning Amendment's differential treatment of male and female topless dancers constitutes a gender-based classification that cannot survive equal protection scrutiny.

Discussion

I. First Amendment Claim

The district court correctly relied on *Young* and *Renton.* Both cases involved ordinances substantially similar to New York City's Zoning Amendment; each ordinance regulated adult business establishments based upon essentially the same definitions of "Specified Sexual Activities" and "Specified Anatomical Areas" as the New York Zoning Amendment, including the differential treatment of male and female toplessness. *See Young,* 427 U.S. at 53 n.4, 96 S. Ct. at 2444; *Playtime Theaters, Inc. v. City of Renton,* 748 F.2d 527, 529 n.1 (9th Cir. 1984), *rev'd,* 475 U.S. 41, 106 S. Ct. 925, 89 L. Ed. 2d 29 (1986). In *Young,* the Court upheld Detroit's adult film zoning ordinance, despite the fact that it singled out one category of expression for special regulation. A plurality of the Court placed importance on the fact that the expression at issue was far from the "core" of First Amendment protections, noting that "even though we recognize that the First Amendment will not tolerate the total suppression of erotic materials that have some arguably artistic value, it is manifest that society's interest in protecting this type of expression is of a wholly different, and lesser, magnitude than the interest in untrammeled political debate." *Young,* 427 U.S. at 70, 96 S. Ct. at 2452 (plurality); *see also Barnes v. Glen Theatre, Inc.,* 501 U.S. 560, 565–66, 111 S. Ct. 2456, 2460, 115 L. Ed. 2d 504 (1991) (plurality opinion) (quoting language from previous cases "supporting the conclusion . . . that nude dancing of the kind sought to be performed here is expressive conduct within the outer perimeters of the First Amendment, though we view it as only marginally so.").

Thus, the *Young* Court held, "even though the First Amendment protects communication in this area from total suppression . . . the State may legitimately use the content of these materials as the basis for placing them in a different classification from other motion pictures." Stressing that "the city must be allowed a reasonable opportunity to experiment with solutions to admittedly serious problems," the *Young* plurality concluded, with specific reference to Detroit's ordinance, that "since what is ultimately at stake is nothing more than a limitation on the place where adult films may be exhibited, even though the determination of whether a particular film fits that characterization turns on the nature of its content, we conclude that the city's interest in the present and future character of its neighborhoods adequately supports its classification of motion pictures."

Renton built directly upon the *Young* framework. The dissent in *Renton* argued that the adult zoning ordinance at issue "discriminated on its face against certain forms of speech based on content" because its restrictions applied only to theaters showing a certain kind of material—i.e., sexually explicit films. *See Renton,* 475 U.S. at 57–58, 106 S. Ct. at 934 (Brennan, J., dissenting). The majority rejected this view. It acknowledged that "regulations enacted for the purpose of restraining speech on the basis of its content presumptively violate the First Amendment," and that "the [Renton] ordinance treats theaters that specialize in adult films differently from other kinds of theaters." *Renton,* 475 U.S. at 46–47, 106 S. Ct. at 928–29 (citations omitted). The *Renton* majority nonetheless viewed the ordinance as content-neutral; "as the District Court concluded, the Renton ordinance is aimed not at the content of the films shown at 'adult motion picture theatres,' but rather at the secondary effects of such theaters on the surrounding community." *Id.* at 47, 106 S. Ct. at 929.

In reaching this conclusion, the Supreme Court looked to the overall purpose of the ordinance. Whereas the district court had found the Renton City Council's "'predominate concerns' [in enacting the ordinance] were with the secondary effects of adult theaters, and not with the content of adult films themselves," the court of appeals had applied a more stringent test, under which "if 'a motivating factor' in enacting the ordinance was to restrict respondents' exercise of First Amendment rights the ordinance would be invalid, apparently no matter how small a part this motivating factor may have played in the City Council's decision." *Id.* (citations omitted). According to the Supreme Court, the court of appeals had erred in not looking to the overall purpose of the ordinance: The District Court's finding as to "predominate" intent . . . is more than adequate to establish that the city's pursuit of its zoning interests here was unrelated to the suppression of free expression. The ordinance by its terms is designed to prevent crime, protect the city's retail trade, maintain property values, and generally "protect and preserve the quality of [the city's] neighborhoods, commercial districts, and the quality of urban life," not to suppress the expression of unpopular views. As a result, the Court ruled, the Renton ordinance is completely consistent with our definition of "content-neutral" speech regulations as those that "are justified without reference to the content of the regulated speech." . . . The appropriate inquiry in this case, then, is whether the Renton ordinance is designed to serve a substantial governmental interest and allows for reasonable alternative avenues of communication.

The appellants argue that *Young* and *Renton* are distinguishable because neither addressed the issue whether the differential treatment of male and female toplessness constituted an impermissible viewpoint restriction. In considering this argument, we need not decide whether appellants have accurately characterized female topless dancing as conveying, for First Amendment purposes, the "viewpoint" of "female eroticism." For even assuming the correctness of plaintiff's contention, we do not think that the Zoning Amendment represents an attempt by New York City to disfavor the viewpoint of female eroticism.

We recognize that "viewpoint discrimination is . . . an egregious form of content discrimination.

The government must abstain from regulating speech when the specific motivating ideology or the opinion or perspective of the speaker is the rationale for the restriction."

We think it clear, however, that the viewpoint of "female eroticism" did not constitute New York City's "rationale for the restrictions" in the Zoning Amendment. As the district court found, "the record does not indicate that the city was aiming to suppress free expression or to disadvantage women who want to perform barechested, as opposed to similarly situated men. Rather, after careful study the city decided to regulate the zoning rights of adult establishments in an effort to address the negative impact such establishments have on the surrounding community." Moreover, the Zoning Amendment by its terms applies both to male and female erotic dancers. All but one of the defined "specified sexual activities" apply to males as well as females, and all but one of the defined "specified anatomical areas" apply to males, as well. Moreover, the definition of "specified anatomical areas" also singles out "male genitals in a discernibly turgid state." Zoning Amendment, § 12–10. In sum, we agree with the district court that the Zoning Amendment is not aimed at suppressing the viewpoint of female eroticism, and is properly viewed, under *Renton,* as a content-neutral time, place, and manner regulation.

We therefore uphold the New York ordinance. With respect to the first requirement for upholding content-neutral regulations, the Supreme Court has made clear that concerns similar to those advanced by New York City, such as preventing crime, maintaining property values, and preserving the quality of urban life and the character of city neighborhoods, constitute "substantial governmental interests." *See Renton,* 475 U.S. at 48, 50, 106 S. Ct. at 929, 930; *see also Young,* 427 U.S. at 71, 96 S. Ct. at 2453 (plurality) ("The city's interest in attempting to preserve the quality of urban life is one that must be accorded high respect."). In addition, *Renton* emphasized that city officials were not required to make particular findings regarding the secondary effects of adult entertainment in

Renton itself, but rather were "entitled to rely on the experiences of . . . other cities." *Renton,* 475 U.S. at 51, 106 S. Ct. at 931; *see id.* at 51–52, 106 S. Ct. at 931 ("The First Amendment does not require a city, before enacting such an ordinance, to conduct new studies or produce evidence independent of that already generated by other cities, so long as whatever evidence the city relies upon is reasonably believed to be relevant to the problem that the city addresses."). Thus, New York City's reliance on studies from a variety of other areas of the country was well-placed. But, as indicated above, New York City went beyond this minimal requirement: the DCP conducted its own detailed study, consulted other studies conducted in particular neighborhoods of New York City, and considered testimony given at public hearings in New York. As the District Court found:

The city has adequately documented the evidence supporting its decision to enact a zoning regulation to help counter the negative secondary effects it believed were caused by adult establishments throughout New York City. . . . Such impacts include increased crime, reduced property value, and a perceived decline in the community character. The negative secondary effects associated with adult establishments and relied on as the impetus for the Zoning Amendment were extensively studied and documented before the Ordinance was adopted. . . . Defendants' interest in preventing crime, maintaining property values, and preserving the quality of the city's neighborhoods is both important and substantial.

Finally, there can be no doubt on this record that the Zoning Amendment allows for "reasonable alternative avenues of communication." The *Renton* Court noted that because the Renton ordinance left "some 520 acres, or more than five percent of the entire land area of Renton, open to use as adult theater sites," even though little or none of it might be "'commercially viable,'" "reasonable alternative avenues" remained. In comparison, as the district court found in the instant case, "Eleven percent of

New York City's total land area remains as permissible locations for adult establishments to operate. The Zoning Amendment certainly allows for alternative sites for adult establishments to operate." Furthermore, the DCP has estimated that the Zoning Amendment "allows for the operation of approximately 500 adult establishments in New York City" in comparison to the approximately 177 adult establishments currently operating in the city; "accordingly, the Amendment permits all of the City's existing adult establishments to continue to operate in the City, either at their current sites or at new locations."

We therefore agree with the district court, under the authority of *Young* and *Renton,* that the New York City Zoning Amendment is a content-neutral time, place, and manner regulation, is justified by substantial government interests and allows for reasonable alternative avenues of communication, and, accordingly, does not violate the First Amendment.

II. Equal Protection Claim

Appellants also argue that the Zoning Amendment's differential regulation of male and female topless dancing constitutes an invidious gender distinction, in violation of the Equal Protection Clause. The Supreme Court has recently "summarized the Court's current directions for cases of official classification based on gender" as follows: Focusing on the differential treatment or denial of opportunity for which relief is sought, the reviewing court must determine whether the proffered justification is "exceedingly persuasive." The burden of justification is demanding and it rests entirely on the State. The State must show "at least that the [challenged] classification serves 'important governmental objectives and that the discriminatory means employed' are 'substantially related to the achievement of those objectives.'" The justification must be genuine, not hypothesized or invented post hoc in response to litigation. And it must not rely on overbroad generalizations about the different talents, capacities, or preferences of males and females.

"It is clear that 'gender has never been rejected as an impermissible classification in all instances.'" *Rostker v. Goldberg,* 453 U.S. 57, 69 n.7, 101 S. Ct. 2646, 2654 n.7, 69 L. Ed. 2d 478 (1981) (quoting *Kahn v. Shevin,* 416 U.S. 351, 356 n.10, 94 S. Ct. 1734, 1737–38 n.10, 40 L. Ed. 2d 189 (1974)). The Court recently reaffirmed in Virginia that "the heightened review standard our precedent establishes does not make sex a proscribed classification. . . . Physical differences between men and women . . . are enduring: The two sexes are not fungible; a community made up exclusively of one [sex] is different from a community composed of both."

Thus, the Court has noted that "because the Equal Protection Clause does not demand that a statute necessarily apply equally to all persons or require things which are different in fact . . . to be treated in law as though they were the same, this Court has consistently upheld statutes where the gender classification is not invidious, but rather realistically reflects the fact that the sexes are not similarly situated in certain circumstances." *Michael M. v. Superior Court of Sonoma County,* 450 U.S. 464, 469, 101 S. Ct. 1200, 1204, 67 L. Ed. 2d 437 (1981) (plurality opinion) (internal quotation marks and citations omitted). Statutes that fairly can be seen as responding to clear sexual differences between men and women are among those laws that courts have upheld, despite the gender-based classifications contained in them. *See, e.g., id.* at 471–73, 101 S. Ct. at 1205–06 (upholding statutory rape law designed, *inter alia,* to prevent illegitimate teenage pregnancies under which only men could be held criminally liable because "only women may become pregnant, and they suffer disproportionately the profound physical, emotional and psychological consequences of sexual activity"; the statute was thus "sufficiently related to the state's objectives to pass constitutional muster"); *Liberta v. Kelly,* 839 F.2d 77, 82–83 (2d Cir.), *cert. denied,* 488 U.S. 832, 109 S. Ct. 89, 102 L. Ed. 2d 65 (1988) (upholding, against equal protection challenge, a New York rape statute criminalizing coerced intercourse with females by males, but not coerced intercourse with males by females; "we find it inconceivable that males who rape should go free solely because the legislature focused on a real problem, rape of women by men, with verified attendant physical and psychological trauma, and failed to act on a hypothetical problem, rape of men by women"); *United States v. Davis,* 785 F.2d 610, 614 (8th Cir. 1986).

Applying these principles to the Zoning Amendment, we conclude that, for the reasons stated in our discussion of appellants' First Amendment claim, New York City's objectives of preventing crime, maintaining property values, and preserving the quality of urban life, are important. We also believe that the Zoning Amendment's regulation of female, but not male, topless dancing, in the context of its overall regulation of sexually explicit commercial establishments, is substantially related to the achievement of New York City's objectives.

In this latter connection, we note first that under the Supreme Court's tests for gender classifications, "the relevant inquiry . . . is not whether the statute is drawn as precisely as it might have been, but whether the line chosen by the [legislature] is within constitutional limitations." *Liberta,* 839 F.2d at 83 (quoting *Michael M.,* 450 U.S. at 473, 101 S. Ct. at 1206 (plurality opinion)). Here, as described above, New York City officials, in addition to canvassing numerous prior studies regarding the secondary effects of adult establishments, also conducted their own study of the problem in New York. One of the adult establishments surveyed as part of the DCP study was, as appellants put it, "the well-known male topless bar Chippendales." *See* DCP Study, Appendix B. After reviewing the results of the DCP study, as well as other studies and public testimony, the city "carefully drafted" the Zoning Amendment "to cover only the types of establishments that have been found to produce negative impacts on the communities in which they are located," according to Joseph B. Rose, the Chairman of the CPC and the Director of the Planning Commission. Rose's uncontradicted affidavit also indicates that "the vast majority of topless clubs in New York City employ female

entertainers exclusively" and "according to studies conducted in New York and in other municipalities, . . . it is those clubs that tend to produce negative impacts, such as a reduction in the value of nearby properties and an impairment in the character of the surrounding community." Having thoroughly examined the problems of adult entertainment, the DCP, Rose reported, "has no evidence that [male topless clubs] create the type of negative community impacts that the adult establishments covered by the Amendment tend to produce."

In short, New York City carefully studied the contours of the problem it was seeking to address and legislated in accordance with its findings. "We simply have no basis on this record for assuming that [New York] will not, in the future, amend its ordinance to include other kinds of adult businesses that [are] shown to produce the same kinds of secondary effects." *Renton,* 475 U.S. at 53, 106 S. Ct. at 931–32.

Moreover, as the district court pointed out in support of its conclusion that the Zoning Amendment was not gender-biased, numerous courts have recognized that the societal impacts associated with female toplessness are legitimate bases for regulation. *See, e.g., United States v. Biocic,* 928 F.2d 112, 115–16 (4th Cir. 1991) (upholding a public indecency statute that applied to topless females but not topless males, and noting that, in our society, the "erogenous zones. . . . still include (whether justifiably or not in the eyes of all) the female, but not the male, breast"). Indeed, courts have considered, and rejected, equal protection challenges quite similar to Buzzetti's and Doe's, against adult entertainment regulations like New York City's Zoning Amendment. *See, e.g., SDJ, Inc. v. City of Houston,* 837 F.2d 1268, 1279–80 (5th Cir. 1988), *cert. denied,* 489 U.S. 1052, 109 S. Ct. 1310, 103 L. Ed. 2d 579 (1989) (considering a similar ordinance regulating adult entertainment, and concluding that "the district court did not err in holding that such regulation of female breasts is substantially related to the City's interest in regulation"); *Tolbert v. City of Memphis,* 568 F. Supp. 1285, 1290 (W.D. Tenn. 1983) ("The only aspect of the ordinance at issue in this case that could be construed as discriminating against women on its face is directed solely against the exposure of the female breast in a public place. In our culture, for the purpose of this type [of] ordinance, female breasts are a justifiable basis for a gender-based classification."); *cf. Hang On, Inc. v. City of Arlington,* 65 F.3d 1248, 1256–57 (5th Cir. 1995) (rejecting a challenge brought under the Texas Equal Rights Amendment to a similar ordinance).

Given New York City's objective, which is not to oppress either gender's sexuality but to control effects that flow from public reaction to the conduct involved, we must recognize that the public reactions to the exhibition of the female breast and the male breast are highly different. The male chest is routinely exposed on beaches, in public sporting events and the ballet, and in general consumption magazine photography without involving any sexual suggestion. In contrast, public exposure of the female breast is rare under the conventions of our society, and almost invariably conveys sexual overtones. It is therefore permissible for New York City, in its effort to achieve the objectives of the Zoning Ordinance, to classify female toplessness differently from the exhibition of the naked male chest. This does not constitute a denial of equal protection.

Finally, although we need not rest our decision on this basis, we note that, given the city's findings, regulating both male and female topless entertainment might have burdened more expressive activity than necessary, thus creating potential First Amendment problems. For example, in *Schad v. Borough of Mount Ephraim,* 452 U.S. 61, 101 S. Ct. 2176, 68 L. Ed. 2d 671 (1981), the Court struck down an ordinance banning all live entertainment within the Borough of Mount Ephraim, New Jersey. "Even if Mount Ephraim might validly place restrictions on certain forms of live nude dancing under a narrowly drawn ordinance, this would not justify the exclusion of all live entertainment. . . ." Mount Ephraim's ordinance regulated too much speech because "the Borough has presented no evidence, and it is

not immediately apparent as a matter of experience, that live entertainment poses problems of this nature more significant than those associated with various permitted uses; nor does it appear that the Borough's zoning authority has arrived at a defensible conclusion that unusual problems are presented by live entertainment." Similarly, in *Erznoznik v. Jacksonville,* 422 U.S. 205, 95 S. Ct. 2268, 45 L. Ed. 2d 125 (1975), the Court invalidated an ordinance prohibiting drive-in movie theaters from showing films containing nudity when the screen was visible from a public street or place. Insofar as the ordinance was aimed at prohibiting youth from viewing the films, it regulated too much expression. "The ordinance is not directed against sexually explicit nudity, nor is it otherwise limited. Rather, it sweepingly forbids display of all films containing any uncovered buttocks or breasts, irrespective of context or pervasiveness. Thus it would bar a film containing a picture of a baby's buttocks, the nude body of a war victim, . . . scenes from a culture in which nudity is indigenous [or] shots of bathers on a beach. . . . Clearly all nudity cannot be deemed obscene even as to minors."

Referring to these precedents, the Court pointed out in *Renton* that "the Renton ordinance is 'narrowly tailored' to affect only that category of theaters shown to produce the unwanted secondary effects, thus avoiding the flaw that proved fatal to the regulations in Schad . . . and Erznoznik. . . ." *Renton,* 475 U.S. at 52, 106 S. Ct. at 931; *see also Young,* 427 U.S. at 82, 96 S. Ct. at 2458 (Powell, J., concurring in part and concurring in the judgment) ("The evidence presented to the Common Council indicated that the urban deterioration was threatened, not by the concentration of all movie theaters with other 'regulated uses,' but only by a concentration of those that elected to specialize in adult movies. The case would present a different situation had Detroit brought within the ordinance types of theaters that had not been shown to contribute to the deterioration of surrounding areas.") (footnotes omitted). By implication, if, after conducting a thorough examination in which only topless entertainment by female performers was "shown to produce" the unwanted secondary effects, New York City nonetheless regulated male topless entertainment, the City might have violated the First Amendment.

In any event, we conclude that appellants have shown no equal protection violation. The Zoning Amendment is substantially related to the City's important objectives in controlling the secondary effects of adult entertainment, and the City has provided the "exceedingly persuasive" justification for its differential regulation of male and female topless performances required under Virginia. "'The gender classification is not invidious, but rather realistically reflects the fact that the sexes are not similarly situated' in this case." *Rostker,* 453 U.S. at 79, 101 S. Ct. at 2659 (quoting *Michael M.,* 450 U.S. at 469, 101 S. Ct. at 1204 (plurality opinion)).

Conclusion

The judgment of the district court is affirmed.

Material has been adapted for this text. Used with the permission of LexisNexis.

SEATING ISSUES

With the passage of the Americans with Disabilities Act (ADA) in 1990, business and service providers throughout the United States are mandated to ensure access to goods for people with disabilities. ADA compliance efforts are focused on removing barriers to access for individuals with mobility concerns. The result of compliance efforts include the installation of elevators, ramps, handrails, and so on.

HEARING ISSUES

The ADA also requires accessibility for individuals with vision and hearing impairments. Since the accommodation needs of hearing-impaired individuals vary, a theatre might also consider various accommodations potentially required by disabled patrons. This includes amplification devices, interpreters who utilize American Sign Language (ASL), and other "reasonable accommodations." The Equal Employment Opportunity Commission (EEOC) has interpreted the ADA to provide a defense to a discrimination claim if the accommodation would expose the disabled individual or others to a significant risk of substantial harm.[124]

BONA FIDE OCCUPATIONAL QUALIFICATION

Under the **bona fide occupational qualification** (BFOQ) exception to what would otherwise be a discriminatory employment relationship, employers

---

[124] *See also* § 504 of the Rehabilitation Act.

(including casting directors and entertainment-based restaurants looking for certain types of people) are allowed to discriminate in hiring workers on the basis of age, race, sex, and other federally protected classifications under certain circumstances. The BFOQ exception, found in Title VII of the Civil Rights Act of 1964, reads as follows:

> it shall not be an unlawful employment practice for an employer to hire and employ employees . . . on the basis of his religion, sex, or national origin in those certain instances where religion, sex, or national origin is a bona fide occupational qualification reasonably necessary to the normal operation of that particular business or enterprise . . . (42 U.S.C. 2000e–2(e)(1)).

When employers want to invoke the BFOQ defense (i.e., exception), they must demonstrate that the employment practice is related to the job, the employee's ability to do the job, and the "essence" of their business. An employer must prove that one of the employee's characteristics that is used as a basis for an employment decision is related to that employee's ability to perform and that those job-related activities are a part of the essence and success of the business. The EEOC has interpreted Title VII as allowing sex as a BFOQ when hiring actors and actresses (see 29 C.F.R. § 1604.2(2) following) if it is necessary for the purpose of authenticity.[125]

TITLE 29—LABOR

SUBTITLE B—Regulations Relating to Labor
CHAPTER XIV—Equal Employment Opportunity Commission
PART 1604—Guidelines on Discrimination Because of Sex

29 CFR § 1604.2

§ 1604.2 Sex as a bona fide occupational qualification.

(a) The commission believes that the bona fide occupational qualification exception as to sex should be interpreted narrowly. Label—"Men's jobs" and "Women's jobs"—tend to deny employment opportunities unnecessarily to one sex or the other.

(1) The Commission will find that the following situations do not warrant the application of the bona fide occupational qualification exception:

(i) The refusal to hire a woman because of her sex based on assumptions of the comparative employment characteristics of women in general. For example, the assumption that the turnover rate among women is higher than among men.

(ii) The refusal to hire an individual based on stereotyped characterizations of the sexes. Such stereotypes include, for

---

[125] *See* B. Chen, *Note: Mixing Law and Art: The Role of Anti-Discrimination Law and Color-Blind Casting in Broadway Theater,* 16 Hofstra Lab. & Emp. L.J. 515 (1999). *See also* H.R. Doc. No. 7152, 88th Cong., 2d Sess., 110 Cong. Rec. 7213 (1964) (comment of Senators Joseph Clark and Clifford Case).

example, that men are less capable of assembling intricate equipment: that women are less capable of aggressive salesmanship. The principle of nondiscrimination requires that individuals be considered on the basis of individual capacities and not on the basis of any characteristics generally attributed to the group.

    (iii) The refusal to hire an individual because of the preferences of coworkers, the employer, clients or customers except as covered specifically in paragraph (a)(2) of this section.

(2) Where it is necessary for the purpose of authenticity or genuineness, the Commission will consider sex to be a bona fide occupational qualification, e.g., an actor or actress.

(b) Effect of sex-oriented State employment legislation.

(1) Many States have enacted laws or promulgated administrative regulations with respect to the employment of females. Among these laws are those which prohibit or limit the employment of females, e.g., the employment of females in certain occupations, in jobs requiring the lifting or carrying of weights exceeding certain prescribed limits, during certain hours of the night, for more than a specified number of hours per day or per week, and for certain periods of time before and after childbirth. The Commission has found that such laws and regulations do not take into account the capacities, preferences, and abilities of individual females and, therefore, discriminate on the basis of sex. The Commission has concluded that such laws and regulations conflict with and are superseded by title VII of the Civil Rights Act of 1964. Accordingly, such laws will not be considered a defense to an otherwise established unlawful employment practice or as a basis for the application of the bona fide occupational qualification exception.

(2) The Commission has concluded that State laws and regulations which discriminate on the basis of sex with regard to the employment of minors are in conflict with and are superseded by title VII to the extent that such laws are more restrictive for one sex. Accordingly, restrictions on the employment of minors of one sex over and above those imposed on minors of the other sex will not be considered a defense to an otherwise established unlawful employment practice or as a basis for the application of the bona fide occupational qualification exception.

(3) A number of States require that minimum wage and premium pay for overtime be provided for female employees. An employer will be deemed to have engaged in an unlawful employment practice if:

    (i) It refuses to hire or otherwise adversely affects the employment opportunities of female applicants or employees in order to avoid the payment of minimum wages or overtime pay required by State law; or

    (ii) It does not provide the same benefits for male employees.

(4) As to other kinds of sex-oriented State employment laws, such as those requiring special rest and meal periods or physical facilities for women, provision of these benefits to one sex only will be a violation of title VII.

An employer will be deemed to have engaged in an unlawful employment practice if:

(i) It refuses to hire or otherwise adversely affects the employment opportunities of female applicants or employees in order to avoid the provision of such benefits; or

(ii) It does not provide the same benefits for male employees. If the employer can prove that business necessity precludes providing these benefits to both men and women, then the State law is in conflict with and superseded by title VII as to this employer. In this situation, the employer shall not provide such benefits to members of either sex.

(5) Some States require that separate restrooms be provided for employees of each sex. An employer will be deemed to have engaged in an unlawful employment practice if it refuses to hire or otherwise adversely affects the employment opportunities of applicants or employees in order to avoid the provision of such restrooms for persons of that sex.

Reprinted with permission of LexisNexis.

CASTING

The hiring of actors and actresses for live (and recorded) performances certainly requires skill and diligence. This process can be intense, grueling, and intimidating. The Casting Society of America (CSA) is the premier organization of theatrical casting directors in film, television, and theatre. Although it is not a union, its members are a united professional society that consistently set the level of professionalism in casting on which the entertainment industry has come to rely. The Casting Society of America was founded in Los Angeles in February 1982 with the intent of establishing a recognized standard of professionalism in the casting field. The CSA is constantly working on improving the standing of casting directors within the entertainment industry. Casting directors are now represented in four Emmy categories by the Television Academy, and it has its own Artios Awards that honor achievements in casting.

Miss Saigon

Concerns over casting, discrimination, and actors' rights came to a head in the 1990 Broadway production of *Miss Saigon*. British actor Jonathan Pryce was hired (i.e., cast) as the male lead in the production of the love affair between an American marine and a Vietnamese bar girl during and after the fall of Saigon in 1975. Pryce's character was an Asian named "Engineer." After the selection was initially rejected by the Actors' Equity Association and after certain Asian Americans and others protested the selection of the actor, Cameron Mackintosh, the

British producer, canceled the $10 million New York production.[126] Realizing that its action would result in the loss of many jobs, the AEA reversed its previous decision, saying that Mackintosh had to be allowed **artistic freedom.** The Broadway production of *Miss Saigon* ended up being one of the most successful shows in the history of live theatre.

HOOTERS

The Atlanta-based Hooters of America, Inc. (Hooters) restaurant chain agreed to pay $3.75 million to settle a sexual discrimination lawsuit brought by seven men turned down for jobs because of their gender.[127] The EEOC charged that Hooters hiring practices discriminated against men, even though Hooters hired only women who best fit the image of their Hooters Girl. The settlement in 1997 (after twenty-three members of Congress requested that the EEOC drop the matter and avoid litigation) allowed Hooters to continue luring customers with its attractive female staff of Hooters Girls. As part of the settlement, Hooters had to create a few support jobs, including bartenders and hosts, that must be filled without regard to gender. While this case created national discourse, it created virtually no law in the traditional sense. As a result, the law with regard to live entertainment and restaurants (not referring to strip clubs or nude dancing) remains unclear.[128]

ART

While one might not initially consider art (pictures, objects, etc.) as a form of entertainment, art displays are highly popular and valuable and often encompass important legal issues. In art, the **Standard Art Consignment Agreement** represents a model contract between an artist and a dealer particularly with regard to **consignment** of the artwork. The contract is flexible, making it ideal for establishing consignment arrangements that are mutually beneficial. It covers agency, consignment, warranties, transportation responsibilities, insurance coverage, pricing, commissions, promotion, return of art, and much more.[129]

---

[126] The Actors' Equity Association allegedly refused to approve a work visa for Pryce on the grounds that a Caucasian actor in this lead role was offensive to the Asian community.

[127] http://www.registerguard.com/news/2003/12/01/f2.bz.grinfas.1130.html.

[128] It appears that the appropriate legal standard is that in a strip club hiring only a single sex (for example, just women) is permitted, while in a restaurant hiring only a single sex (just women) is prohibited. *See Wilson v. Southwest Airlines Co.*, 517 F. Supp. 292 (N.D. Tex. 1981).

[129] The Standard Art Consignment Agreement is one contract for use by artists and art galleries. It is based on a model drawn up by the Artist/Craftsmen's Information Service of Washington, D.C. (A/CIS).

The following is an example of provisions found in a Standard Art Consignment Agreement.

STANDARD ART CONSIGNMENT AGREEMENT[130]

The Artist (name, address, and telephone number):_____

_____
and the Gallery (name, address, and telephone number): _____
hereby enter into the following Agreement:

1. Agency; Purposes. The Artist appoints the Gallery as agent for the works of art ("the Artworks") consigned under this Agreement, for the purposes of exhibition and sale. The Gallery shall not permit the Artworks to be used for any other purposes without the written consent of the Artist.

2. Consignment. The Artist hereby consigns to the Gallery, and the Gallery accepts on consignment, those Artworks listed on the attached Inventory Sheet which is a part of this Agreement. Additional Inventory Sheets may be incorporated into this Agreement at such time as both parties agree to the consignment of other works of art. All Inventory Sheets shall be signed by Artist and Gallery.

3. Warranty. The Artist hereby warrants that he/she created and possesses unencumbered title to the Artworks, and that their descriptions are true and accurate.

4. Duration of Consignment. The Artist and the Gallery agree that the initial term of consignment for the Artworks is to be _____ (months), and that the Artist does not intend to request their return before the end of this term. Thereafter, consignment shall continue until the Artist requests the return of any or all of the Artworks or the Gallery requests that the Artist take back any or all of the Artworks with which request the other party shall comply promptly.

5. Transportation Responsibilities. Packing and shipping charges, insurance costs, other handling expenses, and risk of loss or damage incurred in the delivery of Artworks from the Artist to the Gallery, and in their return to the Artist, shall be the responsibility of the _____ (specify Gallery or Artist).

6. Responsibility for Loss or Damage; Insurance Coverage. The Gallery shall be responsible for the safekeeping of all consigned Artworks while they are in its custody. The Gallery shall be strictly liable to the Artist for their loss or damage (except for damage resulting from flaws inherent in the Artworks), to the full amount the Artist would have received from the Gallery if the Artworks had been sold. The Gallery shall provide the Artist with all relevant information about its insurance coverage for the Artworks if the Artist requests this information.

7. Fiduciary Responsibilities. Title to each of the Artworks remains in the Artist until the Artist has been paid the full amount owing him or her for the Artworks; title then passes directly to the purchaser. All proceeds from the sale of the Artworks shall be held in trust for the Artist. The Gallery shall pay all amounts due the Artist before any proceeds of sales can be made available to creditors of the Gallery.

---

[130] http://www.allworth.com/Articles/article26.htm.

8. Notice of Consignment. The Gallery shall give notice, by means of a clear and conspicuous sign in full public view, that certain works of art are being sold subject to a contract of consignment.

9. Removal from Gallery. The Gallery shall not lend out, remove from the premises, or sell on approval any of the Artworks, without first obtaining written permission from the Artist.

10. Pricing; Gallery's Commission; Terms of Payment. The Gallery shall sell the Artworks only at the Retail Price specified on the Inventory Sheet. The Gallery and the Artist agree that the Gallery's commission is to be _____ percent of the Retail Price of the Artwork. Any change in the Retail Price, or in the Gallery's commission, must be agreed to in advance by the Artist and the Gallery. Payment to the Artist shall be made by the Gallery within _____ days after the date of sale of any of the Artworks. The Gallery assumes full risk for the failure to pay on the part of any purchaser to whom it has sold an Artwork.

11. Promotion. The Gallery shall use its best efforts to promote the sale of the Artworks. The Gallery agrees to provide adequate display of the Artworks, and to undertake other promotional activities on the Artist's behalf, as follows:

_____

The Gallery and the Artist shall agree in advance on the division of artistic control and of financial responsibility for expenses incurred in the Gallery's exhibitions and other promotional activities undertaken on the Artist's behalf. The Gallery shall identify clearly all Artworks with the Artist's name, and the Artist's name shall be included on the bill of sale of each of the Artworks.

12. Reproduction. The Artist reserves all rights to the reproduction of the Artworks except as noted in writing to the contrary. The Gallery may arrange to have the Artworks photographed to publicize and promote the Artworks through means to be agreed to by both parties. In every instance of such use, the Artist shall be acknowledged as the creator and copyright owner of the Artwork. The Gallery shall include on each bill of sale of any Artwork the following legend: "All rights to reproduction of the work(s) of art identified herein are retained by the Artist."

13. Accounting. A statement of accounts for all sales of the Artworks shall be furnished by the Gallery to the Artist on a regular basis, in a form agreed to by both parties, as follows:

_____ (specify frequency and manner of accounting). The Artist shall have the right to inventory his or her Artworks in the Gallery and to inspect any books and records pertaining to sales of the Artworks.

14. Additional Provisions. *(List)*

_____

_____

_____

15. Termination of Agreement. Notwithstanding any other provision of this Agreement, this Agreement may be terminated at any time by either the Gallery or the

Artist, by means of written notification of termination from either party to the other. In the event of the Artist's death, the estate of the Artist shall have the right to terminate the Agreement. Within thirty days of the notification of termination, all accounts shall be settled and all unsold Artworks shall be returned by the Gallery.

16. Procedures for Modification. Amendments to this Agreement must be signed by both Artist and Gallery and attached to this Agreement. Both parties must initial any deletions made on this form and any additional provisions written onto it.

17. Miscellany. This Agreement represents the entire agreement between the Artist and the Gallery. If any part of this Agreement is held to be illegal, void, or unenforceable for any reason, such holding shall not affect the validity and enforceability of any other part. A waiver of any breach of any of the provisions of this Agreement shall not be construed as a continuing waiver of other breaches of the same provision or other provisions hereof. This Agreement shall not be assigned, nor shall it inure to the benefit of the successors of the Gallery, whether by operation of law or otherwise, without the prior written consent of the Artist.

18. Choice of Law. This Agreement shall be governed by the law of the State of _____.

_____
(Signature of Artist)

_____
(Date)

_____
(Signature of authorized representative of the Gallery)

_____
(Date)

Reprinted by permission from the Artist-Gallery Partnership by Tad Crawford and Susan Mellor (Allworth Press, www.allworth.com).

CHAPTER SUMMARY

This chapter represents an amalgamation of issues related to live performances in entertainment law. Understanding the role and importance of the AEA as a union representative for actors and actresses is vital in the study of live theatre, whether the production is for-profit or not-for-profit, Broadway or off-Broadway. One should appreciate the significant impact that live awards presentations have had on the promotion of entertainment among its various industries.

Ticket sales are not simple concerns anymore, as antiscalping laws and laws designed to prevent counterfeit sales of tickets (especially now over the Internet) continue to affect access to certain live events.

Live adult entertainment establishments have forced states and municipalities (and courts) to interpret and apply constitutional issues involving freedom of speech and expression with regard to land use regulations, particularly with regard to zoning laws.

Employment laws, particularly the ADA, have made their way into the entertainment industry. However, major concerns have arisen over choice or selection of actors and actresses as a matter of artistic freedom and discretion, as opposed to qualification or background. Art galleries and artists usually display art under a contract known as the Standard Art Consignment Agreement.

CHAPTER TERMS

99-seat plan
Adult entertainment
Antiscalping laws
Artistic freedom
Bona fide occupational
    qualification (BFOQ)
Civic light opera
Consignment
CORST (Council of
    Resident/Stock
    Theatres)

Counterfeit tickets
Cyberscalping
Dinner theatre
Equity Waiver
    Agreement
Exotic dancing
For-profit
Live theatre
LORT (League of
    Regional Theatres)
Municipal police power

No scalp zone
Non-Equity
Not-for-profit
Nuisance
On-Broadway
Secondary effects/
    impacts
Standard Art
    Consignment
    Agreement

Strip club
Theatre
Theatre for Young
    Audiences (TYA)
Ticket scalping
Variance
Zoning

ADDITIONAL CASES

Barnes v. Glen Theatre, Inc., 501 U.S. 560 (1991)
Broadrick v. Oklahoma, 413 U.S. 601 (1973)
California v. LaRue, 409 U.S. 109 (1972)
City of Colorado Springs v. 2354, Inc., 896 P.2d 272 (Colo. 1995)
Davis-Kidd Booksellers, Inc. v. McWherter, 866 S.W.2d 520 (Tenn. 1993)
DLS, Inc. v. City of Chattanooga, 107 F.3d 403 (6th Cir. 1997)
Dothard v. Rawlinson, 433 U.S. 321 (1977)
Erznoznik v. City of Jacksonville, 422 U.S. 205 (1975)
Ino Ino, Inc. v. City of Bellevue, 937 P.2d 154 (Wash. 1997)
J&B Entertainment, Inc. v. City of Jackson, 152 F.3d 362, 371 (5th Cir. 1998)
Madsen v. Erwin, 481 N.E.2d 1160 (Mass. 1985)

New York State Liquor Authority v. Bellanca, 452 U.S. 714 (1981)
People ex rel. Cort Theatre Co. v. Thompson, 283 Ill. 87, 119 N.E. 41 (1918)
People v. Osborne, 180 Misc. 2d 152 (N.Y. 1999)
Rising Sun Entm't, Inc. v. Bureau of Liquor Control Enforcement, 829 A.2d 1214 (Pa. 2003)
Stringfellow's of New York, Ltd. v. City of New York, 749 N.E.2d 192 (N.Y. 2001)
Threesome Entertainment v. Strittmather, 4 F. Supp. 2d 710 (N.D. Ohio 1998)
Town of Islip v. Caviglia, 540 N.E.2d 215 (N.Y. 1989)
Triplett Grille, Inc. v. City of Akron, 40 F.3d 129 (6th Cir. 1994)
Young v. American Mini Theatres, Inc., 427 U.S. 50 (1976)

REVIEW QUESTIONS

1. Why have off-Broadway and regional theatre productions become so successful?
2. What does the term equity mean in the context of theatre?
3. Are live awards productions genuine, or are they merely designed to make money off of viewers and others interested in entertainment?
4. Should artwork be considered a form of entertainment?
5. Why has the state of Tennessee, for example, decided to regulate beauty pageants, whereas most other states have not?
6. Should swimsuit contests, fitness pageants, and bodybuilding contests be regulated by the government as well?

7. Why do you feel that some cities and states have developed antiscalping and other ticket-related laws, while other cities and states have not addressed the issue?
8. How does the First Amendment of the Constitution relate to live adult entertainment?
9. Discuss the relationship between zoning, exotic dancing, and the *O'Brien* test.
10. What is a "buffer zone" in the context of live entertainment?
11. Should casting directors have the freedom to choose who to hire for a particular role without regard to the gender of the actor or actress? Does this violate general employment law principles?

HISTORY OF RECORDING TECHNOLOGY

In the last twenty-five years, the music industry has been transformed by recording technology that has made millions of records, 8-tracks, and cassette tapes virtually extinct or the subject of nostalgic hobby enthusiasts. The arrival of compact discs (CDs) in 1982 and its use of laser technology provided clearer sound quality than any of the previous recording technologies. Today, digital technology using DVD and MP3 technology has begun to replace the CDs which transformed the industry for many years. Use of MP3s has facilitated the ease of recording and copying sound, too. Still, an understanding of the history of music recording technology advances presents an important perspective for the student of music and law.

The Record

The phonographic "disc" record (created by Edison) became popular among consumers, and the cylinder player faded out in the early 1900s. Victor introduced its Victrola record player in 1906, and it eventually became an American household name.[132] The phonographic record was referred to by various names during this time period, including "gramophone" (in England), phonograph record (in America), record, album, disc, "platter," and vinyl (because that became the most popular substance for making records).

Though the record was powered mechanically through the 1920s, in 1924 Columbia experimented with electronic power and the phonograph. A successful design caused consumers to demand electric-based motors with electronic amplifiers which provided better sound. The record usually consisted of a single, concentric spiraled groove on one side of a disc. The needle attached to a mobile arm would then run in the groove as the record spun at a certain speed, thereby creating sound. The recording industry settled on a diameter of 10 inches for the new vinyl disc format at that time.

Recording Process.   For the first several decades of vinyl disc record manufacturing, sound was recorded directly onto the master disc (also called the matrix or "master") at the recording studio. During the 1950s, it was common to have a song recorded on audiotape (invented after the vinyl record), which would then be processed and/or edited and then dubbed onto the master disc. The master would then usually be electroplated with a nickel alloy metal, and it became the negative master. A negative master mold was used to create a metal positive disc called a mother. The mother would then be used to make more negatives called stampers. The stampers would later be used as the molds for the discs sold to the public.

Recording Speeds.   While the rotational speed varied from one manufacturer to another, most turntables that played vinyl records turned between 75 and 80 revolutions per minute (rpm). Some turntables were made at adjustable speeds. By the end of the 1920s, 78 rpm became the industry standard. The 78 rpm recordings (called "seventy-eights") were only recorded on one side, but

---

[132] Victor ultimately became RCA-Victor in the United States.

Christina Aguilera.
Getty Images, Inc. –Liaison

by 1923, double-sided recordings were common. After World War II, the 78 for-mat was eventually replaced by two other formats: the 33 1/3 rpm (the "thirty-three") and the 45 rpm (the "forty-five"). The 33 1/3 rpm LP ("Long Play") format was developed by Columbia Records and was marketed in 1948. RCA-Victor marketed the 45 rpm format in 1949. A 45-rpm 7-inch was called a 45 (forty-five) or a single because it usually held only one song per side. It took over this role from the older standard of the 10-inch 78. The 45 had a 3/4″ center hole. A 33-rpm 7-inch format was known as an EP ("Extended Play"), with two or three songs per side. However, 45-rpm 7-inch EPs were also produced using narrower groove spacing (and therefore lower sound quality) to carry two songs per side. A 33-rpm 12-inch format was ultimately created to hold five to ten songs on each side. Records in a 16-rpm format, usually 12 inches, were also manufactured. These were generally of lower audio fidelity and mostly used for spoken word recordings. The most common of these were recorded readings of books made for visually impaired persons.

The Tape

Magnetic audiotape recording eventually replaced the phonograph and records in record companies, on radio, and in movies by the early 1950s. Using magnetic heads that could read and record electromagnetic signals, the 3M company (Minnesota Mining & Manufacturing Company), in conjunction with discover-ies made by Americans and World War II Allies of German technology, advanced the use of this technology quite quickly. The first consumer magnetic tape recorders also appeared during this time frame and sold very well. Still, the LP record controlled the marketplace.

Tape allowed one of the greatest impacts on the recording industry: edit-ing. Editing is the process of cutting, splicing, and rearranging recordings and allowing more than one source to be recorded on a tape at a time. This was a very novel concept at that time, but it allowed musicians and other artists to record in a manner that opened up a whole new creative world by allowing studio engineers the ability to splice together two or more recordings to make a better end product. This created "special effects" such as allowing one singer's voice to be recorded on a tape accompanying himself (or herself) by allowing more than one recording (called a multitrack).

For musicians in a studio, this even allowed separate recordings of the same song by different parts of the band, even on different days. The sound engineers could then take the best recordings and mix them together to get the best version of the song or sound on a track. In the 1960s, multitrack recording became so popular that it was not uncommon to have up to twenty-four or more tracks to be recorded on a single tape. Multitrack recordings also allowed for creating the live "stereo sound effect," which created a live effect for the listener. The first stereo recordings available to the public were in the form of a larger reel-to-reel tape. In 1957, however, RCA introduced a recorder with a super-compact tape head that stacked four heads in the place of just two, allowing a stereo tape to be flipped over and played on both sides.

The 4-track Tape

While the 4-track cartridge tape (approximately 1956) format evolved earlier than the more popular 8-track tape, the concept of playing a tape in an automobile intrigued Ford Motors. In the 1960s, Ernie Muntz acquired rights to the 4-track tape format and began marketing his concept to Ford, which eventually offered an in-dash tape cartridge system.

The 8-track Tape

The 8-track tape was designed to make the tape less likely to jam while playing. This format was developed by a joint effort of the Ampex Magnetic Tape Company, Lear Jet Company, and RCA Records. In 1965, Ford Motors offered 8-track players as an option in their line of 1966 model cars. Thus, the 8-track was a by-product of the desire to bring easily accessible recorded sound to American cars. Soon all the American automakers offered this technology as optional equipment, and home and portable versions of the 8-track players appeared. The 8-track took a large proportion of the music market in the late 1960s and peaked in the mid-1970s. The 8-track ultimately became obsolete in the early 1980s, as they were eclipsed by the advent of the rerecordable compact cassette tape systems.

The Cassette Tape

The cassette tape ("cassette") was a small, two-reel cartridge. It was introduced by Phillips in Europe and Norelco in the United States. Although of low quality at first, with a "hissing" sound in the background, hiss reduction technology for cassette tape was introduced in 1968. One of the greatest advantages of the cassette tape was that it allowed users to make copies of records and then replay them in cars or on portable tape players.

Sales of cassette tapes outpaced 8-tracks in the mid-1970s and began to sell more than records in the early 1980s. Iron oxide and then chromium oxide tapes replaced the gamma-ferric oxide tape that had been used in the original reel-to-reel tapes. The 90-minute tape became the best-selling blank tape, and two full record albums could usually be recorded on a single 90-minute cassette.

The rise of the cassette tape pushed the recording industry to an even higher level by creating a better variety of portable and home recorders and tape players. In addition to the small battery-operated portables available since the beginning, larger, more powerful "boom boxes" became mass marketed and were quite versatile. Sony introduced its battery-powered cassette tape machine, the "Walkman," in the late 1970s.

Compact Discs

The compact disc (CD) was introduced in 1982. A CD is made out of plastic and is approximately four one-hundredths (4/100) of an inch (1.2 mm) thick. Most of a CD consists of an injection-molded piece of polycarbonate plastic. During the manufacturing process, this plastic is impressed with microscopic "bumps" arranged as a single, continuous, extremely long spiral track of data. Then, a thin, reflective aluminum layer is sputtered onto the disc, covering the bumps. Finally, a thin acrylic layer is sprayed over the aluminum to protect it.

A CD can store up to 74 minutes of music and requires a CD player. The CD player drive consists of three major components: the **drive motor** that spins the disc, a laser and lens system to read the bumps, and a tracking system that moves the laser assembly so that the laser can follow the spiral track. The tracking system, as it plays the CD, has to continually move the laser outward.

The CD was not an immediate hit, and it took nearly a decade for it to displace the audio cassette. In the 1990s, it became the most popular home format for playing music. Recordable CDs were not generally available until the mid-1990s, and few were sold before approximately 2000. CDs are still popular, but fierce competition from DVDs and MP3s are giving users cause to believe that the CD will fall by the wayside, similar to vinyl records, due to tremendous advances in recording technology.

DVDs

Today, the CD is being challenged by the DVD (which is also used for video) for sales. DVDs are very similar to CDs, but they hold more data—4.7 gigabytes for a DVD as compared to 650 megabytes for a CD. DVD technology offers an optical disc with a much larger capacity than the compact disc and is available as a family of prerecorded, recordable, and rewritable formats to meet the requirements of the industries and applications mentioned previously. DVD-Video and DVD-ROM (Read Only Memory) hardware and software have been available since 1997. DVD-Audio was launched in 2000. DVD writers and DVD video recorders are now available at affordable prices for the general public. The DVD-ROM is beginning to replace the CD-ROM and provide a new high-capacity disc format for the computer industry. New personal computers (PCs) are now often provided with DVD drives instead of CD drives.

MP3s

MP3 is the shortened name for Moving Picture Experts Group Layer-3 Audio (or MPEG Audio Layer III). Since 1999, the popularity of the MP3 has increased tremendously. MP3 is a technology that compresses high-quality sound files into digital audio format so that they can be downloaded quickly from the Internet to a PC hard drive. Early compression formats such as Musical Instrument Digital Interface (MIDI) made music obtainable over the Internet but took hours to download and required the use of many floppy disks, due to the size of the compressed music file. The most popular method of obtaining a MP3 is via peer-to-peer (i.e., "person-to-person") file-sharers such as the Napster.com Web site, which was put out of business but then reappeared legally in 2003.

ATTEMPTS TO CONTROL MUSIC PIRACY

Advances in the recording and delivery of music have also led to the same technologies that have been used to copy (without a fee) the same music that the recording industry wanted consumers to purchase. When the cassette tape became popular, consumers discovered that they were able to record songs from the radio or record songs from other tapes for their own use without paying a fee. The same motivation to copy and record songs exists today, and companies such as Napster were sued to stop the no-fee delivery of music over the Internet. Several laws and initiatives have been spearheaded by the Recording Industry Association of America. Additionally, in 2004 the Federal Bureau of Investigation (FBI) gave Hollywood film studios, music companies, and software makers permission to use its name and logo on their DVDs, CDs, and other digital media as a deterrent to piracy.[133]

Audio Home Recording Act

In 1992, the Audio Home Recording Act (AHRA) was enacted by Congress to address the issue of digital audio recording devices and copyright infringement (17 U.S.C. §§ 1001–1010). The AHRA was designed to allow consumers access to the newest technology, while simultaneously providing incentives to manufacturers and recording companies to develop the products and the media. The Act requires manufacturers of consumer digital audio taping (DAT) machines and tapes to pay a royalty to owners of sound recording and musical composition copyrights.

Secure Digital Music Initiative

At the end of 1998, the RIAA advanced the Secure Digital Music Initiative (SDMI) in conjunction with representatives of BMG, EMI, Sony Music Entertainment, Universal, Warner, RIAA, IFPI, and RIAJ (Recording Industry Association

---

[133] http://www.cnn.com/2004/TECH/ptech/02/20/downloading.music.ap/.

of Japan). The objectives of SDMI are to answer consumer demand for convenient access to high-quality recordings; ensure copyright protection for artists' work; and enable technology and music companies to build successful businesses. Ultimately, the goal of these businesses is to use the SDMI to allow the public to enjoy the ease of access to online music so that pirating music becomes obsolete.

CD Anticopying Software

In 2003, SunnComm (United States) and BMG (German) companies signed a deal to license CD-3 copy protection software to prevent CD copying and "burning." Unfortunately for these companies, a Princeton University student posted on a Web site that all one needed to do to disarm the anticopying software was to hold down the "Shift" key on a keyboard while loading the disc into a CD drive. SunnComm threatened to sue the graduate student but later changed its mind.

Watermarks and Fingerprinting

In addition to the Digital Millennium Copyright Act, additional ways the music industry is attempting to curb the distribution of illegal copies of music is through the use of a **watermark.** A digital watermark is encoded onto the disc itself as an inaudible signal. Even though the signal cannot be heard by the human ear, playback equipment easily detects its presence, and when the user copies a song, the artist's name, song title, and often the serial number identifying the source of the music can be read by the computer and ultimately delivered to licensing bureaus. In theory, this allows the licensing bureaus to monitor the trading of these songs online. The **fingerprint** is another copy protection mechanism and is similar to the watermark. Fingerprinting works to recognize certain aspects of songs by comparing the tracks shared on peer-to-peer (P2P) computer networks. Still, policing of watermarks and fingerprints is not very practical or feasible.

THE RECORDING INDUSTRY ASSOCIATION OF AMERICA AND RIO

Founded in 1952, the Recording Industry Association of America represents 90% of the recording industry. Its mission is "to protect intellectual property rights worldwide and the First Amendment rights of artists; conduct consumer, industry and technical research; and monitor and review state and federal laws, regulations and policies."

In 1998, RIAA sued Diamond Multimedia because it opposed Diamond's creation of Rio, a trademarked portable MP3 player that allowed the downloading of songs from the Internet or CD. In 1999, the Ninth Circuit Court of Appeals (California) ruled that Diamond's Rio MP3 player did <u>not</u> violate the Audio Home Recording Act. The three-judge panel decided in favor of Diamond Multimedia, holding that the Rio player does not qualify as a digital audio recording device (and therefore the law does not apply to it) because it does not reproduce a digital music recording directly from a transmission. It only makes a copy from the computer's hard drive to render portable use.

NAPSTER

In response to the difficulty of finding MP3s, Napster was created by software engineers Sean Parker and Shawn Fanning. The software program allowed people to share recordings via the Internet for free. Fanning created the program, along with Parker, when he was a freshman in college. Napster used a P2P file-sharing system. Napster allowed (enabled) participants to download music from other people's computer hard drives when they were connected to the Internet by essentially "opening" the individual's computer behind the scenes in order for other people to download music from it. Similar music file-sharing Web sites included Kazaa.com, Morpheus.com, and Grokster.com.

In 2000, the band Metallica filed suit against Napster and three universities (University of Indiana, University of Southern California, and Yale University), claiming copyright violations. Metallica's suit claimed that Napster was an "insidious and ongoing thievery scheme" and sought $100,000 per copyright violation. In the suit, Metallica charged that its music had been unlawfully duplicated. That same year, U.S. District Judge Marilyn Hall Patel ordered an injunction against Napster during a hearing in the San Francisco federal court. The ruling handed the recording industry its first major victory against online piracy. Napster eventually filed for Chapter 11 bankruptcy protection in March 2002, after a federal court ruled it was a tool for widespread piracy.

RIAA AND SUBPOENAS

In 2003 and 2004, the RIAA garnered national attention when it subpoenaed hundreds of file-sharers of music. RIAA was able to convince federal courts that the 1998 Digital Millennium Copyright Act allows the recording industry to force Internet Service Providers (ISPs) to turn over the names of suspected file traders with a subpoena from any U.S. District Court clerk's office without a judge's signature. Verizon Internet Services filed two lawsuits against the RIAA and attempted to block the RIAA's requests for customers' personal information. However, the lawsuits failed. The RIAA has settled many of the claims, but under the law, it could seek damages of between $750 and $150,000 for each alleged illegal song under U.S. copyright law. Only time will tell of the impact of the RIAA's pursuit of P2P file-sharers.

NAPSTER 2.0

In late 2003, Napster.com was relaunched as a legal Web site. Napster was acquired in 2002 by music software firm Roxio, which created the new Web site named Napster 2.0. Napster 2.0 allows anyone with a PC to freely sample the company's online collection, "burn" CDs, and transfer music to portable devices with the permission of the true copyright holders for a subscription fee. The Napster 2.0 service has support from Microsoft, being compatible with the software giant's Windows Media Player software. Napster 2.0 competes with Apple Computer's iTunes (www.apple.com/tunes), Musicmatch.com, Rhapsody (www.listen.com), and Buymusic.com, which offer downloads under similar fee-based plans.

INDUSTRY SELF-REGULATION

In May 1985, the Parent's Music Resource Center (PMRC) pursued the regulation of obscene music lyrics. An infamous meeting in front of the U.S. Senate involving Dee Snider, lead singer of the rock group Twisted Sister, and representatives from the Recording Industry Association of America thrust the issue of whether freedom of speech outweighed the public interest in regulating certain types of speech. PMRC originally proposed that record companies rate records "V" for violence, "X" for sex, "D/A" for drugs and alcohol, and "O" for occult. By the time of the Senate hearing, the PMRC wanted record companies simply to voluntarily label "offensive albums." The RIAA complied, and by 1990, the black-and-white "Parental Advisory/ Explicit Content" label had become commonplace in retail stores. The motion picture, music recording, and electronic and video game industries have also taken steps to identify content that may not be appropriate for children by establishing their own voluntary rating systems.

MUSICIAN UNIONS

The two major unions representing musicians are the American Federation of Musicians of the United States and Canada (AFM) and the American Federation of Television and Radio Artists (AFTRA). These unions comprise a network of local chapters that work together to improve wages and working conditions for musicians. The AFM represents musicians, while AFTRA members are vocalists and actors. The AFM is the largest musicians' union in the world (established in 1896) with members from all fields and types of music from studio recording, television, and jingles (television and radio commercial music) to symphony, opera, and other live concerts. Most musicians join this union during their professional careers.

The AFM negotiates and administers agreements with the major recording companies, film and television companies, live music venues and booking agencies, and so on. These agreements designate a basic union scale wage that the companies must pay to musicians at a minimum and provide for employer contributions to the AFM health and pension funds. AFM membership benefits also include local job referrals for session and tour work; group insurance rates for health, life, dental, and music equipment; and collection of unpaid wages owed to members.

include Universal Music and BMG Publishing. Numerous other independent agencies exist as well.

THE RECORDING CONTRACT

While copying music and protecting rights are important, having a record label behind an artist can prove to be an asset: the label can create exposure for the artist by promoting live performances, television appearances, books, merchandise, and, if the artist is also a songwriter, increased publishing royalties. Consequently, the recording agreement remains a vitally important part of an artist's career. It is necessary to be equipped with a general understanding of the terms of the contractual relationship between a record company and an artist (see Chapter 2).

Term of the Recording Contract

The **term** of the recording agreement dictates the period of time during which the artist is under exclusive contract with the record company. A recording commitment is the phrase that places a burden on the artist to produce a certain minimum number of singles, albums, and so forth. If the minimum number is not met, the record company may exercise an option—sometimes called a "suspension"—if the artist breaches, such as the inability to perform or the failure to pursue their career any further.

Single Song Agreements

The **single song agreement** contract is a basic publishing agreement for a songwriter. Once a songwriter has written a song that is attractive to another publisher, artist, producer, film, or television show, a single song agreement can be executed. Under this arrangement, the songwriter usually assigns 50% (or in some cases, 100%) of the publishing rights of a song to the publisher for a certain period of time, usually between one to two years. If the publisher secures a placement with an artist during this period, then the publisher becomes a permanent copyright owner of the song. The contract could also stipulate whether the securing of a film or television usage for the song (instead of a record placement) is sufficient for the publisher to retain a permanent copyright interest. Also, a **copublishing agreement** provides for the co-ownership of songs by two or more parties. It is usually on a 50/50 (sometimes 75/25) basis. An **administration agreement** provides that the songwriter retains the copyright. However, the publisher receives a fee as the administrator.

Right to Use Artist's Name and Likeness

The recording company and artist must agree as to the degree to which the company may use the artist's name and logo for promoting CDs, labels, advertising, and so forth. An artist will normally grant the right to market the name and logo to sell CDs for commercial purposes during the term of the agreement.

Creative Control

Considerations in music contracts involving creative control represent a huge struggle between artists and record and publishing companies. For example, there are often concerns over who selects the studio, producers, and what songs make the final cut on a CD. Additionally, the performer must consider who has the right to control artwork, advertising, promotions, tours, and when a song might even be used on a radio or television commercial.

Exclusivity

Once an artist signs a recording agreement, the artist's activities in every arena of the record industry are exclusive to the record company during the length of the term. The artist cannot perform as a featured artist on other artists' records or a soundtrack album without the record company's consent, which can be withheld for any reason. Two exceptions that record companies typically carve out are to allow the artist to record jingles and to record as a side artist (e.g., studio musician or background vocalist) on other artists' sessions.

Advances

Normally, a recording company will **advance** the costs of recording but will recoup them off the top once an album is created and sales begin. An advance is guaranteed money to the artist (similar to a signing bonus in professional sports, but in most sports contracts the money is guaranteed and is not deducted from other income). The amount of the advance, which includes recording costs as well as the producer's advance, is dependent upon how many albums the artist has released previously and how well those albums performed. In the event the album fares poorly, however, labels do have a clause called a **cross-collateralization** clause that allows them to recoup costs against the advance, so that they do not lose money. In accounting terms, this offsets any money owed by the artist or songwriter to the record or publishing company.

ROYALTIES

Royalties go by various names in the music industry. The concept of royalties can be too complex for those without an accounting background, and the calculation of royalties can be so convoluted that it has been referred to as royalty math.[136] Great concern over accounting practices has led to "royalty workshops" for interested artists and their representatives to help them understand royalty statements. Artists and others should know the difference between the term **wholesale** (the price charged to the seller for a CD) and the term **retail** (the price paid by the consumer). The artist's royalty for this sale is calculated as a percentage of the selling price. It is usually based upon the suggested retail list

---

[136] http://www.usatoday.com/life/music/news/2004-05-16-royalties-main_x.htm.

price (SRLP) or on the wholesale price. Certain deductions and reductions will affect the retail or wholesale price, in order to determine the **base royalty rate**. These include deductions for packaging, freebies or promotional goods, and other items.

Artist Royalties

Artist royalties are generally based on sales and the overall success of the artist. Royalties are based upon unit sales, and the royalty is usually 15%.[137] For example, an artist might get a particular royalty based upon actual sales up to 500,000 units and then get a higher rate (maybe a 1% increase) for sales exceeding 1,000,000 units. Sales in foreign markets may produce a different calculation for royalty purposes as well.

COPYRIGHT ROYALTY TRIBUNALS/PANELS

Under the Copyright Act of 1976 (17 U.S.C. §§ 1–810), a Copyright Royalty Tribunal was established, whose role is to monitor the mechanical royalties paid to songwriters and publishers. The royalty rate stayed the same from 1909 to 1976. In 1993, the Copyright Royalty Tribunal was eliminated and replaced with a system of ad hoc Copyright Arbitration Royalty Panels (CARPs). The CARPs approved the following mechanical royalty rates:

2002–2003—The greater of 8.0 cents per song or 1.55 cents per minute

2004–2005—The greater of 8.5 cents per song or 1.65 cents per minute

2006–2007—The greater of 9.1 cents per song or 1.75 cents per minute

EXHIBIT 9.1

Copyright Royalty Rates since 1909

Section 115, the Mechanical License[138]

Date	Rate	Authority
1909–1977	2 cents	Copyright Act of 1909
January 1, 1978	2.75 cents or 0.5 cent per minute of playing time or fraction thereof, whichever is greater	Copyright Act of 1976
January 1, 1981	4 cents or 0.75 cent per minute of playing time or fraction thereof, whichever is greater	1980 Mechanical Rate Adjustment Proceeding

(continued)

[137] In the music industry, percentages are often referred to as points. Thus, "15 points" equals 15 percent.
[138] http://www.copyright.gov/carp/m200a.html.

January 1, 1983	4.25 cents or 0.8 cent per minute of playing time or fraction thereof, whichever is greater	1980 Mechanical Rate Adjustment Proceeding
July 1, 1984	4.5 cents or 0.85 cent per minute of playing time or fraction thereof, whichever is greater	1980 Mechanical Rate Adjustment Proceeding
January 1, 1986	5 cents or 0.95 cent per minute of playing time or fraction thereof, whichever is greater	1980 Mechanical Rate Adjustment Proceeding
January 1, 1988 to December 31, 1989	5.25 cents or 1 cent per minute of playing time or fraction thereof, whichever is greater	17 U.S.C. 801(b)(1) and 804. Based upon the change in the Consumer Price Index from Dec. 1985 to Sept. 1987
January 1, 1990 to December 31, 1991	5.7 cents or 1.1 cents per minute of playing time or fraction thereof, whichever is greater	Consumer Price Index from Sept. 1987 to Sept. 1989
January 1, 1992 to December 31, 1993	6.25 cents or 1.2 cents per minute of playing time or fraction thereof, whichever is greater	Consumer Price Index from Sept. 1989 to Sept. 1991
January 1, 1994 to December 31, 1995	6.60 cents or 1.25 cents per minute of playing time or fraction thereof, whichever is greater	Consumer Price Index from Sept. 1991 to Sept. 1993
January 1, 1996 to December 31, 1997	6.95 cents or 1.3 cents per minute of playing time or fraction thereof, whichever is greater	Consumer Price Index from Sept. 1993 to Sept. 1995
January 1, 1998 to December 31, 1999	7.1 cents or 1.35 cents per minute of playing time or fraction thereof, whichever is greater	1997 Mechanical Rate Adjustment Proceeding
January 1, 2000 to December 31, 2001	7.55 cents or 1.45 cents per minute of playing time or fraction thereof, whichever is greater	1997 Mechanical Rate Adjustment Proceeding
January 1, 2002 to December 31, 2003	8.0 cents or 1.55 cents per minute of playing time or fraction thereof, whichever is greater	1997 Mechanical Rate Adjustment Proceeding
January 1, 2004 to December 31, 2005	8.5 cents or 1.65 cents per minute of playing time or fraction thereof, whichever is greater	1997 Mechanical Rate Adjustment Proceeding
January 1, 2006	9.1 cents or 1.75 cents per minute of playing time or fraction thereof, whichever is greater	1997 Mechanical Rate Adjustment Proceeding

NET ARTIST ROYALTY RATE

The **net artist royalty rate** is the money that an artist gets per CD. The net artist royalty rate on a CD sold in the United States with a SRLP of $18.98 might be 12% or $2.28. For a new artist, royalty rates payable on sales of top-of-the-line CDs in the United States range from 11 to 13% of the SRLP. The royalty rate for a more significant artist ranges from 16 to 18%, increasing to 18 to 21% of the SRLP for a star artist. In determining the base artist royalty rate, however, most recording companies also deduct 15 to 25% of the SRLP for packaging costs (a jacket, CD jewel box, and booklet, etc.). Of course, that is also before the producer royalty of an additional 3% (see "Producer Royalties" below). Thus, the artist never sees $2.28 per CD. In fact, an artist might make slightly above $1 per CD sold. That is the traditional business model in the music industry. Those involved in the recording industry still refer to recordings as records or albums from time to time, but this text utilizes the term CDs instead.

BUDGET RECORDINGS AND MIDLINE RECORDINGS

Artists' royalty rates are subject to reduction on sales of CDs at less than the "topline" price (i.e., at a reduced price), such as **midline** or **budget-line** sales. Budget CDs sell for a low price usually when the commercial value of the CD has decreased. A midline CD is typically sold at a price halfway between the full SRLP and the budget price to entice the consumer to buy the CD. An artist might attempt to negotiate into his or her recording deal certain restrictions on the recording company's right to release midline or budget-line CDs.

"RECORD CLUB" ROYALTIES

Royalties are reduced to the artist for CD club sales such as Columbia House, Capitol, and RCA, who market thousands of artists at the same time. These third parties promote artists and their works for a fee to the artist and record company. This now includes television clubs and other late-night promotions of collections of music from the 1970s, 1980s, and more.

PRODUCER ROYALTIES

Producers of music have a financial incentive to produce an excellent product. Producers work in the studio with artists to make sure that the final work product sells. As such, producers receive a royalty known as the producer royalty (usually 3%), and it, too, is deducted from the artist's royalty rate.

COMPLIMENTARY GOODS

Recording companies use the distribution of free albums as a sales and promotional tool in an effort to sell its product. The artist receives no royalties on these free goods or **freebies.** Companies will not agree to eliminate these free goods but will agree to limit the number they give away. For example, if asked, most companies will agree to a free goods clause, whereby they will limit free CDs to 20 percent of records purchased and 30 percent of singles purchased. In calculating the artist royalty, some record companies discount the purchase price of a CD up to 15 or 20 percent in the name of **free goods.** Along the same lines are **premium** CDs: those goods given away as the result of a promotional sale such as test driving an automobile and receiving a complimentary CD.

MECHANICAL LICENSE

When an artist writes a song, he or she has a copyright in the song. When the song later is fixed on a CD, the recording company pays a **mechanical license** fee to the copyright owner. The current rate is .085 cents per copy for each song. A mechanical license fee is the fee paid by the recording company to the publisher for the use of copyrighted composition on a recording that is ultimately sold to the public. Depending upon the artist's clout, the rate generally falls between 70 and 100 percent of the rate prescribed in the Copyright Act.

For example, if one writes and records a song and 10,000 copies are made, the company owes $755. Most record companies pay mechanical royalties directly to the copyright owner, but the Harry Fox Agency (owned by the National Music Publishers Association) often collects these mechanical royalties for song owners. Labels have instituted **controlled composition clauses** in recording contracts, which means labels pay only 75 percent of the full royalty rate, especially to new artists.

COMPULSORY LICENSE

A **compulsory license** (sometimes known as a statutory license) forces a copyright owner to permit someone else to use the work for a predetermined fee. It precludes the owner of the copyright from refusing to license his or her work to other people in certain, specified circumstances. A compulsory license fee puts a ceiling on what the publisher can charge a recording company for using copyrighted music. The purpose is to get the music out to the public, as long as the fee is paid for the song.

PRINT LICENSE

A **print license** allows for the reproduction of printed copies of music such as sheet music, concert arrangements, and the printing of lyrics in magazines, advertising, and books. Although not the income producer it once was, print licenses, especially for well-known songs or well-known songwriters, can still generate substantial income. There is a large market in instructional music books for people taking music lessons and for educational uses such as choral, marching band, or orchestral scores. For educational uses, it is not uncommon to grant a royalty-free mechanical license for a recording of the arrangement to be made as a promotional tool by the print publisher.

BLANKET LICENSE

Performing rights organizations grant blanket licenses that allow businesses to use any songs within the catalog of music. For example, when a business obtains a blanket license from ASCAP, that business can play any songs within any of ASCAP's catalogs of music. A blanket license from ASCAP and BMI, for example, allows the licensee to access millions of copyrighted musical works. This is often how **cover bands** and sporting event venues are able to play the myriad of copyrighted songs at their own events without fear of being sued for infringement.[139]

SYNC LICENSE

Another way to profit is through a **sync license,** which is an agreement for the use of a song on television or in a movie. Sync licenses vary from several thousands of dollars for **independent films** (smaller, theatre-like film productions) to tens of thousands of dollars for major Hollywood films and national television advertisement campaigns. There is no fixed fee for this right, and it is usually negotiated by the music publisher.

---

[139] Some cover bands or events might intentionally not comply, or may just not know that they are technically infringing on copyrighted works.

CHAPTER SUMMARY

From the invention of the phonograph to tapes to CDs to MP3s, music is more available to the public than ever. Though profits have driven the music business for decades, the advent of the Internet has caused considerable concern in the recording industry as a whole. Industry leaders such as the RIAA have attempted to regulate downloading of copyrighted songs and have caused a stir among consumers, many of whom have become used to utilizing their home computers to copy songs (illegally) for free. Musicians and recording companies have established performing rights organizations and unions not only to establish minimum standards within the industry, but also to collect royalty fees. Changes in federal law and lawsuits within the music business over copyright infringement issues involving sampling have created a highly regulated industry.

CHAPTER TERMS

Administration
    agreement
Advance
Base royalty rate
Budget-line
Compulsory license
Controlled composition
    clause

Copublishing agreement
Cover bands
Cross-collateralization
Drive motor
Fingerprint
Free goods
Freebies
Hybrid song

Independent film
Mechanical license
Midline
Net artist royalty rate
Performance royalties
Premium
Print license
Recoup

Retail
Sampling
Single song agreement
Sync license
Tape
Term
Watermark
Wholesale

ADDITIONAL CASES

A&M Records, Inc. v. Napster, Inc., 239 F.3d 1004 (9th Cir. 2000)

Baxter v. MCA, Inc., 812 F.2d 421 (9th Cir. 1987)

Bonner v. Westbound Records, 394 N.E.2d 1303 (Ill. App. 1979)

Buffalo Broadcasting Co. v. ASCAP, 744 F.2d 917 (2d Cir. 1984)

Campbell v. Acuff-Rose Music, Inc., 510 U.S. 569 (1994)

Cohen v. Paramount Pictures Corp., 845 F.2d 851 (9th Cir. 1988)

Jarvis v. A&M Records, 827 F. Supp. 282 (D.N.J. 1993)

Northern Music Corp. v. King Record Distrib. Co., 105 F. Supp. 393 (S.D.N.Y. 1952)

Papa's-June Music, Inc. v. McLean, 921 F. Supp. 1154 (S.D.N.Y. 1996)

Phillips v. Playboy Music, Inc., 424 F. Supp. 1148 (N.D. Miss. 1976)

RIAA v. Diamond Multimedia Systems, Inc., 180 F.3d 1072 (9th Cir. 1999)

Robertson v. Batten, Barton, Durstine & Osborn, Inc., 146 F. Supp. 795 (S.D. Cal. 1956)

Sony Corp. of Am. v. Universal City Studios Inc., 464 U.S. 417 (1984)

Three Boys Music Corp. v. Bolton, 212 F.3d 477 (9th Cir. 2000)

Tin Pan Apple, Inc. v. Miller Brewing Co., 737 F. Supp. 826 (S.D.N.Y. 1990)

Waterson, Berlin & Snyder Co., In re, 48 F.2d 704 (2d Cir. 1931)

REVIEW QUESTIONS

1. Discuss the history of music technology from the twentieth century through the present.
2. What is the role of the Recording Industry Association of America?
3. What is Napster and how did that technology affect the music industry?
4. What is sampling?
5. Discuss the role of the various performance rights organizations such as BMI, ASCAP, and SESAC.
6. What is the difference between gross and net with regard to royalties?
7. Why should music producers receive a percent of the royalty of the production of a song?
8. What is a blanket license and what is the benefit of obtaining one?
9. Do you believe that technology will eventually be able to prevent music piracy?

The *ABKCO Music, Inc. v. Stellar Records, Inc.* case follows.

ABKCO Music, Inc. v. Stellar Records, Inc.

96 F.3d 60 (2d Cir. 1996)

UNITED STATES COURT OF APPEALS FOR THE SECOND CIRCUIT

OPINION: OWEN, District Judge:

This is an appeal from an order of the District Court for the Southern District of New York (Batts, J.), entered on August 10, 1995, preliminarily enjoining defendant-appellant Performance Tracks, Inc. ("Tracks") from publishing without authority the lyrics to copyrighted songs owned by plaintiffs-appellees ABKCO Music Inc. and ABKCO Music and Records Inc. ("ABKCO"), thus prohibiting Tracks from distributing its compact discs containing the copyrighted songs. We affirm.

Although this presents a case of first impression in terms of the technology at issue, the applicable legal principles are well-settled. ABKCO owns the copyrights to seven musical compositions by Mick Jagger and Keith Richards of the Rolling Stones, including the rock-and-roll classics "Satisfaction (I Can't Get No)," "Jumping Jack Flash," and "Brown Sugar." Despite many requests, ABKCO has never

licensed these famous songs for use in the "karaoke" or "sing-along" industry.

Tracks, a newcomer in the music field, is in the sing-along industry. It uses a new technology to encode on a compact disc ("CD") not only the audio rendition of a song, but also the contemporaneous video display of a song's lyrics. Thus, for a user who has a CD player with a video output, the lyrics of the songs can be displayed on a video screen in "real time" as the songs are playing so that the viewer can sing the lyrics along with the recorded artist. No other image or information appears, and the user cannot print the lyrics from the screen or control the speed of the music or lyrics. The Tracks discs, called "Compact Discs + Graphics" ("CD+Gs"), will provide audio playback alone when played on standard CD players. These CD+Gs are similar in purpose to the more familiar karaoke laser discs, which are quite popular in this country and abroad for entertainment at parties and nightclubs. Like the CD+Gs, karaoke discs display song lyrics against video images, enabling people to sing in time to the music. The primary difference between traditional karaoke discs and CD+Gs is that CD+Gs display only the lyrics, whereas karaoke discs display some video image, such as a sun-drenched beach, behind the song lyrics. Under the Copyright Act of 1976, 17 U.S.C. § 101 *et seq.*, the producers and distributors of karaoke versions of songs must acquire synchronization or "synch" licenses from the copyright owners of the songs to legally manufacture karaoke discs; a copyright owner may negotiate, if so disposed, the karaoke use of a song and the terms of the authorizing synch license with a karaoke maker.

Tracks did not secure synchronization licenses from ABKCO, but [**5] instead, viewing its products as "phonorecords," obtained "compulsory licenses" for the compositions, pursuant to the Copyright Act, 17 U.S.C. § 115, which permits the manufacture and distribution of new "cover" versions of copyrighted musical works as long as the licensee follows the statutory notice requirements and pays the proper royalty fees. Section 115 of the Copyright Act provides in part:

Compulsory license for making and distributing phonorecords

In the case of nondramatic musical works, the exclusive rights . . . to make and to distribute phonorecords of such works, are subject to compulsory licensing under the conditions specified by this section.

(a)   Availability and Scope of Compulsory License.—

(1)   When phonorecords of a nondramatic musical work have been distributed to the public in the United States under the authority of the copyright owner, any other person may, by complying with the provisions of this section, obtain a compulsory license to make and distribute phonorecords of the work. A person may obtain a compulsory license only if his or her primary purpose in making

phonorecords is to distribute them to the public for private use. . . .

(2)   A compulsory license includes the privilege of making a musical arrangement of the work to the extent necessary to conform it to the style or manner of interpretation of the performance involved, but the arrangement shall not change the basic melody or fundamental character of the work, and shall not be subject to protection as a derivative work under this title, except with the express consent of the copyright owner. 17 U.S.C. § 115 (emphasis added).

Under the Copyright Act, "phonorecords" are defined as material objects in which sounds, other than those accompanying a motion picture or other audiovisual work, are fixed by any method now known or later developed, and from which the sounds can be perceived, reproduced, or otherwise communicated, either directly or with the aid of a machine or device. The term "phonorecords" includes the material object in which the sounds are first fixed. 17 U.S.C. § 101 (emphasis added). "Audiovisual works" are defined as works that consist of a series of related images which are intrinsically intended to be shown by the use of machines or devices such as projectors, viewers, or electronic equipment, together with accompanying sounds, if any, regardless of the nature of the material objects, such as films or tapes, in which the works are embodied. 17 U.S.C. § 101 (emphasis added).

Tracks sent ABKCO a CD+G entitled "Songs of the Rolling Stones" containing the compositions, as well as notices of its intention to obtain compulsory licenses for the compositions. ABKCO thereupon informed Tracks that the Rolling Stones CD+G infringed on its copyrights of the compositions, and shortly thereafter initiated this action.

On July 5, 1995, ABKCO obtained a temporary restraining order. Thereafter, on August 10, 1995, Judge Deborah A. Batts, ruling from the bench, granted a preliminary injunction enjoining Tracks from "further publishing the lyrics of plaintiff's copyrighted Rolling Stones songs without authorization to do so," concluding that the visual depiction of the lyrics constituted an unauthorized publication of the lyrics, infringing ABKCO's copyrights. Tracks appeals pursuant to 28 U.S.C. § 1292(a)(1).

Tracks asserts as error, first, the district court's conclusion that the CD+G's visual display of song lyrics constitutes an unauthorized reproduction in violation of 17 U.S.C. § 106 because the visual feature of the CD+Gs is not within the ambit of the compulsory license provisions of 17 U.S.C. § 11, and second, the court's holding that the irreparable harm requirement had been satisfied.

In granting the preliminary injunction, the court below properly found that Tracks' compulsory licenses do not give it the right to publish the compositions' lyrics on a screen. Song lyrics enjoy independent copyright protection as "literary works," 1 Nimmer § 2.05[B], and the right to print a song's lyrics is exclusively that of the copyright holder under 17 U.S.C. § 106(1). Thus, while a compulsory license permits the recording of a "cover" version of a song, it does not permit the inclusion of a copy of the lyrics. That requires the separate permission of the copyright holder.

The court below correctly viewed *Bourne Co. v. Walt Disney Co.,* 1992 U.S. Dist. LEXIS 11731, No. 91 Civ. 0344, 1992 WL 204343 (S.D.N.Y. Aug. 7, 1992), as supporting its conclusion. Disney had obtained from plaintiff publisher's predecessor-in-interest a license to use the song "Little Wooden Head" from the film *Pinocchio* in synchronization with any Disney motion picture. The court in *Bourne* enjoined Disney, however, from using the song in a "sing-along" format on videocassettes in which the lyrics appeared at the bottom of the screen and a printed copy of the lyrics accompanied the video. The district court held in *Bourne* that the "right to print the lyrics . . . is qualitatively different from the right to synchronize that song with a visual image":

Even if . . . Disney had acquired the right to use the Pinocchio songs on videocassettes, that would not give it the right to print the lyrics of those songs, a right which appears to rest

exclusively with [the plaintiff publisher]. *Id.* at * 4–5. As in *Bourne,* the district court here properly concluded that a compulsory phonorecord license does not give Tracks the right to publish the lyrics on a screen.

A time-honored method of facilitating singing along with music has been to furnish the singer with a printed copy of the lyrics. Copyright holders have always enjoyed exclusive rights over such copies. While projecting lyrics on a screen and producing printed copies of the lyrics, of course, have their differences, there is no reason to treat them differently for purposes of the Copyright Act.

While we hardly need go further to affirm, we deal briefly with Tracks' contention that the court below, applying *Bourne,* was in error because its CD+Gs are "phonorecords," not copies, within the meaning of the Copyright Act, and therefore its compulsory licenses include the right to its limited video display. While the court below did not reach this contention, we do so hereafter and conclude that it is both factually and legally flawed.

Tracks' contention that CD+Gs are "phonorecords" and thus the video aspect is within the grant of its compulsory licenses can be disposed of quickly. The plain language of the Copyright Act refutes Tracks' view. Phonorecords are defined as objects on which "sounds" are fixed; CD+Gs, however, are objects on which sounds and visual representations of song lyrics are fixed. Moreover, the term phonorecord expressly excludes "audiovisual works," yet CD+Gs constitute "audiovisual works," since they "consist of a series of related images"—the lyrics— "together with accompanying sounds"— the music. 17 U.S.C. § 10.

Tracks does not claim that the actual definition of "phonorecord" in § 101 includes the visual capabilities of its CD+Gs, but rather contends that the Copyright Act has not kept pace with new technology, and that Congress, in view of its definition of "digital music recording" in the Audio Home Recording Act of 1992, 17 U.S.C. § 1001 *et seq.* ("AHRA"), would include Tracks' entire CD+G capability within the definition of "phonorecords" if it were to redefine "phonorecord" today. It would, however, seem to be a sufficient answer to Tracks' contention to observe that Tracks' product is not within the statutory definition of "phonorecord," and what Congress may or may not do in the future to redefine the term is not for us to speculate.

We further note that the AHRA itself undercuts Tracks' contention as to congressional leaning. Tracks relies upon the AHRA definition of "digital music recording," as well as the definition of "audiogram" in the legislative history, although the latter term, which appeared in an earlier version of the legislation, does not appear in the AHRA as enacted. *See* S. Rep. No. 294, 102d Cong., 2d Sess. 1 (1992) (hereinafter "Senate Report"). Tracks, arguing from the Senate Report, notes that an "audiogram" is "intended to include such items as the textual and graphic materials commonly embodied on (or inserted inside) album covers, CD boxes and audio cassette packages, such as title and artist information, biographies and still photos of the performers, and lyrics of the musical works." S. Rep. No. 294 at 46 (emphasis added). It is this, Tracks ultimately contends, that evidences that if Congress were to revisit the definition of "phonorecord" in the Copyright Act, it would amend the term to include visual depictions of song lyrics, thereby authorizing Tracks to produce its CD+Gs under the single umbrella of a compulsory license.

Not only have we earlier observed that Tracks' interpretation of the relationship between audiograms and phonorecords contradicts the plain language of the Copyright Act, but also the AHRA has specifically used the term "digital musical recording" instead of "phonorecords" to "avoid any impact on other unamended provisions of the current Copyright Act, such as § 115, which grants a compulsory license. . . ." H.R. Rep. No. 873 at 17, 1992 U.S.C.C.A.N. at 3587. Moreover, the Senate Report states that "the use of the new term 'audiogram' in chapter 10 is not intended to diminish, enlarge, or otherwise affect the scope of the term 'phonorecord' as it is used in . . . title 17." S. Rep. No. 294 at 53 (emphasis added). Tracks' argument founders on this.

Although the court below did not directly address Tracks' contention dealt with above, its observations implicitly—and correctly—rejected Tracks' interpretation of the AHRA: It seems to me that Congress at the time it passed the Audio Home Recording Act . . . was aware of the provision of the Copyright Act and the definitions of the Copyright Act, and that if Congress had intended to amend the Copyright Act, or had it intended that its 1992 Audio Home Recording Act was to have some impact on the Copyright Act, I'm sure that Congress would have said so. . . . J. A. at A211.

Lastly, Tracks contends that the injunction issued by the court below was erroneously granted without an adequate demonstration of irreparable harm. Tracks asserts "it is a dramatic leap in logic to argue that the addition of the lyrics to an indisputably permissible activity [rerecording a copyrighted composition pursuant to the compulsory license provisions of 17 U.S.C. § 115] somehow instantly creates irreparable harm to the copyright holders." We disagree. It is precisely this addition of the lyrics to be projected on the screen that renders the CD+Gs potentially lucrative for Tracks, and at the same time, if not enjoined, would leave ABKCO with a difficult reconstruction of damages should that issue arise at a later time, and would put ABKCO at the risk of disadvantageous exploitation of its artists in ways it would not have authorized. In any event, in a copyright infringement case, once a prima facie case of infringement has been demonstrated, irreparable harm is normally presumed, and substantial deference is given to a district court finding of irreparable harm. Thus, the court below, having a sound legal and factual basis for its assessment of a likelihood of success of on the merits, was justified in relying on the presumption of irreparable harm.

Conclusion

For the foregoing reasons, the order of the district court granting the preliminary injunction is affirmed.

REFERENCES FOR ADDITIONAL RESEARCH AND DISCUSSION

Baker, R.T., *Finding a Winning Strategy Against the MP3 Invasion: Supplemental Measures the Recording Industry Must Take to Curb Online Piracy*, 8 UCLA Ent. L. Rev. 1 (2000).

Beets, R.P., *RIAA v. Napster: The Struggle to Protect Copyrights in the Internet Age*, 18 Ga. St. U. L. Rev. 507 (2001).

Craft, K.L., *The Webcasting Music Revolution Is Ready to Begin, as Soon as We Figure Out the Copyright Law: The Story of the Music Industry at War with Itself*, 24 Hastings Comm. & Ent. L.J. 1 (2001).

Hepler, D.A., *Dropping Slugs in the Celestial Jukebox: Congressional Enabling of Digital Music Piracy Short-Changes Copyright Holders*, 37 San Diego L. Rev. 1165 (2000).

Maynor, D.R., *Just Let the Music Play: How Classic Bootlegging Can Buoy the Drowning Music Industry*, 10 J. Intell. Prop. L. 173 (2002).

Mullen, K.I., *The Rich Man's Eight Track: MP3 Files, Copyright Infringement, and Fair Use*, 5 Marq. Intell. Prop. L. Rev. 237 (2001).

Needham, L.M., *A Day in the Life of the Digital Music Wars: The RIAA v. Diamond Multimedia*, 26 Wm. Mitchell L. Rev. 1135 (2000).

Reese, R.A., *Copyright and Internet Music Transmissions: Existing Law, Major Controversies, Possible Solutions*, 55 U. Miami L. Rev. 237 (2001).

LEGAL ISSUES IN TELEVISION

AFTER STUDYING THIS CHAPTER YOU SHOULD BE ABLE TO:

1. Discuss concerns over fraud and television shows.
2. Compare and contrast quiz shows, reality television, and talk shows.
3. Discuss the specific liability for reality television and talk shows with particular regard to their shock value.
4. Identify concerns related to television cameras in the courtroom.
5. Discuss how the Television Decoder Circuitry Act of 1990 and the Americans with Disabilities Act have impacted television broadcasting.
6. Discuss the impact that the digital video recorder has had on television programming.
7. Explain what a V-chip is.
8. Discuss concerns over television broadcasts and children and related legislation.
9. Identify ways that television has attempted to regulate its programming.
10. Explain the terms pilot and syndication.

INTRODUCTION

Few inventions have had as much effect on American society as the television set and, consequently, the television industry as a whole. Before 1950, the number of U.S. homes with television sets was very few. Today, virtually every American home has at least one television set. Often referred to as the "small screen," television is one of the most governmentally regulated of all the entertainment industries. As studied earlier in the text, the FCC plays the major role in regulating the television industry and broadcasting generally.

A study of the evolution of the television and its regulation mirrors the shape of American history. Progress in technological advances during the twentieth century in television reflects a time line of significant events in American society as well, from sporting events to wars to national tragedies; television has been there to record and transmit images to the general public around the world.

For many, the study of television in the entertainment industry may represent a nostalgic venture. For others, the evolution and impact of television represents a continuing discourse on constitutional and regulatory issues and the role of the government. For some, the study of the television industry is all about ratings and advertising dollars and profits. Regardless of the perspective, television has had an overall positive impact on society and has made the world seem a lot smaller than

Television journalist Tim Russert interviews a guest on the set of the "Meet the Press."
Richard A. Bloom

before its existence, bringing rural viewers to the big city and city dwellers to America's heartland—all from the comforts of home.

Legal issues related to television (broadcasting, production, and so on) vary greatly. This chapter will attempt to break down a large area of the law into its most basic parts. The student should also recall the role that the FCC plays in the federal regulation of television broadcasting. Similarly, legal issues found in other chapters certainly apply in the television industry as well.

THE TELEVISION INDUSTRY

Generally speaking, the television industry consists of three categories: networks, studios, and production companies. Networks are the final medium to television viewers. The networks make the decisions as to what material to program and ultimately broadcast. Aside from the hundreds of cable channels, the noncable networks include ABC, CBS, NBC, Fox (FBC), WB, and UPN. Television studios are the physical production areas for shows, and production companies are usually independent companies that partner with studios to make shows.

Writers are the fundamental backbone of most television projects, and a **development deal** employs a writer to develop a single concept or idea, whereas an **overall deal** is usually longer and requires writing for more than just one project. Some studios hire their own writers in-house.

Beginning in 1949, television awards, called the Emmy awards, were given each September for outstanding television shows, actors, writers, and directing performances. The Academy of Television Arts and Sciences (ATAS), headquartered in Los Angeles, awards Emmys for prime time programs. The National Academy of Television Arts and Sciences (NATAS), in New York City, offers awards for daytime shows and for news and documentary programs.

TELEVISION UNIONS

The television business, like many industries, has its share of unions. Actors, writers, and directors can join unions that bargain collectively for its members. The major unions include the Screen Actors Guild (SAG), Screen Extras Guild (SEG), American Federation of Television and Radio Artists (AFTRA), Directors Guild of America (DGA), Writers Guild of America (WGA), and Actors' Equity Association (AEA). Also, the Associated Actors and Artists of America (AAAA) is an assembly of seven different unions, all of which represent actors and entertainers in the United States, including SAG and SEG.

PILOT

Each new year (January–April), television studios and production companies concern themselves with what is known as **pilot season.** A **pilot** is a term used to describe a sample episode of a television show. Producers, writers, and directors try to sell their show to the networks with the hope that the networks will adopt them for the fall television schedule after they **pitch** their concept. Concepts and pitches change frequently and often reflect themes that society is interested in viewing. During development season (July–November), writers pitch their shows to studios and production companies. Often, if a show works, copycat shows follow attempting to capitalize on a similar concept. The networks generally debut two to six new shows per fall season and possibly a few more at midseason.

Since pilots can be very costly to produce, sometimes shortened versions of pilot shows called **demos** are created using preexisting studio sets and props. Usually demos are only 15 minutes in length as opposed to a standard 22-minute show. The networks view pilots in April and May and make decisions soon thereafter. It is important to decide quickly since networks can then begin to sell advertising to sponsors for a particular show. If a network decides to accept a pilot project, it will then make an offer for a number of episodes, usually between thirteen and twenty-three, though they can be more or less. Once established, a network may choose to **pick up** a long-term contractual agreement of five years or more, much to the liking of writers, actors, producers, agents, managers, and networks who can then sell advertising.

NIELSEN COMPANY RATING SYSTEM

Television ratings provide useful information for advertising companies and producers, and the information is used to buy and sell television advertising time, as well as make program decisions. Not to be confused with quality ratings in terms of television content, the Nielsen television ratings provide an estimate of the numbers of viewers of a television program for just about every program that can be seen on television in over 200 markets. The Nielsen television ratings are the most well-known ratings and are managed by Nielsen Media Research (NMR).

Beginning in 1923, Nielsen was one of the first companies to measure the audience preferences for the radio broadcasting and advertising industry and later for television. The data is collected by means of an electronic measurement system called the Nielsen People Meter (NPM). Nielsen People Meter representatives are recruiters for Nielsen households who will serve as a sample for television ratings and actually train the viewers to use the Nielsen People Meter. The meter measures what program or channel is being tuned in and who is watching. The information is stored in and retrieved by NMR's computer system. NMR uses a sample of more than 5,000 households, containing over 13,000 people who have agreed to participate. The ratings are used on an international basis as well.

Oprah Winfrey stands in front of the cover of the premiere issue of *O, The Oprah Magazine.*
AP Wide World Photos

SYNDICATION

In its most general terms, **syndication** is the process of selling the rights of
presentation of a television program to customers such as individual television
stations and cable channels. Though many shows are syndicated internationally, in the United States the term syndication means repeated sales or reruns.
This can be lucrative for all involved in making a show because the costs of
making the show have already been expensed; there are no more sets to design
and no more writers or producers to pay. The show is simply rebroadcast. The
airing of a syndicated show is often referred to as a **run.**

TELEVISION FRAUD AND QUIZ SHOWS

The race for ratings, advertising, and profits brought some dark days to the television industry beginning in the 1950s. Around that time, contestant game and
quiz shows gathered increasing viewer popularity (and are still popular today)
in shows such as *Jeopardy, Millionaire,* and many others. These shows present intellectual challenges for viewers and can be very exciting to watch.

In the late 1950s, however, *Twenty-One*, *The $64,000 Question*, and *Dotto*, the highest-rated daytime quiz game show at the time, became the focus of scandals. All three shows, however, were eventually pulled from television broadcasts after it was discovered that certain contestants were prepped with answers to questions, even before the show went on the air.

For example, in 1956 on the game show *Twenty-One*, a college professor from Columbia University named Charles Van Doren was set up to beat champion Herb Stempel on the show. Ratings were at an all-time high, and networks and producers were happy. Later, however, Stempel became quite unhappy, especially after Van Doren appeared on the cover of *Time* and *Life* magazines, and he sought revenge by exposing the show's fraudulent conduct. Van Doren, a producer, and seventeen other contestants were ultimately convicted of lying to a grand jury but were only given suspended sentences. Actor Robert Redford produced a movie about the *Twenty-One* scandal titled *Quiz Show*, which won an Academy Award in 1994.

■ REALITY TELEVISION

The term **reality television** is a phrase used to describe a relatively recent phenomenon in television broadcasting. These unscripted shows display persons acting in real-world situations where their words and behaviors are not scripted.[140] Reality television shows include *Cops* (FOX), *Fear Factor* (NBC), and many others. Reality television can provide some of the most fascinating forms of entertainment for television viewers.

Ratings of other reality television shows, such as *American Idol* (FOX), *The Bachelor* (ABC), *The Bachelorette* (ABC), and *Survivor* (CBS), demonstrate the success and profitability of such ventures. While some shows have their roots stemming from programs such as *Candid Camera* and its "hidden camera" technique of filming people in the real world without them knowing they were on camera, today's shows have also exposed producers of the shows to a whole new world of potential lawsuits as well. Some of the most outrageous examples of reality television include MTV's *Punk'd* and TNN's *Oblivious*.

Reality shows that follow persons twenty-four hours per day for a period of time might invade the privacy of an individual by following a contestant into the bathroom.[141] Shows that are fixed to surprise or present "shock value" to unknowing participants could lead to claims involving the tort of intentional infliction of emotional distress. While the television shows will usually have a contestant sign a waiver (and possibly provide a fee) before the show is ultimately broadcast, concerns remain as to whether such waivers are even valid (for example, waiving the right to sue in the event of serious injury or death).

In 2001, former *Survivor* contestant Stacey Stillman sued producer Mark Burnett, his production company SEG Inc., and CBS, alleging that the show was

---

[140] This includes faux-reality television, where all are actors in a somewhat scripted scenario and all are aware of the scripted scenario except one unsuspecting participant.

[141] One may waive one's rights via a waiver or release, sometimes referred to as an exculpatory clause (see Chapter 3). Of course, the ultimate broadcast goes through the natural editing process before it is presented.

rigged. SEG filed a $5 million countersuit claiming defamation and breach of contract. Similarly, CBS sued the Fox broadcast network and LMNO Productions over the Fox show *Boot Camp*, alleging that Fox had stolen the idea for its show from *Survivor*.

For those involved in the legal aspects of these unscripted reality television shows, consideration must be given to damage control or risk prevention, including the purchase of liability insurance. Additionally, consideration must be given to requiring the signing of a confidentiality clause and other appropriate waivers and disclaimers. Finally, conducting thorough background checks on participants to ensure that the shows themselves have not been lied to about the qualification or identity of a contestant is important. This could avoid negative press subsequent to the broadcast of the show.

TALK SHOWS

Similar to reality television shows, daytime and nighttime talk shows usually go unscripted and are quite entertaining, whether they are politics-based, celebrity-based, or simply entertainment-value-based. *The O'Reilly Factor*, *The Oprah Winfrey Show*, *The Maury Povich Show*, and even the *Late Show with David Letterman* have become American household staples of an unscripted yet entertaining model of television programming.

Though such shows often have decent television ratings, legal issues in recent years involving violent behavior and embarrassment have given pause to producing talk shows, for example, the former *Jenny Jones Show* and *Jerry Springer*. Some outcomes of the talk shows can be characterized as tragic. Lawsuits involving tortious conduct during a talk show have become characterized as a **talk show tort** or even **ambush television.**

Jenny Jones Show

On March 5, 1995, Jonathan Schmitz and Scott Amedure were participants in the live taping of an episode of the *Jenny Jones Show* that dealt with revealing secret crushes. This particular crush involved a same-sex crush. Though the show never aired nationally, a mere three days after the taping Amedure was killed, and Schmitz turned himself in to the police. Schmitz was eventually convicted of second degree murder in 1996 and received a sentence of twenty-five to fifty years.[142]

Defense attorneys for Schmitz argued that the show's producers "ambushed" Schmitz with the news of the secret crush and that a shocked, embarrassed, and unpredictable reaction was exactly what the show's producers had in mind. In late 1998, the murder verdict was overturned in the Michigan Court

---

[142] *People v. Schmitz*, 586 N.W.2d 766 (Mich. Ct. App. 1998).

of Appeals, though a retrial in 1999 resulted in a similar verdict.[143] Amedure's representatives subsequently filed a $50 million lawsuit against the *Jenny Jones Show*. Also sued was Warner Brothers television, and the plaintiffs were awarded $25 million and burial costs in 1999. The show was found to be negligent in the guest's killing.

In 2002, the Michigan Court of Appeals reversed that 1999 decision and ruled that the show's owner, Warner Brothers, and its distributor, Telepictures, had no civil liability in the death of Scott Amedure. The court of appeals stated that the show "may be regarded as the epitome of bad taste and sensationalism," but that was not enough to create legal liability. In a dissenting opinion, Judge William Murphy said the show failed to check Schmitz's personal history, which included mental illness, alcohol and drug abuse, suicide attempts, and anger management problems.[144]

Talk shows, quiz shows, and reality television all offer interesting and sometimes shocking perspectives on American life. While it is doubtful that any of these categories of television will be phased out in the near future, tragic results and embarrassing scenarios have given audiences pause as to the role such unscripted programs will continue to play in television.

The following recent New York case represents the issue of talk shows and potential tort liability. Numerous torts previously discussed in this text are also analyzed by the court.

Sheila C. v. Povich

2003 N.Y. Misc. LEXIS 1439

OPINION: DIANE A. LEBEDEFF, J.

At the outset of what appears to be the first New York case falling into an emerging category of "Talk Show Torts," the named defendants move to dismiss the complaint brought on behalf of Sheila C., a minor who appeared on the *Maury Povich Show* (the "Show"). Plaintiff alleges the defendants' negligent acts connected with the Show set in motion a chain of events which concluded with her rape. Plaintiff cross-moves for leave to amend, should the court find the complaint is inadequate.

Background

In 2001, the Show solicited "out-of-control teen" guests. The plaintiff's mother contacted the Show. During conversations with plaintiff's mother and grandmother, the Show's staff was advised that plaintiff was fourteen years old, undergoing counseling, and taking medication for emotional illness, as well as that she recently had attempted suicide, lost a close immediate family member, and reported sexual intercourse with one twenty-nine-year-old man and five boys who were under age sixteen. It was agreed that the teen would appear on the Show and that the Show would provide the teen with follow-up psychological counseling and a corrective "teen boot camp," make transportation and hotel arrangements, and pay related expenses. After being told the teenager lived with her grandmother, the Show asked that both plaintiff's mother and grandmother

[143] http://www.datalounge.com/datalounge/issues/?storyline=288.
[144] *Graves v. Warner Bros.*, 656 N.W.2d 195 (Mich. Ct. App. 2002).

accompany the plaintiff on the trip. On December 5, 2001, plaintiff, her mother and her grandmother were picked up by a limousine in their hometown of Lemphill, Texas, flown to New York City, and transported by limousine to a midtown hotel.

On December 6, 2001, the day of the taping at the studio, defendant Polly Corman and Show staff allegedly told the teen to act sexually provocative and requested that plaintiff look "sexier" by wearing her thigh-length top without slacks. In accord with that theme, plaintiff claims her sexual experience was exaggerated five-fold during the Show.

While plaintiff was watching the taping of other guests on the Show with staff members, a man approached and exchanged greetings with Show personnel. In their presence, he introduced himself to plaintiff as "Maury's limo driver," complimented plaintiff's looks and asked for contact information so that he could show her around town at night. When plaintiff's mother inquired about this exchange, an unidentified staff member told the mother not to worry because the staff had "everything under control."

Later that evening, the driver called upon plaintiff at the hotel. After being turned away by plaintiff's mother and grandmother, he persuaded plaintiff to sneak away. The complaint alleges that the driver drove plaintiff up in a limousine to a dark area, climbed in back with her, and raped her.

Based on the factual allegations summarized above, the complaint asserts causes of action for negligence, negligent infliction of emotional distress, slander, negligent hiring and retention, and negligence *per se.* The moving defendants seek dismissal of all claims.

Negligence and the Duty of Care

Movants urge they owed no duty of care to the plaintiff at the time of the alleged rape and that all negligence claims must fail. The issue of the "existence and scope of a duty of care is a question of law" to be approached with recognition that "negligence is not a stereotyped thing, but, as courts have wisely said, it is a matter of time, place and circumstance; and the same act of a defendant may be a breach of duty toward one person while not a breach of duty toward another."

The defendants' argument has its seeds in *Graves v. Warner Bros.,* 253 Mich. App. 486, 656 N.W.2d 195 (2002), *app denied* 469 Mich. 853, 666 N.W.2d 665 (2003), *reconsideration denied* Mich., 669 N.W.2d 552 (2003) (the "Jenny Jones case"), which held that the *Jenny Jones Show* owed no duty to a former show guest who was murdered by another person who participated in the same taping session. The murder occurred several days after the show and after both guests returned to their homes in another state. The appellate court emphasized the distance of time and place, concluded that "under the circumstances defendants owed no legally cognizable duty to protect plaintiffs' decedent from the homicidal acts of a third party" and vacated the $29 million jury verdict. The court applied tort rules governing commercial premises where the owners and operators have a duty to use reasonable care which "is triggered by specific acts occurring on the premises that pose a risk of imminent and foreseeable harm to an identifiable invitee," and ruled that the relationships between the talk show and its guests were "of business invitor to invitee" and that "any duty ends when the relationship ends."

The facts pleaded by the instant complaint are distinctly different from the Jenny Jones case. The complaint describes an active relationship between the Show and the plaintiff at the time of the claimed rape, in that the plaintiff was subject to the Show's travel, care and chaperone arrangements at the very time of the assault. Further, the Show is described as having a continuing bargained-for future obligation to provide plaintiff with counseling, to send her to a remedial camp, and to return her to her home State (*see,* for a description of psychological screening and aftercare provided by television talk shows, Jason S. Schlessel, *The Deep Pocket Dilemma: Setting the Parameters of Talk Show Liability,* 20 Cardozo Arts & Ent. L.J. 461,

481–483 [2002]). A fair summary of the complaint's allegations, and its inferences, is as follows: (1) for the Show's commercial purposes and as a result of the Show's solicitation and selection, an "out-of-control" minor with disclosed emotional difficulties was brought into this State; (2) the Show presented itself as having special expertise in remedying the problems of an "out-of-control" teen, with the capability of choosing and providing an appropriate remedial therapist and camp program; (3) while the child was under the Show's direct supervision, the Show staff allowed a person allegedly known to them to approach the minor and successfully learn how to contact the minor, notwithstanding that there was no facially proper purpose for such a contact; (4) after being taped—and it is unclear that all taping was fully completed—the minor was left under the supervision of the two adults who admitted they could not control the minor and who had asked the Show to help them correct this problem; and, (5) no other steps having been taken to protect the infant, to assist the guardians, or to prevent the driver from pursuing his desire to contact the minor, the child was lured away from the guardians by the driver and was raped. Clearly, the pleading states a fact pattern very different from the Jenny Jones case.

As to the law, also unlike the Jenny Jones case, no great legal scrutiny is required to identify a legally cognizable duty which underlies the negligence claim. The pleading asserts negligent supervision of a child, a claim well-recognized in New York. A non-parent may be held responsible for negligent supervision of a child when the non-parent undertakes the care and supervision of a child, the child is injured, and such injuries foreseeably are related to the absence of adequate supervision. *Shante D. v. City of New York,* 83 N.Y.2d 948, 615 N.Y.S.2d 317, 638 N.E.2d 962 (1994). As a matter of law, a high standard of care is imposed upon the supervisor of a minor and no lower standard of care may be utilized, such as the invitee standard used in the Jenny Jones case (*Zalak v. Carroll,* 15 N.Y.2d 753, 754, 257 N.Y.S.2d 177, 205

N.E.2d 313 [1965], duty to infant in defendants' care "not measured by what their duty would have been to a social guest or a mere licensee" and caretakers "were required to use reasonable care to protect the infant plaintiff from injury"; *Willis v. YMCA of Amsterdam,* 28 N.Y.2d 375, 379, 321 N.Y.S.2d 895, 270 N.E.2d 717 [1971], "Although persons having children entrusted to their care are 'not the absolute insurers' of their safety, they are 'charged with the highest degree of care'").

Further, although movants request consideration of a number of other factors, none defeat the pleaded cause of action. First, the fact that the Talk Show's personnel were not directly supervising the minor at the time of the injury is not fatal to the pleading. A caretaker is not automatically exempt from responsibility merely because of a suspension of physical supervision of an injured minor where, as here, the conditions created by the caretaker are still in effect (*Ernest v. Red Creek Central School,* 93 N.Y.2d 664, 671, 695 N.Y.S.2d 531, 717 N.E.2d 690 [1999], school district may be responsible for injury after child released from custody when student was "released into a potentially hazardous situation" and hazard was partially of defendants' "own making"). Once a claim of lack of adequate supervision is pleaded, it must be left to a later date to weigh whether the facts are such that the duty to supervise no longer lay with defendants (compare *Berlin v. Nassau County Council, Boy Scouts of America,* 229 A.D.2d 414, 645 N.Y.S.2d 90 [2d Dept. 1996], summary judgment determination dismissing claim against trip supervisor for permitting slingshot purchase on trip when injury was one week after child returned home).

Second, describing a rape as an unanticipated voluntary act offers no safe harbor defeating the pleading. The proper inquiry here is whether the complaint claims that deficient supervision was a substantial contributing factor to injury to a minor by the harmful action of a third party, outside the presence of the supervisor, in a setting arising from the supervisor's failure to anticipate an obvious, inherent danger (*Bell v. Board of Education of the City of New York,* 90

N.Y.2d 944, 947, 665 N.Y.S.2d 42, 687 N.E.2d 1325 [1997], student separated from supervised class trip, rape held reasonably foreseeable consequence of earlier inadequate supervision, court noting "the very purpose of the . . . supervision was to shield [a] vulnerable schoolchild[] from such acts"; *Kush v. City of Buffalo,* 59 N.Y.2d 26, 33, 462 N.Y.S.2d 831, 449 N.E.2d 725 [1983], minors injured by dangerous chemicals stolen from playground premises, "the intervening, intentional act of another is itself the foreseeable harm that shapes the duty"). The pleading clearly meets this standard, for this contention is the very essence of the claim raised by plaintiffs.

Third, defendants' contention that the involvement of the plaintiff's mother and grandmother insulates them from liability is unavailing. Even assuming *arguendo* that the mother and grandmother bore some responsibility to supervise the plaintiff in the hotel, any contributory negligence on their part cannot, as a matter of law, defeat or impair a minor's claim (General Obligations Law § 3–111, "In an action brought by an infant to recover damages for personal injury the contributory negligence of the infant's parent or other custodian shall not be imputed to the infant"; *Holodook v. Spencer,* 36 N.Y.2d 35, 49, 364 N.Y.S.2d 859, 324 N.E.2d 338 [1974], statute indicates "that the parent's failure to provide adequate supervision . . . [is not] permitted to diminish or bar a child's recovery against a third party").

Finally, it is not fatal to the claim that plaintiff was a teenager. All caretakers of minors have a duty of care, even if the minor is a teenager (*Mary A. 'ZZ' v. Blasen,* 284 A.D.2d 773, 726 N.Y.S.2d 767 [3d Dept. 2001], neighbor who agreed to "keep an eye" on teenage girls, one of whom was sexually assaulted, was "required to use reasonable care to protect the child from harm and may be liable for injury proximately caused by . . . negligence"). Whether the teenage plaintiff herself was contributorily negligent cannot be weighed on a motion to dismiss and likely not even on a motion for summary judgment (*Carmen P. v. PS&S Realty Corp.,* 259 A.D.2d 386, 388, 687 N.Y.S.2d 96 [1st Dept. 1999], in relation to 14 year old, "Whether a child has exercised reasonable care for a person of her age and maturity and development level is typically a jury question"; *Adolph E. by Susan E. v. Lori M.,* 166 A.D.2d 906, 560 N.Y.S.2d 567 [4th Dept. 1990], "whether defendant, then 12 years of age, was negligent presents issues of fact which cannot be resolved on a motion for summary judgment").

Based upon the foregoing, it is determined that plaintiff has adequately pleaded a cause of action for negligence.

Emotional Distress

The emotional distress cause of action sets forth in its text mixed claims of both intentional and negligent infliction of emotional distress. An intentional infliction of emotional distress claim must rest upon allegations that a defendant's behavior was "extreme and outrageous" to such extent that the action was "atrocious and intolerable in a civilized society." The same legal standard is generally applicable to negligent infliction of emotional distress (*Longo v. Armor Elevator Co., Inc.,* 307 A.D.2d 848, 850, 763 N.Y.S.2d 597 [1st Dept. 2003], plaintiffs must "establish the element of extreme and outrageous conduct for a negligent infliction of emotional distress claim [by] . . . evidence that the . . . defendants' conduct was so outrageous in character and extreme in degree as to go beyond all possible bounds of decency").

Alternatively, a negligent infliction of emotional distress claim may rest upon an assertion that "defendants' conduct unreasonably endangered plaintiffs' physical safety" or, albeit irrelevant here, "that untruthful information regarding death was transmitted or that a corpse was negligently mishandled" (*Dobisky v. Rand,* 248 A.D.2d 903, 905, 670 N.Y.S.2d 606 [3d Dept. 1998], summarizing *Johnson v. State of New York,* 37 N.Y.2d 378, 381–382, 372 N.Y.S.2d 638, 334 N.E.2d 590 [1975]). Where endangerment of physical safety is pleaded, the physical danger supporting a negligent infliction of emotional distress claim involves direct and immediate jeopardy, not a danger later arising as a consequence of a defendant's action. Neither alternate basis for a negligent infliction of emotional distress claim applies here.

No other standard being applicable, the pivotal factor upon which the emotional distress claim must rest is the conduct of the defendants as pleaded. No movant is the alleged rapist. These movants are described as participants in various aspects of production of a television show, and no language in the pleading identifies any of the actions of an individual movant as "intolerable in a civilized society."

Given that the actions attributed to each movant fail to meet the requisite standard, this claim against each movant is severed and stricken.

Slander

Defendants also seek dismissal of the slander *per se* claim, on the ground that the complaint fails to allege the exact defamatory words, the speaker, and the time and place of the allegedly defamatory statements and the pleading fails to meet the particularity requirements of CPLR 3016(a).

Movants rightly argue that the pleading must set forth the exact words used, which also is necessary so that the court may perform a threshold review to determine if the exaggerating words are defamatory or, alternatively, are "rhetorical hyperbole" that "cannot reasonably be interpreted as stating actual facts about an individual" (*Milkovich v. Lorain Journal Co.,* 497 U.S. 1, 20, 111 L. Ed. 2d 1, 110 S. Ct. 2695 [1990], citing *Hustler Magazine v. Falwell,* 485 U.S. 46, 50, 99 L. Ed. 2d 41, 108 S. Ct. 876 [1987]). Such a review must be undertaken carefully when a claimed defamatory statement is made in the course of a public discussion, where both parties may use "non-literal, figurative language in expressing their views" (*Horsley v. Rivera,* 292 F.3d 695, 702 [11th Cir. 2002], suit dismissed against talk show host Geraldo Rivera arising out of his exchange with anti-abortion activist). Further, in the context present here, an exact quotation is required to identify whether a statement made in relation to a talk show was aired to the general public (*Peter Scalamandre & Sons, Inc. v. Kaufman,* 113 F.3d 556, 563 [5th Cir. 1997], "It is common knowledge television shows . . . shoot more footage than necessary and edit the tape they collect down to a brief piece"; *see,* for a description of editing process for a television show, *Texas Beef Group v. Winfrey,* 201 F.3d 680, 689 [5th Cir. 2000], rehearing en banc den 212 F.3d 597 [5th Cir. 2000], suit against Oprah Winfrey Show involving product disparagement claims of the Texas cattle industry).

Because the offending words are not set forth in the complaint, the slander claim is dismissed with leave to replead, if plaintiff be so advised.

Negligent Hiring and Retention

A cause of action for negligent hiring or retention requires allegations that the employer "knew or should have known of the employee's propensity to commit injury," or the employer failed to investigate a prospective employee notwithstanding knowledge of "facts that would lead a reasonably prudent person to investigate that prospective employee." The complaint contains the necessary allegations.

Negligent hiring and retention concepts do have sufficient flexibility to cover relationships which are not those of a typical employer-employee arrangement, especially where a named defendant is alleged to have selected or controlled persons placed in contact with minors (*see Koran I. v. New York City of Bd. of Educ., supra,* 256 A.D.2d at 191, school volunteer screened by teachers and principal, claim dismissed only upon proof defeating substantive claim). It is not ignored that the role and status of each moving defendant—and, indeed, of the alleged limousine driver and rapist—within the Show's organization and structure must be clarified in the course of discovery. These relevant facts are necessarily "within defendants' exclusive knowledge" and "it would be premature to grant dismissal" for a failure to plead full supporting facts at this early stage of the proceeding (*Parsons & Whittemore, Inc. v.*

Abady Luttati Kaiser Saurborn & Mair, P.C., 299 A.D.2d 156, 753 N.Y.S.2d 36, 2003 WL 22435220 [1st Dept. 2003]). Accordingly, the requests to dismiss this branch of the pleading are denied.

Negligence Per Se (Child Endangerment Statute)

The negligence *per se* claim is based on allegations that the conduct of several of the defendants violated Penal Law § 260.10(1). The statute states a "person is guilty of endangering the welfare of a child when . . . [such person] knowingly acts in a manner likely to be injurious to the physical, mental or moral welfare of a child less than seventeen years old or directs or authorizes such child to engage in an occupation involving a substantial risk of danger to his life or health. . . ."

In relation to the mandate of Penal Law § 260.10(1) that adults refrain from acting in "a manner likely to be injurious to the physical, mental or moral welfare of a child," it has been observed that "the statute is broadly written" and it "does not require a particular outcome or actions aimed at a specific individual" but only that the defendant have "an awareness of the potential for harm" to a child (*People v. Johnson,* 95 N.Y.2d 368, 372, 718 N.Y.S.2d 1, 740 N.E.2d 1075 [2000]; *see,* similarly, *People v. Hitchcock,* 98 N.Y.2d 586, 590, 750 N.Y.S.2d 580, 780 N.E.2d 181 [2002]). This duty is clearly general, and harkens to custom and reasonableness.

Indeed, there is no independent support for plaintiffs' argument that the statute gives rise to negligence *per se.* No New York case has interpreted this particular statutory language as giving rise to negligence without fault. In the one jurisdiction where this argument was also raised, absolute liability was held to be unsupported by similar language (*Hite v. Brown,* 100 Ohio App. 3d 606, 612, 654 N.E.2d 452, 456 [Ohio App. 8th Dist. 1995], *app denied* 73 Ohio St. 3d 1414, 651 N.E.2d 1311 [1995], negligence *per se* inapplicable because "statute requires one to employ reasonable conduct under the circumstances, it does not describe a specific act but instead states a rule of conduct."). Nationwide, similar broadly

worded child endangerment provisions are the basis for criminal and custody termination disputes, and they are almost never invoked in a negligence context.

It is helpful to contrast provisions in relation to which negligence *per se* does arise. Typically involved is a "flat and unvarying duty," such as is found in worker protection provisions of the Labor Law, which involve "a hazard of definable orbit" (*Koenig v. Patrick Constr. Corp.,* 298 N.Y. 313, 317–318, 83 N.E.2d 133 [1948]). Strikingly, because of the confined nature of the duty, the second branch of the child endangerment statute—the bar of employment of a minor in an "occupation involving a substantial risk of danger"—and kindred statutes limiting employment of a minor at dangerous tasks have been held to support absolute liability (*see Stenson v. J. H. Flick Const. Co.,* 146 A.D. 66, 130 N.Y.S. 555 [1st Dept. 1911], *app dismissed* 203 N.Y. 553, 96 N.E. 1131 [1911], case brought under child endangerment provision, plaintiff required to establish employer knew child was a minor to claim negligence *per se; Karpeles v. Heine,* 227 N.Y. 74, 124 N.E. 101 [1919], collecting cases, statutory prohibition against minor operating freight elevator).

Based on the above, the court determines that the statutory duty to refrain from acting in a manner "likely to be injurious to the physical, mental or moral welfare" of a minor child does not give rise to a negligence *per se* claim. Accordingly, this claim is severed and dismissed as to each moving defendant.

Other Requests

Movants also present heavily redacted contracts as documentary evidence indicating that individual defendants Kemmer and Corman were employed by or were independent contractors of Studio USA Talk Television and they urge that the claims against Mr. Povich and the other corporate defendants should fail on that basis. The proffered contracts shed no light on the actual degree of control any defendant had over any other defendant, and they reveal no information on the relationship of Studio USA Talk Television to Mr. Povich or the other corporate defendants. Accordingly, these documents are inadequate to support dismissal of the complaint as requested.

Plaintiff's cross-motion for leave to amend is denied except as to the slander claim. The balance of plaintiff's request is not supported by a proposed amended pleading nor by evidentiary supporting material.

_____

Material has been adapted for this text. Used with the permission of LexisNexis.

TELEVISION IN THE COURTROOM

At one time, the thought of a camera in the courtroom was considered preposterous. Today, however, all fifty states currently allow some form of audio/video coverage of court proceedings under a variety of rules and conditions. With few exceptions, federal courts do not allow cameras in the courtroom. In 2003, a bill was introduced called the "Sunshine in the Courtroom Act," after attempts in 1999 and 2001 failed to pass in Congress. As of the time of this writing, the bill has not become law. However, it is only a matter of time before federal courts, including the Supreme Court, will no longer hide behind walls of justice inaccessible to television or Internet (webcam) feeds.

Court TV

Television in the state courtrooms became quite popular beginning with retired California Judge Joseph Wapner presiding over *The People's Court* in 1981. Successful imitations followed with reality television shows such as *Judge Judy*, *Judge Joe Brown*, *Judge Mathis*, *Divorce Court*, and *Judge Mills Lane*, among others. Litigants (plaintiffs and defendants) are paid as part of their appearance.[145]

Similarly, the popular cable show *Court TV* began in 1991, using the television in the courtroom as its own form of reality television. The first trial aired was a murder case in which the defendant was acquitted of murdering his stepmother-in-law. In order to protect privacy concerns, *Court TV* uses a 10-second broadcast delay for all trials in order to prevent the airing of information such as the addresses of witnesses, names of jurors, and private conversations between a lawyer and his or her client. Litigants in *Court TV* are not compensated by the program.

CLOSED CAPTIONING

Closed captioning (CC) means that within a television broadcast signal there is a hidden caption not viewable unless the viewer selects it to be opened. Closed captioning is akin to subtitles in a movie theatre (such as when viewing a foreign film and not understanding the foreign language). Closed captioning

_____

[145] http://www.usfca.edu/pj/articles/realcourt.htm.

provides access to television for persons with hearing disabilities. **Online captioning** can be done from a script or actually created in real time. **Offline captioning** is done after the fact, in a studio.

Through closed captioning, the audio portion of programming is displayed as text superimposed over part of the video.[146] In 1990, Congress required television receivers to contain circuitry designed to decode and display closed captioning. In 1993, the FCC required that all analog television sets with screens 13 inches or larger sold in the United States contain built-in decoder circuitry that allowed any viewer to display closed captions. This was known as the **Television Decoder Circuitry Act (TDCA)** of 1990.[147] The TDCA was passed the same year as the Americans with Disabilities Act (ADA), discussed further in Chapter 11.

As part of the Telecommunications Act of 1996, Congress instructed the FCC to require video program distributors (cable operators, broadcasters, satellite distributors, and other multichannel video programming distributors) to phase in over time, the closed captioning of their television programs. In 1997, the FCC implemented rules to provide a transition schedule for video program distributors to follow in providing even more captioned programming. The rules required that distributors provide an increasing amount of captioned programming according to a set schedule. Beginning July 1, 2002, the FCC also required that digital television (DTV) receivers include closed caption display capability.

AMERICANS WITH DISABILITIES ACT (ADA)

The Americans with Disabilities Act (ADA) is a law designed to protect disabled people from discrimination in employment, transportation, and public accommodation. While the ADA does not require all television programming to be captioned, all public service announcements produced or funded by the federal government for television must be closed captioned. Public accommodations, including (but not limited to) hotels, hospitals, bars, convention centers, shopping centers, libraries, museums, day care centers, health spas, and bowling alleys, must provide access to the audio portion of programs. Presidential and vice presidential candidates may not obtain federal campaign money unless they caption their commercials (26 U.S.C. § 2006(e)).

EMERGENCY PROGRAMMING

The FCC also has specific rules requiring that all video programming distributors that elect to provide emergency information do so in a format that is accessible to people who are deaf or hard of hearing, blind, or have low vision. Emergency information is information that helps to protect life, health, safety,

---

[146] For news broadcasts, the term electronic newsroom technique (ENT) creates captions from a news script computer or teleprompter used for live newscasts.
[147] 47 U.S.C. § 303(u).

or property. Examples include hazardous weather situations such as tornadoes, heavy snows, hurricanes, earthquakes, and dangerous community situations such as the discharge of toxic gases, widespread power failures, civil disorders, and school closings. In order to provide access, emergency information that is provided in the audio portion of the programming must be provided using closed captioning or other methods of visual presentation, such as open captioning, crawls, or scrolls that appear on the screen.[148]

■ PIRACY AND RETRANSMISSION ISSUES

Similar to piracy issues in the music industry, the pirating and retransmission of television broadcasts is a major concern in the television industry. The advent of the Internet has created interesting twists as well with regard to pirates. In 2000, movie and television companies including Twentieth Century Fox Film, Disney Enterprises, Columbia TriStar Television, Columbia Pictures Television, Columbia Pictures Industries, Metro-Goldwyn-Mayer Studios, Orion Pictures, Paramount Pictures, Universal City Studios, Time Warner Entertainment (Warner Bros.), ABC, CBS Broadcasting, and Fox Broadcasting filed a lawsuit against the Canadian company iCraveTV.com for sending copyrighted television programs over the Internet without prior permission. The lawsuit sought an injunction in federal district court in Pennsylvania. The company allegedly took seventeen over-the-air television signals in Toronto and retransmitted them over the Internet. An injunction was granted, an agreement was reached, and the case was settled out of court.

Los Angeles-based RecordTV.com allowed customers, for a short time, to record television shows and play them back online. The idea of RecordTV.com was to allow a user to record content from local television and basic cable programs and stream it via their computers. In 2001, the company settled a lawsuit with the Motion Picture Association of America (MPAA), which accused RecordTV.com of violating copyright laws by recording movies and then streaming them online without prior permission.[149]

In late 2003, the FCC instituted a mandate that by July 1, 2005, makers of digital television receivers must recognize an electronic marker that broadcasters can embed in their programs to limit piracy. Known as a "broadcast flag," the signal does not prevent consumers from copying programs but would make it very difficult to transfer the copies to the Internet, where users could download the shows for free, interfering with international and syndication profits.

■ DIGITAL VIDEO RECORDER (DVR)

Recent technological advances in recording television programming have made the VCR's days numbered. It has also changed the way some consumers (a small but growing number) watch television. One of these advances is termed a digital

---

[148] http://www.fcc.gov/cgb/consumerfacts/emergencyvideo.html.
[149] http://www.mpaa.org/Press/RecTVSettlementRelease.htm.

video recorder (DVR), which is like a VCR but with a hard drive that can record up to 80 hours of television shows automatically without videotape.

Services such as TiVo, ReplayTV, and Echostar allow consumers to record television shows for a fee, and there are no videotapes. Few American households have the service, but the number is growing. TiVo invented a method for recording one program while playing back another, watching a television program as it is recording, and allowing for "TrickPlay" capability which allows live television broadcasts to be paused, fast-forwarded, replayed, or shown in slow motion. Commercials can be skipped over or eliminated entirely, and consumers can watch programs on their own terms at their own times. Competition is so fierce that TiVo filed a patent infringement suit in 2004 against EchoStar, alleging that it violated TiVo's multimedia time-warping system, also known as Time Warp, patent acquired in 2001.[150] Additionally, in late 2004 TiVo received FCC approval for TiVoToGo, which enables a user to record and then send a digital broadcast show to up to nine other registered people (against the wishes of organizations such as the MPAA).

VIOLENCE AND TELEVISION

One major concern over the television industry is its violent programming content. In response to nationwide complaints over the increased violent content of television shows and as a matter of self-regulation, the television industry submitted a system of voluntary parental guidelines to the FCC in 1997. In § 551 of the Telecommunications Act of 1996, Congress gave the broadcasting industry the first opportunity to establish voluntary ratings. The industry established a system for rating programming that contains sexual, violent, or other material parents may deem inappropriate and committed to voluntarily broadcast signals containing these ratings.

The rating system, also known as TV Parental Guidelines, was established by the National Association of Broadcasters, National Cable Television Association, and Motion Picture Association of America. These ratings are displayed on the television screen for the first 15 seconds of rated programming and, in conjunction with the V-chip, permit parents to block programming with a certain rating from coming into their home.

TELEVISION RATING SYSTEM

(The TV Parental Guidelines)[151]

FOR PROGRAMS DESIGNED SOLELY FOR CHILDREN

TV-Y (All Children—This program is designed to be appropriate for all children.) Whether animated or live-action, the themes and elements in this program

---

[150] http://www.tivo.com/5.3.1.1.asp?article=193.
[151] http://www.fcc.gov/parents/parent_guide.html

CHAPTER SUMMARY

The advent of the television had a huge impact on American society. From the early black-and-white days to the modern era of HDTV and plasma television sets, few Americans can live without a television. The television industry has informed and entertained the world for years and has brought rural and urban areas together. At one time, only three broadcast networks existed. Today, hundreds of channels on color cable television dominate households and provide all-day entertainment.

A highly regulated industry, the FCC has played a major role in regulating, licensing, and enforcing its rules for television broadcasts. The federal government has kept a keen eye on possible antitrust violations in the television industry as well.

Television unions such as SAG and AFTRA were established to protect and assert fundamental rights for performers, writers, and directors. Though viewer ratings drive the advertising game, violence in television brought angry viewers to push for a quality rating system called the TV Parental Guidelines. Contemporary issues in television include dealing with piracy and retransmission issues and how the Internet and television have become intertwined.

CHAPTER TERMS

All-Channel Receiver Act (ACRA)
Ambush television
Analog
Cable Television Consumer Protection and Competition Act of 1992
Children's Television Act of 1990
Closed captioning
Demos
Development deal
Digital
Must carry
Offline captioning
Online captioning
Overall deal
Pick up
Pilot
Pilot season
Pitch
Reality television
Run
Syndication
Talk show tort
Television Decoder Circuitry Act (TDCA)
V-chip

ADDITIONAL CASES

American. Broad. Cos. v. Writers Guild of Am., West, Inc., 437 U.S. 411, 424 (1978)

Association of Maximum Service Telecasters v. FCC, 853 F.2d 973 (D.C. Cir. 1988)

Buckley v. Am. Fed'n of Television and Radio Artists, 496 F.2d 305 (2d Cir. 1974)

Eastern Microwave, Inc. v. Doubleday Sport, Inc., 691 F.2d 125 (2d Cir. 1982)

Electronic Industries Ass'n Consumer Electronics Group v. FCC, 636 F.2d 689 (D.C. Cir. 1980)

Metromedia Broadcasting Corp. v. MGM/UA Entertainment Co., 611 F. Supp. 415 (C.D. Cal. 1985)

Orth-O-Vision, Inc. v. Home Box Office, Inc., 474 F. Supp. 672 (S.D.N.Y. 1979)

Ralph C. Wilson Industries, Inc. v. American Broadcasting Cos. Inc., 598 F. Supp. 694 (N.D. Cal. 1984)

Schurz Comm., Inc. v. FCC, 982 F.2d 1043, 1050 (D.C. Cir. 1992)

Shulman v. Group W Productions, 955 P.2d 469 (Cal. 1998)

Twentieth Century Fox Film Corp. v. ICRAVETV, 2000 U.S. Dist. LEXIS 11670, 53 U.S.P.Q. 2d (BNA) 1831, Copy. L. Rep. (CCH) P28, 030, Feb. 8, 2000)

United States v. Loew's, Inc., 371 U.S. 38 (1962)

United States v. National Ass'n of Broadcasters, 536 F. Supp. 149 (D.D.C. 1982)

Writers Guild of Am. W. v. American Broadcasting Co., 609 F.2d 355 (9th Cir. 1979), *cert. denied*, 449 U.S. 824 (1980)

REVIEW QUESTIONS

1. Cite specific examples of fraud in television.
2. What are some legal issues particular to live talk shows?
3. What is closed-captioning?
4. Are DVRs legal?
5. How does the Americans with Disabilities Act relate to television broadcasting?
6. What is a V-chip?
7. What is the meaning of the term syndication in television?
8. How has cable television affected American life?
9. How are children protected from certain television broadcasts?
10. Do you believe that televisions should be allowed in state and federal courtrooms?

REFERENCES FOR ADDITIONAL RESEARCH AND DISCUSSION

Famoso, R., *Ambush TV: Holding Talk Shows Liable for the Public Disclosure of Private Facts*, 29 Rutgers L.J. 579 (1998).

Fecteau, A., *NFL Network Blackouts: Old Law Meets New Technology with the Advent of the Satellite Dish*, 5 Marq. Sports L.J. 221 (1995).

Fornos, C.A., *Inspiring the Audience to Kill: Should the Entertainment Industry Be Held Liable for Intentional Acts of Violence Committed by Viewers, Listeners, or Readers?* 46 Loy. L. Rev. 441 (2000).

Forouzan, M. K., *Television Violence: Legislation to Combat the National Epidemic*, 18 Whittier L. Rev. 219 (1996).

Fucci, M. J., *Facing the Future: An Analysis of the Television Ratings System*, 6 UCLA Ent. L. Rev. 1 (1998).

Green, D., *Almost Famous: Reality Television Participants as Limited-Purpose Public Figures*, 6 Vand. J. Ent. L. & Prac. 94 (2003).

Neikirk, K.E., *Fore! The Americans With Disabilities Act Tees Off at Professional Sports in Martin v. PGA Tour, Inc., But Will It Make the Cut?* 36 Hous. L. Rev. 1867 (1999).

Schlessel, J.S., *The Deep Pocket Dilemma: Setting the Parameters of Talk Show Liability*, 20 Cardozo Arts & Ent. L.J. 461 (2002).

Scott, D.V., *The V-Chip Debate: Blocking Television Sex, Violence, and the First Amendment*, 16 Loy. L.A. Ent. L.J. 741 (1996).

Wolff, J.L., *The V-Chip: Giving Parents the Ability to Regulate Television Violence*, 37 Santa Clara L. Rev. 785 (1997).

CHAPTER 11

LEGAL ISSUES IN MOTION PICTURES

AFTER STUDYING THIS CHAPTER YOU SHOULD BE ABLE TO:

1. Discuss the various guilds particular to the motion picture industry.
2. Identify the impact and role of the Motion Picture Association of America.
3. Describe various concerns that the Hays Production Code addressed.
4. Discuss the voluntary movie rating system of today.
5. Address whether the adult film industry has been legitimized by Hollywood.
6. Discuss why colorization is no longer a legal issue for film traditionalists.
7. Discuss the development and promotion of a movie script.
8. Describe the role of the Visual Artists Rights Act of 1990.
9. Discuss piracy issues and prevention related to the motion picture industry.
10. Describe what a True Name and Address statute is.

INTRODUCTION

Most individuals consider motion pictures (also referred to interchangeably today as movies, film, and often video and now even DVD productions) as the heart of Hollywood's entertainment industry. Though the term **Hollywood** has now become the general term used to describe the amalgamation of the various industries of traditional entertainment, including television, music, video, and video games, Hollywood still maintains film production as its primary (and most costly) driving force.

Though the rest of the globe has its own share of entertainment production facilities, creative forces, writers, actors, directors, and so on, particularly in Europe and Australia, American entertainment products that derive from this Southern California community still rule the world and control the largest market share of the entertainment pie. The advent of technological advances, such as VCRs, DVDs, and big-screen televisions with cable and satellite reception, have given Hollywood pause as to the role that public theatre will play in the future. Consumers continue to purchase products that bring movies to the home, changing the entertainment landscape.

The motion picture industry continues to affect individuals and influences perceptions and perspectives of reality throughout the world. Hollywood's production of motion pictures has allowed moviegoers to pay a relatively small fee to watch a film in a theatre that exposes them to an artificial world lasting a mere two hours or so. The cinema world educates, provides thrills, and can create horrors.

Always somewhat controversial, Hollywood has been accused of glorifying sex and violence, allegedly leading to the demise of societal values. Not all films, however, promote nonconservative values. Hollywood has promoted globalization of ideas, broadcast the English language and American culture generally, and provided continued impetus for freedom of thought and expression. Hollywood productions have allowed today's viewers to visit the world of their parents or grandparents, and special effects have made moviegoing more exciting than ever.

Motion pictures have their own financial, legal, and ethical issues, just like every other entertainment industry. Huge conglomerates of studios, films with incredible budgets, and actors, actresses, and writers demanding more rights and a greater share of the financial pie continue to challenge Hollywood and its players to entertain and create successful ventures that employ thousands of people. The motion pictures industry must be concerned over piracy issues, just like the music and television industries.

After harsh criticism of its contribution to the decline of societal values, the movie industry instituted a rating system similar to that of the music and television industries. The adult film industry, once thought of as a stepchild to the movie industry, is now not only profitable, but also arguably the fastest growing category of film, due to the explosion of the cable television, home video/DVD, and Internet industries.

HOLLYWOOD

Hollywood is a district of the city of Los Angeles, California. Founded officially in 1857, its name comes either from imported English holly bushes or because the wife of real estate developer Harvey Henderson Wilcox named it in the late 1880s, after having met someone on a train who hailed from a town with the same name. Due to better weather and longer days, motion picture production companies moved to California from the east coast states such as New York and New Jersey. The first movie studio in the Hollywood area was founded in 1911, and shortly thereafter fifteen more companies settled in the same area. Interestingly, the famous Hollywood sign actually read Hollywoodland and was erected in 1923 to advertise a housing development. The sign is now a registered trademark and cannot be used without the permission of the Hollywood Chamber of Commerce.

Hollywood Sign, high above Los Angeles in the Hollywood Hills in California.
Neil Setchfield © Dorling Kindersley

WRITERS GUILD OF AMERICA

The Writers Guild of America (WGA) is the sole collective bargaining representative for writers in the motion picture, broadcast, cable, interactive, and newer forms of entertainment media industries. It is a large collection of numerous writers, guilds formed throughout the twentieth century in America. In 1912, an Author's Guild was organized to protect writers of books, short stories, and eventually drama. The **Dramatists Guild** merged with the Author's Guild and became the **Author's League.** In 1921, the Screen Writers Guild emerged to protect writer's rights and wages and eventually became the collective bargaining agent for writers in the motion picture industry.

The Screen Writers Guild had helped to organize the Radio Writers Guild and in 1950 began organizing a group of television writers within its own body. A Television Writers Group was organized within the Author's League as well. However, in 1949, meetings took place in New York between representatives of the Author's Guild, Dramatists Guild, Radio Writers Guild, Television Writers Group, and Screen Writers Guild, which led to a revised organizational structure becoming known as the Writers Guild of America (1954).

The WGA today is made up of the Writers Guild of America (West and East), with offices in Los Angeles and New York. The Mississippi River is used as the dividing line for administrative jurisdiction between the two guilds. Obtaining a **screen credit**—the credit that goes on the print of the movie you see in the theatre, after the "Produced by" credit and before the "Directed by" credit—is decided only by the Writers Guild of America.

DIRECTORS GUILD OF AMERICA

The Directors Guild of America (DGA) is an organization consisting of directors, their assistants, production managers and their staffs, and managers of the stage in film and television and represents these individuals in negotiating their contracts. The DGA represents more than 12,000 members working in U.S. cities and abroad. Their creative work is represented in theatrical, industrial, educational, and documentary films and television, as well as videos and commercials.

SCREEN ACTORS GUILD

The Screen Actors Guild (SAG) is the labor union representing film actors in the United States. It ensures its members a minimum daily wage on union productions (scale) and handles payment of residuals. SAG members may not work on nonunion productions without special dispensation, but many film schools have waiver agreements with the guild to allow SAG actors to work free of charge in student films. This organization was created in 1933 and should not be confused with the Actors' Equity Association (mentioned earlier in the text).

PRODUCER'S GUILD OF AMERICA

In 2001, the Producer's Guild of America (PGA) and the American Association of Producers (AAP) merged into a single organization. This was a major shift for producers in America, and today's PGA now represents the entire producing team. This includes producers and executive producers to postproduction supervisors and production coordinators. Producers have many responsibilities.

A producer initiates, coordinates, supervises, and controls all aspects of the motion picture or television production process. This includes creative, financial, technological, and administrative aspects of the production. Producers have numerous names, including **executive producer** (supervises one or more producers in the performance of all of their functions) on single or multiple productions. In television, an executive producer may also be the creator or writer of a series. There are also associate producers, coproducers, and supervising, segment, and line producers, all with various supervisory roles.

MOTION PICTURE ASSOCIATION OF AMERICA

The Motion Picture Association of America (MPAA) is an organization that advocates on behalf of the motion picture, home video, and television industries. It has an international arm known simply as the Motion Picture Association (MPA). This organization's influence is especially important since U.S. films are shown in over 150 countries in over 125 international television markets. The MPAA was founded in 1922 and focused much of its original efforts on silent films. (MPA was founded in 1945 after World War II.) The MPAA has offices in Los Angeles and Washington, D.C. The leaders of the seven major producers and distributors of motion pictures and television programs are on the MPAA's board of directors. This includes Walt Disney Company, Sony Pictures Entertainment, Inc., Metro-Goldwyn-Mayer Inc., Paramount Pictures Corporation, Twentieth Century Fox Film Corp., Universal Studios, Inc., and Warner Bros.

OTHER PROFESSIONAL ASSOCIATIONS AND UNIONS

Affiliated Property Craftspersons, Grip/Craftservice, International Cinematographers Guild, Motion Pictures Editors Guild, Motion Picture Costume, Make-Up Artists & Hairstylists, Motion Picture Set Painters & Sign Writers, and the Scenic, Title & Graphic Artists are examples of other unions found in Hollywood.

HAYS PRODUCTION CODE

In the 1920s, the public-at-large became quite concerned over the increasingly frequent portrayal of violence, sex, and lawlessness on movie screens. Wishing to avoid government regulation, the Motion Picture Producers and Distributors of America created their own regulatory body and appointed Postmaster General Will H. Hays as head. His influence became so great that this body became known as the Hays Office and was also known as the Hays Code, **Hays Production Code,** or Hays Production Office. The Hays Production Code for Motion Pictures was introduced in 1934 and was extremely strict, governing violence, sex, and criminal conduct on film. Creative moviemakers felt restrained by this code of conduct. For example, under the Hays Production Code, a filmmaker could not depict details of how crimes were committed or show a criminal profiting from crime.

VOLUNTARY MOVIE RATING SYSTEM

Believing the Hays Production Code to be a form of censorship, Jack Valenti of the Motion Picture Association of America developed a formal **voluntary movie rating system** in November 1968. The MPAA rating system replaced the Hays Production Code. The MPAA rating system today relies on a voluntary agreement of the movie producers to seek a MPAA rating prior to releasing a movie. The purpose of the MPAA rating system is strictly limited to warning parents and really serves no other purpose. Between 1968 and 1990, the MPAA rating system underwent a few revisions. In September 1990, the MPAA rating system was finalized as it stands today. Input was considered from the National Association of Theatre Owners (NATO) and the International Film Importers & Distributors of America (IFIDA).

The original plan had only four categories: G (General Audiences—all ages admitted); M (Mature Audiences—all ages admitted, but parental guidance suggested); R (Restricted—children under 16 and later under 17 were not admitted without a parent or adult guardian); and X (no one under 17 admitted).

Confusion between the M and R categories called for a change in the rating system. As a result, PG (Parental Guidance Suggested) was added, and in 1984, PG was split into PG (Parental Guidance Suggested. Some Material May Not Be Suitable For Children) and PG-13 (Parents Strongly Cautioned. Some Material May Be Inappropriate For Children Under 13). Two subsequent revisions included the phrase R rating (Restricted, Under 17 Requires Accompanying Parent or Adult Guardian), and the X rating was changed to NC-17 (No One 17 and Under Admitted).

A ratings board makes its decision based upon a majority vote considering several factors including theme, violence, language, nudity, sensuality, drug abuse, and other elements actually found on-screen and viewed as a whole.

If a producer or distributor of a film does not agree with the rating, they may edit the film or appeal to the Rating Appeals Board made up of fourteen to eighteen members of men and women from various industry organizations. Producers and distributors are not forced to submit films for ratings. It is entirely voluntary.

EXHIBIT 11.1

Motion Picture
Association of America
Rating System[153]

G: General Audiences
  • All ages admitted.
PG: Parental Guidance Suggested
  • Some material may not be suitable for children.
PG-13: Parents Strongly Cautioned
  • Some material may be inappropriate for children under 13.
R: Restricted
  • Under 17 requires accompanying parent or adult guardian.
NC-17: No One 17 and Under Admitted

The ratings symbols are registered at the federal level as certification marks. Interestingly, the video game industry regulates itself under the Entertainment Software Ratings Board (ESRB). The system is designed, once again, for parents and falls into one of five categories: EC: Early Childhood, E: Everyone, T: Teen, M: Mature 17+, and AO: Adults Only 18+.

PROMOTING FILMS AND TRAILERS

In order to generate interest, production companies and distributors advertise new films via print advertisements, radio, television, and in what are characterized as **trailers**—short snippets of a film to generate interest. Trailers, too, use rating systems either approved for all audiences, which means they may be shown with all feature films and has a green background or approved for restricted audiences, having a red background, which limits their use to feature films rated R or NC-17. Each trailer carries at the front a tag which tells two things: (1) the audience for which the trailer has been approved and (2) the rating of the picture being advertised. The color is to alert the projectionist against mismatching trailers with the film being shown on the theatre screen.

STUDIOS AND DISTRIBUTION

Walt Disney, Warner Bros. Studios, Paramount Studios, Sony Pictures Studios (Columbia/Tristar), MGM/UA Studios, Universal Studios, and Twentieth Century Fox Studios are considered the major studios of today. Numerous independent studios and production companies exist as well. In addition to producing films, studios play a prominent role in distributing movies to the public. The power and influence of the film industry often lies in the distribution companies that have the finances to promote films.

While some films, such as *Titanic*, may cost over $100 million to produce, others, such as *The Blair Witch Project*, may be produced for $15 million or

---

[153] http://www.mpaa.org/movieratings/. See also The Classification and Rating Administration (CARA) at http://www.filmratings.com

Paramount Studios.
Max Alexander © Dorling Kindersley.

less. The studios and distributors receive income from U.S. theatre rentals (the movie theatre renting a copy of the film of a new movie), foreign theatres, home video, and television.

MOVIE SCRIPTS

As in television, a film starts with an idea and then follows with a script. Unless a writer is employed by the studio, independent writers must pitch their screenwriting ideas to the studios. Considerations such as theme, main characters (protagonist), possible actors, and the target audience are factors in developing a film from the early stages.

Before the script is written, a **treatment** must be developed: a short story with a scene-by-scene description of the story about to be told, including the emotional responses the movie intends to invoke. The script must have an introduction, a middle, and an ending. It must also have stories within the story, conflict, and so on. After the treatment, a step outline follows, and later the actual **screenplay** itself emerges.

Once accepted, a script starts with development of the script (finding actors, directors, producers, distributors). This can take several years. Then, **preproduction** begins. Preproduction is the activity before a filming. This includes location scouting, crew hiring, equipment securing, casting, and so forth. It also includes creating storyboards, production boards, and production schedules, getting permits, setting the budget, and the production designer, art director, costume designer, and screenwriter all sitting down together and making sure they all have the same vision for the film. This also includes renting sound stages. After preproduction, shooting begins and often takes up to three months. **Postproduction** is everything from lab (film processing), editorial, sound mixing, and online (video) or negative cut (film finishing). Dubbing and special effects including sounds are also part of postproduction. Finally, distribution takes place in order to get the film out to the public.

MOVIE BUDGETS

In the movie industry, **above-the-line** expenditures are those that are negotiated or spent before filming begins. These costs include rights for the material on which the screenplay is based and salaries for the screenwriter, director, producer, and actors. The **below-the-line** budget is usually fixed and includes the salaries of the nonstarring cast members and crew, studio, equipment, trailer (meaning advertising trailer), and location costs.

Salaries and perks for famous actors, director, and producer are only part of the necessaries when considering a budget for a film. Vehicles, airplanes, stunt men and women, location scouts, transportation for talent, cast, and crew, insurance considerations, animal trainers and handlers, special effects personnel, explosives experts, sound effects, costume, makeup, hair, script supervisor, stills photographer, special permissions, translators, crowd control, craft services, parking permits, shooting permits, electricity, weather reports, and so on all go into preparing a budget. All people and egos must be dealt with and managed.

ADULT FILM INDUSTRY

Hollywood did not wish to recognize the adult film industry as a separate, distinct, and legitimate form of moviemaking from its beginning. Often referred to as the "Other Hollywood" and characterized as a sleazy industry with poor writers, directors, and performers on a shoestring budget, this industry has gained considerable momentum in recent years due to the exposure given to it by the Internet and home video and DVD rentals and sales. While not known for their plots, the adult film industry (once recognized only as pornography) no longer is considered extreme entertainment or morally offensive by many.

The vast majority of this industry is not found in Hollywood, but rather in the San Fernando Valley (sometimes referred to as Silicone Valley). Costs to produce such films are a mere pittance next to traditional film budgets, but the films can be quite profitable. The growth of the Internet and changing social mores and values power the $4 billion adult film (or **porn**) industry. This industry has proved seemingly impervious to the bean-counting, cost-cutting culture seeping into Hollywood. Most adult films are shot in a few days or a week.

Similar to the more traditional Hollywood movie industry, the adult film and entertainment industry produces features with catchy titles, sequels, and diverse settings. The adult film industry rewards its leading women the most. Few theatres offered adult films, and if they did, it was at odd hours of the day or night. Video stores would have separate rooms for adult films.

Today, with the advent of Internet and video-on-demand services, adult films are almost (but not quite yet) considered mainstream entertainment.

An exotic dancer performs at Club Fantasy in South Burlington, Vermont in this September 28, 1995 photo.
AP Wide World Photos

Some, however, still refer to the adult film industry as porn, short for pornography, and concerns over obscenity issues still perpetuate a negative stigma in this industry generally.[154] However, profits continue to soar in this industry, and a recent survey showed that porn Internet Web sites are visited three times as much as traditional search engines.[155]

■ CHILD PROTECTION RESTORATION AND PENALTIES ENHANCEMENT ACT OF 1990

Related to adult films, videos, and DVDs is a part of the federal law known as the Child Protection Restoration and Penalties Enhancement Act of 1990.[156] Of

---

[154] Concerns over transmission of sexually transmitted diseases continues to haunt this industry as well. *See* http://www.sltrib.com/2004/Apr/04162004/nation_w/157707.asp.
[155] http://www.usatoday.com/tech/webguide/internetlife/2004-06-03-popular-porn_x.htm
[156] Other important laws related to child pornography include the Child Pornography Prevention Act of 1996 (CPPA), 18 U.S.C. § 2251; Prosecutorial Remedies and Other Tools to End the Exploitation of Children Today Act of 2003 (PROTECT Act), Pub. L. No. 108-21; and the Children's Online Privacy Protection Act of 1998 (COPPA).

particular interest is 18 U.S.C. § 2257 (Recordkeeping requirements). This section requires that producers of depictions of actual sexual activity must obtain required information and documentation of the participant's age and keep and index those records and make them available to the Attorney General's delegate upon demand. Moreover, the depictions must have associated with them a label (a "statement") describing where the records are kept. Noncompliance with the federal law is a felony. The purpose behind the act was to prevent underage performers from engaging in child pornography. The Act does not apply to visual depictions made before November 1, 1990, however.

For example, an adult label might read:

---

18 U.S.C. § 2257 STATEMENT:

In compliance with the Federal Labeling and Recordkeeping Law (also know as 18 U.S.C. § 2257), all models located within our domains were eighteen years of age or older during the time of photography. All models' proof of age is held by the custodian of records, which is listed below, organized by producer. All content and images are in full compliance with the requirements of 18 U.S.C. § 2257 and associated regulations.

COLORIZATION

The process of **colorization** is a computerized process that adds color to black-and-white movies and television programs. Color is added by computer after an original negative is converted to a videotape that can be watched on television. Obvious colors are added while other less obvious colors are added only after some guidance has been offered by investigation of photographs and costume vaults maintained by the studios. Colorization still has its issues, particularly with historians, film critics, and directors who maintain that the original black-and-white films should be left alone and not colorized as a matter of ethical (rather than legal) principles. Colorization, though controversial from the late 1980s to the mid 1990s, faded as an issue after Congress established the National Film Registry in 1988 that had to label (via a disclaimer) whether a film had been colorized or not.

VISUAL ARTISTS RIGHTS ACT OF 1990

On October 27, 1990, Congress passed the Visual Artists Rights Act (VARA) (17 U.S.C. § 101). This amendment was put into the Copyright Act of 1976 as § 106A. VARA covers only limited, fine art categories of works of visual art: paintings, sculptures, drawings, prints, and still photographs produced for exhibition by painters, sculptors, and other graphic artists. Sometimes known as **moral rights,** VARA allows authors of visual art to control the use of their names in conjunction with a work of art. The Act provides for the right of **attribution** and for protection of the physical integrity of certain works of visual art. Attribution includes the right to claim authorship of a work to prevent attachment of an artist's name to a work which he or she did not create and, where there has been a subsequent distortion, mutilation, or modification (i.e., integrity) of the work prejudicial to the artist's honor or reputation, the right to disclaim authorship and to prevent identification of the artist's name with the work.

ART LICENSES IN MOVIES

Licenses permitting the use of art in motion pictures are usually obtained either from the artist or the artist's representative and are usually granted in exchange for either a flat fee or a rental payment. A higher fee is charged for a major use (i.e., more than a few seconds, full frame, or close-up) than for a minor use. License fees are not usually paid for merely incidental uses (i.e., less than two seconds or less than 20 percent of the work shown on screen).

PIRACY

The Motion Picture Association of America and its international counterpart, the Motion Picture Association, estimate that the U.S. motion picture industry loses in excess of $3 billion due to piracy. In 2000, the MPA launched over 60,000 investigations into suspected pirate activities and more than 18,000 raids against pirate operations in coordination with local authorities around the world. The MPAA/MPA directs its worldwide antipiracy activities from headquarters in Encino, California.[157] In late 2004, the MPAA began a fierce campaign to slow the illegal downloading of movies off the Internet.

The Copyright Act of 1976 (an amended in 1982) increases the penalties for the illegal duplication of copyrighted material including movies and videos, making such offenses felonies on the first offense. Copyright owners may also file civil lawsuits against copyright infringers, and the government may file criminal charges. The Communications Act of 1984 and later amendments provide comparable penalties and remedies for cable television and satellite pirates. Today, more than eighty nations have copyright laws. Outside of the United States, where copyright laws are often powerless, successful charges have been brought against pirates under other statutes, such as receiving stolen goods, trademark violations, smuggling, and failure to pay customs duties.

It is a violation of federal law (17 U.S.C. § 106(1)) to distribute, rent, or sell illegally duplicated copies, even if the copies are made by someone else (17 U.S.C. § 106(3)). The Communications Act of 1934, as amended (47 U.S.C. § 605), and related statutes also prohibit the unauthorized reception of films via

---

[157] http://www.mpaa.org/anti-piracy/index.htm

satellite or cable television. Various states have so-called truth-in-labeling laws and other statutes that can be used to prosecute film and video pirates.

TRUE NAME AND ADDRESS STATUTES

Forty-five states have **True Name and Address** statutes which can be used to combat video piracy and **bootlegging.** True Name and Address statutes make it illegal for anyone to manufacture, distribute, sell, or possess for any of these purposes any video, compact disc, audiocassette, or phonograph record whose packaging does not contain the actual name and address of the manufacturer and, in some states, the actual name of the performer or group.

CAMCORDING

As of January 1, 2004 in the state of California, the illegal recording of a feature film in a movie theater with a camcorder is a crime. The MPAA is lobbying to enact similar laws in other states. California's anticamcording law was designed to combat this form of digital piracy, making it a misdemeanor to operate a recording device in a movie theater for purposes of taping a movie and punishable up to one year in jail and/or $2,500 fine. A few months later, a Los Angeles resident was sentenced to over one month in jail for a violation of the new law.[158]

PENAL CODE
PART 1. Crimes and Punishments
TITLE 15. Miscellaneous Crimes
CHAPTER 2. Other and Miscellaneous Offenses
Cal. Pen. Code § 653z (2004)

§ 653z. Operation of recording device in theater while motion picture is being exhibited without authority

(a) Every person who operates a recording device in a motion picture theater while a motion picture is being exhibited, for the purpose of recording a theatrical motion picture and without the express written authority of the owner of the motion picture theater, is guilty of a public offense and shall be punished by imprisonment in a county jail not exceeding one year, by a fine not exceeding two thousand five hundred dollars ($2,500), or by both that fine and imprisonment.

---

[158] http://www.cnn.com/2004/SHOWBIZ/Movies/05/10/pirate.jail.reut/index.html.

(b) For the purposes of this section, the following terms have the following meanings:

    (1) "Recording device" means a photographic, digital or video camera, or other audio or video recording device capable of recording the sounds and images of a motion picture or any portion of a motion picture.

    (2) "Motion picture theater" means a theater or other premises in which a motion picture is exhibited.

(c) Nothing in this section shall preclude prosecution under any other provision of law.

CHAPTER SUMMARY

From the fundamental cameras invented in the late 1800s and early 1900s to the high-definition cameras of today, the motion picture industry has grown into one of the largest industries in the world. Production of a film requires such basics as a script, preproduction and postproduction issues, and a studio with distribution channels to get the film to potential viewers. The distribution of U.S. films has promoted American values and the English language around the world.

Much goes into the making of motion pictures and hundreds of people are involved along the way, including actors, their agents, various unions and guilds, and forms of self-regulation including the Voluntary Rating System. Recent issues involving films include colorization issues, the rapid growth of the adult film industry, and, of course, piracy issues.

CHAPTER TERMS

Above-the-line
Attribution
Author's League
Below-the-line
Bootlegging
Colorization

Dramatists Guild
Executive producer
Hays Production Code
Hollywood
Moral rights
Porn

Postproduction
Preproduction
Screen credit
Screenplay
Trailers
Treatment

True Name and Address
Voluntary movie rating
   system

ADDITIONAL CASES

Allied Artists Picture Corp. v. Rhodes, 679 F.2d 656 (6th Cir. 1982)

Astaire v. Best Film & Video Corp. 116 F.3d 1297 (9th Cir. 1997), *amended and superseded on reh'g by* 136 F.3d 1208 (9th Cir. 1998)

Famous Players-Lasky Corp., In re, 11 F.T.C. 187 (1927)

General Cinema Corp. v. Buena Vista Distrib. Co., 532 F. Supp. 1244 (C.D. Cal. 1982)

Lamb v. Starks, 949 F. Supp. 753 (N.D. Cal. 1996)

Maljack Productions, Inc. v. UAV Corp., 964 F. Supp. 1416, 1427 (C.D. Cal. 1997)

Motion Picture Patents Co. v. Universal Film Manufacture Co., 243 U.S. 502 (1917)

United States v. Capitol Service, Inc., 756 F.2d 502 (7th Cir. 1985)

United States v. Loew's Inc., 783 F. Supp. 211 (1992)

United States v. Paramount Pictures, Inc. 334 U.S. 131 (1948)

REVIEW QUESTIONS

1. What is the role of Hollywood movie studios?
2. Discuss the various unions involved in the motion picture industry.
3. What is the Motion Picture Association of America, and how has it impacted film production concerns?
4. What was the Hays Production Code? Why was it enacted?
5. What is the Voluntary Movie Rating System? Why was it developed?
6. What is the colorization process, and what are some legal and ethical concerns related to this process?
7. Has the adult film industry become mainstream Hollywood, and what are some concerns unique to this industry?
8. What does the Visual Artists Rights Act of 1990 protect?
9. How are piracy issues, including camcording, affecting the motion picture industry?
10. What are True Name and Address statutes?

REFERENCES FOR ADDITIONAL RESEARCH AND DISCUSSION

Campbell, A.J., *Self-Regulation and the Media*, 51 Fed. Comm. L.J. 711 (1999).

Frumes, H.M., *Surviving Titanic: Independent Production in an Increasingly Centralized Film Industry*, 19 Loy. L.A. Ent. L.J. Rev. 523 (1999).

Honicky, D.A., *Film Labelling as a Cure for Colorization [and Other Alterations]: A Band-Aid for a Hatchet Job*, 12 Cardozo Arts & Ent. L.J. 409 (1994).

McCoy, S., *The Government Tunes in to Tune Out the Marketing of Violent Entertainment to Kids: The Media Violence Labeling Act, the Media Marketing Accountability Act and the First Amendment*, 4 Vand. J. Ent. L. & Prac. 237 (2002).

Mosk, R.M., *The Jurisprudence of Ratings Symposium Part I: Motion Picture Ratings in the United States*, 15 Cardozo Arts & Ent. L.J. 135 (1997).

Above-the-line: In movies, expenditures that are negotiated or spent before filming begins.

Abuse of discretion: A standard of judicial review found in the Administrative Procedure Act (APA) which prohibits agency decisions that are arbitrary, capricious, and unreasonable.

Acceptance: A basic element of a contract in which the offeree communicates assent to agreeable terms to the offer.

Actors' Equity Association (AEA): The stage actor's union.

Actual malice: Standard of proof required for public figures or officials when alleging defamation.

Addenda: Additional material terms to a contract, sometimes called a rider.

Administration agreement: Agreement whereby a songwriter maintains the copyright.

Administrative agencies: Federal or state agencies; part of the executive branch of government and include the FCC and FTC.

Administrative law: Area of law governing decisions involving administrative agencies.

Adult entertainment: General term often used to describe exotic or nude dancing.

Advance: Similar to a signing bonus; a sum of money paid to an artist that is often recouped later by the publisher.

Advertising: Similar to solicitation, but not in-person; term associated with acceptable conduct under MRPC 7.3.

Agent: An intermediary such as a lawyer, booking agent, talent agent, and so forth, owing certain fiduciary duties to the principal.

Agreement for representation: A synonym for a contract in the context of agency law.

Agreements to agree: A contract is not effective if the offeror and offeree agree to agree, since such arrangement lacks definiteness.

All-Channel Receiver Act (ACRA): 1963 Act which gave the FCC the power to require new television receivers to include the capability to receive both VHF and UHF channels.

Ambush television: Phrase used to describe talk show torts and television shows involving unexpected humiliation to guests.

Amendments: Subsequent additions to the Constitution, statute, or code.

Analog: Type of broadcast signal that varies continuously, as opposed to digital signals which are based on combinations of 0s and 1s.

Annotated: A book that has explanatory footnotes or endnotes for clarity.

Anti-Cybersquatting Consumer Protection Act (ACPA): Enacted on November 29, 1999, the Act amended the

276

Lanham Act by adding a new Section 43(d); provides trademark owners with a civil remedy against cybersquatting.

Antiscalping laws: Laws designed to prevent the resale of tickets for higher than face value.

Antisiphoning: Legislation enacted by the FCC to protect free broadcast programming (as opposed to cable) as a matter of public interest.

Antitrust: Anticompetitive arrangements or conduct that restrict competition and promote monopolies.

Antitrust laws: The Sherman and Clayton Acts, which are designed to prevent contracts, combinations, and conspiracies that restrain trade.

Arbitrary: Term used in conjunction with illegitimate administrative agency decisions that do not pass judicial review.

Arbitrary trademark: Sometimes called a fanciful trademark; a trademark that had no meaning before becoming a trademark.

Arbitration: Type of alternative form of dispute resolution involving a final decision by an arbitrator rather than by a judge.

Artistic freedom: A right that casting directors and other artists claim is inherent to producing their work without interference from private or governmental influence.

Assigned: A contract involving a third party; one assigns rights, while one delegates duties.

Attorney general: The official and chief lawyer for a state or the federal government.

Attribution: The right by an artist to claim authorship of a work.

Author's Guild: Precursor organization to the Writer's Guild of America.

Author's League: Another precursor organization to the Writer's Guild of America.

Automatic stay: Legal protection afforded to petitioners under the Bankruptcy Code which prohibits contact with debtor by creditors after filing under the Code and enforced by the Trustee.

Bankruptcy: Code that protects debtors from creditors in order to give the debtor a fresh start.

Base royalty rate: Royalty calculation for musical artists after certain deductions such as packaging.

Basic Agreement: Another term for a union contract.

Below-cost: Illegal form of predatory pricing by a competitor.

Below-the-line: Accounting term describing fixed costs in movie production such as equipment.

Benefit of the bargain: Phrase used when a plaintiff sues for breach of contract under the theory of promissory estoppel, often alleging the breach of an oral promise and desiring what was bargained.

Beyond a reasonable doubt: The burden of proof in a criminal case that the government (state) must overcome to prove a defendant guilty of a crime.

Big four: The big four professional sports of football (NFL), basketball (NBA), baseball (MLB), and hockey (NHL).

Bill of Rights: The first ten amendments of the U.S. Constitution.

Blanket license: Gives a licensee the right to perform any and all of the compositions owned by the members or affiliates as often as the licensee desires for a stated term.

Block booking: Illegal and anticompetitive practice by studios requiring theatres to buy and show subpar films as a condition of showing the "A" film as well.

Blogging: Posting thoughts on the Internet; a Web log.

Blurring: The unauthorized use of a mark on dissimilar products or services that causes the mark to no longer be a unique identifier of the mark owner's goods.

Boilerplate: A preprinted and standard form of contract.

Bona fide: Latin—in good faith.

Bona fide occupational qualification (BFOQ): A defense to a claim of employment discrimination in which employers (including casting directors and entertainment-based restaurants looking for certain types of people) are allowed to discriminate in hiring workers on the basis of age, race, sex, and other federally protected classifications under certain circumstances.

Booking agency: Specific type of talent agency that sets up live performance dates and tours.

Booking agent: Type of agent whose sole role is to set up live performance dates for an artist.

Bootlegging: Unauthorized and illegal copying of music, video, or DVD for resale.

Bottleneck: A vertical merger that ultimately harms competition and consumers by having the supplier-distributor relationship maintain a virtual monopoly over a component part, for example.

Boutique: A relatively small law firm that specializes in an area of the law.

Brand name: A name that identifies certain goods.

Breach of contract: A violation of the terms of an agreement between two or more parties to a contract.

Bright-line test: The lack of clear-cut rules in a fair use case.

Broadcasts: Transmission of radio, television, and other signals over the air that are regulated by the FCC.

Budget-line: Music that sells for a low price, usually when the commercial value of the album has decreased.

Business manager: Type of agent who focuses on profits and losses and finances involving talent.

Cable Act of 1992: *See Cable Television Consumer Protection and Competition Act of 1992.*

Cable Television Consumer Protection and Competition Act of 1992: An amendment to the Communications Act of 1934, Congress directed the FCC to conduct an ongoing study on the carriage of local, regional and national sports programming by broadcast stations, cable programming networks, and pay-per-view services.

Call letters: Four-letter codes identify the geographic origin of broadcast of the radio station, usually beginning with K or W.

Capacity: The legal capability of entering into a contract.

Capricious: An illegitimate administrative agency action under the process of judicial review.

Case law: English and American tradition of utilizing precedent and previous judicial decisions (common law) to interpret statutes or simply making law when a statute is not involved.

Celebrity: A famous person.

Censorship: Governmental regulation of speech.

Certification: Process of being approved through training or education by a private organization.

Certification mark: Any word, name, symbol, device, or any combination used or intended to be used in commerce with the owner's permission by someone other than its owner to certify regional or other geographic origin, material, mode of manufacture, quality, accuracy, or other characteristics of someone's goods or services or that the work or labor on the goods or services was performed by members of a union or other organization.

Child Performers Education and Trust Act of 2003: New York State's attempt to protect child (minor) actors' and actresses' finances, among other things.

Children's Television Act of 1990: Established a specific programming obligation for every commercial television station to serve the educational and informational needs of children through overall programming and at least three hours per week of "core" programming specifically designed with educational and informational content.

Circuit: Federal geographic and regional classification of the tiered system of appeals.

Civic light operas: Type of live theatre performance.

Civil law: Private lawsuits involving a plaintiff and a defendant, as opposed to criminal law involving the state.

Clayton Act: Passed by Congress in 1914, the Act provides that labor unions and labor activities are exempt from the Sherman Act.

Clear and convincing evidence: Standard of proof used in some courts.

Closed captioning: Within a television broadcast signal there is a hidden caption not viewable unless the viewer selects it to be opened.

Clout: A way to describe the intangible social status of talent or a talent agent as a career advances; used to create more opportunities.

Code of Federal Regulations (C.F.R.): Administrative agency regulations are published here.

Codes: Sometimes referred to as statutes or ordinances; the published representation of the law enacted by a legislature or Congress as opposed to common law judicial interpretations of the law.

Collective bargaining agreement: The contract between management and a labor union.

Collective mark: A trademark or service mark used or intended to be used in commerce by the members of a cooperative, an association, or other collective group or organization, including a mark which indicates membership in a union, an association, or other organization.

Collude: The process of creating an anticompetitive and illegal arrangement between two or more persons or organizations.

Colorization: A computerized process that adds color to black-and-white movies and television programs.

Commercial misappropriation: A court-based legal doctrine that prevents the unauthorized commercial use of an individual name, likeness, or other recognizable aspects of one's persona; also known as the tort of right of publicity.

Commission: A fee earned based upon a percentage of a sale.

Commissioned: A specially ordered work for hire.

Common law: Judicial interpretations of the law; used to fill in the gaps left untouched or unclear by statutes and codes.

Communications Act of 1934: Act which established the Federal Communications Commission.

Compensatory damages: Type of damages in a breach of contract or tort claim to be compensated for the breach or injury.

Compulsory license: Forces a copyright owner to permit someone else to use their work for a predetermined fee and prevents the owner of the copyright from refusing to license their work to other people in certain, specified circumstances.

Confidentiality agreement: An agreement to keep something secret; sometimes referred to as a covenant not to compete or a no compete clause.

Conflict of interest: A situation in which the question of whose best interest is being served is at issue; often financial in nature.

Congress: The combined efforts of the House of Representatives and the Senate.

Consent decree: An out-of-court legal settlement whereby the accused party agrees to modify or change their behavior rather than plead guilty or go through an administrative hearing on charges brought before a court.

Consequential damages: Damages that result as a consequence of a breach of contract or personal injury.

Consideration: A vital element of a contract; the price of a promise.

Consignment: The temporary or permanent transfer of the possession but not the ownership of a good.

Conspicuous: Clearly visible and noticeable to the eye with little effort.

Constitution: The fundamental legal document in the United States.

Contingency fee: A fee contingent upon the occurrence of an event or condition.

Controlled composition clause: Record labels shall pay only 75 percent of the full royalty rate, especially to new artists.

Conventional broadcast: Noncable television broadcast.

Copublishing agreement: An agreement that provides for the co-ownership of songs by two or more parties.

Copyright: Term of intellectual property that gives the copyright owner the exclusive right to reproduce the copyrighted work, prepare derivative works, distribute copies of the copyrighted work, and perform or display the copyrighted work publicly.

Corporation for Public Broadcasting (CPB): A private, government corporation that funds over 1,000 public television and radio stations nationwide using an annual appropriation from Congress.

***Corpus Juris Secundum* (C.J.S.):** Literally, "second body of law"; a legal encyclopedia considered a secondary source of law.

CORST (Council of Resident/Stock Theatres): Form of equity production.

Counterfeit tickets: Fraudulent tickets.

Counterfeiting: A crime consisting of the use of a substantially identical copy of a registered trademark on the same goods or services for which the original mark is registered.

Courts of Appeal: Intermediary court; court subsequent to a trial court but prior to the Supreme Court at both federal and state levels.

Covenants not to compete: No compete clause; an agreement not to compete with a prior employer after termination.

Cover bands: Bands that play songs usually copyrighted by other bands.

Creditors: Those that are owed, as opposed to debtors who owe.

Criminal law: As opposed to civil law, the goal of this area of the law is to punish the wrongdoer.

Cross-collateralization: Allows a label to recoup costs against the advance so that they do not lose money; in accounting terms, this offsets any money owed by the artist or songwriter to the record or publishing company.

Cross-ownership: Regulations which prevent owners of daily newspapers or multiple broadcast facilities within a single local market from acquiring a license to operate a television station in the same market. Also prevents mergers that might undermine antitrust laws.

Curt Flood Act of 1998: An attempt by Congress to legislatively override the antitrust ruling in *Federal Baseball.*

Cybercasters: Individuals who are broadcasting over the Internet.

Cyberscalping: Resale of tickets over the Internet.

Cybersquatters: Those who purchase an Internet domain name with the intent to extort money from an otherwise legitimate claimant.

Cybersquatting: The act of registering an Internet address, such as a company name or the name of a famous individual, with the intent of selling it (i.e., extortion) to the person whom the real world would perceive to be the rightful owner of that address.

Cyberstalking: Stalking via the Internet.

De Havilland law: A seven-year limitation on certain contracts as a result of the favorable ruling handed down by California courts in Olivia de Havilland's lawsuit against Warner Bros. Studios in 1945, in which her studio contract could not be extended beyond seven years.

De minimis defense: Defense to a claim of infringement on the grounds that the amount copied was so small.

Dead celebrity: California law that protects the right of publicity for a time for a celebrity in § 3344.1.

Debtor: One who owes money.

Deceptive acts and practices: Illegal acts that deceive consumers; sometimes called "bait and switch" advertising.

Declaration of use: Pursuant to Section 8 of the Lanham Act, 15 U.S.C. § 1058, the owner of a trademark registration is required to periodically submit a declaration attesting to and demonstrating that the mark is still in use in commerce.

Defamation: The act of making untrue statements about another which damage his or her reputation and/or deter others from working with or association with the defamed party; forms include slander (spoken) and written (libel).

Defendants: Those who are sued by plaintiffs.

Demos: Shortened versions of television pilot shows.

Deregulation: Policy of less governmental regulation.

Derivative work: A work based upon one or more preexisting works, such as translation, musical arrangement, or any other form in which a work may be recast, transformed, or adapted.

Descriptive trademark: A trademark that actually describes the goods.

Development deal: Employs a writer to develop a single concept or idea, as opposed to a longer overall deal.

Digital: Type of broadcast signal that is based on combinations of 0s and 1s, as opposed to analog (continuous) signals.

Digital Millennium Copyright Act: 1998, the DMCA had as its primary purpose the goal of updating United States copyright laws to deal with the digital information age.

Dilution: The lessening of the capacity of a famous trademark to identify and distinguish goods or services.

Dinner theatre: A play or musical takes place for customers in addition to dinner being served.

Disaffirm: The ability to discharge a contractual obligation either due to status as a minor or to bankruptcy.

Disclaimer: A waiver, release, or exculpatory clause.

Dispute resolution or Alternative dispute resulution (ADR): As opposed to litigation, dispute resolution or alternative dispute resolution is the process of mediation or arbitration to resolve a dispute.

Distinctiveness: Characteristic of a mark that distinguishes it from other marks.

Dramatists Guild: Merged with the Author's Guild and became the Author's League.

Drive motor: Spins the disc on a CD player.

Driver's Privacy Protection Act (DPPA): Enacted by Congress, the Act prohibits states from disclosing personal information that their drivers submit in order to obtain driver's licenses.

Due process: One is entitled to a hearing before one's life, liberty, or property can be taken away from them by a state action under American jurisprudence; found in the Fifth and Fourteenth Amendments.

Duties: Includes the various duties of accounting, care, loyalty, and good faith; owed by an agent to a principal.

Duty of Accounting: An agent must keep an account (and be able to account for) of all money and property received and paid out on behalf of a principal.

Duty of Care: An agent must use reasonable skill and diligence when working for the principal.

Duty of Good Faith: An agent must be truthful and faithful to promoting the interests of the principal.

Duty of Loyalty: The principle that an employer or employee may not divert a business opportunity to themselves or a competitor.

Emancipated: A minor who has legally been separated from the bounds of parents and may enter into legally binding agreements.

Employment agencies: Regulated in some states, their role is to match an employee with an employer.

Enabling legislation: A statute passed by Congress that enables the enactment and establishment of an administrative agency.

Endorsement: Sponsorship for an athlete beyond salary from a professional team.

Enforcement Bureau: The Enforcement Bureau of the FCC pursues written complaints of indecent or obscene broadcasting received from the public at large.

Entertainment law: The general term associated with the legal aspects of a variety of business industries and the players within those industries, which include music, radio, television, live performances, movies, videos, publishing, and the like. Entertainment law has its legal and developmental roots in California and New York jurisprudence primarily.

Entertainment Work Permit: In California, minors seeking employment in the entertainment industry must also obtain this work permit.

Equal protection: Fourteenth Amendment clause that guarantees equality and the right to be judged on the basis of individual merit without discrimination based upon race, color, religion, sex, or national origin.

Equity: In the judicial system, decisions based on what is "fair" rather than what is necessarily "right"; developed from English chancery courts.

Equity Waiver Agreement: The 99-seat plan, which evolved into the City of Los Angeles small theater plans of 1988 and 2000, in which actors receive minimal compensation, rehearsal times are limited, and production runs are restricted.

Ex parte: On behalf of one party only; usually without the presence or knowledge of another party, at least at first.

Exculpatory clauses: Clauses in a contract that take the blame away from one in the event of negligence; synonymous with a waiver or a release.

Executed: A complete performed contract, though in the entertainment industry it can mean a "signed" contract even if performance is not yet complete.

Executive branch: The branch of government involving the president and administrative agencies.

Executive producer: Supervises one or more producers in the performance of all of their functions.

Executory: A contract still being performed and not yet complete.

Exemplary damages: Sometimes called punitive damages; not available in contract law but available in tort law to punish (make an example of) the defendant.

Exotic dancing: Synonym for nude or adult dancing.

Extra benefits: Violation of NCAA rules in which, usually, sports agents give benefits to a student-athlete with remaining eligibility and the benefits are not given or available to the students at large.

Extreme and outrageous: If conduct is extreme and outrageous, one may recover for the tort of intentional infliction of emotional distress; must shock the conscience of society.

Fair use doctrine: Allows someone to use a copyrighted work without fear of being sued; a defense to a claim of copyright infringement; often used in the educational context, but it has some limitations.

Fairness doctrine: FCC policy from 1949 until 1987; this doctrine required broadcasters, as a condition of getting their licenses from the FCC, to report controversial issues in their community by offering balancing viewpoints.

False light: Related to the tort of invasion of privacy (right to privacy) where the plaintiff alleges that a false and defamatory statement was made and places the plaintiff in a false light.

Fanciful trademark: Sometimes called an arbitrary trademark; has no obvious association with a mark relative to a good or service.

Federal Circuit: The various district courts, the Courts of Appeal, and the Supreme Court of the United States.

Federal Communications Commission (FCC): The federal agency that reports to Congress and regulates interstate and international radio, television, wire, cable, and satellite broadcasts.

Federal Trade Commission (FTC): A consumer protection agency with mandates under the Federal Trade Commission Act (15 U.S.C. §§ 41–51) to guard the marketplace from unfair methods of competition and to prevent unfair or deceptive acts or unfair business practices that harm consumers.

Federalism: The concept whereby federal laws and state laws coexist.

Fiduciary: One who owes another a duty of good faith; for example, an agent is a fiduciary of a principal.

File-sharers: Those who swap files from computers over the Internet.

Fingerprint: Similar to a watermark, designed to track files on a peer-to-peer (P2P) or person-to-person network.

First sale doctrine: Ownership after a legal purchase (i.e., a first sale) of a physical copy of any copyrighted work, such as a book, compact disc, and so on; permits lending, reselling, disposing, or doing whatever the owner wishes to do with it, but does not allow a complete copying of it.

Flat fee: As opposed to a commission, a flat fee is usually a one-time fee or in some cases an hourly fee for services by an agent such as a lawyer.

For-profit: IRS tax classification of a business which is in business to make a profit.

Franchise license: Various unions do not allow talent agents to procure employment for any union member without a certification from that union.

Fraud: Intentional misrepresentation.

Free goods: Freebies under a contract for the artist.

Freebies: Free goods given to an artist under contract.

Freedom of contract: Legal theory that says anyone can contract for anything as long as it is for a legal purpose in addition to the elements of offer, acceptance, consideration, and capacity.

Freedom of speech: Clause found in the First Amendment of the Constitution; sometimes called Free Speech.

Freedom of the press: Clause found in the First Amendment of the Constitution; sometimes called Free Press.

General damages: Damages for pain, suffering, mental anguish, disability, and disfigurement.

Generic name: Name given to a formerly trademarked name that has lost its distinctiveness (e.g., "aspirin").

Generic trademark: Weakest of all the types of trademarks; for example, the phrase "personal computer" cannot be trademarked.

Goods: Tangible and moveable items at the time of sale.

Gross earnings: Earnings before any deductions are taken.

Guarantor: One who guarantees something for another; in contract law, often referred to as a surety.

Guardian: One who represents the affairs of another, particularly a minor.

Guilds: A synonym for a union.

Handshake deals: Agreements reached between studio executives and others in Hollywood that were not reduced to writing.

Hart-Scott-Rodino Antitrust Improvements Act of 1976: Provides that certain larger companies seeking to acquire or merge with another company must file advance notice of its intentions with the FTC and the Assistant Attorney General in charge of the Antitrust Division of the Department of Justice at least thirty days prior to consummation of such a transaction.

Hays Production Code: The Hays Production Code (for Motion Pictures) was introduced in 1934 and was extremely strict, governing violence, sex, and criminal conduct on film.

Hollywood: Term used to describe the amalgamation of the various industries of traditional entertainment, including television, music, video, video games, and such, particularly in the area near Los Angeles.

Horizontal merger: The acquisition of a competitor, increasing market concentration and the likelihood of collusion; the elimination of head-to-head competition between two leading firms resulting in possible anticompetitive effects.

Hourly fee: Fee charged by the hour.

Hybrid song: Merging an original song with a sampled song.

Incidental booking exception: New York law's exception to licensing for managers; it applies only to representatives who function primarily as managers for their clients.

Indecent speech: Speech that the government, via the subjective opinion of the FCC, says violates the bounds of decency in a radio or television broadcast.

Independent film: A small, theatre-like production not directly tied to a major studio.

Infant: Synonym for a minor; someone under the age of 18.

Infomercial: A radio or television commercial trying to sell a product or service in the form of an interview or education.

Infringement: Unlawful use of someone's copyrighted, patented, or trademarked material.

Injunction: A court order requiring someone to act or, alternatively, to refrain from doing an act.

Intangible property: Property not moveable or touchable; a protected idea.

Intellectual property: Copyrights, patents, and trademarks.

Intentional infliction of emotional distress: Tort alleging the extreme and outrageous misconduct by the defendant.

Interstate commerce: Commerce (trade or travel) that crosses state lines.

Invasion of privacy: Tort of violating someone's right to be left alone; includes the public disclosure of otherwise nonpublic facts.

Inventor: The owner of a patent.

Judge: The arbiter in a trial or an appeal, as opposed to a justice, who presides over the supreme court of a given jurisdiction.

Judicial activists: Pejorative term for judges who believe that their role is to make the law, rather than interpret and apply the laws.

Judicial branch: The branch of government involving the trial, appellate, and supreme courts.

Judicial review: The right to appeal an administrative agency decision to a court of appeals on the condition that the decision will not be overruled unless it can be shown that the decision was arbitrary, capricious, unreasonable, or an abuse of discretion.

Jurisdiction: The power of a court to hear a case.

Justices: Judges who preside over a supreme court (state or federal).

Lanham Act: The federal trademark act.

Legislative branch: The branch of government including Congress that proposes and passes laws and statutes.

Letter of inquiry: If it appears that a violation of rules against indecent or obscene broadcasting may have occurred, the Enforcement Bureau staff of the FCC commences an investigation by sending a letter of inquiry to the broadcast station.

Libel: Written defamation.

Libel per se: Defamation in and of itself; for example, a false publication that someone has a communicable disease or is a criminal when in fact they are not.

License: The formal granting of permission to do an act.

Licensee: One who receives the grant of permission to do an act; usually requires formal training, continuing education, and/or a fee by the government or a private party.

Licensor: One who grants a license.

Liquidated damages: Agreed upon damages in a contract, usually prior to the performance of a contract, in the event of a breach by a party to the contract.

Live theatre: General term used to describe the various settings of live theatrical performances.

LORT (League of Regional Theatres): Form of equity production.

Madrid Protocol: The 1996 Madrid Agreement (Madrid Protocol) is a treaty that facilitates the international registration and maintenance (extensions) of trademarks.

Magistrates: Judges who preside primarily over administrative agency hearings.

Malpractice: Negligence of a professional or other licensed individual.

Manager: General term used to describe someone who handles the affairs of another.

Marca Registrada: A federally registered mark.

Mask work: A blueprint of a semiconductor chip.

Mechanical license: When the song later is fixed on a CD, cassette, or vinyl record, the record company pays a mechanical license fee (royalty) to the copyright owner.

Media Bureau: The FCC's Media Bureau administers the rules governing radio and television stations.

Mediation: A form of dispute resolution that is nonbinding, as opposed to arbitration; the parties themselves attempt to resolve their differences with the assistance of a mediator.

Meeting of the minds: When an offeror and an offeree have agreed to the terms of a contract.

Merchant: Someone who is regularly involved in the buying or selling of goods.

Midline: A record typically sold at a price halfway between the full SRLP and the budget price, to entice the consumer to buy the album.

***Miller* test:** In *Miller v. California*, 413 U.S. 14 (1973), the Supreme Court established a three-pronged test for obscenity prohibitions which would violate the First Amendment.

Misappropriation of a trade secret: Theft of a trade secret.

Misdescriptive: Misleading or deceptive description of goods.

Model Code of Professional Responsibility (MCPR): The American Bar Association (ABA) 1969 model act for professional conduct for lawyers.

Model Rules of Professional Conduct (MRPC): The American Bar Association (ABA) 1983 draft of the model act for professional conduct for lawyers.

Monopoly: Situation in which there is only one seller of a product or service.

Moral rights: Allows authors of visual art to control the use of their names in conjunction with a work of art.

Municipal police power: The power of a city or county to enact regulations in order to protect the public health, safety, and welfare.

Must carry: Mandatory provisions allow a broadcaster to require a cable operator to retransmit a local (free) station's signal on the cable system.

National Association of Broadcasters: Founded in 1923 and based in Washington, D.C., the National Association of Broadcasters (NAB) serves as the broadcast lobbying representative organization for radio and television stations.

National Collegiate Athletic Association (NCAA): A voluntary governing athletic association of over 1,200 member colleges and universities in the United States headquartered in Indianapolis.

National Conference of Commissioners on Uniform State Laws (NCCUSL): A private organization that drafts uniform laws for adoption by states.

National Reporter System: A set of law reporters (books) that divides the fifty states and the District of Columbia into seven regions: Atlantic, North Eastern, North Western, Pacific, South Eastern, South Western and Southern.

Necessary and Proper Clause: Article I, section 8, states that Congress shall have the authority "To make all Laws which shall be necessary and proper for carrying into Execution" the various powers allotted to the federal government by the Constitution.

Negligence: The failure to act as a reasonable person would in the same or similar situation.

Negligent infliction of emotional distress: The unreasonable infliction of emotional distress due to negligence.

Net artist royalty rate: The money that an artist gets per record, cassette tape, or CD.

Netpaks: Student course packets (packs) that utilize PDF files rather than paper.

Newsworthy: Term describing media speech that is protected due to the public interest involved; related to the First Amendment.

NFL blackout rule: Exemption to antitrust laws in which NFL games may not be broadcast in home markets (i.e., within a 75-mile radius) unless they are sold out 72 hours in advance.

99-seat plan: Special equity contract sometimes referred to as Equity Waiver, specific to the Los Angeles area.

No scalp zone: A geographic area normally found around an arena or venue in which scalped tickets may not be sold.

Nondisclosure agreement: Synonymous with a trade secret or confidentiality clause.

Nonequity: Theatre productions not supported by the AEA; equity actors may not work in such productions unless they are granted a waiver.

Not-for-profit: IRS tax designation for a nonprofit organization.

Nuisance: Tort of interference with one's use and enjoyment of property.

O'Brien test: As a result of the Supreme Court decision in *United States v. O'Brien*, 391 U.S. 367 (1968), the government's regulation of freedom of expression must further an important or substantial governmental interest.

Obscene speech: Speech not protected by the First Amendment, unlike indecent speech.

Offer: Made by an offeror, it creates the power of acceptance in the offeree.

Offeree: One who receives an offer.

Offeror: One who makes an offer to the offeree.

Offline captioning: Captioning done after the recording of a television program in a studio.

On-Broadway: A live theatrical performance in the Times Square area of New York, usually with the highest production costs yet also the most significant and the broadest public appeal.

Online captioning: Captioning done live, usually in a studio.

Opinions: Decisions rendered by judges or justices.

Option: Grants the holder the right to do or refrain from doing something upon the occurrence (or lack) of a condition.

Option contract: The right of one of the parties to accept a contract at their option for a limited period of time.

Oral contracts: Contracts not made in writing; not enforceable if a writing is required by the statute of frauds.

Order of protection: Court order telling someone to stay away from another; often involved in stalking or domestic abuse cases.

Overall deal: Unlike a development deal, employs a writer to write for more than just one project over a longer term and sometimes hired in-house by a studio.

Paparazzi: Overzealous photographers who take pictures of celebrities and other famous or infamous people; sometimes called stalkerazzi.

Parody: Similar to satire, but found in literature, music, art, or film for humorous purposes.

Patent: The formal grant of a property right for an invention to the inventor, issued only by the federal government's Patent and Trademark Office (USPTO).

Per se: Latin—in and of itself.

Per se rule: Antitrust analysis which invalidates any labor practices that are inherently unreasonable restraints of trade.

Performance royalties: Royalties earned by an artist for a live performance.

Personal manager: A manager that handles the daily affairs of talent or an artist; often the manager closest to the artist as opposed to a business manager.

Personal service: A contract for someone's unique talent, abilities, or skills.

Pickup: A network television contract usually for longer than five years, after the pilot has been proven successful.

Pilot: A sample episode of a television show.

Pilot season: January through April of every year.

Piracy: Theft of music, video, and so forth by pirates, often done over the Internet.

Pirates: Those who take music, video, and so forth without permission.

Pitch: Marketing attempt by producers, writers, and directors to try to sell their shows to the networks with the hope that the networks will adopt them.

Plaintiff: One who brings a civil lawsuit against a defendant.

Political programming: Controversial yet free speech and commentary in the arena of broadcast journalism related to politics.

Porn: Short for pornography.

Postproduction: Sometimes called post, it includes everything from lab (film processing), editorial, and sound mixing to dubbing and special effects.

Precedent: Concept in U.S. law which holds that lower courts must follow the decisions of previous and higher courts with all things being equal.

Predatory: Illegal acts designed to squeeze out competition.

Premium: Those goods given away as the result of a promotional sale, such as test driving an automobile and receiving a complimentary CD.

Preponderance of the evidence: Burden of proof in a civil case; is it more likely than not that the defendant was responsible for the act in question that allegedly caused damages to the plaintiff?

Preproduction: The numerous activities involved before filming a movie or television show begins.

Price-fixing: A form of an illegal restraint of trade between competitors.

Principal: A person who hires an agent to act in his or her best interest.

Print license: Allows for the reproduction of printed copies of music, such as sheet music, folios, concert arrangements, and the printing of lyrics in magazines, advertising, and books.

Privileges and immunities: A clause found in the Fourteenth Amendment which states that no state shall make or enforce any law abridging the privileges or immunities of citizens of the United States.

Procure employment: Find employment for another.

Professional associations: Nonunionized organizations that regulate conduct and fight for the rights of their members.

Promissory estoppel: A legal claim that one has relied on the oral promise made by another.

Prosecutor: The plaintiff in a criminal case who acts on behalf of the state or society at large.

Public domain: Material free for all to use without permission; works in the public domain include a lost copyright, an expired copyright, and those works owned or authored by the federal government, specifically granted to public domain, or just noncopyrightable.

Public figure: One who has become a matter of public discussion or debate, for a variety of reasons.

Public interest: Government may regulate broadcast speech if such regulation serves the health, safety, and welfare of the public at large.

Public official: A publicly elected official.

Punitive damages: Also known as exemplary damages; designed to punish the defendant for intentional misconduct.

Quantum meruit: Latin—as much as he or she deserved.

Quick look: Abbreviated or quick-look rule of reason antitrust analysis designed for restraints that do not fall within the narrow categories of restraints deemed *per se* unlawful, but that are sufficiently anticompetitive that they do not require a full-blown rule of reason inquiry either.

Reality television: Television shows displaying persons acting in real-world situations where their words and behaviors are not scripted.

Reckless: Conduct that is so lacking in care that it is considered intentional.

Recoup: Recover costs that were advanced to an artist.

Regulations: The laws of administrative agencies. Also referred to as "regs."

Release: A waiver or disclaimer.

Restatement of Contracts: Treatise that summarizes contract law principles and cases.

Restatement of Torts: Treatise that summarizes tort law principles and cases.

Restrain trade (Restraint of trade): Any anticompetitive behavior that undermines competition.

Restraining order: Also known as an order of protection; prevents someone from certain types of conduct, such as stalking.

Retail: The price offered to the general consumer, as opposed to wholesale.

Retraction: An affirmative recanting of a statement made by a publication due to error.

Rider: An addendum to a contract.

Right of privacy: The right to be left alone as long as one's actions are not newsworthy.

Right of publicity: Synonymous with commercial misappropriation.

Routing: The process of establishing a logical logistical plan for an artist's tour.

Rule of reason: A court must examine the alleged anticompetitive practice at issue and determine whether it is reasonable or unreasonable.

Run: The airing of a syndicated show.

Safe harbor: An exception to the rule.

Sampling: The act of taking a portion of one sound recording and reusing it as an instrument in a new recording; this is done with a sampler, a piece of hardware or a computer program on a digital computer.

Satellite Digital Audio Radio Service (SDARS): Broadcast system that utilizes digitally encoded technology to broadcast to Earth-based receivers.

Satire: A form of literature that uses humor and imitation to ridicule an individual's moral and character traits and flaws.

Screen credit: A credit for a writer that is displayed on a movie screen.

Screenplay: The script for a movie.

Secondary effects/impacts: Crime, drug use, and lowering of property values often associated with adult entertainment establishments.

Secondary meaning: When a name, such as a person's last name, has a meaning associated with a distinct product or service.

Service mark: A trademark that involves a service rather than a good.

Seven Year Statute: California's Labor Code § 2855 limits the amount of time anyone can be held to a contract for personal services to a maximum of seven years; also known as the De Havilland law.

Sherman Antitrust Act of 1890: One of the two major antitrust laws that promotes competition and deters monopolistic practices that ultimately hurt consumers.

Single song agreement: A songwriter assigns part or all of the publishing rights of a song to the publisher for a certain period of time, usually between one to two years; if the publisher secures a placement with an artist during this period, then the publisher becomes a permanent copyright owner of the song.

Siphoning off: Drawing the audience away from viewing.

Slander: Spoken defamation, as opposed to written defamation (libel).

Slander per se: Spoken defamation about someone's criminality, inability to perform a job, or having a communicable disease.

Solicitation: Similar to advertising, but usually face-to-face meetings in an attempt to obtain business.

Special damages: Damages peculiar to that particular plaintiff.

Specific performance: A court order requiring that a contract be performed.

Spectrum: The various invisible frequencies associated with broadcasting radio, television, cellular phones, and so on.

Sports agent: An individual who manages and markets professional athletes.

Sports Broadcasting Act of 1961: Generally exempts television agreements entered into by professional football, baseball, basketball, and hockey leagues from the federal antitrust laws.

Sports entertainment: The merger of sports and entertainment, such as professional wrestling.

Sports law: The study and development of the law in the context of sports.

Stalking: Crime of repetitive misconduct involving harassing, annoying, threatening and sometimes potentially deadly behavior.

Standard Art Consignment Agreement: Agreement between an art gallery and an artist to display art, usually for a fee and for a limited time.

Stare decisis: Latin—let the decision stand.

Statute: A law that has been codified in books.

Statute of frauds: The principle that certain contracts must be in writing to be enforceable.

Statute of limitations: The amount of time within which one may bring a lawsuit.

Strip club: A club that allows nude or exotic dancing.

Subliminal: Not noticeable to the conscious self.

Subliminal speech: Speech that influences the behavior of someone without them being aware of the influence.

Suggestive trademark: A trademark that suggests in the name itself an association between the name and the good or service.

Summary judgment: A decision made by a court based upon the pleadings only and prior to a trial.

Surety: Someone who promises to answer for the debt of another.

Surname: A person's last name.

Sync license: An agreement for the use of a song on television or in a movie.

Syndication: The process of selling the rights of presentation of a television program to customers such as individual television stations and cable channels.

Talent: The artist or celebrity.

Talent agencies: Regulated businesses that promote talent, usually for a commission.

Talent Agencies Act (TAA): California's strict licensing requirements for talent agents.

Talent agents: Arrange and negotiate clients' employment opportunities.

Talk show tort: The shock value associated with the emotional distress related to guests on a show who act violently after being subjected to humiliation in front of an audience.

Tangible: Something that can be touched.

Tape: The product involved in a devolving, yet still effective, form of audio and visual recording.

Tarnishment: When a trademark becomes linked with poor quality, unsavory, or unwholesome goods or services.

Technical riders: Another name for a rider.

Telecommunications Act of 1996: Act that affected broadcast radio and television regulation and other forms of communication, including telephone services. As a result, ownership of broadcast radio and televisions began to consolidate as national ownership limits for radio were eliminated and local ownership restrictions were based on market size.

Television Decoder Circuitry Act (TDCA): 1993 Act in which the FCC required that all analog television sets with screens 13 inches or larger sold in the United States contain built-in decoder circuitry that allowed any viewer to display closed captions.

Term: A specific period of time.

Theatre: A live stage performance.

Theatre for Young Audiences (TYA): An equity contract for children.

Ticket scalping: Selling a ticket in a secondary market for higher than face value.

Tort: Personal injury.

Tour: The orderly geographic dates and times of live performance for an artist.

Trade dress: Represents the total image of a product as opposed to a product's individual parts or aspects; may deal with the totality of features such as size, shape, color, color combinations, texture, or graphics.

Trade secret: Consists of any formula, pattern, device, or compilation of information which is used in one's business and which gives an opportunity to obtain an advantage over competitors who do not know or use it.

Trademark: A word or brand name, logo, or package design, or a combination of the two used by a merchant or a manufacturer to identify and distinguish its goods from those of others.

Trademark Act: Also known as the Lanham Act (federal).

Trademark availability search: A search done to ensure that a name has not yet been trademarked.

Trailers: Short snippets of a film to generate interest.

Treatises: Secondary sources of law such as a legal encyclopedia.

Treatment: A short story with a scene-by-scene description of the story about to be told for film or television, including the emotional responses the movie intends to invoke.

True Name and Address: Statutes that make it illegal for anyone to manufacture, distribute, sell, or possess for any of these purposes any video, compact disc, audio cassette, or phonograph record whose packaging does not contain the actual name and address of the manufacturer.

Trustee: The person in charge of a proceeding in bankruptcy.

Typosquatting: A form of cybersquatting in which an owner speculates that someone will misspell an otherwise legitimate domain name and purchasing that variation on the name in order to make a profit.

Unfair competition: The creation of a false impression as to the source, origin, sponsorship, or endorsement of products or services without the use of a trademark.

Uniform Athlete Agent Act (UAAA): Model act adopted by numerous states in order to regulate sports agent conduct in relation to student athletes.

Uniform Commercial Code (U.C.C): Model act established by the National Conference of Commissioners on Uniform State Laws governing the sale of goods among other things.

Unions: Also called guilds; the bargaining representative for a group of individuals.

United States District Courts: The trial courts in the federal circuits.

Unreasonable: Broad term noting either negligent or unfair conduct by a party.

Valid: A contract that satisfies all elements of formation.

Variance: An exception to a zoning ordinance.

V-chip: Enables parents to block television programming from their children if the program has a certain rating.

Venues: The actual physical location of a performance.

Vertical merger: A merger between two firms, one of which is a supplier or distributor for the other.

Voice of America (VOA): In addition to the Armed Forces Radio Network, began during World War II to keep soldiers and citizens informed of the status of battles, the war generally, and conditions back home in the United States.

Void: An illegal contract or one that lacks all the elements of a contract.

Voidable: A type of contract that allows one party to avoid their obligations under the contract; sometimes referred to as an option.

Voluntary movie rating system: System of rating movies established by the Motion Picture Association of America to replace the Hays Production Code.

Waiver: The voluntary relinquishment of a right.

Watermark: An inaudible signal on a song that can be sent over the Internet to show the source of the playback.

Webcasting: Broadcasting over the Internet.

Wholesale: As opposed to retail, the price charged to the seller for a CD or other good.

Work for hire: Sometimes abbreviated WMFH (work made for hire); a work prepared by an employee within the scope of their employment or a work specially ordered or commissioned under certain specified circumstances.

Writ of certiorari: Order granted by the Supreme Court to hear a case from a Court of Appeals.

Zoning: Governmental classification of land in terms of residential, commercial, industrial, and so on.

index